Tropical Multiculturalism

A book in the series
Latin America Otherwise:
Languages, Empires, Nations
Series editors:
Walter D. Mignolo, Duke University
Irene Silverblatt, Duke University
Sonia Saldívar-Hull, University of California
at Los Angeles

TROPICAL
MULTICULTURALISM

A Comparative History of Race in Brazilian

Cinema and Culture

∞

ROBERT STAM

DUKE UNIVERSITY PRESS   *Durham and London 1997*

© 1997 Duke University Press

All rights reserved

Printed in the United States of America on acid-free paper ∞

Typeset in Carter and Cone Galliard

Library of Congress Cataloging-in-Publication Data

appear on the last printed page of this book.

To Arlindo Castro,
Axé

CONTENTS

∞

About the Series

Latin America Otherwise: Languages, Empires, Nations is a critical series. It aims to explore the emergence and consequences of concepts used to define "Latin America" while at the same time exploring the broad interplay of political, economic, and cultural practices that have shaped Latin American worlds. Latin America, at the crossroads of competing imperial designs and local responses, has been construed as a geocultural and geopolitical entity since the nineteenth century. This series provides a starting point from which to redefine Latin America as a configuration of political, linguistic, cultural, and economic intersections that demands a continuous reappraisal of the role of the Americas in history, and of the ongoing process of globalization and the relocation of people and cultures that have characterized Latin America's experience. *Latin America Otherwise: Languages, Empires, Nations* is a forum that confronts established geocultural constructions, that rethinks area studies and disciplinary boundaries, that assesses convictions of the academy and of public policy, and that, correspondingly, demands that the practices through which we produce knowledge and understanding about and from Latin America be subject to rigorous and critical scrutiny.

Stam's *Tropical Multiculturalism: A Comparative History of Race in Brazilian Cinema and Culture* offers an innovative and critical methodology to cultural studies. Stam's focus is Brazil, but his analytical eyes are on the global processes that both join and distinguish the United States from the former Portuguese colony. Urging a comparative perspective, he highlights connections built on a shared history of conquest, colonization, slavery, immigration, and modernity. He also insists on the methodological consequences of that shared history. Analysis of ethnic or racial representations must proceed by placing them with the "larger matrix of the ethnic ideologies and representations of-fered by the other racially plural societies of the Americas."

By framing contemporary Brazilian cinema in the history of colonialism, Stam underlines the colonial side (past and present) of Latin American his-tory, blurred more often than not by the emphasis on modernity. The study of Brazilian cinema allows him to explore a variety of crucial issues at the inter-section of modernity and coloniality, from race to technology, from slavery to anthropology, from indigenous communities to the urban favelas.

Walter D. Mignolo, Duke University
Irene Silverblatt, Duke University
Sonia Saldívar-Hull, University of
California at Los Angeles

ACKNOWLEDGMENTS

∞

Tropical Multiculturalism is the culmination of a long period of research, teaching, and curatorial work on Brazilian cinema. At the same time, it is the fruit of a long personal connection to Latin America due to an important part of my family living in Costa Rica and Brazil. Finally, the book is the product of three decades of intense, palimpsestic cohabitation with things Brazilian, such that it is virtually impossible to thank all the people who have been helpful to me. Since the debts accumulated over the years defy any easy accounting, I can only refer to a few of the innumerable people who have in some way contributed to this work. While my intellectual debts are documented in the copious footnotes and extended bibliography, I would also like to thank a number of people in a more personal way.

I dedicate the book to the late Arlindo Castro. I learned of Arlindo's tragic and untimely death due to heart failure just as I was putting the final touches on these acknowledgments. Arlindo was a close friend of mine and very much loved by the many who knew him both in Brazil and the United States. Arlindo gave me the benefit of an extremely close and informed reading of the manuscript, and the reader will note frequent "thank-yous" to Arlindo for his insights and observations. We will miss Arlindo immensely for his kindness, his intelligence, and his *bom astral*. He encapsulated as well as anyone the spirit that animates this book.

I would also like to call attention to a number of people with whom I have shared not only friendship but also a passion for the analysis of Brazilian culture: Randal Johnson, João Luiz Vieira, Richard Pena, and Ismail Xavier. My ongoing conversations with these four people—three of whom have also been my occasional coauthors—have infinitely enriched this work. Ismail

Xavier gave me the benefit of his theoretical and historical skills. Randal Johnson read the manuscript with his usual precision and attention to detail. Richard Pena is deeply knowledgeable about Brazilian Cinema and has always been collaborative. And my dialogue with João Luiz Vieira has been incessant, pleasurable, and productive.

I would also like to acknowledge other individuals who read the manuscript, in part or in its entirety, and who made useful suggestions. Michael Hanchard helped with his profound understanding of Afro Brazilian political movements, as did the various readers engaged by the University of Minnesota Press and Duke University Press—notably Julianne Burton and Ruby Rich.

José Gatti, professor at the Federal University of Santa Catarina, has also been an important interlocutor over the years. João Carlos Rodrigues, one of the pioneer scholars of racial imagery in Brazilian cinema, was helpful in the earliest stages of this research. My son Gilberto (a.k.a. Giba) was helpful in bringing books, articles, videotapes, and CDs from Brazil on his innumerable trips to the United States. (We too have had our evolving dialogue about Brazilian culture.) I also thank the students who attended the various courses on Brazilian cinema I have taught both in Brazil (at the Federal University of Rio de Janeiro, Niteroi, at the University of São Paulo, at the University of Bahia, and at the Federal University of Minas Gerais) and in the United States (at the University of California at Berkeley, at New York University, and at the University of California at Los Angeles). I would also like to acknowledge the wonderful collaborative efforts of Duke University Press, especially of Ken Wissoker and Pam Morrison.

I have benefited from ongoing discussion with many of the directors examined in this book. Glauber Rocha came to live with me in Berkeley on two occasions before his untimely death in 1981; we had extensive conversations about his work on Brazilian cinema generally. I have also had engaging discussions with Suzana Amaral, Karim Ainouz, Yom Tov Azulay, Carlos Blajsblat, Vincent Carelli, Francisco Cesar Filho, Tania Cipriani, Eduardo Coutinho, Carlos Diegues, Jorge Duran, Vera de Figuereido, Monica Frotta, Rui Guerra, Eunice Guttman, José Joffily, Leon Hirszman, Arnaldo Jabor, Arthur Omar, Nelson Percira dos Santos, Rogerio Sganzerla, Elena Solberg-Ladd, Andrea Tonacci, and Tizuka Yamasaki. During the course of my research, I also managed to talk to a number of key performers, notably Zózimo Bulbul, Marpessa Dawn, Milton Gonçalves, Paulo Betti, Zezé Motta, Antonio Pitanga, and Ruth de Souza. I also discussed issues of racial representation with black activist leaders such as the late Lelia Gonzales and Fernando Conceicao, both of whom addressed my classes at New York University. My work has also been enriched over the years by dialogue with Brazilian artists, activists, theorists, and journalists, such as Sergio Augusto, José Carlos Avellar, Jean-Claude Bernardet, Nelson Brissac, Augusto Carlos Calil, José Celso Martinez Correia, Raquel Gerber, Walnice Galvão, Helio Goldstein, Nelson Hoineff, Amir Labaki, Lucia Nagib, Heloisa Buarque de Holanda, Fernão Ramos, Helena Salem, Roberto Schwarz, Jorge Schwarz, João Silverio Trevisao, David Tygel, and Carlos Verissimo.

I would also like to thank other "interlocutors," such as Catherine Benamou, Isa Castro, Edir de Castro, Luiz Antonio Coelho, Marcello Dantas, Joan Dassin, Carol Boyce Davies, Dan Dawson, Christopher Dunn, Jean Franco, Monica Frotta, Faye Ginsburg, Lucia Guimaraes, John Hess, Patricia Hofbauer, Chuck Kleinhans, Augustin Lao, the late Paul Lenti, Julia Lesage, Ana Lopez, Tomás Pumarejo Lopez, Lloyd MacNiell, Ivone Margulies, Roberto Moura, Robin Nagle, Vinícius Novarro, Richard Pena, Ana Pessoa, Marcelle Python, José Roberto, George Sanchez, Clyde Taylor, and George Yúdice. And I would like to make a special tribute to the late Warren Dean, my colleague at New York University, for his historical rigor, his unassuming generosity, and his principled pedagogy.

I am also indebted to the cooperative staffs of the Fundacao Cinemateca Brasileira (São Paulo), the Museu Lesar Segall (São Paulo), the Cinemateca of the Museu de Arte Moderna (Rio de Janeiro), and the Museum of Image and Sound (São Paulo).

Although most of the material in this book is new, certain sections were published, in preliminary and usually quite different form, in various journals. My general approach was first sketched out in an essay entitled "Slow Fade to Afro," published in *Film Quarterly* 36, no. 2 (Winter 1982–1983). Some of the material on music, religion, and the *quilombos* was first published as "Samba, Candomblé, Quilombo: Black Performance and Brazilian Cinema," in *Journal of Ethnic Studies* 13, no. 3 (1985). The material on Orson Welles first appeared as "Orson Welles, Brazil, and the Power of Blackness," published in

Persistence of Vision, no. 7 (1989). My comparative method was first outlined in some detail in "Mutual Illuminations," published in *Iris* no. 13 (Summer 1991).

A number of institutions and foundations offered grants which directly or indirectly aided this project. Two Fulbright Lectureships allowed me to teach in Brazil (at the School of Communications of University of São Paulo in 1985 and at Federal University in Rio, Niteroi, in 1985 and again in 1995) while also doing research for this project. Some of my primary research was done with the aid of a Guggenheim Fellowship (1987–88). My work as a Rockefeller Fellow at SUNY–Buffalo (1992–93) largely went to completing *Unthinking Eurocentrism: Multiculturalism and the Media* (with Ella Shohat), but also indirectly furthered my work on *Tropical Multiculturalism*.

I am grateful to the following individuals for stills: Ana Maria Galano provided production stills from *Casa Grande, Senzala e Cia* (The Big House, the Slave Quarters, and Company/Incorporated), a film project by Joaquim Pedro de Andrade; Tania Cipriani provided stills for *Odo Ya! Life with AIDS*; Vera Figueiredo provided stills for *Samba da Crição do Mundo* (Samba of the Creation of the World); Eduardo Coutinho provided stills for *O Fio da Memoria* (The Thread of Memory) and *Boca de Lixo* (The Scavengers); Elena Solberg-Ladd provided stills from *Bananas Is My Business*. Tizuka Yamasaki provided stills from *J.S. Brown: O Último Heroi* (J.S. Brown: The Last Hero). Bernardo T. S. Magalhaes provided the still for "Tropical Anthropophagy: Caetano Veloso" and the photo of Caetano Veloso. Vincent Carelli provided the stills which became photo 117 (The "Technicized Indian")and photo 118 (The Spirit of TV). Francisco Cesar Filho provided stills from *Hip Hop São Paulo*. Fabiano Canosa provided stills of *A Mulher de Todos* (Everybody's Woman). The stills from *It's All True: Based on an Unfinished Film by Orson Welles* were provided by Catherine Benamou and Balenciaga Productions. Richard Pena and the New York Film Festival provided stills of *Sixteen, Oh Sixty*.

The following stills were provided by Embrafilme/Fundação do Cinema Brasileiro: *O Descobrimento do Brasil* (The Discovery of Brazil); Grande Otelo at Atlantida; *Moleque Tião* (Street Kid Tião); *Anchieta, José do Brasil*; *As Aventuras Amorosas de um Padeiro* (Amorous Adventures of a Baker); *As Aventuras de Robinson Crusoe* (The Adventures of Robinson Crusoe); *Na Boca do Mundo* (In the World's Mouth); *Compasso de Espera* (Marking Time); *Cordão de Ouro* (Gold Belt); *Chico Rei*; *A Deusa Negra* (The Black Goddess);

Faustão: O Cangaceiro Negro (Faustão: The Black Cangaceiro); *A Força de Xangô* (The Force of Xangô); *J.S. Brown: O Último Herói* (J.S. Brown: The Last Hero); *Jubiaba*; *Ladroes de Cinema* (Cinema Thieves); *A Marcha* (The March); *O Negrinho do Pastoreio* (The Black Boy of the Pasture); *Pindorama*; *Pixote*; *A Prova de Fogo* (Trial by Fire); *Rainha Diaba* (Devil Queen); *Tenda dos Milagres* (Tent of Miracles); *Uira: Um Indio a Procura de Deus* (Uira: Indian in Search of God); *Na Boca do Mundo* (In the World's Mouth); *Xica da Silva.*

Cine-World provided stills for *Deus e Diabo na Terra do Sol* (Black God, White Devil) and *Terra em Transe* (Land in Anguish).

New Yorker Films provided stills from *Barravento; Como Era Gostoso Meu Francês* (How Tasty Was My Little Frenchman); *Eles Não Usam Black Tie* (They Don't Wear Black Tie); *Ganga Zumba; A Grande Cidade* (The Big City); *Quilombo; Fome de Amor* (Hunger for Love); and *Xica da Silva.* Gary Crowdus and Cinema Guild provided stills from *Iracema* (1975). Janus Films provided stills from *Black Orpheus.* Cinema Guild provided stills from *Iao* and *Iracema* (1975). New Line Films provided stills of *Macunaíma.* The Saul Zaentz Distributor provided stills for *At Play in the Fields of the Lord.*

The following stills were provided by the Cinemateca Brasileira in São Paulo: *Casei-me com uma Xavante* (I Married a Xavante); *O Cangaceiro; Caicára; Bandido da Luz Vermelha* (Red Light Bandit); *Bahia de Todos os Santos; O Canto do Mar* (Song of the Sea); *João Negrinho* (John the Black Boy); *Macumba; A Mulata Que Queria Pecar* (The Mulatta Who Wanted to Sin); *Otália da Bahia* (Otália from Bahia); *O Saci; Sinhá Moça* (The Plantation Owner's Daughter); *Asalto ao Trem Pagador* (Attack on the Pay Train); *Cinco Vezes Favela* (Five Times Favela); *A Grande Feira* (Big Market); *O Pagador de Promessas* (The Given Word); *Iracema* (1920); Benjamin de Oliveira; *Os Guaranis* (1908); *O Guarani* (1916); *A Escrava Isaura* (The Slave Isaura).

The Cinemateca of the Museum of Modern Art in Rio provided me with the following stills: *Amuleto de Ogum* (The Amulet of Ogum); *Carnaval Atlántida; Os Cosmonautas* (The Cosmonauts); *Um Desconhecido Bate à Porta* (A Stranger Knocks, alternately titled *Pista de Grama*); *Gimba; Matar ou Correr* (To Kill or to Run); *De Pernas Pro Ar* (Upside Down); *Rio Fantasia; Rio 40 Graus* (Rio 40 Degrees); *Rio Zona Norte* (Rio Northern Zone);

Também Somos Irmaos (We Are Also Brothers); *Triste Tropico*; and *A Mulata Que Queria Pecar* (The Mulata Who Wanted to Sin). Thanks to João Luiz Vieira for helping me to procure the stills.

To my *companheira* Ella, thanks for everything.

Tropical Multiculturalism

Historical Preamble:
The European/Indigenous
Encounter

∞

For North Americans, the image of Brazil is both reassuringly familiar and disconcertingly alien. Writing about Brazilian culture is not, therefore, a matter of a distant exploration of a completely foreign geography. Indeed, the underlying assumption of this book is that Brazil and the United States are deeply interconnected in a specular play of sameness and difference, identity and alterity. The two countries offer distorting images of each other. Although in no way identical, the two countries are eminently *comparable*. The same elements exist, but reshuffled. What is a major chord in one country becomes a minor chord in the other.

As a vast, continent-size New World country, similar to the United States in both historical formation and ethnic diversity, Brazil constitutes a kind of southern twin whose strong affinities with the United States have been obscured by ethnocentric assumptions and media stereotypes. Eurocentric misapprehensions about Brazil go at least as far back as 1500 and Pedro Cabral's misrecognition of northern Brazil as an island, which he called "Vera Cruz." Over the centuries, misconceptions about Brazil, and about Latin America generally, have become intertwined with sedimented prejudices that are at once *religious* (Christian condescension toward African and indigenous religions); *social* (poverty as a sign of degradation); *sexual* (the view of Latin women as sultry temptresses); and *racial* (reproducing Eurocentric hierarchies of white European over African "black" and indigenous "red").[1] After at least 30,000 years of indigenous culture (patronizingly labeled "pre-Columbian"), both Brazil and the United States were "discovered" as part of Europe's search for a trade route to India. Though the land was called "virgin"—a gendered trope implying availability for defloration and fecundation—it was peopled by what are now estimated to have been 7 million indigenous people, in Brazil, mistakenly called "Indians," and from 10 to 20 million in what is now the U.S. and Canada.[2] Even the Amazonian basin was not "virgin" when the Europeans arrived, nor was it "undeveloped." Aerial photographs of the Amazon region have revealed vestiges of advanced agricultural systems, featuring drainage canals and man-made embankments, dating from the first centuries of our era.[3] And though it was once believed that indigenous civilization spread from the Andes into the Amazon, it is now thought that Amazonian ceramics antedate, by over a thousand years, the oldest ceramics in Peru and Ecuador.

The histories of Brazil and the United States run on parallel tracks. Both countries "began" their official histories as European colonies, one of Portugal, the other of Great Britain. In both countries, colonization led to the occupation of vast territories and the subjugation and dispossession of indigenous peoples. In the United States, the occupiers were called pioneers; in Brazil they were called *bandeirantes* and *mamelucos*. Subsequently, both countries massively imported Africans to form the two largest slave societies of modern times, up until slavery was abolished, with the Emancipation Proclamation of 1863 in the United States and the Lei Áurea (Golden Law) of 1888 in Brazil. Both countries received similar waves of immigration from all over the world, ultimately forming multicultural societies with substantial indigenous (in Brazil Tupi, Bororo, Nambaquara, in the United States Cree, Mohawk, Seminole), African (in Brazil Bantu, Hausa, Yoruba, Fon), Italian, German, Japanese, Slavic, Arab, and Jewish (Ashkenazi and Sephardi) populations and influences. As a result of these palimpsestic histories, Brazil and the United States are (1) "multination states" (whose cultural diversity arises from the incorporation of previously self-governing indigenous territories into a larger state); (2) polyracial (whose diversity arises as well from the incorporation of formerly self-governing people imported from Africa; and (3) polyethnic (whose diversity arises from immigration).[4]

In spatial terms, both countries cover vast territory—if one omits Alaska, Brazil is larger than the continental United States—and both countries display a wide variety of landscapes and climates. Although often thought to be a "young" country, Brazil's colonization actually began almost a century before that of the United States; whereas Jamestown was founded in 1607, São

Vicente, the first Portuguese settlement, was founded in 1532. (Jamestown was preceded by the settlement in 1526 of parts of South Carolina by 500 Spaniards and 100 African slaves.) In their political history, both countries sought independence from Europe. In 1820 Thomas Jefferson even contemplated a Pan-American alliance based on the convergence of aspirations and interests.[5] The literary histories of both countries are also marked by a parallel struggle for cultural independence from Europe. Emerson's "American Scholar" address in 1836, which Oliver Wendell Holmes called "our intellectual declaration of independence," came just one year after a similar declaration by Brazilian poet Gonçalves de Magalhães. The same literary movements and genres characterize both countries: religious literature (Padre Vieira in Brazil, Jonathon Edwards in the United States); romanticism (José de Alencar in Brazil, Edgar Allan Poe in the United States); abolitionist literature (Joaquim Nabuco; William Garrison); naturalism (Júlio Ribeiro; Frank Norris); "local color" regionalism (José Lins do Rego; Bret Harte); poetic Modernism (Mário de Andrade; T. S. Eliot). Both countries, finally, are given to patriotic excess, as reflected in the "greatest-country-of-the-world" jingoism of U.S. politicians, and in the Brazilian conviction that "God is Brazilian."

Despite the roughly parallel contours of historical development—conquest, slavery, immigration—important differences separate the two countries. The colonial formation of the two societies, for example, was quite distinct. Although each conducted an implacable ethnocide of indigenous peoples—reduced from an estimated 7 million in Brazil to 300,000 and from many millions to a few million in the United States (with a modest demographic resurgence in both countries in recent years)—that ethnocide took distinct forms. In the initial period of colonization, the Portuguese exploited an abundant supply of subjugated labor (Indians, blacks, and *mestiços*), while the 13 North American colonies relied not only on slave labor but also on the European peasants, artisans, and professionals who became the free workers forming the basis of the new society. Whereas many European settlers in North America were fleeing from religious or political oppression, the Portuguese who settled Brazil were usually loyal servants of the Portuguese crown. Brazil was colonized by soldiers of fortune in search of legendary treasure, but the United States was settled by pilgrims who hoped to reproduce in the New World the style of life they had practiced in the Old but which persecution had threatened, and who inscribed onto their own migration a messianic

1. Digesting the foreigner: *Como Era Gostoso Meu Francês* (1971)

scriptural thrust rooted in the language of the Exodus story and of a "New Israel," a narrative subsequently given insurgent significance by African Americans.

Gendered differences played a role in the distinct nature of settlement in the two countries. Whereas husbands and wives traveled together to North America, men came alone to Brazil, resulting in a much higher degree of European intermarriage with Indians and African Brazilians. Thus the first wave of *mestiçagem* (miscegenation) in Brazil took place between Europeans and Indians to an extent unheard of in North America. But this racial mixing in Brazil was less a sign of "tolerance" than a technique for domination. In a few decades the indigenous villages of the Brazilian coast disappeared, replaced by missionary-dominated reserves and production-oriented *fazendas* (plantations), where European male colonizers, responding both to the demographic imperative and to corporeal desire, impregnated Indian women in order to populate and assert control over the land. Thus miscegenation, whether in the form of involuntary rape or voluntary unions, generated the mass of the population. A system called *cunhadismo,* based on the Indian practice of incorporating strangers into their communities by providing wives—a variant practice of which is shown in the 1971 film *Como Era Gostoso Meu Francês* (How Tasty Was My Little Frenchman; see photo 1)—generated people of European and indigenous ancestry called *mamelucos*.[6] At first a matter of Europeans being incorporated into the Indian group, *cunhadismo* later metamorphosed into a general *mestiçagem* dominated by European interests and desires.

Although early U.S. history offers occasional examples of a three-sided *mestiçaje*—the Lumbee of North Carolina, the Wampanoags in Massachusetts, the Seminoles in Florida, in Brazil the very domination of the frontier was the product of a mestiço people. It was these *mamelucos* who extended the Lusitanian-dominated territories to the Tordesillas line, always looking for gold, precious stones, and Indian slaves. As half-Indians, they were familiar with the land and its customs: they knew how to make ceramics, to cut paths through the forest, to weave hammocks and papooses, to pierce their lips and ears. Politically ambiguous, they sometimes aligned with Indians against European enemies and sometimes worked with the white elite. Examples of what Ronaldo Vainfas calls "cultural disjunction," people dilacerated by colonialism, *mamelucos* spread their own ambivalence around Brazil.[7] The *mamelucos* were riven in their allegiances between their indigenous ancestors, whom they often despised, and the Europeans, who despised them; they were, in a sense, the first victims of the "ideology of whitening." The "generic Indians" produced by Jesuit schooling, meanwhile, suffered a deculturation by which the process of Christianization served to efface the traces of Indian cultures.

The United States and Brazil also display distinct attitudes toward the frontier. Edmundo O'Gorman contends that Latin America generally was never really a frontier land in the North American sense. Depending on state favoritism, Latin Americans never engaged in any "tenacious effort to transform forests and deserts into cultivable areas."[8] Whereas North Americans moved westward as free and independent agents, motivated by land hunger and material ambition, Brazilians, like Latin Americans generally, appropriated the frontier only after reaching an agreement with the central government. While the American frontier urged "the emancipated being on toward the unrelenting conquest of nature as the means to sustain economic independence," as Fredrick Pike puts it, "the Latin American hinterland with its large private estates fostered the subordination and dependence of a collectivist labor force."[9] Brazilian cinema gives voice to these differences. Unlike American cinema, it does not feature any Conquest-of-the-Frontier theme, nor is it interested in "homesteading" or "settling" à la *Drums Along the Mohawk*. Nor does it prominently depict an Indian "enemy."

The colonizing process in both the United States and Brazil had an important linguistic dimension. In each country, a high proportion of state names (Piauí, Ceará in Brazil; Alabama, Arizona in the United States), cities (Curitiba; Tallahassee), and rivers (Tietê; Potomac), carry native names.[10] In both countries, early religious figures learned Indian languages in order to proselytize: John Eliot translated the Bible into Indian tongues; José de Anchieta devised a Tupi grammar. Although some of the American founding fathers learned Indian languages, and while Indian words came to enrich English vocabulary, in Brazil the Tupi Guarani language, first used as a language of communication between the Portuguese and the Tupinambá, spread along the coast and even became the lingua franca, or *língua geral*, called *nheengatu*, up until the eighteenth century, including among non-Tupi indians. As late as the nineteenth century, there were proposals to make Tupi the national language of Brazil, an idea comically recapitulated in Lima Barretto's novel *O Triste Fim de Policarpo Quaresma*.

In both countries, indigenous culture provided inspiration for emancipatory currents of thought. Indeed, the ideal of the egalitarian communal freedom of the native peoples, however romanticized, has served as an intellectual yeast or ferment in Brazil and in North America. In the United States, revisionist scholars have called attention to the native influence on American democratic institutions, emphasizing salient features of Iroquois (Haudenosaunee) social life subsequently adopted by the founding fathers, such as the suspicion of authoritarian power ("that government governs best which governs least"), and the notion of checks and balances to prevent its concentration. Ben Franklin's idea of a "confederation" was reportedly borrowed from the confederation of the six Iroquois nations.[11] This same appreciation for indigenous freedom induced Jefferson to substitute the "pursuit of happiness" for "property" as the third leg of the natural rights tripod defended by followers of John Locke. Of course this appreciation did not prevent the founding fathers from also appropriating Indian land, or keep Benjamin Franklin from sponsoring a Pennsylvania law paying bounty for Indian scalps.[12]

In both countries, Indian-inflected symbolism became associated with independence movements. The anti-British discourse of the American revolution appropriated the Indian as symbol of national difference, whence the figure of a native chief on an earlier American nickel, the symbolism of the quiver of arrows on the dollar bill, and the statue of an Indian gracing the Capitol. It is no accident, Native American scholars point out, that the revolutionary Sons of Liberty disguised themselves as Mohawks, or that the word "caucus" comes from the Algonquian language. In Brazil, too, the Indian became a symbol of national resistance to European domination; a statue in a Salvador Bahia square, for example, depicts a Native figure crushing a snake symbolizing Portuguese colonialism. Thus a tentative Brazilian national unity coalesced around the figure of the idealized Indian. The Brazilian modernists of the 1920s updated and radicalized nineteenth-century Indianismo, taking as their national symbol not the well-behaved "noble savage" but rather the rebel Tupinambá who devoured the foreigner to appropriate his force. In Indian communality, the modernists saw a utopian model of a society free of coercion and hierarchy, without police or capitalism. As it did for the European *philosophes,* philo-indigenism enabled a deep anthropological critique of the political and moral bases of Eurocentric civilization. In any case, despite ethnocide, the native peoples in both countries still exist and struggle daily for their basic rights, struggles registered in countless documentary films (*Incident at Oglala* in the United States; *Kayapó: Out of the Forest* in Brazil), and fiction films *(Thunderheart; Avaeté)* as well as in the work of "indigenous media," that is, indigenous peoples' use of audiovisual technology (camcorders, VCRs) for their cultural and political purposes.

Brazilian cinema does not present a univocal vision of the European-indigenous encounter. This becomes obvious when we compare two cinematic versions of the same historical event, a kind of "primal scene" for settler colonialism in the New World—the moment of "first contact," and more specifically Pedro Álvares Cabral's arrival in Brazil in 1500 and the celebration of the "first mass." Humberto Mauro's O *Descobrimento do Brasil* (The Discovery of Brazil, 1937) relays the official version (photo 2). The film's presentation is based on the letter from Pero Vaz de Caminha, official scribe of the Portuguese fleet, to the Portuguese monarch, where he describes exuberant landscapes and docile natives. Sponsored by the Cocoa Institute, an organization of large landowners—quite literally the heirs of the *capitanias,* or land grants, distributed by

2. Colonial idyll: *O Descobrimento do Brasil* (1937)

the *conquista*—*O Descobrimento do Brasil* idealizes the European role. The film's staging of the European-indigene encounter was partially inspired by a famous 1861 painting by Victor Meirelles, entitled "The First Mass." The Portuguese discoverer is generally center frame, with the infantilized Indians in the background. Like the Hollywood films devoted to Columbus, the Mauro film sacralizes European conquest. The choral music by Villa-Lobos "blesses" the conquest with a religious aura. (Unlike Hollywood films, however, the "Indians" actually speak in their indigenous Tupi language.)[13] The natives spontaneously applaud the conquest of their own land and seem to acquiesce in their own dispossession. They abandon their own beliefs, it is suggested, and embrace Christianity and the culture of Europe as irresistibly persuasive. Their genuflections translate into a veristic audiovisual representation the fantasy of the conquistadores: that reading a document in a European language to uncomprehending natives signifies a legitimate transfer of ownership.

Glauber Rocha's *Terra em Transe* (Land in Anguish, 1967), a baroque allegory about Brazilian politics set in the imaginary land of Eldorado, offers a contrasting, "unofficial" representation of Pedro Alvares Cabral. The right-wing figure of the film (named Porfirio Diaz after the Mexican dictator), arrives from the sea with a flag and a crucifix, suggesting a foundational myth of national origins. The sandy stage is bare; there is no picturesqueness as in the Mauro film (see photo 3). Dressed in an anachronistic modern-day suit, Diaz is accompanied by a priest in a Catholic habit, a sixteenth-century conquistador, and a symbolic feathered Indian. Unlike in the conventional representations of European "discovery," here there are no genuflections; the "Indian" receives the conqueror with dignified pride and confidence, on a basis of apparent equality. Diaz approaches a huge cross fixed in the sand and lifts a silver chalice, a ritual that evokes, once again, Cabral's "first mass," but in an anachronistic manner that stresses the continuities between the conquest and contemporary oppression; the contemporary dictator is portrayed as the latter-day heir of the conquistadores.

Rocha further destabilizes meaning by making Africa a textual presence. The very aesthetic of the sequence, first of all, draws heavily from the Africanized forms of Rio's yearly samba pageant, with its polyrhythms, delight in extravagant costume, and zany forms of historicism; indeed, the actor who plays the conquistador is Clóvis Bornay, a historian specialized in carnival "allegories," and a well-known figure from Rio's carnival. Second, the mass is accompanied not by Christian religious music, but by Yoruba religious chants, evoking the "trance" of the Portuguese title. Rocha's suggestive referencing of African music, as if it had existed in Brazil prior to the arrival of Europeans, reminds us not only of the "continental drift" theory that sees South America and Africa as once having formed part of a single land mass, but also of the theories of Ivan Van Sertima and others that Africans arrived in the New World "before Columbus."[14] The music suggests that Africans, as those who shaped and were shaped by the Americas over centuries, are in some uncanny sense *also* indigenous to the region.[15] At the same time, the music enacts an ironic reversal, since the chants of exaltation are addressed to a reprehensible, dictatorial figure. Although Eurocentric discourse posits African religion as irrational, the film suggests that in fact it is the European elite embodied by Porfirio Diaz that is irrational, hysterical, entranced, almost demonic. The presence of a mestiço actor representing the Indian, furthermore, points to a frequent practice in Brazilian cinema, where Indians, whose legal status as "wards of the state" prevented them from representing themselves, were often represented by blacks. While in the United States white actors performed in blackface, in Brazil blacks performed, as it were, in "redface." That the entire

3. Cabral's "first mass": *Terra em Transe* (1967)

scene is a product of the narrator-protagonist's delirium as he lies dying, finally, adds still another layer of meaning, as the protagonist sees the past (the "discovery") and the future (the coup d'état) flashing up before his eyes. The scene's fractured and discontinuous aesthetic stages the drama of life in the colonial "contact zone," defined by Mary Louise Pratt as the space in which "subjects previously separated" encounter each other and "establish ongoing relations, usually involving conditions of coercion, radical inequality, and intractable conflict."[16] Rocha's neobaroque Afro-avant-gardist aesthetic here figures the discontinuous, dissonant, fractured history of the nation through equally dissonant images and sounds.

Brazil and the United States offer variations on the same racial theme: the shifting relationalities of the fundamental triad of indigenous "reds," African "blacks," and European "whites," augmented by immigrants from around the world.[17] Eurocentric assumptions, however, lead many North Americans to look to Europe for self-definition rather than to the multiracial societies of our own hemisphere. Although it has become commonplace to see Latin America as a "mestiço" continent, it is not always recognized that "United

Statesian" culture is *also* mestiço, mixed, hybrid, syncretic. While the syncretic nature of Latin American societies is "visible," the syncretic nature of U.S. society is often overlooked. And even the currently fashionable academic discussions of postcolonial "hybridity" usually ignore the long history of such discussions within Latin American cultural criticism. Whereas the North American vision of national identity has been surreptitiously premised on an unstated yet nonetheless normative "whiteness," the Brazilian vision of national identity has usually been premised on the notion of racial *multiplicity*. North American historians have explored the national character in terms of the puritanical religious formation of its founders (Perry Miller), or the impact of the frontier experience on the national personality (Frederick Jackson Turner, R.W. B. Lewis), or the shaping power of relatively egalitarian political institutions (Alexis de Tocqueville), but they have downplayed the specifically racial dimension of national identity. In contrast, Brazilian intellectuals have tended to conceive national identity in racially plural terms. I am not suggesting that Brazilian theorists were less racist; indeed, many excoriated the African and indigenous presence as a source of "degeneracy," or deployed the notion of *mestiçagem* to camouflage oppressive racial hierarchies. I am simply suggesting that Brazilian theorists were more conscious of the primordial role of racial diversity within the national formation.

In Brazil, miscegenation with native people was quasi-official policy, whereas the occasional U.S. proposals to assimilate Indians through intermarriage were officially rejected.[18] The romantic poets and novelists of the Indianist movement of the mid-nineteenth century saw Brazil as the product of the fusion of the indigenous peoples with the European element, a fusion figured in the marriage of the Indian Iracema (photo 4) and the European Martins in Alencar's *Iracema* (1865), or the love of the indigenous Peri and the European Ceci in the same novelist's *O Guarani* (1857). Thus while North American ideology promoted myths of separation, and the doomed nature of love between white and Indian (for example in the novels of James Fenimore Cooper), Brazilian ideology promoted myths of fusion through what Doris Sommer calls "foundational romances" of love between European and indigene. Whereas U.S. tradition venerates the Euro American founding fathers, the Brazilian includes an indigenous mother. The Thanksgiving holiday ritual includes the Indian, but, as befits Puritans, without the sex.[19] While Brazilian literature lauded cross-racial heterosexual romance—Indian men loving white

4. Foundational romance:
Iracema (1920)

women *(O Guarani)* or Indian women loving white men *(Iracema)* — as the generative matrix of a mestiço nation, American literature stressed male bonding between white frontiersmen and the native American male.[20] Even now, the cultural industries of both countries return obsessively to the theme of European-indigene romance. Just as the Disney *Pocahontas* was being released in the United States, Norma Benguell was putting the final touches on her adaptation of *O Guarani*. But the love affair between Pocahantas and John Smith, in the recent Disney version, ends with his return to England, even though the real-life Pocahantas did marry the Englishman John Rolfe; miscegenation remains taboo.

In the 1920s, the Brazilian modernists reconceptualized Indianism by envisioning Brazil as an irrevocably syncretic polyphony of ethnic and cultural voices. In the 1930s, Gilberto Freyre saw Brazil's racial diversity as the key to its originality.[21] Freyre's "New World in the Tropics" reflected the cultural fusion of three genetically equal races, each of which made an invaluable contribution, even if Freyre romanticized slavery and "folklorized" the black and indigenous role. Far from being an obstacle to "progress," the miscegenation, fostered by the eroticized cohabitation of three cultures, was a progressive mechanism. In this myth of national origin, as Dain Borges sums it up, "the mestiço Brazilian son accepted and transcended his Portuguese, Indian, and African parents."[22]

Brazilian filmmaker Joaquim Pedro de Andrade's planned adaptation of Freyre's *Casa Grande e Senzala* (translated as *The Masters and the Slaves*), never finished because of the director's untimely death, would have dramatically staged (and critically updated) Freyre's theories (photos 5a and 5b).[23] An examination of the script reveals that the film would have orchestrated a polyphonic encounter among Brazil's various source cultures, with their conflicts, alliances, and wars. Instead of presenting history as closed and uncontested, de Andrade planned to have the film envision Brazilian history through a polycultural grid. Through this "fictional story based on facts," moving from 1500 to 1635, from the arrival of Cabral to the Dutch invasion of Olinda in 1635,[24] he hoped to use film as the vehicle for a serious reflection on multicultural historiography. The modified title of the film—*Casa Grande, Senzala e Cia* (The Big House, the Slave Quarters, and Company/Incorporated)—already conveys a revisionist attitude toward Freyre's work, in that the "and Company" makes room not only for issues of political economy but also for the Indians. In Freyre's book, in contrast, history was quite literally marginalized—the historical episode of the maroon community Palmares, for example, is relegated to the footnotes—in favor of a protostructuralist approach that made the patriarchal *engenho* (sugar mill) the generating nucleus of Brazilian culture.

5a/5b. Designs for *Casa Grande, Senzala e Cia*

The film version was to provide a space for indigenous resistance (warfare, anthropophagy), black resistance (the *quilombos,* or maroon republics) and "new Christians" (Sephardic Jews forced to convert) fleeing the Inquisition. Instead of succumbing to the reverential awe typical of most costume dramas, the film would approach the past with a parodic, Dadaesque, anthropophagic irreverence. The film was to satirize the Jesuit efforts to catechize the Indians, while restaging the incident, much beloved by the modernists, in which the Caetés Indians devoured a Portuguese bishop, ironically named Sardinha (sardine), in a "memorable meal." (*Casa Grande, Senzala e Cia* in this sense would have continued the director's dialogue with Brazilian Modernism begun in *Macunaíma* [1969] based on Mário de Andrade's modernist novel, and continued in *O Homem do Pau-Brazil* [The Brazil-Wood Man, 1982], the film devoted to modernist Oswald de Andrade.) In a sequence entitled "Indian Political Breakfast," a young priest inadvertently becomes the leader of an Indian protest against the worthless trinkets that the Portuguese insist on giving them. Liberation theologian *avant la lettre,* the priest is subsequently accused of "subversion." The Indians, in the film, undermine European domination even when they appear to acquiesce. Three Indians declare themselves God the Father, Jesus, and the Virgin Mary, while another declares himself the Pope. And whereas Freyre "sweetened" the history of slavery by emphasizing the relation between the black nanny and the white child, the film was to give a sense both of the physical, sexual, and psychological violence of slavery, and of the dignity of black efforts to lead an independent cultural life. The film's finale was to consist in a polyphonic series of rival celebrations—the *quilombolas* would celebrate the founding of a maroon community, the Portuguese would celebrate their victories over the Indians, and so forth, while the final intertitle was to link indigenous resistance (in the form of cannibalism) to the Africanized spirituality of the *orixás* (spirits): "On this day in 1635, the Dutch began to occupy the Brazilian province of Pernambuco, where they have remained thirty years until they were expelled. Before and since, from 1500 on, foreign colonizers replaced each other in Brazil. But with Oxalá's help we will eat them all."

As Joaquim Pedro de Andrade's proposed film suggests, the United States and Brazil are in no way identical societies; the point is that they are eminently *comparable.* But despite this comparability, one often encounters a "refusal of the mirror" on the part of both Brazilian and American intellectuals.

The North American side often rejects the mirror out of ethnocentric ignorance and provincialism, as if it were offensive to national pride to compare a superpower like the United States with a Third World country like Brazil. Indeed, it is symptomatic that Pat Buchanan, during his 1996 campaign for the Republican presidential nomination, warned that demographic changes favoring people of color would turn the United States into "the Brazil of North America."[25] Brazilians, meanwhile, look in the cross-cultural mirror with mingled admiration and resentment, combined with a resistance to multiculturalism à l'Americaine, partially because the Brazilian media tend to buy into, and often literally translate, the neoconservative caricature of multiculturalism as separatist, puritanical, and "politically correct." For Brazilians, the United States represents both the admirably "successful" country to the north, and the arrogant hegemony that exploits Brazil. If Americans fear "Brazilianization," Brazilians fear "Americanization," "dollarization," and "Disneyization." Both right and left in Brazil resist the view of the United States and Brazil as mirror societies. Since the right sometimes internalizes the United States as ego ideal, it rejects the comparison for the same reason as North American national chauvinists. To schematize shamelessly, for the Brazilian right, multiculturalism is a "black thing," that evokes what for the Brazilian elite is a frightening prospect: people of color demanding their rights. For the Brazilian left, meanwhile, multiculturalism is "a gringo thing," that is, just another North American cultural export. The leftist analysis confuses issues of economic hegemony, widely resented and correctly critiqued, with issues of culture and history. It also forgets that the very term "multiculturalism" itself represents a "Latinization" or "Brazilianization" of North American self-conceptualization, in that it opts out of the binary black-white model in order to insist, in the Latin American manner, on ethnic multiplicity. It also forgets that as the United States becomes increasingly multiracial, mestiço Brazil might well represent the demographic as well as the cultural future of the United States.

The "refusal of the mirror" reflects a process of twinned essentializations, a desire to heighten differences in order to more clearly demarcate the cozily familiar from the nastily alien. Even such an astute observer as anthropologist Darcy Ribeiro, in his *O Povo Brasileiro* ignores the powerful analogies between the United States and Brazil:

Some New World nations—the United States, Canada, Australia—are merely European transplants in the ample spaces across the seas. They do not present any novelties in this world. They consist of excess populations for whom there was no longer room in the Old World and who came to repeat Europe here, reconstituting its native landscapes with more verve and freedom, in order to feel at home. At times, admittedly, they become creative, reinventing the idea of Republican government and Greek democracy. But rarely. In the end, they are the opposite of us. Our destiny is to unite with all Latin Americans in our common opposition to the same antagonist: Anglo Saxon America.[26]

The spirit of this uninformed conclusion to an otherwise illuminating book could not be further from my method here. Darcy Ribeiro conflates the political level of legitimate resistance to domination with the cultural level of national difference, on the basis of undertheorized "grain of truth" contrasts of putative national personality: Brazilian cordiality and Anglo Saxon frigidity, Brazilian flexibility and American rigidity, Brazilian polychronism and American monochronism. Apart from the fact that it is a misnomer to call the United States Anglo-Saxon (Ribeiro's dichotomies are generally premised on an Anglo-dominant), it is ironical that many of Ribeiro's claims about Brazil—the role of the colonizer, the impact of slavery, the syncretic forms of the national culture—apply equally to the United States. Ribeiro seems unaware of the racial diversity of the United States, its constitutive multiplicity and its inexorable march toward an ever-more mixed cultural formation. He seems blind to the comparable dispossession of the Indian in both countries, to the roughly parallel enslavement of Africans, to the cultural affinities between samba and jazz, soul food and *feijoada* (black-bean stew), break dancing and capoeira. He seems unaware as well of the diversity of the African American community, now become what Ali Mazrui calls "a microcosm of global Africa," embracing Haitians, Jamaicans, Nigerians, Senegalese, Cubans, Dominicans, and even black Brazilians.[27] Ribeiro also ignores the symptoms of convergence: the Brazilianization of the United States and the Americanization of Brazil. Thus Catholicism and African religions grow in the United States, while Protestantism grows in Brazil. Despite his passionate denunciation of Brazilian-style racism, Ribeiro falls back in the end on the outdated Eurocentric notion of Brazil as a "new Rome" (a notion ironically not at all alien to the North American founding fathers) but "one washed in Indian and black blood."[28] Ribeiro's discourse carries the vestiges of an outdated nationalist discourse that refuses to see Brazil as part of a colonial pattern common to all the Americas, a discourse that indirectly renders innocent the Brazilian elite, and culpabalizes a demonized North American other, not for political but for cultural, even ethnic, reasons.

My method in *Tropical Multiculturalism,* in contrast, assumes that cultural analysis, to achieve depth, must move beyond the restrictive framework of the blinkered narcissisms of nation-states. It also assumes that multiculturalism, far from being a "United Statesian" monopoly, is a Pan-American, and indeed a worldwide, phenomenon. *Tropical Multiculturalism* is based on the methodological presupposition that a shared history of colonialism, conquest, slavery, and immigration makes it essential to study the question of ethnic and racial representation within the larger matrix of the ethnic ideologies and representations offered by the other racially plural societies of the Americas. I distinguish, therefore, between the multicultural "fact"—the multiplicity of mutually impacting cultures within and between nation-states—and the multicultural "project"—the attempt to restructure knowledge and cultural relations in function of an antiracist perspective that assumes the radical equality of peoples, communities, and cultures. As a critical method, multiculturalism places diverse peoples and communities in relation, always bearing in mind the history of European domination over the last five centuries.[29] In this sense, many Brazilian artistic movements—Modernismo in the 1920s, Tropicalismo in the 1960s—can be seen as multiculturalist *avant la lettre.*

The crucial point is that the two cultures have much to learn from one another. "United Statesians" can learn from Afro-Brazilian culture, from the artistic practices of Brazilian multiculturalism, and from Brazil's nonessentialist approach to issues of identity. Brazilians, meanwhile, can learn from African American and Native American political activism and from the American academic theorizations of the multiculturalist project. Both countries need to "take in" the lessons of a critical, relational, antiracist multiculturalism. The Brazilian educational system, for example, is every bit as Eurocentric as the American system, and perhaps even more so, since it has only rarely been challenged, whether institutionally or intellectually, by a multiculturalist or an Afrocentric movement. It was only in 1986 that some participants in the Constituent Assembly, charged with drafting a new constitution, proposed a reformulation of "the teaching of Brazilian history, with the goal of contemplating on an equal basis the contributions of different ethnic groups to the Brazilian people's multicultural and pluriethnic formation." In the end, however, the multicultural proposal was reduced to a paternalistic "protection by the State of Afro-Brazilian and indigenous culture" with no specific reference to education.[30]

This book tries, above all, to make connections. It makes connections, first, in temporal terms, between past and present, both within and between countries. It is not well known, for example, that the first Jews who came to North America came via Brazil, or that Afro Brazilians, as I explain in the next chapter, owned land in New York City (then New Amsterdam) in the seventeenth century. Second, it makes connections in spatial and geographical terms, placing debates about representation in a broader context that embraces Brazil and the United States, North and South America. In this sense, it forms part of a larger wave of diasporic and comparative studies that speak of "black Atlantic civilization" (Robert Farris Thompson), "the Black Atlantic" (Paul Gilroy) and of "circum-Atlantic performance" (Joe Roach). Rather than segregate historical periods and geographical regions into neatly fenced-off areas of expertise, in sum, it explores their interconnectedness. Third, the book makes connections in disciplinary terms, forging links between usually compartmentalized fields (media studies, literary theory, reflexive ethnography, feminism, postcolonial studies, Afro-diasporic studies, "area studies"); and fourth, in intertextual terms, envisioning the cinema as part of a broader discursive network ranging from the erudite (poems, novels, history, performance art, cultural theory) to the popular (commercial television, pop music, journalism). Fifth, the book tries to make connections in communitarian and political terms, hoping to link the multiculturalist and antiracist struggles in the United States and Brazil. (One of the paranoid obsessions of the Brazilian dictatorship of 1964–1985, symptomatically, was that the black movements in the United States and Brazil would somehow "hook up" and foment revolution.)

My specific focus is on the multicultural problematic within the Brazilian fiction film, especially foregrounding the Afro Brazilian presence but also examining that presence in relation to the portrayal of other groups: indigenous peoples, European immigrants, and so forth. Within a larger relational context of co-implicated ethnicities, then, I will sketch out the outlines of the multicultural presence in Brazilian Cinema, reflect on some of the issues raised by that presence, and draw some tentative conclusions within a transcultural and multidisciplinary perspective. What are the dynamics of the transformations of racial imagery, and how are those transformations related to larger historical and discursive mutations?

Although issues of race and ethnicity are culturally omnipresent in Brazil, they are often textually submerged. It is therefore important to pay attention to the racial undertones and overtones "haunting" all texts.[31] The challenge is to render visible, or at least audible, the repressed multiculturalism even of dominant texts. Indeed, the very notion of the nonethnic text is questionable. In the end all people are "ethnic"; projecting some groups as "ethnic" and others as "beyond ethnicity," as has often been pointed out, has the effect of normativizing whiteness as transcendental signifier, buttressing the Eurocentric assumption of white self-sufficiency and transparent normative value.[32] How, then, is "whiteness" thematized within Brazilian cinema? How is whiteness implicitly idealized, or, at times, exposed? Many of the more conservative filmic representations of the history of slavery and abolition, for example, idealize whiteness by "fudging" the question of final responsibility for slavery. Films like *Sinhá Moça* (The Plantation Owner's Daughter, 1953) give the impression that slavery was opposed by most whites and that blacks had only a subordinate role in the abolition struggle. The cruelest roles in slavery, meanwhile, are relegated to mestiço subalterns. Unlike many "ethnic image" studies, then, this book does not assume a silently normative whiteness, from which perspective films about native Brazilians and Afro Brazilians are covertly being judged. I assume that films by white directors about blacks and Indians are also "about" whites; the groups are co implicated historically and methodologically. In portraying blacks and Indians, for example, Euro Brazilian directors are also portraying themselves and their own projections, fantasies, allegories, identifications.

At the core of this study is a fairly extensive corpus of hundreds of films and videos featuring multicultural themes and performers, works screened by me over many years in commercial theaters, in film festivals, in the cinematheques of Rio and São Paulo, in the screening rooms of the (now defunct) Embrafilme, in classrooms, on television, and in homes on VCRs. After sketching out the broad historical and cultural parallels between the United States and Brazil, I will examine the progressive metamorphoses of multicultural imagery beginning in the silent period, moving through the comic *chanchadas* (musicals) of the 1930s and 1940s (pausing for a North American interlude concerning Orson Welles's never-completed *It's All True*), and moving on to the Hollywood-style films from São Paulo in the 1950s, and finally through the diverse phases of Cinema Novo in the 1960s and 1970s up to the present. A final chapter concentrates on questions of methodology. At times I depart from chronology in order to follow a theme or figure into a later period. Since Cinema Novo has been discussed extensively, by Randal Johnson in *Cinema Novo x Five* and by Randal Johnson, myself, and others in *Brazilian Cinema,* I have favored films not previously analyzed. Well over half of the book is devoted to the period prior to Cinema Novo, and many of the more recent films and videos have little to do with the Cinema Novo movement per se. Many of the films have never been written about in English, some have never been written about seriously even in Portuguese. Since few readers will have seen all the films in question, Duke University Press has generously allowed me to include numerous stills so as to give a sense of the visual "feel" of the films. Regarding quotes from the movies and secondary sources in Portuguese, all translations are mine unless noted otherwise.

Tropical Multiculturalism deals primarily with the relation between Euro Brazilian and Afro Brazilians, and only secondarily with the relationship between both groups and indigenous Brazilians, and this for both demographic and filmic reasons. Demographically, indigenous people form a tiny minority within Brazil, whereas people of African ancestry form a demographic majority. And in cinematic terms, there are many more films featuring black directors, themes, and performers than there are "Indian" films. Unlike some other countries in the Americas, Brazil has rarely had indigenous filmmakers, or filmmakers with strong indigenous orientation such as the Mexican Emilio "Índio" Fernández or the Bolivian Jorge Sanjines.[33] Indigenous filmmakers did emerge in the 1980s, but the focus was collectivist and activist, not individualist and auteurist. The Indian thematic, meanwhile, is important during the silent period (a time when black themes are absent), but then largely disappears during the 1930s, 1940s, 1950s, and 1960s (at a time when black themes are becoming more common). Indian themes emerge again in the 1970s through the 1990s, when both Indian and black themes are at their height.

We will encounter a wide spectrum of representations of the Brazilian In-

6. *Casei-me com um Xavante* (1957)

dian: the "noble savage" of the Indianist films *(O Guarani);* the "primitive" to be "modernized" in the early ethnographic films (Luiz Thomas Reis); the comic Indian of the 1950s *(Casei-me com um Xavante* [I Married a Xavante, 1957]; see photo 6); the modernist cannibal of the 1960s *(Macunaíma);* the allegorical rebel of the 1970s *(Como Era Gostoso Meu Francês);* the "victim-Indian" of the denunciation documentaries of the 1980s; and finally the self-representing, camcorder-wielding Indian of the "indigenous media" of the 1990s. For those interested in the indigenous peoples of Brazil, Sílvio Back's *Índio do Brasil* (1995) offers a precious anthology of documentary and feature film representations of the Brazilian Indian—counterpointed with ironic, poetic commentary—with segments from the following films: George Dyott's *The River of Doubt* (1913–1927); Aloha Baker's *The Last of the Bororos* (1930); Jorge Konchin's *Iracema* (1931); Vittório Capellaro's *O Caçador de Diamantes* (The Diamond Hunter, 1933); Franz Eichorn's *Eine Brasilianische Rapsodie* (A Brazilian Rhapsody, 1935); Humberto Mauro's *O Descobrimento do Brasil* (The Discovery of Brazil, 1937); Genil Vasconcelos's *Frente à Frente com os Xavantes* (Face to Face with the Xavantes, 1948); Eichorn's *Mundo Estranho* (Strange World, 1948); Eurico Richer's *Tabu* (1949); Vladimir Kozak's *Xetas na Serra dos Dourados* (Xetas in the Dourados Mountains, 1956); Alfredo Palacios's *Casei-me com um Xavante;* William Gerick's *O Segredo de Diacui* (Diacui's Secret, 1959); Nelson Pereira dos Santos's *Como Era Gostoso Meu Francês;* Marco Altberg's *Noel Nutels* (1975); Andre Luiz Oliveira's *A Lenda de Ubirajara* (The Legend of Ubirajara, 1975); Placido de Campos's *Curumim* (1978); and Luiz Paulino dos Santos's *Ikatena* (1983).

Tropical Multiculturalism superimposes a number of projects: a history of Brazilian cinema from the standpoint of race, a history of Brazil itself through its cinematic representations, a reciprocally comparative study of the racial formations in Brazil and the United States, and a theorized essay on the analysis of racialized representations. Although the book places Brazilian cinema and culture in a comparative perspective, I do not systematically compare Brazilian cinema with Hollywood. Whereas Hollywood is well financed, prolific, and internationally disseminated, Brazilian cinema is underfinanced, precarious, and dominated even within its own domestic market, partially because of Hollywood hegemony over film distribution and exhibition in Brazil. My comparisons between Brazilian films and Hollywood films, as a result, are intermittent and provisional rather than sustained and systematic. Indeed, one of my hopes here is to combat the Hollywoodcentrism that makes Hollywood the symbolic center, the *primum mobile* of global film culture. Despite its hegemonic position, Hollywood still contributes only a fraction of the annual worldwide production of feature films. Like many other Third World countries such as India, Egypt, Mexico, and Argentina, Brazil has a long cinematic tradition (going back to 1898). My goal here, in this sense, is to offer culturally informed readings of a fascinating and underappreciated body of film. Fortunately, the films discussed here are becoming increasingly available for screening. Some of the films, such as *Black Orpheus* (1959) and *O Cangaceiro* (The Cangaceiro, 1953) are now international classics. Many of the Cinema Novo films by Carlos Diegues, Glauber Rocha, Joaquim Pedro de Andrade, Rui Guerra, and Leon Hirszman, are in distribution. Some post–Cinema Novo films like *Pixote* (1980) and *Bye Bye Brazil* (1980) won commercial release in the United States. Films such as *Tenda dos Milagres* (Tent of Miracles, 1977) and *Sixteen, Oh Sixty* (1995) have been screened in film festivals. Many films (*Quilombo* [1984], *Black Orpheus* [1959], *Terra em Transe, Deus e Diabo na Terra do Sol* [literally God and the Devil in the Land of the Sun; released as Black God, White Devil; 1964]) can be rented on video,[34] and many documentary shorts are available through distributors like Cinema Guild and Icarus/First Run Features. The Oscar nomination for Fabio Barreto's *O Quatrilho* (1996) should call renewed attention to Brazilian cinema. And the advent of new technologies, one hopes, will facilitate the "digital redemption" that will make this vast archive available on a more democratic basis.

CHAPTER I

Comparative Diasporas:

The Aftershocks of

Slavery

∞

Over recent decades, the image of Brazil presented by the U.S. mass media has morphed from a "positive" (albeit patronizing) image of Brazil as the vibrant scene of carnival, samba, and soccer to a clearly negative image of Brazil as the cataclysmic site of massacres of children, apocalyptic devastation of forests, and the anthill-like prospecting of Serra Pelada. In both the "positive" and "negative" cases, a factual grain of truth is transformed by dominant cinema and the international news industry into something terribly partial and misleading. Films such as *Blame It on Rio* (1984) and *Wild Orchid* (1989) present a caricatural version of Afro Brazilian religion in order to spice up bland narratives, while *Lambada: The Forbidden Dance* (1990) mingles indigenous and African culture in bizarre ways, and *Moon over Parador* (1988) uses Brazil as location to portray all Latin American nations as banana republics ruled over by Ubuesque dictators. In films like *Medicine Man* (1992), noble Americans struggle against irresponsible Brazilians to save the rain forest and protect the Indians. The "Indians" in *The Emerald Forest* speak a bizarre dialect of English (*tutei*/today), and *Amazon in Flames* (1989) obliges Sônia Braga to adopt a Hispanic accent even in a film set in *her* own Portuguese-speaking country.[1]

What is missing in such representations is a relational sense of Brazil as a country with links to the United States and with a comparable history. To further lay the groundwork for our discussion of Brazilian multiculturalism, therefore, I will now delineate in more detail the analogies and disanalogies between the U.S. and the Brazilian historical experiences. In economic terms, for example, Brazilian and U.S. history differ dramatically. Whereas the Portuguese who went to Brazil were agents for Portugal, the American colonists went on their own behalf. And while the fledgling American colonies had products that duplicated those of the mother country, Brazilian products were complementary to those of the metropole and therefore more jealously watched over. Thus Brazil was ironically "cursed" by its wealth, whereas the United States was "saved" by its (relative) poverty. Portugal forbade Brazil to produce anything, including toothpicks, but England tolerated some limited manufacture. While Brazil has tended toward the serial monoculture of lucrative crops on vast land-grant plantations—with a succession of booms and busts (sugar in the Northeast, silver and gold in Minas Gerais, rubber in the Amazon, and coffee in São Paulo)—the United States has had fairly diversified agriculture on relatively small property from the beginning. Moreover, in cultural terms, whereas Portugal discouraged education and even publishing in Brazil—the first legal printing press was in 1808—England was less "touchy" about cultural independence; it was unperturbed, for example, by the founding of Harvard in 1636.

The global economic context of Brazil and the United States as colonies was also quite distinct. The United States was linked to the dynamic capitalism of Britain; Brazil in contrast, was tied to the decadent capitalism of a Portugal itself subordinated to British mercantile interests. As a consequence, Brazilian formal independence in 1822 led only to British free-trade imperialism throughout the nineteenth century and to American neocolonialism in the twentieth, while North American independence in 1776 led to substantive independence, the historical ground for subsequent hegemony over Latin America. (Independence in both countries did not mean freedom for either blacks or indigenous people.) And if Brazilian independence was bloodless and diplomatic—the visiting Portuguese Prince Pedro declared himself emperor and resolved to stay in Brazil—U.S. independence was wrought through a bloody revolution. As a result, the United States became a nation where the white majority enjoyed substantial political rights, while Brazil became a land where a tiny minority of landowners, along with civil, military, and religious authorities, lorded over an oppressed mestiço mass with virtually no rights whatsoever.[2]

The Brazil-U.S. connection is not only a metaphorical one of comparison and analogy; it is also metonymic, a question of concrete historical links going far back in time. The first Jews to come to what is now the United States came by way of Brazil. Portuguese Jews fleeing the Inquisition went to Brazil with the Dutch, ended up fleeing the Inquisition once again in Recife in 1636 and going to New York, then called New Amsterdam, where they founded the first Sephardi Synagogue on West Seventieth Street. Afro Brazilians, also arriving with the Dutch from Brazil, were among the very first black people to arrive in New York City. At that time, New York was a moderately prosperous Dutch colony founded by the East India Company in 1624. Envious of the material wealth of the Portuguese colonies, the Dutch had already placed Salvador under siege in the same year, and took over Recife in 1630. In need of agricultural workers, New Amsterdam invited Dutch landowners with their slaves and thus inaugurated a small-scale slave system into the city. The first Afro Brazilians arrived in New Amsterdam in chains. Historian Warren Dean tells us their names: Paulo d'Angola and his wife, Clara; Grande Manuel, Simão Congo, Antônio Português, Manuel Trompete, and many others. When New Amsterdam was undergoing a food shortage simultaneous with increased Native American attack, Governor Klieft decided to liberate the productive forces of the East India Company's slaves. He granted the slaves land, situated in the place the Indians called "Sapohanican," an area that would now run from Eighth Street to Grand Street, that is, much of contemporary Greenwich Village. Along with land, the governor offered contingent freedom: the blacks would have all their rights as long as they produced 800 liters of corn or beans per year. (The proposal did not apply to their children.) The newly freed blacks apparently prospered under this regime: Simão Congo owned 20 hectares, while other Afro Brazilians had land going from what is now Twenty-third Street to Chatham Square, a total of 20 sites owned up until 1660. In sum, "almost all of Greenwich Village in those times belonged to blacks, including what is now Washington Square, much of what is now New York University, and Soho."[3] The current site of S.O.B.'s (Sounds of Brazil), where Afro Brazilian musicians like Gilberto Gil, Djavan, and Jorge Benjor often play, was then the property of the Simão Congo. New Amsterdam was also the site of *mestiçagem* à la Brésilienne, since some of the sons of Afro Brazilians married white women, while their children adopted Anglo names; for example, Susannah Anthony Roberts, the daughter of Antônio Português. When the British took over New Amsterdam in 1664, the Afro Brazilians had their children declared free, but they were slowly forced to sell their land to whites.

Both Brazil and the United States have been slave-holding societies longer than they have been free. But although Brazil and the United States developed systems of racialized slavery, the institution was hardly identical in the two countries. Slavery in Brazil began almost a century before slavery in the United States and was abolished over two decades later. The Portuguese initiated the trans-Atlantic slave trade and for a century virtually monopolized it. Indeed, the word "negro" in American English is borrowed from Portuguese, as is "pickaninny" (from Portuguese *pequeninho*). In what became the United States, the first Africans were not slaves but indentured servants, while Indian enslavement died out relatively early. In Brazil, Indians were enslaved before Africans and were enslaved longer than they were in the United States; indeed, Brazilian Indians were sometimes called *negros da terra* (home negroes) as opposed to *negros de Guine* (Guinea negroes). In both countries, slaves were largely taken from West Africa. In Brazil, slaves were taken from very diverse African groups: (1) Bantu, from Congo and Angola; (2) Islamized Africans, notably the Peul, the Mandinga, and the Hausa, from the north of Nigeria and in Brazil called *malê* in Bahia and *alufa* in Rio de Janeiro; and (3) Yoruba (called nagô), especially those from Dahomey (called *gegê*). Early on, the *mamelucos* and the Africans together composed a racially mestiço proto-Brazil, no longer completely African or Indian but a mixture of both with the Portuguese and other Europeans, changing the overall appearance of Brazil from one that was Indian and Portuguese to one that was black, Indian, and European.

There exists a substantial tradition of comparative slavery studies between Brazil and the United States, going back to the nineteenth century but reaching vast proportions in the twentieth century. Frank Tannenbaum argued in *Slave and Citizen* (1947) that Latin American slavery was less harsh than the Anglo Saxon model. In the Spanish and Portuguese territories, the heritage of Roman law, tempered by Christian ethics, led to a recognition of the moral and spiritual personality of the slave, who was regarded as temporarily degraded rather than as essentially and eternally dehumanized. More than a decade later, Stanley Elkins, in the same vein, claimed in *Slavery: A Problem in American Institutional Life* (1959) that Latin American slavery was tempered by religious institutions that prevented the reduction of blacks to mere commodities. The theories of Tannenbaum and Elkins were subsequently disputed by North American as well as Brazilian scholars. Eugene Genovese pointed out that the Catholic model of slavery did not prevent violent revolutions, as in Haiti, or slave insurrections, as in Brazil.[4] Marvin Harris mocked the "myth of the friendly master," arguing that the Brazilian slaveholding class created an intermediate group of mestiços as soldiers and slave drivers (a phenomenon registered in the film *Sinhá Moça* [1953]) only because whites were not available for such services.[5] And whatever the church's abstractly theological respect for the slave's soul, it was pointed out, the slave's body was treated with relentless cruelty. Indeed, in some respects Brazilian slavery was physically more rigorous than North American slavery. Whereas the slave population in the United States endured and even expanded on the basis of reproduction alone, slaves in Brazil were not guaranteed sufficient health or well-being to reproduce in large numbers. A number of practices documented in Brazil, furthermore, found little or no counterpart in the North American experience. Female slaves were often exploited as prostitutes, and in some cases masters lived off the earnings of these slaves. Suicides were also apparently more common in Brazil than in the United States.[6] The academic discussion of the relative "humanity" of slavery in North and South America, in any case, partakes of the obscene, as if one were coolly assessing the relative comfort of the accommodations at Auschwitz versus Treblinka. New World racialized slavery, in all its modalities, constituted an excruciatingly prolonged commodification of human beings, and no discussion of comparative amenities can alter that fact.

It is tempting, but dangerous, then, to overdraw the contrasts between slavery in the two countries. Both systems shared an ideological substratum rooted in colonialist and racist hierarchies that first justified slavery and subsequently underwrote the political, economic, and social exclusion of those of African descent. At the same time, slavery and its sequels were also distinct in important respects. First, there were differences in the cultural attitudes of the colonizers. The Portuguese came from a Mediterranean world, which from time immemorial had been the site of the intermingling of peoples, from Africa, Asia, and Europe, whereas the English, of all the major colonizing powers, were the most isolated, with the least experience of people of color prior to settlement in the New World. While blacks regularly accompanied the Spanish and Portuguese on their New World explorations, often in subordinate yet important positions (one need only think of Coronado's

Moorish emissary Estevanico), the English sailed alone. On the other hand, both the English and the Portuguese had prior experience in quasi-colonial domination; the English "practiced" racism first with the Irish, while the Portuguese practiced with Muslims and Jews during the *reconquista* and the Inquisition.[7] Second, in Brazil, slavery existed across the entire national territory, while in the United States it was after a time confined to the South, although it clearly *implicated* the entire national territory. (It was only in the United States, consequently, that the prospect of abolition led to *sectional* conflict.) Third, the United States abolished slavery with a swift legislative stroke in 1863, during a traumatic civil war, but Brazil abolished the institution only gradually, first freeing children born of slaves in 1871, then freeing slaves of more than 60 years of age (in 1885), and culminating in unconditional abolition in 1888. Indeed, abolition itself constituted a belated recognition by the state that the vast majority of Afro Brazilians had already obtained their own emancipation. A large number of free blacks enjoyed a status, both before and after abolition, not very different from that of lower-class whites. Several Brazilian films call attention to the role of these free blacks. Thus *Chico Rei* (1982) portrays a freed black mining entrepreneur in eighteenth-century Minas Gerais, and *Xica da Silva* (1976) explores the historical case of a black woman whose liaison with a Portuguese official made her a kind of power behind the throne.

Fourth, whereas in the United States the "one-drop rule" made all those with some African ancestry "black," racial classification in Brazil as early as the nineteenth century was pluralistic, involving not an epidermic dichotomy based on descent, but rather a subtle (if nonetheless racist) schema involving a complex interplay of color, facial features, occupation, education, and social status. (In the United States the one-drop rule functioned in the opposite direction for Native Americans, seen as "mixed" if they had even minimal European ancestry; in both cases the law reinforced white domination, by multiplying slaves in the case of blacks and by weakening community land claims in the case of Native Americans.) By assigning perpetual servitude to all those of any African descent, Anglo-colonists cut off hope for social mobility, suggesting that blacks would always be at the bottom of the social hierarchy. Whereas in Brazil many of the enslaved (domestic slaves, urban slaves, trusted slaves in the mines) were manumitted or able to buy their freedom and thus move up and out of slavery, in the United States black-white relations were more rigid

7. The appraisals of slavery: *Chico Rei* (1982)

and more polarized. And those whites who fathered children with black slave women disavowed them in order to maintain a (fictitious) color line. Fifth, the two countries differed in ideological terms. Abolitionism began earlier in the United States. Some Puritans, although ethnocidal toward Indians, were philosophically opposed to slavery, and already in 1775 the Quakers of Philadelphia organized the first abolitionist society, the Society for the Relief of Free Negroes Unlawfully Held in Bondage.[8] On the other hand, the elite of the antebellum South, on the defensive against Northern Abolitionists, mounted a more vigorous defense of the "peculiar institution," promoting the idyllic vision of slave society, subsequently recycled in films like *Gone with the Wind* (1939) and *Song of the South* (1946). Brazilian proslavery ideologists, in contrast, rarely went beyond a pragmatic, economic rationale for slavery's continuation, a fact reflected in Brazilian films like *Sinhá Moça* (The Plantation Owner's Daughter, 1953) and *João Negrinho* (John the Black Boy; shot 1954, released 1958).

The postslavery period, similarly, features congruencies and contrasts. In both countries, the historical inertia of colonialism and slavery, and an abolition negotiated on ruling-class terms, favored the maintenance of archaic social hierarchies even under a free-labor regime. In each of the countries, the ruling elite favored European immigrants over blacks. And in both countries, self-exculpatory myths "covered" the fact of racialized oppression: in the United States, myths of the American dream and equal opportunity; in Brazil, the myth of "racial democracy." However, Brazilians generally rejected segregationist racism as not only inhuman but also counterproductive.[9] Brazilian paternalism opted for an "ideology of whitening," which "allowed" a mixed population to gradually "cleanse" itself through intermarriage. Faith in the likelihood of whitening, in other words, led Brazilian elites to partially encourage miscegenation, rather than proscribe it in the phobic North American manner.[10] And while North American racial segregation ironically favored the development of parallel institutions—black colleges, the black Church, an independent black press, sports organizations—the Brazilian situation encouraged a paternalistic dependency on elite (i.e., white) institutions.[11] Although American blacks were relegated to the "basement" of American society, in sum, they at least dominated the basement.

Brazilian culture is irrevocably mestiço. Many of the foods, place-names, and customs are indigenous in origin. Brazilians trace their love of taking showers to the indigenous custom of frequent bathing in rivers. The minimalist bikini, or *tanga,* derives from indigenous dress. Lévi-Strauss's description of the Nambiquara as "expressing tenderness in broad daylight" evokes the penchant of present-day nonindigenous Brazilians to spontaneously embrace, kiss, and caress. Brazilian culture is also highly and consciously Africanized. All of Brazilian culture, its *jeito,* its way of walking and talking and touching, of making music and telling stories, its flexible, sinuous style, subtle like the feints of the Afro Brazilian martial art/dance *capoeira,* is thoroughly inflected by Africa-derived cultural patterns. Brazil's improvisational samba soccer, in this sense, corresponds to America's jazzistic basketball. Roger Bastide points out that many Africanisms, such as rubbing hands to show pleasure, have become generalized in Brazil.[12] Forms of collective survival and solidarity, such as the *mutirão* (the collective construction of favela homes) are also highly Africanized. Even the celebrated Brazilian *jeitinho,* the ingenious manner of bypassing apparently insuperable legal and bureaucratic obstacles, can be seen as a form of survivalist improvisation, expressed not musically but rather as part of the creativity of everyday life. Brazilians' expansive orality and capacity for collective enthusiasm, whether during carnival, a soccer game, or a political rally, can be seen, in some measure, as shaped by an

African inheritance, part of what Basil Davidson calls the "art of social happiness."[13]

The African presence pervades all moments of Brazilian history and all areas of Brazilian culture. A kind of Yoruba hegemony often results in the slighting of other African strains within Brazilian culture. Yet words and concepts of central cultural importance *(senzala, quilombo, macumba, candomblé, maconha, samba, bunda)* all come from Bantu languages. Nor can African influence be restricted to the question of African "survivals"; Africanicity also reshaped other ethnic identities. The Brazilian version of the Portuguese language, for example, is thoroughly Africanized. As the black activist Lélia Gonzalez once punningly put it, Brazilians do not speak Portuguese but "Pretoguês" ("Blackoguese").[14] The African influence on the Brazilian language is at once phonetic, morphological, and lexical. Words from African languages such as Fon, Hausa, and Yoruba have enriched the Brazilian Portuguese vocabulary and made the language more musical and mellifluous. Indeed, it was ironically thanks to enslaved Afro Brazilians that Portuguese became disseminated as the national language. As mentioned in the historical preamble, in the early centuries of European colonization, Tupi-Guarani served as the *língua geral* (general language) for commerce and communication. It was only when Africans, coming from widely divergent cultures and languages, learned Portuguese from the shouted commands of the slave drivers and used it as a common denominator among themselves, that Portuguese became the national language of Brazil.[15]

Brazilian cultural life, both erudite and popular, is deeply informed by the black presence. Many of the greatest Brazilian literary figures, whose works have frequently been adapted for the cinema, were black or mulatto. The mulatto writer Machado de Assis, for example, wrote the novels adapted in Paulo César Saraceni's *Capitu* (1968; based on *Don Casmurro*), Nelson Pereira dos Santos' *Azyllo Muito Louco* (1970; based on "O Alienista"), and Júlio Bressane's *Brás Cubas* (1985; based on *Memórias Posthumas de Brás Cubas*). Lima Barreto, Jorge de Lima, and Mário de Andrade were also black or mulatto. Although these writers enjoyed more prestige than their black counterparts in the United States, they were less likely to be "race men." Hemmed in by taboos, they were often forced into the ambiguous position of "honorary whites." Maria Emília de Azeredo's *Alva Paixão* (White Passion, 1995) traces the tragic destiny of one of these black writers: Cruz e Souza, son of freed slaves and the most accomplished representative of the symbolist movement in Brazil. (Cruz e Souza died in 1898, the year in which Brazilian cinema began.) In his polished, gemlike poems, the "spiritualizing beauty" of whiteness becomes the transcendent symbol of an existence far from his own life of poverty, discrimination, and sadness with his mentally unstable wife (Zezé Motta). As a prompter in the theater, Cruz e Souza is the man who knows the lines but who cannot appear on the stage. His poetry is appreciated, but his blackness is out of place in the literary milieu of Santa Caterina, one of the "whitest" regions of Brazil. The film ends with a flash-forward to the present with a shot of a young black boy sitting pen in hand in an impoverished schoolhouse. What is the fate, this ending implicitly asks, of the *contemporary* Cruz e Souzas? Can they avoid the kinds of tragedies that befell earlier black writers?

In the realm of popular culture, meanwhile, many of the most highly prized symbols of Brazilian nationhood are Afro Brazilian in origin. The national dish is *feijoada,* the black-bean stew improvised by enslaved blacks from low-quality materials, and the national music is samba, whose Africanized polyrhythms have long thrown down the basic beat of the Brazilian musical idiom. In the privileged moments of Brazilian life, as we see in films like *Xica da Silva* (1976) and *Tenda dos Milagres* (Tent of Miracles, 1977), Brazil might be said to celebrate its own blackness. (We will address the limits of this "celebration" subsequently.)

Africa also influenced Brazilian religiosity irrevocably. Whereas African Americans largely adopted the formal robes of Christian religion—even if "read" in a critical, subversive manner and expressed in a transcoded African spiritualism—Afro Brazilians managed to maintain clearly African and Africanized religions. The symbolic architecture of the religion *candomblé*—the temples, the groves of sacred trees, the spring of Oxalá—represent a "reconstruction of the lost Africa."[16] Africa not only sent religions such as *candomblé* to Brazil; it also syncretized with popular Catholicism and European spiritism to form such religions as *umbanda.* The African influence, furthermore, shaped Catholic practice in Brazil, making it more humane, affective, and sentimental rather than dogmatic, formalist, and inquisitorial. (African spirit religions were usually not exclusivist and had no objection to its adepts simultaneously practicing other religions.) African religious practices left many traces in everyday language; *fazer a cabeça* (literally, make the head, figuratively, to influence) is drawn from *candomblé* initiation; *baixar o santo* (literally, the saint descended, figuratively, to get inspired) refers to trance possession. African "magical" practices became common among all Brazilians, thus contributing to folk Catholicism and to popular therapeutic religion. The charismatic appeal of Africanized religions becomes strikingly visible on New Year's Eve on Copacabana beach, as thousands of devotees of Iemanjá, all dressed in white, place their offerings on small hand-made boats in honor of their *orixá*.

African religions in Brazil are as diverse as the cultural complexes (Yoruba, Bantu, Hausa) that gave birth to them and even more diverse because they historically syncretized not only with Christianity, Judaism, and European spiritism but also with indigenous religions and with one another. Some African religions are relatively "pure" or traditional, whereas others are highly, and multiply, syncretic. Syncretism with Catholicism has sometimes led to a double system of rough equivalences between *orixás* and saints. Oxalá is often associated with Christ, although in African terms Oxalá is androgynous, so Oxalá is elsewhere identified with a woman saint, Saint Anne. Iemanjá, the water goddess, is sometimes identified with the Virgin Mary. In *O Pagador de Promessas* (The Given Word, 1962) Iansã, a goddess of storms, is linked to Saint Barbara, seen in popular Catholicism as a saint who protected people from storms and lightning. In general, Brazilian films proliferate syncretic traces. One sequence in *O Pagador de Promessas* shows white-clad women washing the steps of a Church of Nosso Senhor do Bomfim, a practice that mingles a Portuguese custom with the African custom of washing cult objects and shrines. The time has passed, we should add, when "syncretism" can be used as a pejorative; all religions are syncretic. European Christianity, for example, borrowed many elements from so called pagan pre-Christian religions, whence the ritual use of Christmas trees to celebrate Christmas.

African religions are the partial subject of fiction films such as *Pagador de Promessas* (The Given Word, 1962), *Barravento* (The Turning Wind, 1962), *A Força de Xangô* (The Power of Xangô, 1979), *Samba da Criação do Mundo* (Samba of the Creation of the World, 1979), *O Amuleto de Ogum* (The Amulet of Ogum, 1974), and *A Prova de Fogo* (Trial by Fire, 1981), as well as of innumerable documentaries such as Tina Espinheira's *Bahia de Todos os Exus* (All Exu's Bahia, 1978), Leão Rozenberg's *Candomblé* (1969), Geraldo Sarno's *Espaço Sagrado* (Sacred Space, 1975) and *Iao* (1978), Orlando Senna's *Ilê Aiyê/ Angola* (1985), Roberto Moura's *Sai Dessa Exu* (Cut It Out, Exu, 1972), Maria

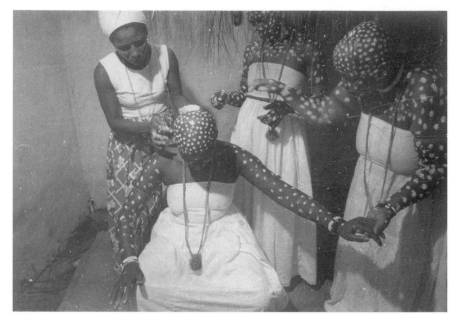

8. Religious initiations in *Iao* (1978)

Lúcia Aboim's *Teu Nome Veio da Africa* (Your Name Came from Africa, 1979), Raquel Gerber's *Ylê Xoroquê* (1981), and José Aranjo's *Salve Umbanda!* (Hail Umbanda!, 1996). Geraldo Sarno's *Iao* (photo 8) documents the initiation rites into a *nagô gegê terreiro* (*candomblé* house of worship) in Bahia, especially foregrounding the slow transformation of three young women *(abians)* into *iaos,* or brides of the spirit. The duty of the *abians* is to "seat" their *orixás,* to bring them into their lives. The film shows the *catulagem,* or cutting, of the *abians'* hair. The priestesses chant as they cut the hair close to the scalp. Each *abian* is given armlets, bracelets, anklets, and necklaces. Their heads become the mediums open to the *orixás;* the blood of a dove is poured over conse-crated heads, and feathers are placed in the drying blood. A shallow cross is cut in the center of the head, opening up a point of connection between the inner and outer worlds. Finally, the *iaos* publicly present themselves three times before the community, each time wearing different costumes and fol-lowing different drum rhythms, the third time appearing in full regalia.

The African element also shaped the protean vitality of Brazilian carnival, making it more dynamic than the relatively petrified forms of European carni-val. African Brazilians brought to carnival their totems (*ranchos* in Bahia) and their tradition of royal pageants (*maracatu* in Recife), turning carnival into a secularized religion, what Oswald de Andrade called in one of his manifestos "the religious event of the Brazilian race." Carnival and Afro Brazilian religious practice thus display both metonymic and metaphoric links. In metonymic terms, Afro Brazilian religious groups have actively shaped carnival's style of pageantry, music, dance, and costume. And in metaphoric terms carnival and the West African trance religions share a comparable play with identity, whether through the *fantasias* of carnival (the *favelada* costumed as an aristocrat, the man in drag) or through the possession trances of *candomblé*, where a man can be possessed by a female *orixá*, a young white person by a *preto velho* (old black man), and so on. Carnival and Afro Brazilian religion meet in Vera Figueiredo's *Samba da Criação do Mundo* (see photo 9), where the Beija Flor Samba School stages Yoruba cosmology. The breath of Olorum, as primal energy, transforms air first into water, then into mud, and finally into stone, which turns red and gives birth to Exu. Olorum then orders Obatalá, the masculine principle, to create the world, but Obatalá forgets to pay homage to Exu. Once Oduduá, the feminine principle, pays homage to Exu, she is aided in creating the world. Finally, both Obatalá and Oduduá give birth to the various *orixás*. The film is punctuated by cosmological poems

9. *Samba da Criação do Mundo* (1978)

and danced poetic tributes to the *orixás:* Nana, *orixá* of fertility; Oxum, *orixá* of waterfalls and rivers; Ogum, warrior god and hunter. Each *orixá* figure is set in an appropriate decor. Iemanjá, goddess of salt waters, for example, whose colors are white and blue, performs against a shimmering backdrop of surf and sand. At the finale, the union of Oduduá and Obatalá is celebrated, as is usual in *candomblé,* with a banquet, after which the *sambistas* return to their daily life.

Africa not only provided many of the instruments featured in Brazilian music (the *cuíca* [friction drum], the *agogô* [double cowbell struck with wooden stick], and the *berimbau* [consisting of a long bow, gourd, and string, and played with wooden sticks]), but also furnished the cardinal aesthetic principles on which Brazilian music in general, and popular music in particular, are built. In the Brazilian tradition, percussion has independent signification. It is not the "servant" of melody or harmony; rather, the rhythms provide a complex, variegated vocabulary of moods and emotions. Brazilian music, like African music, constitutes a collective form of active creation, linked to polyphony and communitarian dance; it is the dynamic expression of a community, gregarious rather than introspective. The principles of the dominant Brazilian musical style include a percussive performance style based on the synergistic dialectic of multiple rhythms existing in intricate and constantly changing relationships to one another, a frequency of overlapping call and response patterns (e.g., between the *puxador* [caller] of samba and the responding chorus); offbeat phrasing and suspended accentuation; and the assumption that music has the right, even the duty, to speak to its time and community through social commentary and allusion.[17] Brazilian music has also existed in a symbiotic relation with American music. Among the American musicians who have played or been influenced by Brazilian music are Charlie Byrd, Stan Getz, Zoot Sims, Paul Winter, Stanley Turrentine, Coleman Hawkins, Lalo Schifrin, Nat King Cole, Ella Fitzgerald, Ray Charles, Elvis Presley, Dionne Warwick, Gil Evans, Frank Sinatra, George Duke, Herbie Hancock, Chick Corea, Don Cherry, Ron Carter, George Duke, Sarah Vaughan, Wayne Shorter, Paul Simon, David Byrne, George Benson, Patti Austin, Lee Ritenour, Pat Metheny, Stevie Wonder, Michael Franks, Joni Mitchell, and Quincy Jones. (My final chapter will offer some modest proposals about what Brazilian cinema might learn from Brazilian popular music.)

Brazilian popular music is not only dominated by Afro Brazilian and Afro-influenced composers and singers, but it also increasingly addresses, in its lyrics, Afro Brazilian themes and preoccupations. Singers and composers of all colors (Gal Costa in "Raça Negra," Caetano Veloso in "Ilê Ayê," Gilberto Gil in "Filhos de Gandhi," Daniella Mercury with her *axé* [energy, power of realization] music) pay tribute to Afro Brazilian cultural expression. Doryval Caymmi's "Oração à Mãe Menininha" (Prayer of Praise for Mãe Menininha) is dedicated to the beloved *candomblé* priestess from Bahia known as Menininha de Gantois, called in the song "the most beautiful star," "the mother of sweetness," and the "solace of the people." In her ode to blackness, "Abraço Negro," Ivone Lara speaks of the consolations of negritude—

> A black embrace
> A black embrace
> Brings Happiness
> —along with its sorrows—
> Blacks without jobs
> Black without relief
> Black is the root of freedom.

The brilliant composer and performer Gilberto Gil, inspired both by a Pan-Africanist vision and by an anthropophagic openness to world musical culture, speaks of and himself embodies what he calls the immense "tribalizing" power of Afro-derived music. His albums *Refazenda* (1975) and *Refavela* (1978) were already clear calls for Afro Brazilian political consciousness; indeed, Gil called the latter album a "report on the black population of the cities." The lyrics of Gil's more politicized sambas make them the equivalent of the socially conscious reggae of Jamaica, although without that movement's Rastafarian underpinnings. Gil's song "From Bob Dylan to Bob Marley: A Samba Provocation" forges a creative counterpoint between Jewish, Rastafari, and Afro Brazilian culture: "When the peoples of Africa arrived in Brazil, there was no freedom of religion." The European Enlightenment concept of "freedom of religion," Gil's lyrics remind us, did not extend to African religions, just as it did not extend to Judaism or Islam. The refrain indexes two forms of syncretism, one liberating, the other alienated:

> Bob Marley died
> Because besides being black

He was also Jewish
Michael Jackson
Is still around
Because besides becoming white
He's become very sad.[18]

It would be wrong to "folklorize" the African contribution. The influence of Afro Brazilians, like that of African Americans, has also been economic, political, and even military. First, Afro Brazilians had an indispensable role in economic production; they were crucial to the project of exploring, dominating, and cultivating a tropical territory larger than all of Europe. Afro Brazilians "realized" the economic goals of white entrepreneurs, generating the surplus capital that not only fueled Brazilian internal development but which also indirectly helped finance a fledgling European capitalism. Slaves worked everywhere and in very varied capacities: they cut cane in the Northeast, mined silver and gold in the central west, and planted coffee in the south; they were the real producers and fashioners of Brazilian modernity.

Second, Afro Brazilians, like African Americans from Crispus Attucks to Colin Powell, have played a crucial military role. In seventeenth-century Brazil, the former slave Henrique Diaz helped expel the Dutch then occupying the north of Brazil. In a later period, the empire's army maintained its numbers by forced conscription among the poorest sectors of the population, mostly black African, Indian, and mestiço. Slaves enlisted under false names as a way of gaining freedom, or at least a better life. Thousands of black soldiers died in the "War of the Triple Alliance" (1865–1870), in which Paraguay fought against the combined forces of Brazil, Argentina, and Uruguay. "In the rank and file of the army, as in the crews of the fleet," wrote Oliveira Lima, "one sees only blacks and mestiços."[19]

Third, as the most egregious victims (along with the indigenous peoples) of the Brazilian historical process, Afro Brazilians played a crucial role in the ideological critique of the dominant system. Who better than blacks and Indians perceived the hollowness of official proclamations of "order and progress," in an earlier period, and "racial democracy" in a later? Who better than blacks knew the regime's limitations and hypocrisies? As Henry Louis Gates put it in a North American context, blacks were the "first deconstructionists"; they were exotopically positioned to "call the bluff" of official ideologies and idealizations. Caetano Veloso evokes this idea in his song "Milagres do Povo":

> Arriving as survivors in the slave ships
> It was blacks who discovered Brazil
> They saw cruelty face to face
> Yet still produced miracles of faith
> In the Far West.

Because of their radical oppression, blacks were well positioned to discern the urgency of thoroughgoing solutions, and blacks in both countries have often formed a hard core of support for proposals of radical structural change. In Brazil, there were hundreds of slave rebellions, for example the Muslim Malê Revolt in 1835 in Salvador, when some 600 enslaved blacks together with freedmen, bearing talismans containing passages from the Koran, rose up against the government. In Brazil, these revolutionary energies have often been suppressed or diverted, including by blacks themselves, but the potential is always there.

Fourth, Brazilian blacks provided the first New World prototype of what might be called a utopian republic, in the form of Palmares, a community founded in the seventeenth century by runaway slaves, and the subject of at least two major feature-fiction films, *Ganga Zumba* (1963) and *Quilombo* (1984); of many documentaries, notably Linduarte Noronha's *Aruanda* (1960), Vladimir Carvalho's *Quilombo* (1975), and Samin Cherques and Moisés Weltman's *Zumbi dos Palmares* (Zumbi of Palmares, 1963); and most recently of a TV miniseries: *Zumbi, O Rei dos Palmares* (Zumbi: King of Palmares). Palmares at its height counted roughly 20,000 inhabitants spread over numerous villages in the northeastern interior, covering an area roughly one-third the size of Portugal. (In the United States only the black-Indian collaboration of the Second Seminole War approached the scale of Palmares.) To reconstruct the truth about Palmares, historians such as Artur Ramos and Décio Freitas have had to rely on the accounts of the very officials and soldiers who sought to destroy it, but an impressive picture emerges even from the reports of its enemies. Palmares bears witness not only to the capacity of Afro Brazilians to revolt against slavery but also to mobilize an alternative life. Palmares was economically self-sufficient because it practiced the diversified

10. Palmares incarnate: *Quilombo* (1984)

agriculture the slaves remembered from Africa rather than the monoculture characteristic of colonial Brazil. The Palmarinos of this "Little Angola" planted corn, beans, manioc, potatoes, and sugarcane on communally shared land (as had been the pattern in much of Africa). A Portuguese chronicler, Governor Pedro de Almeida, described them as "very hard working."[20] Palmarino kings were kings in the African rather than the European sense, not absolute monarchs but rather custodians of the common wealth. Although the penal code, especially in the later period, was harsh—legislation stipulated the death penalty for theft, homicide, or desertion—the Palmarinos enjoyed basic civic and political equality.

The recent research of the Palmeres Archaeological Project has shown that Palmares welcomed—along with the black majority—Indians, mestiços, renegade whites, Jews, Muslims, and heretics, ultimately becoming a refuge for the persecuted of Brazilian society and thus the prototype of a "multicultural" society long before the term was coined.[21] Although the Portuguese authorities described the whites of Palmares as "criminals," in fact they were impoverished people attracted to the political tolerance and economic well-being of this liberated area. The Palmarinos spoke a syncretic language that fused Portuguese, African, and indigenous Brazilian languages, just as their religion fused African religions with Christianity. They traded with neighboring settlements, and at one point (November 5, 1678) their leader Ganga Zumba (Great Chief), went together with his entourage to Recife to sign a peace treaty with the Portuguese and was received with great solemnity by the Portuguese governor.

As a magnet for fugitive slaves, as a barrier to western expansion, and as a challenge to white domination, Palmares became a prime target for colonial authorities. Numerous military expeditions were mounted against it; indeed, between 1672 and 1694, Palmares withstood an average of one Portuguese attack every 15 months. Knowing that any defeat would be apocalyptic, the Palmarinos resisted by every means possible, fighting with bows and arrows as well as firearms, conducting what was perhaps the world's first guerrilla war. One of the *ganga zumbas*, specifically Zumbi, had entire villages removed to more remote places as a means of self-defense. Palmares was destroyed, finally, by a combination of internal dissension and external assault. Zumbi opted for a decisive battle that would mean either clear victory or defeat. In 1684, the Palmarinos lost; only women and children remained, and many of the women starved themselves to death rather than return to slavery. At one point, it was rumored that Zumbi, preferring death to captivity, had thrown himself off a cliff with his brothers, but he was subsequently sighted by the Portuguese when he attacked a village in order to get arms and ammunition. On November 25, 1695, Furtado de Mendonça cut off the head of Zumbi, the "black Spartacus," and had it brought to Recife. Melo e Castro had it placed on a skewer in the public square until it decomposed in order to terrorize the blacks, who thought him immortal. Shortly thereafter, however, refugees from Palmares formed another *quilombo* called Cumbe in Paraiba, which itself repelled numerous attacks before it was destroyed in 1731. Resistance in the region continued until 1797, more than a century after the death of Zumbi. Indeed, black farmers still cultivate the land that their ancestors settled, and a "*quilombo* clause" in the recent Constitution ceded land titles to 500,000 descendants of the diverse free black communities, providing a precedent for the more than 500 territories inhabited by the remnant of the maroon communities. A number of contemporary musical groups from Bahia, such as Olodum and Ilê Aiyê, have organized support for the "*quilombo* clause," composing lyrics such as the following:

> *Quilombo,* here we are
> my only debt is to the *quilombo*
> my only debt is to Zumbi.[22]

(We will return subsequently to the filmic representations of Palmares.)

For many Brazilians, the *quilombos* have come to symbolize the tradition of black resistance. It is hardly coincidental that black liberationist Abdias do Nascimento called his movement Quilombismo, or that popular musician Milton Nascimento composed a Quilombo Mass, or that politicized black artists like Paulinho da Viola founded a black consciousness carnival group called the Quilombo Samba School, or that the Olodum Theater Group in Salvador presents a play entitled "Zumbi Is Alive and Struggling," or that every year dozens of festivities commemorate the anniversary of Zumbi's death on November 20, now rebaptized the "National Day of Black Consciousness." In fact, many blacks and their supporters have proposed substituting the celebration of Zumbi's Black Consciousness Day on November 20 for the traditional commemoration of the end of slavery on May 13, 1888, the day Princess Isabel signed the Lei Áurea emancipating the slaves.

Over the centuries, roughly three and a half million blacks survived the Middle Passage to arrive in Brazil, six times the number that arrived in the United States, and the largest contingent sent to any New World destination. As a result, blacks in the United States have always formed a minority in terms of numbers and in terms of power, whereas black, mulatto, and mestiço Brazilians form part of a marginalized *majority* of Brazilian citizens. It is thus a Eurocentric misnomer, as Abdias do Nascimento points out, to call Brazil a "Latin" country; it might better be called an indigenous, African, Lusitanian country.

The globalized geography of race, as Howard Winant points out, makes it especially susceptible to comparative analysis.[23] Racial categories in Brazil, as elsewhere, are not natural but constructs, not absolutes but relative, situational, even narrative categories, engendered by historical processes of differentiation. Since race is a sociogenic rather than a phylogenic category, the categorization of the same person can mutate over time, location, and context. Enslaved Africans, prior to colonialism, did not think of themselves as black but only as members of specific groups: Bantu, Fon, Hausa, Igbo, just as Euro Brazilians, prior to the invention of "whiteness," thought of themselves as Castilian, Portuguese, Galicians, and so forth.[24] Even the definition of blackness differs between Brazil and the United States. The North American vision has traditionally inclined toward binarism: a person is *either* black or white; there is no intermediate position. This binaristic thinking is reflected in the "zebra journalism" (Ishmael Reed) that "racializes" events like the Los Angeles rebellions according to simplistic black-white dichotomies. In the United States, even partial African ancestry has historically defined a person as black, whereas in Brazil partial European ancestry defines a person as of mixed race or white. In the United States the one-drop rule allowed the Southern white elite, despite white men's miscegenational proclivities, to turn mixed-race children into coerced laborers rather than potential heirs. Although miscegenation clearly existed in both countries, its social construction was distinct. (Indeed, the English word "miscegenation" itself comes wrapped in a taboo aura of racial terror while its equivalent in Portuguese *[mestiçagem]*, like its cognates in other Latin languages *[metissage, mestizaje]*, now has a vaguely celebratory ring.)

The Brazilian system is less concerned with ancestry than with appearance; its racial spectrum nuances shades from *preto retinto* (dark black) through *escuro* (dark) and *mulato escuro* (dark mulatto) to *mulato claro* (light mulatto), *moreno,* and *branco de Bahia* (Bahia-style white), not to mention all those terms that have to do with European indigenous and African indigenous mixtures—*cafuso, caboclo, mameluco*—indeed, a 1976 survey listed 135 such categories.[25] These differences in racial perception are linked to the distinct modalities of Brazilian racism, which consists less in a binary, supremacist white-over-black than in the superimposition of an official integrationist ideology ("racial democracy") on a power structure that subtly (and often not so subtly) enforces and promotes the idea that "white" is "better." Incorporating an image common in high school geography textbooks, a Brazilian 500-cruzeiro bill from the 1970s visualized this prejudice through a frieze of five faces "progressing" from a clearly black face in profile on the left to a full-front light *moreno* on the right.[26] The perception of race in Brazil focuses on appearance (color, hair, features) and on social and cultural cues (accent, education, dress, body language). It is often said in Brazil that "money whitens," which Oracy Nogueira translates as meaning "In Brazil, money buys anything, including even status for blacks."[27]

The 1980 Brazilian census lists four basic racial groups: *brancos* (whites), *pardos* (browns, mulattoes), *pretos* (blacks), and *amarelos* (yellows, Asians). The population percentages of the respective groups were whites 54.8 percent, mulattoes 38.6 percent, blacks 5.9 percent, and yellows 0.67 percent[28] Combining the figures for blacks and mulattoes brings a total of 45 percent of people who would be considered black within an American spectrum, a conservative number given the Brazilian tendency to "whiten" one's self-definition; Pelé's children, as the product of an interracial marriage, for example, are classified as "white." (A 1991 black movement campaign [Campanha Censo 91] warned blacks against *auto-embranquecimento* [self-whitening] in responding to the official census. The campaign's punning slogan was "Não deixe a sua cor passar em branco," or "Don't let your color be passed off as white/be a null vote.") The term *pardo* (roughly "dark" or "swarthy") has also triggered widespread dissatisfaction because of its pejorative tone and because in fact almost no one uses the term as self-descriptive. *Moreno,* meanwhile, seems agreeable to a large segment of the population, whereas *mulato,* despite its etymological origins in the word "mule," is accepted, although somewhat less enthusiastically. (President Fernando Henrique Cardoso called himself a "mulatinho" in 1995.) At the same time, we find a present-day convergence of racial spectra. In Brazil, rappers like Fernando from Disciplina Urbana, doubtless influenced by Afro American popular culture, argue that Brazilians of mixed race should see themselves as simply "black."[29] The racial spectrum in the United States, meanwhile, is becoming "Brazilianized," as a segregationist model gives way to an assimilationist model, and as people of mixed race begin to see themselves as separate from blacks, with Middle Easterners, Asians, and Latinos as intermediary groups.

In economic terms, statistics reveal the existence of a large black middle class in the United States, expressed in the media through such television shows as *The Cosbys* and *Good Times,* whereas in Brazil the term "black" is often synonymous with "poor." (Many Brazilians were surprised when the *Ebony*-style black periodical *Raça* sold out almost immediately with its inaugural issue in October 1996; Helena Solberg Ladd's *Brazil in Living Color* describes the work of this journal.) In 1995, the TV soap opera *A Próxima Vítima* (The Next Victim) was hailed for featuring the first middle-class prime-time black family, even if only as part of a subplot. Indeed, statistics suggest that the situation of the black middle class has been slowly improving in the United States, while the situation of blacks of all classes has been getting worse in Brazil. According to 1987 census statistics, the median salary for Brazilian whites was two and a half times that of blacks.[30] Blacks are the most egregious victims of a radically stratified system characterized by what a World Bank Report has called "the most unequal distribution of income in the world."[31] In any case, middle-class blacks in both countries complain about public hostility and police harassment. For whites, says Josafa Mota, one of the founders of the United Negro Movement, "every group of five blacks or more is a quilombo."[32]

As white-dominated multiracial societies, both Brazil and the United States are profoundly racist societies. They offer variations on a racial theme: the differences have to do with the specific modalities of domination. The comparison also turns on how one defines racism. More than merely an "opinion," racism is above all a social relation—"systematized hierarchization implacably pursued," in Fanon's words[33]—anchored in material structures and embedded in historical relations of power. In fact, traditional definitions of racism, premised on one-on-one encounters between racist and victim, do not fully account for more abstract, indirect, submerged, even "democratic" forms of racism. Since racism is a structured ensemble of social and institutional practices and discourses, individuals do not have to actively express or practice racism to be its beneficiaries. Racism in Brazil, like racism in the United States, comes thoroughly commingled with class, often taking the paternalistic form of role stereotyping, of assuming that blacks are inevitably poor or subaltern, that they are mainly good for samba and soccer; in short, that they do not deserve substantive empowerment.[34]

Like many Latin American countries, Brazil is what Chilean anthropologist Alejandro Lipschutz calls a "pigmentocracy," a social pyramid where the light skinned dominate the top and where indigenous people, blacks, and mestiços constitute the base. Brazilian society is "open" only in the sense that the "exceptional" person of color can "rise" and thus undergo symbolic "whitening."[35] (In Brazil, for example, Colin Powell would not be seen as "black.") In a society like Brazil, even the victims of racism are subject to engaging in hegemonic racial discourse. Racism thus "trickles down" and circulates laterally; oppressed people can perpetuate the hegemonic system by scapegoating one another "sideways," ultimately benefiting those at the top of the hierarchy. Whereas most African Americans have adopted a posture of racial pride, some black Brazilians still buy into the "ideology of whitening," an ideology that generates arrogance and complacency on the part of whites and self-rejection on the part of blacks and mulattoes. "Racial hegemony," as Michael Hanchard puts it, "has effectively neutralized racial identification among non-whites."[36] The mulatto "places the photo of his black mother in the kitchen, but puts the photo of his white father in the living room."[37] Half of those who define themselves as black, according to recent polls, agree with the assertion that the "good black is the black with a white soul" and almost half of the blacks agree that "blacks are only good at music and sports."[38] At times, racism constitutes a disguised form of genealogical self-rejection. When Brazilian racial ideologists like Nina Rodrigues, himself mulatto, excoriated Africans as the source of Brazilian inferiority, he was indulging in a form of self-hatred. Hence if Malcolm X was right to say that "the white man's greatest crime was to make the black man hate himself," that crime has been extensively committed not only in the United States but also in Brazil.

The introjection of the ideology of "racial democracy" leads to what Fernando Conceição calls "the dissolution of black identity."[39] Thus a series of practical and ideological pressures dissuade the majority population of color from defining itself as "black," despite the shared memory of slavery and exploitation. In Jorge Bodansky and Orlando Senna's film *Iracema* (1975), the indigenous title character (photo 11), whose name evokes the heroine of Alencar's Indianist novel, pathetically insists that she is "white." Among blacks, the introjection of racism is reflected, as in the United States, by the use of hair straighteners and gels and other forms of aesthetic (and at times even physical) self-violence. Although there is as yet no Brazilian equivalent to such films as *Hairpiece* (1985) and *A Question of Color* (1993), which probe the psychic devastation caused by the introjection of white aesthetic norms, Silvana Afram's documentary *Mulheres Negras* (Black Women of Brazil, 1986) does address some aspects of the question.

As in other white-dominated societies, racial attitudes in Brazil are multiform, fissured, even schizophrenic. Indeed, Brazil is in this sense pathogenic, the breeding ground par excellence of racial schizophrenia. The same Europeanized elite that conveniently invokes its mestiço culture and its "foot in the kitchen" steadfastly refuses to empower the mestiço majority.[40] In privileged moments, as in carnival, Brazil celebrates its blackness, yet the country's "ideal ego" in many ways remains white. The ideological legerdemain implicit in the standard cultural genealogy—for example, the founding fable of the "racial

11. *Iracema* (1975)

triangle" that declares Brazil at once Indian, African, and European—ob
scures present-day inequalities. Issues of "culture" are artificially segregated
from issues of power. Thus racism in Brazil often takes the complementary
forms of paternalism and self-hatred, unlike the United States, where racism
has often taken the form of an almost metaphysical otherization rooted psy-
chically in white fear of the "other" (associated with a suppressed animalic
"shadowy" self) and to phobic attitudes toward nature and the body.[41]
Whereas Brazilian racism tends to be pragmatic and paternalistic, U.S. racism
is very much linked to irrational fears, often taking bizarre forms, as when the
blood plasma of blacks was "segregated," or when white-owned clothing
stores in Harlem obliged blacks to use shower caps when they tried on hats,[42]
or when a white juror can fantasize that Rodney King, as he is being ruth-
lessly beaten by a cohort of white cops, is actually "controlling the situation."

Although the sexually phobic side of racism is certainly less strong in Brazil
than in the United States, it is not completely inoperative, especially when it
involves intermarriage. In such films as *Também Somos Irmãos* (We Are Also

Brothers, 1949) and *Jubiabá* (1987), white heads of households expel adopted black male children when they show romantic interest in their daughters. When black actress Zezé Motta portrayed a character involved in an interracial relationship in a 1980s soap opera, similarly, the TV station received angry letters. Even popular language and aphorisms—*ovelha negra* (black sheep), *dia negro* (black day)—encode racist prejudice by positing blackness as negative. Gilberto Gil and Chico Buarque satirically upend one of these racist aphorisms in their music-video performance of the song "Mão de Limpeza" (Hand of Cleanliness). The phenotypically white singer Chico appears in blackface, while Gil, the black, appears in whiteface. The lyrics respond to the racist proverb "blacks either make a mess at the entrance, or at the exit." Calling that view "a damned lie," the singers proceed to undo the association between blackness and dirtiness, linking it instead to the history of white oppression. Both during and after slavery, they argue, it was blacks who cleaned up the mess that whites made, and "black," therefore, "is the hand of cleanliness" and "immaculate purity."

In Brazil, the apparent inclusionism of "racial democracy" masks fundamental exclusions from social power. Indeed, the phrase "racial democracy" itself encodes a blame-the-victim strategy. If Brazil is democratic, the phrase implies, then blacks have only themselves to blame if they do not succeed.[43] Brazilian racism is in this sense closer to the assimilationist Portuguese colonial model, which allowed a minuscule elite into the charmed circle of inclusion, than to the segregationist British model carried on under *apartheid* in South Africa or under de jure segregation in the American South. Brazilian racism tends to be covert, without obvious or explicit hostility, rather than overt, expressed in hostile actions and words. If American-style racism can be a slap in the face, Brazilian-style racism can be a suffocating embrace. In Brazil, racism is muffled, camouflaged, disguised, hard to detect. When it occurs, the official discourse can always assert "plausible deniability" or insist on the exceptional nature of the case. Brazilian racism is largely "inferential" (Stuart Hall), that is, consisting in "those apparently naturalized representations of events and situations . . . which have racist premises and propositions inscribed in them as a set of unquestioned assumptions."[44] "Inferential racism" pervades everyday language in Brazil, which valences kinky hair as "bad" hair. A certain euphemization of race makes it more polite to call a black person *moreno,* as if the latter were more flattering; the "compliment" of a chromatic "upgrade" encodes white supremacist assumptions.

Racism in Brazil, like racism everywhere, is both individual and systemic, at once grindingly quotidian and maddeningly abstract. Racism, as Carlos Hasenbalg puts it, "permeates every stage of the life cycle of blacks and mestiços. It is in the family, the first socializing unit; it is in the schools . . . it is in the labor market, in police violence. It affects all of daily life.[45] Many black Brazilian professionals report that white Brazilians do not recognize them as *the* professor, *the* doctor, *the* lawyer, and misrecognize them as the assistant, the nurse, the janitor. This pattern of misrecognition is criticized in dos Santos's *Tenda dos Milagres,* where the journalist-poet Fausto Pena insists that the mulatto scholar Pedro Arcanjo "doesn't look like a scientist"; only the white American anthropologist Dr. Livingston (named after one of the archetypal European imperialists) really incarnates Pena's conception of the correct physiognomy for a scientist. A similar set of assumptions underlies the incidents in which a person of color is told to use the service rather than the social elevator—a phenomenon that itself inscribes a racially inflected class structure onto domestic architecture—the assumption being that people of color can only be in a "white" building or neighborhood in some sort of subaltern capacity. (Recently laws have been proposed to ban such practices.)

Although Brazil has rarely had an officially declared "color line," some analysts claim that Brazil has procured all the advantages of *apartheid* for its white elite, while avoiding the racial tensions that accompany apartheid per se.[46] Both Brazilian and "United Statesian" society reflect the dumb historical inertia of slavery, resulting in what Joel Kovel calls "metaracism," that is, a racism that requires little active human agency to sustain itself.[47] In both countries, blacks were freed and then promptly marginalized. Just as blacks inhabited the "holds" of the slave ships, they now inhabit the "holds" of civil society.[48] In Brazil, black and mulatto citizens remain oppressed, since the structural mechanisms of the Brazilian social formation largely deprive them of economic, social, and political power. Roughly 40 percent of the nonwhite population is illiterate, whereas the white illiteracy rate is 20 percent. Only 1 percent of black Brazilians define themselves as *patrões* (bosses, owners) while 79 percent of whites so define themselves.[49] Blacks are vastly underrepresented in positions of prestige and projection; they are virtually nonexistent in the higher echelons of the military, the diplomatic corps, and the government. Only a dozen black representatives, out of 559, served in the recent

Constitutional Assembly, and among those few were some who did not identify with black causes. Even in Salvador, Bahia, where blacks and mulattoes compose 80 percent of the population, the mayors and members of the city council have been overwhelmingly white. And if blacks are underrepresented in the universities and the legislature, they are overrepresented in the favelas, the prisons, and the ranks of the unemployed.

The Brazilian racial formation features what Anani Dzidzienyo calls an "etiquette" of race,[50] a complexly choreographed pas de deux of cordiality and deference whereby blacks repress their anger and militancy in exchange for minimal politesse and cultural compliments from whites, who for their part hide their condescension and scorn for black powerlessness, while assuming the right to be the nation's official mouthpiece.[51] The majority of both blacks and whites, for diverse reasons, cling to the myth of "racial democracy." For blacks and mestiços, it is a standard of hope and promise, a reminder of the way things *should* be. For whites, it rationalizes their advantages, conjuring away their fear that what already amounts to an undeclared social civil war (in cities like Rio), would become truly explosive if exacerbated by the incendiary fuel of racial hatred.

Despite its racial problems, Brazil has enjoyed a "positive image" abroad. From the turn-of-the-century through the 1940s, Michael Hanchard points out, many prestigious African Americans, such as Booker T. Washington and W. E. B. DuBois, wrote glowingly of the black experience in Brazil, while Henry McNeal Turner and Cyril Biggs went so far as to advocate emigration to Brazil as a haven for American blacks.[52] And the occasional belief in "racial democracy" on the part even of some Afro Brazilians is somewhat less surprising when we remember that certain features of Brazilian life and society do lend a humane face to what is, in structural terms, a racist society. Unlike the United States and South Africa under *apartheid,* Brazilian history has not been marked by a tradition of ghettos, or segregation, or lynching, or racialized rioting, or by Ku Klux Klan–style white supremacist groups. Unlike the United States of slavery days, where white exploitation of black women was masked by a neurotic obsession with racial purity and a hypocritical phobia about sexual mixing, in Brazil no special onus has generally been attached to interracial sex or marriage (although here the exceptions may be more frequent than Brazilians might like to admit). The carnivalesque festivities that greet the sexual liaison of the ex-slave Xica and the powerful Portuguese official on the Minas diamond frontier in *Xica da Silva*, would be quite simply unthinkable in a North American context. Indeed, the legendary power Xica temporarily amassed in eighteenth-century Brazil would be inconceivable in the United States of the same period. (It would be as if Thomas Jefferson's black mistress Sally Hemmings were to be acknowledged as the informal wielder of power in the White House.) Nor is racial scapegoating, such a prominent feature of the American political process, a normal part of the Brazilian scene. In the United States, many whites often have little contact with blacks and seem ready to believe the worst about them, while Brazilian racism operates within a kind of intimacy and thus on some levels resembles sexism rather than racism.

At the same time, many analysts point to a kind of convergence, as the United States moves from black-white polarity to a more multipolar system and as Brazil moves toward the politicization of racial identities.[53] The comparative racial perspective, once considered flattering to Brazil, is becoming less and less so in the light of political evolution in the world. Now that South Africa has moved to black majority rule under Nelson Mandela and now that it has become commonplace in the United States to have not only black celebrities but also black generals, black mayors, black millionaires, and black "public intellectuals," Brazilian society is looking more and more retrograde in comparison. Brazilian racial dynamics now seem, as Howard Winant puts it, "ossified and anachronistic, plagued by something like a false consciousness."[54] As long as one speaks of epidermic appearances ("We are all mixed") or of atmospherics—the lack of tension, the presence of cross-racial affection—the Brazilian situation seems more "livable," but as soon as one poses the crucial question of economic, political, and cultural power, the Brazilian model seems far less impressive. It is no longer possible to confuse the absence of racial tension with the presence of equality and justice. Nor can the appeal to physiognomy and *mestiçagem* be brandished as "proof" of lack of racism. On the other hand, interpersonal "atmospherics" do shape the lived texture of everyday life.

The causal relation between oppression and skin color in Brazil is obscured by the lack of apparent racial tension and by the fact that blacks and mulattoes often share similar living conditions with many lower-class whites and near-white mestiços. If in the United States race obscures class, it has become a commonplace to say that in Brazil class obscures race. Poverty is also at times shared by blacks and poor whites in the United States, but in a situation of segregation where divisions have been demogogically exploited by the white power structure. Indeed, mulattoes in Brazil arguably serve the same social function as poor whites in the United States; that is, as an intermediate or buffer group granted a modicum of social status contingent on their disaffiliating with those just below them on the social scale, a process allegorized in the film *Na Boca do Mundo* (In the World's Mouth, 1977).

The neighboring of blacks, mulattoes, and poor whites also implies a wide range of social intercourse between the two groups (evidenced in films like *Rio 40 Graus* [Rio 40 Degrees, 1954]), ranging from friendly and superficial contacts on the job and in racially mixed neighborhoods to more intimate friendships and marriages. Nevertheless, this partial sharing of living conditions does not mean that this oppression is not *also* racial. Race, in this sense, is both a kind of salt rubbed into the wounds of class and a wound in itself. Indeed, the Brazilian elite cliché that blacks are discriminated against only because they are poor, forgets that (a) the nonblack poor do not carry the stigma generated by racialized slavery and white supremacist ideology; and (b) that the perception of blackness as an index of poverty (and thus powerlessness) is itself an oppressive burden to bear in a stratified society.

Brazilian racism is a racism that dares not say its name: its most distinctive feature is its nondistinctiveness. A barely concealed racial subtext clearly lurks behind the everyday inequities of Brazilian social life, however; for example, in the parapolice murder of street children, most of whom are black and mulatto. What is confusing in the Brazilian case is that those who kill the children might *also* be people of color. Historically, the major confrontations of Brazilian history have not pitted black against white; there have been people of color on both sides. The situation lacks the stark clarity of a Rodney King–white police confrontation. Yet, murder of people of color by other people of color can also be a form of self-rejection, analogous to the fratricidal violence in the inner cities of America. And the echoes of disenchantment with the Brazilian racial model sound out in popular music, where rappers denounce racism and the former celebrants of *mestiçagem* begin to turn a critical eye on racial practices and ideologies. The Urban Discipline song "High Tech Violence" says that the police

> go up into the favelas
> invade your home

without shame
and the treatment you receive
will depend on the color of your skin

The Gilberto Gil and Caetano Veloso rap video "Haiti," from *Tropicália II* (1993), compares Brazil, unflatteringly, to the Haiti of the generals. The song's lyrics musically depict the intersection of race and class in a country where

soldiers, almost all black
beat up black *malandros*
beat up mulatto thieves and other thieves, almost white
but treated like blacks
just to show to the others, almost black
and they *are* almost all black
and to the almost white, but poor like blacks
how it is that blacks, poor people, and mulattoes
and almost white, almost black from being so poor
how it is that they are to be treated.

The song's refrain—"Haiti is here, Haiti is not here"—alludes to a famous 1881 quotation from the racist philosopher Sílvio Romero. Still frightened by Haiti's black majority revolution, Romero said that "Brazil is not, and should not be, Haiti."[55] The same song evokes the historical memory of the "massacre of 111 defenseless prisoners" in São Paulo, where

prisoners are almost always black
or almost black, or almost white
almost black from being so poor.

At the same time, the song hears reverberations of hope in the drumming of the *bloco-afro* organization Olodum, which conveys "the epic grandeur of a people in formation."

Many of these issues came up at the time of the *centenário*, the one hundredth anniversary of the abolition of slavery. For the first time, "the manifold forms of racial inequality against Afro-Brazilians became a principal theme in national debate."[56] Protest manifestos and position statements bore such titles as "100 Years of Lies" and "Discommemoration," and a persistent editorial leitmotif was the idea that "slavery has not really ended." In 1988, even the samba schools protested the "farce of abolition." The Mangueira school's theme was "100 Years of Freedom: Reality or Illusion," while the champion school Vila Isabel, with its "Kizombo: Feast of the Race," favored Zumbi over Princess Isabel:

> Zumbi's the one
> The strong shout of Palmares
> Crossing land, and air and sea
> shaping Abolition.

This same critical spirit animates two documentaries by Afro Brazilian directors. Zózimo Bulbul's *Abolição* (Abolition, 1988) uses interviews with scholar-activists such as Joel Rufino, Beatriz Nascimento, Lélia Gonzalez, Edmar Morel, Muniz Sodré, and Benedita da Silva in order to expose the limits of "racial democracy" a century after abolition. Silvana Afram's *Mulheres Negras* (Black Women of Brazil, 1986) critiques the media's implicitly white aesthetic and its effect on black Brazilian women, while also explaining their creative ways of coping with both racism and sexism by exploring collective identity through African-derived religion and music.

Eduardo Coutinho's *O Fio da Memória* (The Thread of Memory, 1992), begun on the eve of the centenary of abolition celebration on May 13, 1988, and completed three years later, also reflects on the sequels of slavery and abolition in the present. Instead of history as a coherent narrative, the film offers a history based on scraps and fragments, disjunctive images and data. The film weaves together various strands or fragments, which together become emblematic of the fragmentary interwovenness of black life in Brazil. One strand consists of the diary of Gabriel Joaquim dos Santos, an elderly black man who had died in 1985 at the age of 92 and who had constructed his own dream house as a work of art made completely out of garbage and detritus: cracked tiles, broken plates, burned-out lightbulbs, empty cans. For Gabriel, the city of Rio represents the "power of wealth" and his house, constructed from the "city's leftovers," represents the "power of poverty." His "aesthetics of garbage" remind us of the ways that the black diaspora has always transformed detritus (e.g., discarded oil barrels or scraps of cloth into the art of steel drums or quilting). As the camera slowly dips and pans, caressing the contours of Gabriel's house, we hear excerpts from his diary concerning historical events (the beginnings of slavery, a strike in the salt flats where Gabriel worked, the death of the Pope, the coup d'état of 1964). The excerpts mingle the personal and the political, the past and the present, the quotidian and the grand. As José Carlos Avellar points out, the discontinuous structure of both "texts"—Gabriel's house and his diary—provides an allegorical model not only for the structure of the film itself, also composed of fragments and detritus, but also for the Afro Brazilian experience as a whole:

> One might say that Gabriel, who created his house out of broken pottery taken from the garbage because he didn't have money but wanted to decorate the house, and that Eduardo Coutinho, who created his film as a montage of fragments gathered here and there from what the system left on the margins as urban leftovers, one might say that both the character and the director of *Fio da Memoria* are not heroes but rather common people, common expressions of our culture, and that in Brazil everything is like that including the cinema—fragmented, destructured, created on the margins of the force of wealth.[57]

Gabriel's two texts become the thread of memory along which are strung the various incidents and materials of the film as a whole, all of which have something to do with slavery, abolition, social oppression, and the contemporary life of Afro Brazilians. The voice-over reminds us that abolition threw the largely illiterate Afro Brazilians onto the free market, shorn of their culture, portrayed as not ready for salaried labor, obliged to collect the shards of their identity. The fragmentary materials gathered by the film itself include a white teacher explaining the brutalities of the Middle Passage to young black pupils and interviews with abandoned children, all institutionally renamed (à la slavery) "da Silva." Shots of a May 13 abolition celebration featuring the Queen of the Centenary of Abolition in front of the Church of Rosário and of Saint Benedict (two patron saints of slaves) give way to another party, for Slave Anastácia, seen by some blacks as the person who *really* put an end to slavery, rather than Princess Isabel, who merely signed a law. When a black woman claims that racism is alive and well, a white man repeatedly tries to respond that blacks are 51 percent of the country and that "in any business those who control 51% of the shares control the country, and if blacks are not able to control the country—" He is widely booed by the largely black crowd because

12. The sequels of slavery: *O Fio da Memória* (1992). Photo: Luiz Morier.

they don't like the drift of his argumentation. Other materials include a demonstration by black activists, in front of the statue of Zumbi at Praça Onze (the square whose destruction was protested in Orson Welles's *It's All True*) in favor of November 20 (anniversary of Zumbi's death) as Black Consciousness Day, along with interviews with members of an *umbanda* congregation, a samba group (Cacique de Ramos), and a liberation theology church service mingling homages to Christ and Zumbi. Black congresswoman Benedita da Silva speaks of her family's May 13 celebration and about how her mother washed clothes for the president's family. A photograph of shackled suspects points to police repression as another sequel to slavery (photo 12). The final sequences contrast the mystery of death as treated in African religion with the unceremonious burial of Gabriel, whose body seems to have also become detritus, a numbered corpse in a garbage bag. The film begins and ends with the same "naive" diary entry from Gabriel: "Brazil used to be bossed around by Portugal. Brazil was a Portuguese farm. Here there existed a very dangerous kind of captivity, with the Portuguese carrying blacks from the coast of Africa to work here in the bush. But all this passed. The Portuguese gave all this up. Dom Pedro created Independence, leaving Portugal over there and Brazil over here. And Brazil's fate was left up to us."

CHAPTER 2

The Structuring Absences of
Silent Cinema,
1898–1929

∞

With the preceding historical preamble in mind, we can begin to trace the trajectory of multicultural imagery within Brazilian Cinema. The silent era (1898–1930) was the belle epoque of Brazilian Cinema, when Brazilian films dominated the internal market, reaching an annual production of 100 films a year. Since precious little of the silent era production still exists, however, we must rely on press accounts, stills, memoirs, advertisements, and other archival materials. At times we are reduced to making historically informed inferences from the titles themselves. For example, Afonso Segreto's *Dança de um Baiano* (Dance of a Bahian, 1899) presumably presents a black dancer, since Bahia was then, and remains now, an overwhelmingly black city. Similarly, Cardisbourg's *Dança de Capoeira* (Capoeira Dance, 1905) probably featured black practitioners of the Afro Brazilian martial art/dance *capoeira,* as that form became fashionable among whites only at a much later period. The films about the typical activities of a São Paulo coffee plantation reportedly screened in the Largo do São Francisco in 1904, also most likely featured blacks, along with European immigrants, as workers on the *fazendas.*

The many films documenting Rio's carnival celebrations, going as far back as 1901, with titles such as *O Carnaval da Avenida Central* (Central Avenue Carnival, 1906), *Pela Vitória dos Clubes Carnavalescos* (Victory to the Carnival Clubs, 1909) and *O Carnaval Cantado* (Carnival of Song, 1918), and *Carnaval Cantado de 1933* (1933 Carnival Song, 1933), by the same token, may be assumed to have featured the Afro Brazilians who then formed a majority of the Carioca population. Blacks also presumably appeared in Antônio Leal's adaptation of Harriet Beecher Stowe's *Uncle Tom's Cabin* (A Cabana de Pai Tomas, 1909), a book that enjoyed wide popularity in Brazil. The film reportedly ended with an homage to the heroes of the liberation of the slaves: Viscount Rio Branco and José do Patrocínio, which suggests that the film foregrounded both white (Rio Branco) and black (Patrocínio) abolitionists. A 1915 documentary is dedicated to the celebrated nineteenth-century mulatto sculptor Aleijadinho, whose works dot the once wealthy state of Minas Gerais, but we have no idea whether the film emphasized the sculptor's blackness. A São Paulo documentary, *Os Tres Dias do Carnaval Paulista* (Three Days of São Paulo Carnival, 1915), according to press reports, features "black Pierrots." We also know of adaptations of novels featuring black characters. Felipe Ricci adapted Júlio Ribeiro's naturalist novel *A Carne* (Flesh, 1925); an *Estado de São Paulo* reviewer (November 15, 1925) recommended the film as "effectively conveying the nature of slavery," an ambiguous recommendation given that the novel is in many ways antiblack.

A perusal of the photographs included in the various books about Brazilian Cinema in the silent period, for example, Vicente de Paulo Araújo's *A Bela Época do Cinema Brasileiro* and *Salões, Circos e Cinemas de São Paulo,* and Jurandyr Noronha's *No Tempo da Manivela,* suggests that black Brazilians were at least to be found in the movie theaters if not on the screen. Photos of silent era cinema audiences show a white majority but also a sprinkling of black and mulatto faces. Blacks also performed as musicians in the movie theaters. According to the composer Pixinguinha, black musicians like himself or Nelson Alves were allowed to play only in the "second orchestra," that is, the one that welcomed the moviegoers in the lobby, but not the "first orchestra," which accompanied the films.[1]

In postabolition Rio de Janeiro, blacks found jobs not only as dockers, artisans, factory workers, and clerks, but also as performing artists in the circus, vaudeville, cabarets, and café-theaters. One of the earliest protests against racial prejudice occurred in 1904 with complaints that a Rio theater was discriminating against blacks in its hiring practices.[2] The first black actor known to have performed in a Brazilian fiction film was the popular clown Benjamin de Oliveira (photo 13), principal attraction of the Spinelli Circus in Rio de Janeiro. He played the role of the Indian Peri in Antônio Leal's *Os Guaranis* (1908), an adaptation of an Indianist novel by José de Alencar. Although the film no longer exists, still photos show Oliveira's proud, handsome face,

13. Benjamin de Oliveira

garbed in an Indian headdress for the role of Peri (photo 14). The film was shot on the stage of the Spinelli Circus, as de Oliveira mimed a role he had previously performed as a regular part of the circus show. Before acting in film, he was already a well-known performer even outside Rio de Janeiro. A notice about a 1902 São Paulo performance calls him a "much-beloved clown," and another calls him "without peer both in comic roles and in mime." One 1902 notice speaks of the participation in the Spinelli Circus show of "the black clown Benjamin de Oliveira, who conquered the affection of everyone in São Paulo, and indeed in all the different states where he has performed." But his role in the Spinelli Circus went beyond performing, and another São Paulo notice speaks of his "careful mise-en-scène" of the circus show.[3] In fact, Benjamin de Oliveira began by presenting theatrical sketches as part of the circus. He went on to write up sketches based on novels and musicals, and even composed a miniversion of Shakespeare's *Othello*.

Early Brazilian cinema also featured the multitalented Eduardo das Neves, songwriter, mime, actor, theatrical writer, and impresario, who performed with some regularity in São Paulo under the auspices of the Pavilhão Brasileiro Circus-Theater. Reviews of his work from 1905 speak of his "enormous repertoire" and of a piece ("Father Virgolino Carrapato Dancing a Cakewalk") written especially for him.[4] Das Neves also worked behind the screen as singer-dubber in such films as *Sangue Espanhol* (Spanish Blood, 1914). Black performers also appeared in other films of the silent period. In *O Guarani* (1916), Vittório Capellaro painted seminude black men with yellow paint to perform as "Indians," although he himself used "redface" for the key role of the Indian Perí.[5] In 1908, José Labanca and Antônio Leal filmed *Os Capadócios da Cidade Nova* (New City Imposters), a portrait of the social world of Praça Onze, a square popular among blacks and the place of encounter of Brazilians of all colors along with foreign immigrants from Portugal, Italy, and Spain. (Orson Welles was to memorialize the square's disappearance in *It's All True* more than 30 years later.)

Real-life events also led to the appearance of blacks in documentaries and fiction films. On November 22, 1910, the black corporal João Cândido led a group of sailors in a revolt against inadequate food and corporal punishment, in the historical episode known as A Revolta da Chibata (the Whip Revolt). In this incident, abused sailors, largely black and mestiço, commandeered several warships recently purchased from England. João Cândido took control of the cruiser *Minas Gerais,* killing an official to demonstrate his seriousness while demanding an end to corporal punishment, which for blacks carried the visceral memory of the pillories of slavery. The capital, the governmental palace, and the armed forces were at the mercy of the mutineers led by João Cândido. After the sailors returned the ships, Congress amnestied the mutineers, but later the government reneged on its promises, arresting the rebels and murdering most of them. Corporal punishment, in any case, was henceforth abolished from the Brazilian navy.

A Revolta de Chibata, a kind of Brazilian Potemkin mutiny, generated a flurry of documentaries. According to Vicente de Paulo Araújo, at least four directors filmed events linked to the incident. In *Revolta da Esquadra* (Revolt of the Squadron, 1910), the spectator was shown "the naval movements and the incidents of the last days. At the end, we see a life-size image of João Cândido himself."[6] *Revolta no Rio* (Revolt in Rio, 1910), similarly, also shows João Cândido's arrival in Rio. In 1912, Director Carlos Lambertini staged a fictional account of the episode, entitled *A Vida do Cabo João Cândido* (The Life

DUKE

UNIVERSITY

PRESS · PUBLICITY

BOX 90660

DURHAM, NC

27708-0660

Barb Short
PUBLICITY

(919) 687-3639
TELEPHONE

(919) 688-4391
FAX

bshort@acpub.duke.edu
EMAIL

REVIEW COPY

Robert Stam

TROPICAL MULTICULTURALISM

A Comparative History of Race in Brazilian Cinema and Culture

Price:

Paper	(0-8223-2048-7)	$19.95
Unjacketed cloth	(0-8223-2035-5)	$59.95

(Please note that unjacketed cloth editions are primarily for library use. Non-library reviewers should quote the paperback price.)

Publication Date: January 21, 1998

Latin America Otherwise Series

*Please send two copies of the published review.

of Corporal João Cândido), but the Naval Ministry confiscated the film, thus making it the first Brazilian film to receive the ambiguous compliment of official censorship. (João Cândido makes a reappearance in the 1980s within Sílvio Tendler's documentary *Jango*, where the João Cândido revolt is quite logically juxtaposed both with sequences from Eisenstein's *The Battleship Potemkin,* and with images of the real-life sailors' revolt [Rebellion of the Marujás] in 1964.) The memory of João Cândido as the black sailor struggling for justice on the high seas, and his literal attendance of a rally in support of the sailors, anticipates Paul Gilroy's discussion of the "chronotope of the ship" as a conduit for Pan-African communication and revolt within the history of the black Atlantic.[7]

Generally, however, despite a high proportion of black and mulatto citizens, Afro Brazilians did not figure prominently in the symbolically "white" cinema of the first decades of this century. A number of factors account for this "structuring absence." First of all, the beginnings of Brazilian cinema coincided with the heights of European imperialism. The pioneer filmmaking countries (England, France, the United States, Italy) were all colonial powers who predictably painted the colonized as lazy and villainous and therefore rightly subject to Europe's "benevolent" rule. The tendency within Brazil was to project the country as merely a tropical appendage of Europe in which non-Europeans could only have a minor and subaltern role. These prejudices were embodied in the 1890 immigration laws, which welcomed "all healthy individuals able to work . . . except for people from Asia and Africa, who will require special authorization from the National Congress."[8] Baron Rio Branco, Brazilian Foreign Minister from 1902 to 1912, tried to project an international image of a white Brazil by stocking his diplomatic corps with "white men whom foreigners would consider civilized and sophisticated—to reinforce the image of a Europeanized country growing whiter and whiter."[9] Second, the beginnings of cinema also coincided with the dissemination of racist ideologies of the kind lampooned in Dos Santos's *Tenda dos Milagres* (Tent of Miracles, 1977) ideologies rooted ultimately in colonialism but more immediately in scientific racism and Social Darwinism, doctrines used to legitimate European domination by arguing the innate, almost ontological "superiority" of European races. "Scientific" racism came to infect such diverse fields as history, geography, law, and criminology. Books such as Gobineau's *Essais sur les Inegalités des Races* (1853–1855) came to influence Brazilian intellectuals such as Sílvio Romero, Euclides da Cunha, and Nina Rodrigues. For Nina Rodrigues, in his 1905 book *Os Africanos no Brasil,* the black element contributed to Brazil's racial "degeneracy" and formed "the basis of our inferiority as a people." Oliveira Vianna, in his introduction to the 1920 Brazilian census, called for the "Aryanization" of Brazil, placing his faith in the combined forces of European immigration, high mortality rates among blacks, and the progressive whitening of mulattoes. In his *Retrato do Brasil* (Portrait of Brazil, 1928), Paulo Prado portrayed Brazil as a futureless country made up of three sad and inferior "subraces": Indians, blacks, and Portuguese. (He makes an exception of the Paulistas.) The image of Africa, meanwhile, was still largely negative. Few favorable ethnographic accounts about Africa were available to counter the flood of derogatory propaganda issuing from the colonizing powers as they scrambled to divide up the continent.

Not every medium or voice in this period was so uniformly hostile to black Brazilians. Black newspapers, such as the ironically named *Bandeirante* in 1910, and *O Menelik* in 1915, somewhat timidly asserted black rights, thus anticipating such later black periodicals as *O Clarim da Alvorada* in 1924, self-proclaimed as the "the legitimate organ of black youth," and *O Quilombo* in 1929. At the same time, politician-writer Alberto Torres, governor of the State of Rio (1898–1900) ridiculed the Aryanist caricature of Brazil, noting that the thrust of the Teutonic theories coincided exactly with the imperial interests of Germany.[10] Manuel Bonfim's *America Latina: Males de Origem* (Latin America: Originary Problems, published in Paris in 1903, similarly, denounced doctrines of racial superiority as part of European and North American ideological domination. The backwardness and poverty of Brazil, for Bonfim, derived less from a racially handicapped people than from the irresponsible greed of the dominating elites. Sílvio Romero, in *O Alemanismo no Sul do Brasil* (Germanism in the South of Brazil) "answered" Bonfim's thesis with "scientific" arguments drawn from racist European theorists; the Brazilian intellectual elite, although itself often mestiço, generally sided with Sílvio Romero. In 1911, João Batista de Lacerda, director of the National Museum, presented his thesis on Brazilian mestiços to the First Universal Congress on Race in London; for him, the history of Brazil revealed the productive capacity of mulattoes and mestiços. Although he found blacks inferior, he was among the first to preach *mestiçagem* as a way of whitening and Europeanizing Brazil. Five years later, Álvaro Bomilcar's *O Preconceito de Raça no Brasil*

(Race Prejudice in Brazil), excoriated the racial intolerance evidenced in the physical abuses practiced by the navy, catalysts for revolts and mutinies like that led by João Cândido. The anthropologist Edgar Roquette Pinto, a vehement antiracist, also questioned such Eurocentric doxa as the "necessary degeneration" of mulattoes. The brave performance of black soldiers in World War I, for Roquette Pinto, definitively disproved the myth of black inferiority.[11] In 1919, finally, Rui Barboso anticipated the idea of "racial democracy" in a speech to the Commercial Association, where he describes Brazil as a "leveling" society, where "the vestiges of slavery are constantly diminishing in a fusion of all races."[12]

Brazil in the silent period was nothing, then, if not contradictory. On the one hand, black or mestiço writers like Machado de Assis and Lima Barreto enjoyed enormous prestige. The modernist movement, meanwhile, emerging in the teens but really flourishing in the 1920s when the Semana de Arte Moderna (Modern Art Week) in 1922 called attention, if ambiguously, to the racial multiplicity of Brazilian culture. In the realm of popular culture, meanwhile, the figure of the *mulata sambista* was becoming a national ideal of enticing vivaciousness, an ambiguous valorization in some ways parallel to the French cult of Josephine Baker and *la femme noire*. The 1920s also witnessed the inauguration of the first center of *umbanda,* a syncretic religion fusing Catholicism, spiritism, and Afro Brazilian trance. At the same time, discrimination was real and pervasive. The elite banned Africanized cultural practices like *capoeira* and *candomblé,* and other discriminatory measures sometimes became law. In 1920, for example, the government prohibited the inclusion of black athletes as part of the official Brazilian soccer team. But São Paulo teams such as Corinthians, for their part, did incorporate blacks.

Once the *bela época* came to a close, the Brazilian film market came to be dominated by the Americans. In 1921, the proportion of American films screened in Brazil reached 71 percent, rising to 86 percent in 1929.[13] In the same period, a colonized mentality dominated Brazilian film journals such as *Cinearte* (founded in 1926), a tropical version of Hollywood's *Photoplay*. Largely financed through advertisements for Hollywood films, *Cinearte* defined itself as "the natural intermediary between the Brazilian market and North American producers." The journal, which featured articles on "The Real Greta Garbo" and "What Hollywood Stars Can't Tell You," proclaimed its cinematic and social ideals in an editorial:

A cinema which teaches the weak not to respect the strong, the servant to respect his boss, which shows dirty, bearded, unhygienic faces, sordid events and extreme realism is not cinema. Imagine a young couple who go to see a typical North American film. They will see a clean-faced, well-shaven hero with well-combed hair, agile, a gentleman. And the girl will be pretty, with a nice body and cute face, modern hair-style, photogenic . . . the couple which sees such a film will comment that they had already seen such images twenty times before. But over their dreaming hearts, there will not fall the shadow of any shocking brutality, any dirty face which might take away the poetry and enchantment. Young people to-day cannot accept revolt, lack of hygiene, the struggle and eternal fight against those who have the right to exercise power.[14]

Here the notion of *photogénie,* developed by French filmmaker-theorists like Jean Epstein to advance the specific potentialities of the "seventh art," becomes an epidermic notion of beauty, associated with youth, luxury, stars, and, at least implicitly, with whiteness. Although the passage does not mention race, its call for "clean" and "hygienic" as opposed to "dirty" faces, and its generally servile stance toward the lily-white Hollywood model, suggests a coded reference to the subject.[15]

On some occasions, the racial reference becomes more explicit. One editorialist calls for Brazilian cinema to be an "act of purification of our reality," emphasizing "progress," "modern engineering," and "our beautiful white people." The same author warns against documentaries as more likely to include "undesirable elements": "We should avoid documentaries, for they do not allow for total control over what is shown and therefore might allow for the infiltration of undesirable elements: we need a studio cinema, like that of Hollywood, with well-decorated interiors inhabited by nice people."[16] Thus racial hierarchies impact even on issues of genre and production method.

Although no Brazilian film of the first few decades advances an explicitly racist perspective—there is no Brazilian equivalent to *Birth of a Nation* (1914–1915)—one is struck by the frequent, almost obsessive adaptation of Indianist novels such as *O Guarani* (four versions in the silent period) *Iracema* (three versions), and *Ubirajara* (one version), in contrast with the general slighting of Afro Brazilian themes. Indeed, it is significant that black actors like Benjamin de Oliveira and Tácito de Souza (and occasionally white actors like

14. Benjamin de Oliveira as Peri in *Os Guaranis* (1908)

Vittório Capellaro) performed Indian roles in "redface," while female Indian roles were played by white actresses like Ilka Soares. Indeed, at that time it was illegal to hire Indians as actors because they had the legal status of children. (The law was changed only with the 1988 Constitution.)[17] Thus blacks played Indians in a situation where neither black nor Indian had power over self-representation (see photo 14). Here, too, the cinema simply played out the chosen themes of the dominant ideology. Within the nineteenth-century Indianist movement,[18] the Indian was celebrated as "brave warrior," as the naively good and deeply spiritual source and symbol of Brazil's nationhood. Perí, the "good Indian" from *O Guarani,* is amorously enslaved to the white Cecília and more loyal to her family than to his own tribe. As a result of this "positive" stereotyping, both blacks and whites rushed to claim Indian ancestry. Genealogist-*bricoleurs* created the fiction of the "Indian princess"—daughters of chiefs who married the first colonists—as legitimate forebears, resulting in those bizarre amalgams of European titles of nobility with indigenist names (Viscount de Araguaia), a tendency that even today takes the form of naming non-Indian Brazilian children after the heroes and heroines of indigenous novels.

The exaltation of the Indian involved an element of bad faith toward both Indian and black. By celebrating the fusion of an idealized noble Indian with an equally idealized noble European, such novels as *Iracema* and *O Guarani* (photo 15) prettified the *cunhadismo* described in the preamble and neglected the black, seen at that time purely as a source of labor, shorn of all rights of citizenship, and an iconic reminder of the brutal heritage of slavery, hardly an image the elite wanted to project. Some Indianists, like José de Alencar, saw black slavery as a "necessary social fact," whereas others such as Gonçalves Dias, himself the son of a mestiço slave, took a position against slavery.[19] But to valorize blacks within a slave-holding society would be to cast whites as villains. At the same time, the exaltation of the disappearing Indian was dedicated to the very group being victimized by a process of literal and cultural genocide. The Indians of Ceara celebrated in *Iracema* were virtually extinguished when Alencar published his novel. But although the real Indian was destroyed, marginalized, or "dissolved" through miscegenation, the remote, literary Indian was idealized.

A number of historical factors contributed to this "positive" image: the Jesuit tradition of recognizing the humanity of Indians; the abolition of Indian slavery by the middle of the eighteenth century; the Portuguese custom of conferring nobility on collaborationist *caciques;* and the international vogue of the "noble savage."[20] The ambiguous "compliment" toward the Indian became a means of avoiding the vexed question of slavery. The proud history of black rebellions, of Palmares, and the *quilombos* was ignored; the brave Indian, it was subtly insinuated, resisted slavery while blacks did not. The white filmmakers of the early decades of this century, in sum, took the cue from their literary antecedents, choosing the safely distant and mythically connoted Indian over the more problematically present black, victim of a slavery abolished just 10 years before Afonso Segreto filmed the first Brazilian "views" in 1898.

There is a tension, in the silent period, between the "Indianist" adaptations

15. "Foundational fictions": Peri and Ceci in *O Guarani* (1916)

and the "documentary" record provided by the films of Silvino Santos, the director of *No País das Amazonas* (In the Country of the Amazon, 1922), where we see Euro Brazilians measuring the bodies of Amazonian indians and dressing them with European clothes, and the films of Luis Thomaz Reis, the director of *Rituais e Festas Bororo* (Bororo Rituals and Feasts, 1906) and *Os Sertões de Mato Grosso* (The Backlands of Mato Grosso, 1916), a record of the installation of telegraph lines in the interior of Brazil, featuring "the pacification of numerous Indian tribes encountered in a primitive, Stone Age state."[21] The 1920s also featured another version of the Brazilian Indian, that of the modernist movement in literature and the arts. This movement, which unfortunately only rarely linked up with Brazilian Cinema, deserves as much attention as that given to the historical avant-gardes of Europe, yet the canonical texts on Modernism and the avant-garde favor Paris, London, and Zurich over São Paulo, Havana, and Mexico City.[22] Seeing themselves as surpassing both communism and surrealism, the modernists slighted the "noble savage" of the romantics in favor of the bad, ignoble savage: the cannibal, the devourer of the white colonizer. If the romantics saw the Indian as the exotic exemplar of primitive virtue, the modernists saw the Indian as the irreverent avatar of counterculture. The modernists made the trope of cannibalism the basis of an insurgent aesthetic, calling for a creative synthesis of European avant-gardism and Brazilian "cannibalism" and invoking an "anthropophagic" devouring of the techniques and information of the developed countries in order to better the struggle against domination. Just as the aboriginal Tupinambá Indians devoured their enemies to appropriate their force, the modernists argued, Brazilian artists and intellectuals should digest imported cultural products and exploit them as raw material for a new synthesis, thus turning the imposed culture back, transformed, against the colonizer. The modernists also called for the "de-Vespucciazation" of the Americas (the reference is to Amerigo Vespucci) and the "de-Cabralization" of Brazil (referring to Pedro Cabral, Brazil's Portuguese "discoverer").[23] The *Revista de Antropofagia* (Cannibalist Review) laments that Brazilians continue to be "slaves" to a "rotting European culture" and to a "colonial mentality."[24]

The currently fashionable talk of postcolonial "hybridity" and "syncretism" often elides the fact that artists and intellectuals in Brazil and the Caribbean were theorizing hybridity over half a century earlier. In two manifestos — "Manifesto of Brazilwood Poetry" (1924) and "Cannibalist Manifesto" (1928) — Oswald de Andrade pointed the way to an artistic practice at once nationalist and cosmopolitan, nativist and modern. In the earlier text, de Andrade called for an "export-quality" poetry that would not borrow imported "canned" European models but would find its roots in everyday life and popular culture. Where colonialist discourse had posited the Carib as a ferocious cannibal, as diacritical token of Europe's moral superiority, Oswald de Andrade called in the "Cannibalist Manifesto" for a revolution infinitely "greater than the French revolution," the "Carib revolution," without which "Europe wouldn't even have its meager declaration of the rights of man."[25] Although the cannibalist metaphor was also circulated among European avant-gardists,[26] cannibalism in Europe, as Augusto de Campos points out, never constituted a cultural movement, never defined an ideology, and never enjoyed the profound resonances within the culture that it did in Brazil. The nihilism of Dada had little to do with what de Campos calls the "generous ideological utopia" of Brazilian Anthropophagy.[27] Radicalizing the Enlightenment valorization of indigenous Amerindian freedom, it highlighted aboriginal matriarchy and communalism as a utopian model. "The Indian," de Andrade wrote, "had no police, no repression, no nervous disorders, no shame at being nude, no class struggle, no slavery."[28] Synthesizing insights from Montaigne, Nietzsche, Marx, and Freud, along with what he knew of native Brazilian societies, he portrayed indigenous culture as offering a more adequate social model than the European one.[29]

The 1920s were the period of studies of "primitive" cultures (Frazer, Levy-Bruhl, Freud), of the African researches of the ethnologist Leo Frobenius, and of the appropriations of African and Afro American cultures by the likes of Picasso, Brancusi, and Klee. Oswald de Andrade noted that those who were exotic for the European, that is, the Indian and the black, were a quotidian, unexotic reality for Brazilians.[30] Whereas European artists like Paul Gauguin, Blaise Cendrars, and Georges Bataille looked for a primitive world as an antitype to decadent Europe, Brazilian artists were more knowledgeable about that world and more aware of the limitations of European primitivism. Although the indigenous peoples formed the primary reference for Modernism, the movement did not entirely neglect blacks. Modernist Raul Bopp, author of "Poemas Negros," expressed a desire, in somewhat exoticizing terms, to create poetry out of the "cries of pain of black people. On one side, Africa: prehistoric, sexual, mystical. On the other slavery, field work."[31] But even when the modernists were not directly dealing with blacks, their choice of themes bore indirectly on black issues. Their anticolonialism was by implication an antislavery and an antiracism, and their artistic embrace of popular speech and the "creative errors of the people" inevitably meant incorporating a speech inflected by black Brazilians.

Mário de Andrade's *Macunaíma,* written in 1928 and adapted for the cinema four decades after it was first published, formed the novelistic epitome of the modernist movement and the powerful precursor of what later came to be called "magic realism." That Mário de Andrade is not as famous as a James Joyce or a Marcel Proust, whose poetic universes are no more rich than his own, is merely a matter of historical accident and of writing in the "wrong" language. Although de Andrade declared himself "very optimistic about the creativity of our literature and other contemporary arts," he doubted Brazilian texts would win the applause they deserve due to "factors which have nothing to do with the artistic merit." Some countries, he pointed out, "weigh in with great force in the universal scale; their currency is valuable or pretends to be valuable, and their armies have the power to decide in the wars of the future

. . . the permanence of the arts of any given country in terms of the world's attention exists in direct proportion to the political and economic power of the country in question."[32]

Although de Andrade wrote *Macunaíma* in a week of jazzlike improvisation, the novel was the product of long and scrupulous preparation. An anthropologist and musicologist as well as composer, poet, and novelist, de Andrade compiled Amerindian, Luso-Brazilian, and African legends to create *Macunaíma*. He called his text a "rhapsody" both in the musical sense of a "free fantasy on an epic, heroic or national theme" and in the etymological sense of "stitcher" since the novel "stitches" tales to form a kind of artistic crazy-quilt. In what amounts to an anthology of Brazilian folklore, a *mestiçagem* of mythologies, de Andrade combines oaths, nursery rhymes, proverbs, and elements of erudite literature with the indigenous legends collected by German anthropologist Theodor Koch-Grunberg in the headwaters of the Orinoco between 1911 and 1913 and published in his two-volume *Vom Roroima zum Orinoco: Ergebnisse einer Reise in Nord Bresilien und Venezuela in den Jahren 1911–1913* in 1923.[33] The very language of the novel is ethnically syncretic, weaving African, indigenous, and Portuguese words; it is an imagined speech that carries the linguistic "genes," as it were, of all the blacks, the Indians, and the immigrants of Brazil.[34]

Macunaíma's oxymoronic protagonist is a larger-than-life composite character, a summa of Brazil, who epitomizes the ethnic roots as well as the qualities and defects of an entire people. A composite of several heroes found in the American source-legends, his very name is oxymoronic, composed of the root *maku* (bad) and the suffix *ima* (great). Macunaíma, "the hero without any character" as the novel's subtitle has it, lacks character not only in the conventional moral sense but also in lacking the psychological "coherence" of the autonomous ego and the sociological coherence of the verisimilar character. Ethnically, he is at once black, white, and indian, and morally he is by turns selfish, generous, cruel, sensual, and tender. As a representative of "the grotesque body of the people" rather than a rounded personage, his character consists, as de Andrade explained in a letter to Manuel Bandeira, in "not having any character and his logic . . . in not having any logic."[35] Unlike the romantic Indianist movement, which favored a symbolically idealized Indian over the "inconvenient" black, the Modernism of de Andrade places in relation Indian, black, and white, seeing Brazil as a synthesis of all three races.

But this synthesis was not purely abstract and speculative, since much of de Andrade's anthropological research had to do with such issues as the amalgamation of African and indigenous elements in *pajelanca,* in the Amazon, where the Indian *pajé* (priest) and the African *pai de santo* (priest) are joined, or the amalgam of Euro-Catholic and African elements in macumba in Rio.[36] But syncretism too is power laden. De Andrade described the "sickness of America" (i.e., Latin America) as deriving from the domination of African and indigenous identities by a white identity artificially emboldened by cultural and economic power and by European immigration.[37] Anticipating what would later be called the antiessentialist critique of race, de Andrade offers us a protagonist who has no fixed racial identity, who is born black to an Indian mother, but who becomes phenotypically and culturally whitened when he goes to São Paulo. Artists of an indecisive race, de Andrade wrote in his 1928 "Essay on Brazilian Music," "become equally indecisive." The word *indecisa* (indecisive) in this context is ambiguous; the reference could be to *ethos* (morality) or to *ethnos* (ethnicity).

Both de Andrade and Russian literary theorist Mikhail Bakhtin, without each other's knowledge, were elaborating theories of artistic "polyphony" in the 1920s. For Bakhtin, polyphony refers to the coexistence, in any textual or extratextual situation, of a plurality of voices that do not fuse into a single consciousness but rather generate dialogical dynamism among themselves.[38] De Andrade, in *A Escrava que Não É Isaura* (The Slave Who Is Not Isaura, 1925)—the title itself rejects the sentimental approach to slavery of Benardo Guimaraes's novel—speaks of *polifonismo* as referring to the "theorization of certain procedures employed by certain modernist poets." "Poetic polyphony," for de Andrade, is "the simultaneous artistic union of two or more melodies whose temporary effects of sonorous conflict collaborate to create a total final effect," a definition not terribly distant from Bakhtin's.[39] And although neither author was thinking specifically of a polyphony of ethnic and racial voices per se, an ethnic interpretation is in no way excluded by the term.[40] The concept of multiple and simultaneous racial identities, at once personal and national, then, made it possible for de Andrade to imagine the self as a polyphonic orchestration of racial and cultural identities, lived, of course, within the asymmetries of social power evoked by Bakhtin's "heteroglossia" or "many-languagedness."

The case of de Andrade exemplifies some of the ambiguities of modernist attitudes toward race. The author, it is sometimes overlooked, was himself of mixed racial ancestry; he culturally and phenotypically embodied the indigenous, African, and European inheritance, and multiplicity of identity was one of the leitmotifs of his work. Conflicted about his racial identity in an age where "race men" were few and far between, de Andrade formed an unstable amalgam of black pride and the assumption of honorary white status. Echoing Walt Whitman, de Andrade proclaimed that he contained multitudes: "I am three hundred, three hundred and fifty."[41] He had a proleptic sense of what later was to be called "nomadic" and "palimpsestic" identity. In "Improvisations on the Sickness of America," written in 1928, the same year as *Macunaíma,* de Andrade spoke of the red, black, and white strands "that weave my harlequinate costume." His identity was self-declaredly multiple: indigenous, African and European through ancestry, but also French, through his schooling, and Italian, because of his love of music.[42]

But because of his status as an upper-class Paulista from an artist milieu, the author was also ashamed of his mixed identity.[43] In a poem that begins by speaking of the "imperious shout of whiteness within me," he writes:

> But I cannot feel myself black or red!
> Even though these colors also weave my Harlequinate costume,
> But I don't feel black, but I don't feel red,
> I feel only white . . . I feel only white now, without air in
>   this open-air America
> I feel only white, only white in my soul forged of many races.[44]

On the other hand, Mário de Andrade spoke with admiration of Rio's carnival with its "blacks doing the samba in cadence / So sublime, so Africa!" He was also capable of mocking the Eurocentric ideal of whiteness as the quintessence of beauty. In "Lembranças do Losango Caqui" (1924) he writes:

> My God how white she was!
> How much like snow,
> But I don't know what snow is like
> I've never seen snow
> I don't even like snow
> And I didn't like her.

As Christopher Dunn suggests, the poem not only mocks Eurocentric aesthetics but also expresses a preference for the same tropical climate that racist theory posited as one of the "causes" of Brazil's underdevelopment. In some ways de Andrade qualifies as an early example of James Clifford's "ethnographic surrealist," with the difference that de Andrade was as much an insider as he was an outsider. His status as an anthropologist and musicologist became a way of probing, with mingled distance and identification, his own roots. Indeed, of all the modernists it was he who demonstrated the greatest intimacy with African and Afro Brazilian culture. *Macunaíma* is replete with references to African culture and legends, to Ogum and Exu, to Rei Nago, to *babalaôs* (honored priests), to Iemanjá, to Obatalá, to African dances like *Bamba Quere*, and to "Tia Ciata," the Bahian woman whose home near Praça Onze was reportedly the site of the birth of Rio's samba. Nor was this intimacy with African culture merely bookish. De Andrade visited scores of *terreiros* as part of his research on Afro Brazilian music. He speaks in *O Turista Aprendiz* (The Apprentice Tourist) of undergoing the African *catimbó* ceremony of "closing the body." In his travels in the Northeast, he distinguishes between "Caboclinhos" ceremonies, dedicated to the Indian, and the "Congos," where "everything is African."[45] In *O Empalhador de Passarinho*, he analyzes the northeastern *desafio* (rhymed poetic challenge, which some see as a precursor of rap), insisting on the African as well as the European (medieval) origins of the form.[46] In *Música de Feitiçaria no Brasil* (Witchcraft Music in Brazil), posthumously compiled from his notes, de Andrade offers a global tour of music, whether erudite or popular, European, African, Asian, or Native American, insisting always on the dignity and complexity of Afro-religious music. (We will return to Mário de Andrade in our discussion of the film version of *Macunaíma*.)

The differences between the representation of the Indian and of the Afro Brazilian, in this historical period, are correlatable with distinct differences in official policy. While Indians were symbolically favored but concretely marginalized, blacks were discriminated against by a Europhile immigration policy designed to "whiten" Brazil. The indigenous peoples were the continuing object of genocidal policies and at the same time the ambiguous (and merely symbolic) beneficiaries not only of the romantic Indianist movement but also of a positivist philosophy that preached a certain "progressive" tolerance. For example, it was during the silent period of Brazilian cinema that Cândido Mariano da Silva Rondon, inspired by the ideas of August Comte, founded the Indian Protection Service. Rondon himself was mestiço; his father was descended from *bandeirantes,* his mother from diverse indigenous groups. The Rondon commission, which constructed telegraph lines linking Rio to Mato Grosso and the Amazon, was organized as a scientific and anthropological expedition whose slogan was "To die, yes, to kill, never." The National Museum inaugurated its cinematheque in 1912 with films about the Nambicuara indians that Roquette Pinto brought back from Rondónia along with the films of the Rondon Commission.[47] Teddy Roosevelt also had contact with the Rondon Commission from 1913 to 1914, as a result of which he became an enthusiast of the "ideology of whitening." Seeing Brazilians as basically a white people, Roosevelt praised the indigenous element as having a positive effect and believed European immigration would turn black blood into an "insignificant element."[48] Surprisingly, given the extreme racism of Roosevelt's earlier writing, he recorded favorable impressions of Brazil's mulattoes and mestiços.[49]

The lack of black filmmakers in this period is hardly surprising, given that filmmaking was generally a middle-class activity and that blacks in Brazil were rarely middle class. Much of the early film production, furthermore, was the work of Portuguese or Italian immigrants like the Segretos. And although these immigrants bore no responsibility for the institution of slavery and were often themselves the objects of exploitation—a situation critically registered in Tizuka Yamasaki's 1980 film *Gaijin* (Japanese for "Foreigner")—collectively they were the winners, and blacks the losers, of this period of Brazilian history. At the end of the nineteenth century and the beginning of the twentieth, European immigration, rather than the employment or training of blacks, was consciously encouraged as a way of providing labor for postslavery Brazil. Between 1888, the year of abolition, and 1930, almost 4 million European immigrants arrived in Brazil, more than half of them Italian. As a result Afro Brazilians found themselves at a disadvantage in competition with foreign workers, partly due to racial prejudice and partly due to a relative lack of qualifications in the wake of an "abolition" that was more effective in abolishing the burdensome responsibilities of slaveowners than in preparing black Brazilians for a free future. Whereas artisan slaves and domestics were fairly well equipped for the aftermath of slavery, other blacks without special training were forced into unemployment or the most menial jobs. Thus the black population was economically marginalized, while Europeans

Cinema
Brasileiro

16. Marques Filho's
A Escrava Isaura (1929)

occupied the social and economic space that normally would have been available for blacks. (In the United States, similarly, blacks repeatedly served as a kind of "welcome mat" for European immigrants, who marched to prosperity while blacks remained mired in poverty, with the difference that in the United States the abolition of slavery preceded by many decades the height of European immigration.)

Brazilian Cinema of the silent period did not completely shy away from the subject of slavery. In 1929 Marques Filho adopted Bernardo Guimaraes's sentimental abolitionist novel *A Escrava Isaura* (The Slave Isaura), published in 1875 (photo 16). Like many North American abolitionist novels, where the slave protagonists are often quadroons or octoroons, *A Escrava Isaura* emphasizes the heroine's light skin, under the assumption that white middle-class readers would more readily empathize with a quasi-white figure. The novel concerns a beautiful and well-educated slave who narrowly misses her chance for manumission. Fleeing from the lust of her master's son Leoncio, she is punished by forced heavy labor in the fields. But a young abolitionist, Alvaro, buys her freedom and ultimately marries her. Often referred to, somewhat inaccurately, as the "Brazilian *Uncle Tom's Cabin*," the novel devotes more energy to the romantic aspects of the intrigue than to depicting the depredations of slavery. The implicitly racist novel regarded the title character's enslavement as uniquely tragic because of her "ivory" skin—"Its texture is like the ivory of the keyboard, a whiteness which doesn't dazzle, that you would be unable to say if it was a light pallor or a faint pink"—and her "exceptional qualities," not to mention her noble lineage on her father's side.[50]

The film version perpetuates the novel's elitist perspective of "not-like-the-others" racism by having the white actress Elisa Betty play the title role, much as later North American films such as *Pinky* cast white actresses as "tragic mulattoes." Nevertheless, an *Estado de São Paulo* reviewer (October 6, 1929), called the film a "poem of love and suffering in the *black* era of slavery" (italics mine). The reviewer, like the novelist, simultaneously laments slavery and resorts to a racist notion of blackness as negative. (*A Escrava Isaura* was adopted again in 1949 by Eurides Ramos, and in the 1980s it was adapted and amplified as a *telenovela* [soap opera] by the Globo Network, resulting in a phenomenal commercial success both in Brazil and abroad, where it was shown in 93 countries, making an international star of its leading [white] actress Lucélia Santos.) In the United States and in Brazil, as illustrated by the success of *Roots* in the former country and of *A Escrava Isaura* in the latter, black historical subjects have at times provided the key to domestic and international popularity.

Summing up the silent period, we find a predominance of Indianist themes and a paucity of Afro Brazilian characters and themes. A high proportion of the early films consisted of stock European fare, remakes of *The Merry Widow*, *Tosca*, and so forth. Like the cinema throughout much of the world, Brazilian cinema searched for bourgeois respectability, adopting Brazilian and international classics, few of them featuring black themes. Although Brazil had an even higher proportion of black and mulatto citizens than did the United States, these people rarely appeared on movie screens. Brazilian cinema projected a vision of Brazil as a tropical branch of European civilization. The ideological climate was generally hostile to blacks, while blacks themselves were economically and culturally marginalized, hardly in a position to make films in which to represent themselves as they wished.

CHAPTER 3

Carmen Miranda, Grande Otelo, and the Chanchada,

1929–1949

∞

In the 1930s, the situation of blacks improved somewhat as immigration declined and ideological winds shifted. The 1930s were the era of the Afro-Brazilian Congresses in Recife (1934) and Bahia (1937) and of the Black Brazilian Conference (1940).[1] It was in 1934 that Article 113 of the Brazilian Constitution declared that "All are equal before the law" and that "there will be no privileges or distinctions by reason of birth, sex, race, profession, country, social class, wealth, religious belief or political ideas." It was also in the 1930s that Afro Brazilians in São Paulo formed A Frente Negra Brasileira (The Black Brazilian Front) to protest precisely the same discriminations based on race, wealth, and social class presumably prohibited by the Constitution, in a movement that mobilized thousands of blacks before it was banned by the populist dictator Vargas in 1938.

At the same time, anthropologist Gilberto Freyre, a student of the anti-racist Franz Boas, formulated the theory of "racial democracy" in his 1933 *Casa Grande e Senzala* (literally, "Big House and the Slave Quarters" but translated as "The Masters and the Slaves"). Rather than see Afro Brazilians as the cause of Brazil's "inferiority," Freyre emphasized the many-faceted contribution of blacks and Indians to Brazil's cultural mix. In the patriarchal system typical of Brazilian slavery, according to Freyre, African influences, "carried" by black cooks and mammies, allowed for a certain cultural democracy. Unlike other multiracial societies in the Americas, Brazilian social life was characterized by exceptional familiarity between the races. The tropics softened everything, including racial relations. Freyre's Luso-Tropicalism, as Emília

Viotti da Costa points out, discarded two pillars of European racist theories: the innateness of racial difference and the degeneracy of mixed blood.[2] But Freyre's vision of a "slaveholding utopia" was sentimental and, ultimately, colonialist.[3] A Brazilian variant of what Michael Hanchard calls "the Iberian model of racial exceptionalism," it traces its roots to the nineteenth century, when antiabolitionist Brazilian elites "began concocting favorable representations of Brazilian slavery for foreign consumption."[4] Freyre's rosy picture of rampant interracial mating in tropical hammocks ignored the asymmetrical power relations within which such mating took place. The black contribution to Brazilian culture, furthermore, was reduced to the picturesque and the folkloric, more a matter of dance and cuisine than of fundamental political or economic achievements. (The cinema, as we shall see, often recapitulates this paternalistic culturalism.)

The 1930s also witnessed the resurgence of racist thought. The Integralist Party, a Brazilian variant of fascism especially strong in the European-dominated South of the country, grew rapidly after its founding in 1932. (The pro-Nazi movement among German immigrants in the South is portrayed in Sílvio Back's *Aleluia Gretchen* [1976].) Anti-Semitic and implicitly antiblack and Aryanist, Integralism provoked well-known intellectuals such as Roquete Pinto, Artur Ramos, and Gilberto Freyre to sound an alarm in their "Manifesto against Racial Prejudice," published in 1935, warning against "the transplantation of racist ideas, and especially their social and political corollaries" as a grave risk for a country like Brazil, "whose ethnic formation was decidedly heterogenous."[5]

The 1930s also witness the transformation of "ethnic" practices—samba, carnival, capoeira—into national symbols. Although the cinema cannot be seen as reflecting in any direct way the thinking of ideological elites, the 1930s do bring a changed atmosphere and altered conceptualizations of the Afro Brazilian presence. And if Brazilian cinema of the silent period was symbolically "white," the cinema of the ensuing decades might be called *moreno* (Freyre's ideal) or even "light mulatto." As in the United States, the advent of sound brought new possibilities for black participation; black sounds opened the way for black images. Blacks became a significant presence within the musical review films and later in the *chanchadas,* which dominated production from the 1930s through the late 1950s. Partially modeled on American musicals, and particularly on the "radio broadcast" musicals, the Brazilian musical film had roots as well in popular "review" theater and in Brazilian radio. The "Alô" in Adhemar Gonzaga's *Alô Alô Brasil* (1935) and *Alô Alô Carnaval* (1936), for example, derived from the annual radio salutes to carnival revelers. Both films feature Carmen Miranda, already famous from radio and records. The 1930s films generally favored white stars and a white aesthetic, while featuring occasional blacks and mulattoes in minor or background roles, such as the black drummer with the Simon Boutman orchestra accompanying Carmen Miranda in *Alô Alô Brasil* or the black guitarist with the Conjunto Regional de Benedito Lacerda accompanying Aurora Miranda in *Alô Alô Carnaval.*

It was also in the 1930s that cinema first began to examine the favelas of Rio, the place of origins of the *samba de morro* (samba of the hills). The favelas were created when the poorer population of Rio was pushed out onto the hills by the real-estate boom created by the construction of Avenida Central (now Rio Branco) at the turn of the century. Rio's samba was born in the homes of elderly Bahian matriarchs, or *tias* (aunts), like Tia Ciata, who lived in Praça Onze, and where musicians such as Pixinguinha, Donga, and Sinho gathered to create music. The first song officially recorded as a samba ("Pelo Telefone" [By Telephone]), was composed at Tia Ciata's house and released in 1917. In the early decades of the century, samba was socially despised and even repressed. "Whoever loved samba," said one veteran, "had to sing it far from the police."[6] But as Samba slowly became disseminated through musical recording—the first was the "Isto É Bom" in 1902—and through radio beginning in the 1920s, its popularity gradually spread to other classes of Brazilians. Samba took a number of forms, from the grittier favela versions themselves to the more "sophisticated" orchestrations of singers like Carmen Miranda and Linda Batista. It was thus in the poor milieus that we find the origins of the Afro-inflected popular music of the diaspora and ultimately even of the "world music" now disseminated by multinational companies, as largely poor and discriminated black people—whether in Chicago, New York, or New Orleans, Havana or Rio de Janeiro—created their music, amidst generally hostile populations that only slowly learned to appreciate the musical gifts.

The advent of sound happened to coincide with the social emergence of "samba schools," previously known to the inhabitants of the *morros* (hills) but unfamiliar to Rio's elite. The samba schools amalgamated preexisting traditions like the *entrudo* (carnivalesque slapstick pranks), masked balls, and *cordões* (carnival groupings) into a new and dynamic formation. The name of the first samba school in 1928—Deixa Falar (Let Us Speak)—evokes a preexisting repression and the finding of voice. A 1932 newspaper account from *Mundo Sportivo* describes the newly "discovered" samba school pageant:

> The sonorous soul of the morros descends into the city. All the slopes, all the morros filter into Praça Onze, now become the arena of a beautiful contest. The public can hear various instruments unfamiliar to most people in this city, for example the cuica, with its unique and unmistakable sound . . . they say also that a matchbox, in the hands of a samba master, becomes the equivalent of a complete orchestra . . . with their barbarous instruments, the "schools" achieve veritable miracles. To judge, one must see for oneself. In the morros of this city, there exist many previously unknown melodies.[7]

This passage, at once admiring and patronizing, "translates" the surprise, on the part of the middle-class white Brazilian, at the high quality of Afro Brazilian music, testifying to a greater degree of cultural segregation than is usually acknowledged. According to Sérgio Cabral, MGM producer Hal Roach witnessed the 1932 carnival, but without seeing the samba schools, and announced to the Brazilian newspaper *Correio da Manha* that he would make a film called *Carnavalescos* featuring Laurel and Hardy, with Hardy singing "a very popular samba from Rio's carnival."[8] Humberto Mauro's *Favela dos Meus Amores* (Favela of my Loves, 1935) was the first film to really look at the life and music of the favelas. The plot revolves around two well-heeled gentlemen who, with the help of a mulatta-loving Portuguese man, decide to set up a cabaret in the Morro da Favela. Shot in the Providéncia favela, the film features 300 "passistas" from the Portela Samba School. Alex Viany hailed *Favela dos Meus Amores* as the "first Carioca film to take advantage of the one of the most tragic, exuberant, and musical aspects of Rio: the favela."[9] And Jorge Amado praised the film for not "distorting the character of the favela": "Mauro managed to show the atmosphere of the favela, its misery and at the same time its tremendous beauty. The blacks and mulatos who animate the film show themselves to be admirable artists, acting with an astonishing naturalness, as if there were no camera present. . . . We can only admire the introduction of the Samba Schools, the *maxixe* danced in the cabaret, and all the excellent songs."[10] In *Favela dos Meus Amores,* we note again the direct correlation between documentary-style location-shooting and a higher proportion of black people on the screen.

Although the *chanchada* has its origins in the *filmes cantantes* (sung films) of the silent period, the genre only "took off" in the 1930s. The musical films were intimately linked to the cultural universe of carnival, in that they were timed to be released around the carnival, featured carnival songs, and had an imaginary deeply imbued with carnivalesque values. Alex Viany defines the *chanchada,* succinctly and somewhat pejoratively, as "popularesque comedies, generally made carelessly and in haste, with musical interpolations."[11] Many of the *chanchadas* were produced by the Cinédia Studio, founded in 1930 by Adhemar Gonzaga and still producing films up to the present day. But the most famous *chanchada* studio was Atlântida, founded in 1941, which ultimately produced 62 fiction films in its 20 years of existence. Although immensely popular with the public, the *chanchadas* were the object of all sorts of critical scorn. Even the Brazilian dictionary *Novo Dicionário Aurélio* defines the *chanchada* as "a play or film without value, in which predominate crude devices, vulgar jokes and pornography." The definitions of the *chanchada* vary widely, from a narrow one that includes only the musical comedies of the later period, to a broader one, such as Jean-Claude Bernardet's, which regards the *chanchada* as all "the popular comedies and musical comedies made in Brazil from 1900 to 1960."[12]

The first film to anticipate the *chanchada*'s typical mixture of carnival music and comedy was Wallace Downey's *Coisas Nossas* (Our Things, 1930), modeled after the "all-singing" studio musicals then arriving from Hollywood. Humberto Mauro and Adhemar Gonzaga's *A Voz do Carnaval* (The Voice of Carnival, 1931), the first film to use the optical sound equipment freshly imported from North America, meanwhile, combined carnival reportage with production numbers. The black presence in these films, if always discrete and ephemeral, takes many forms, such as music on the soundtrack, for example, Dorival Caymmi's "O Que É Que a Baiana Tem?" (What Is It That the Bahian Woman Has?) in *Banana da Terra* (Banana of the Earth, 1939); background musicians or dances; or visits to samba schools, as in *Berlim na Batucada* (Percussion in Berlin, 1944). Most of the musicals use blacks largely as background and foil for the love intrigues of white stars like Eliane Macedo and Cyl Farney. Although samba was fundamentally an Afro Brazilian creation, the product of the primarily black *morros* of Rio, film after film gave the impression that samba was a white cultural product.[13] The exclusion of black performers from the Brazilian musical seems especially anomalous in those musicals that exploit Afro Brazilian music and dance. The veiled presence of Afro Brazilian music and dance in numerous films paradoxically marks Afro Brazilian *absence* from the screen.[14] Brazil offers a less extreme version, then, of the same Eurocentric appropriation that led the symptomatically named Paul Whiteman to make the film *King of Jazz* (1930), which paid tribute to the putative origins of jazz by "pouring" (via superimposition) a series of musical ensembles, representing diverse European ethnic groups (Swedes, Italians, Spaniards) into a gigantic melting pot, completely bypassing both Africa and the Afro-Americans who were the driving force behind jazz.

In this sense, the epidermically white performer Carmen Miranda, a star in many of the 1930s musicals, plays a highly ambiguous role. For North Americans, Miranda is the "Brazilian bombshell," a zany emblem of pan-*latinidad,* as well as a gay camp icon. In American musicals, Miranda performed extravagantly flamboyant numbers involving swaying hips, exaggerated facial expressions, kitschy sexy costumes, and "think-big" style props. Her final idealized image as fertility goddess in *The Gang's All Here* (1943) reverberates textually in the opening of the number where raw materials from the South are unloaded in the United States; the North here celebrates the tropical South as the fecund feminine principle that gives birth to the raw materials that the North consumes. The bananas in Miranda's song not only enact the agricultural reductionism of Brazil's monocultural products but also form phallic symbols, here raised by voluptuous latinas over circular, quasi-vaginal forms.[15] Miranda's "excessive" performances allowed her to undercut and parody stereotypical roles, but did little to gain her substantive power.

Whereas for non-Brazilian audiences, the ethnicity of the Miranda persona was submerged, invisible, dissolved into that of a generic *latina,* within a Brazilian context her music and performance style can be seen to be deeply indebted to Afro Brazilian culture. This debt is multidimensional, having to do with her body language and kinetics, with her samba dance steps, with the use of her voice as an instrument, with her percussive approach to tongue-twisting lyrics (a distant cousin to "scat" singing), with her talking-style singing (as in blues), and with her capacity for improvisation. Miranda sways like Iemanjá and has the vanity of Oxum. Miranda grew up in Rio's bohemian district, called "Lapa," where she absorbed Afro Brazilian slang and musical styles. She drew on the repertory of songs by the best samba composers, most of them of African ancestry—Ismael Silva, Ary Barroso, Assis Valente, Dorival Caymmi—and she benefited from the arrangements of an important black composer-performer: Pixinguinha.

Miranda's famous "tutti-fruti" costume, furthermore, stylized and even hyperbolized the already stylized costume of the *baianas*—the female figures dressed in white who sell ritual African foods like *acarajé* (bean fritters with shrimp fried in palm oil) in the streets of Salvador, who became absorbed into Rio's carnival and into Carioca burlesque theater in the early decades of this century and who are even today an obligatory presence in the Carioca samba pageants. Like the typical *baiana* costume, Miranda's outfit comprises turban, necklaces, bracelets, and *balangandas* (jewelry, ornaments). Aloísio Oliveira, one of the members of Carmen's band originally brought by Sudanese slaves of Islamic faith relates that Miranda originally fashioned the costume to illustrate the Doryval Caymmi song "O Que É Que a Baiana Tem?" Broadway producer Lee Shubert saw the performance and brought Miranda to the United States. Hoping to capitalize on her success in *Streets of Paris* (1940), Claude Gleneker launched a fashion campaign, including at Saks Fifth Avenue, featuring Carmen's *baiana* costume.[16] The Afro-Brazilian origins of her *baiana* costume were acknowledged by Miranda herself. Indeed, the lyrics of songs like "O Que É Que a Baiana Tem?" explicitly address the *baiana* and her costume: "She's got a silk turban / A golden necklace"), which is why she turned to the *baiana* costume in the first place, as a way of dramatizing the ethos voiced in the song's lyrics. (In a sequence of Disney's *The Three Caballeros* [1945] Carmen's sister Aurora performs in *baiana* costume as she sings of the sacred delicacies of *candomblé*.) As Zeca Ligiero points out, Carmen's costume drew on the proud tradition of fabrics and design that the Fon and the Yoruba brought to Brazil. (By the end of the nineteenth century, Brazil was importing each year around 50,000 pieces—objects, fabrics and so on—from Yoruba areas of Africa.) Black women in Bahia, some of them slaves, were long famous for their gala dresses and sumptuous jewelry.[17] The *baiana tias* who made their way to Rio de Janeiro were also central figures in the formation of the samba schools, since they organized the parties where the sambistas first got together. Tia Aciata, for example, lived in the Praça Onze neighborhood, then known as Little Africa, and was famous for her elegant dress.

As Ligero points out, the lyrics of Carmen Miranda's sambas proliferated in references to Afro Brazilian culture, to *batuque* (Afro Brazilian celebration, as in the song "Se Gostares do Batuque"), to samba schools like Mangueira (in "Alvorada"), to African instruments like the *cuíca,* and to the "baptism of smoke" from Afro Brazilian religions (in "Batucada da Vida"). Even Carmen's use of jewelry has an African religious precedent, in the use of amulets and charms as protection; female mediums in *candomblé,* for example, wear bracelets and armlets after possession by the *orixás.* The cornucopia of fruits in Carmen's costume, similarly, recalls the *baiana's penca,* the silvery collection of simulacral fruits, each with its own symbolism. In "O Nego no Samba," Carmen adopts the black perspective by making fun of the white ways of dancing samba:

> Black folk's samba
> Always on the tips of your toes
> Black folks samba, my love
> It makes me dizzy
> In samba, white folks get screwed up
> but black folks spread around
> In samba, whites haven't got it, my love
> While blacks are to the style born.

As Ligiero points out, the song references the arrival of whites on the samba scene, reminiscent in a way of the white "slumming" in Harlem nightclubs in the same period. Carmen did not, however, bring black musicians with her from Brazil; her "banda da lua" was all-white. Although most Brazilians were excited about Carmen's success in the United States, some accused her of becoming "Americanized." At the same time, Assis Valente's song "Brazil is a Tambourine," Ligiero reminds us, "insinuates that Carmen Miranda's *baiana* has transformed the austere Uncle Sam into a samba enthusiast":

> It's time for
> the dark skinned people
> to show their value
> I want to see Uncle Sam
> playing tambourine
> for everyone to play samba.

17a/17b. Carmen Miranda before and after:
From *Bananas Is My Business* (1995)

The figure of Miranda was subsequently reinvoiced by the tropicalists of the 1960s, affectionately valued by them as an object for artistic recycling. As she was the first "export-quality" Brazilian star to enjoy international success, she prepared the way for the subsequent successes of bossa nova, samba, and *axé* music. Carmen Miranda also figures into two recent documentaries. Dee Dee Halleck's *Gringo in Mañanaland* (1994) juxtaposes Miranda's spectacular banana numbers with archival footage of actual workers on banana plantations, calling attention to the hard labor effaced by the Hollywood image. Helena Solberg-Ladd's *Bananas Is My Business* (1995), meanwhile, a highly personal and poetic mediation on Carmen's life and career (see photo 17), offers a dazzling melange of news footage (including of Miranda's huge public funeral in 1955), film clips, TV footage, staged scenes (with Erick Barreto impersonating Carmen), and interviews with friends, relatives, and artistic collaborators. The film skillfully registers Carmen's collaboration with Afro Brazilian musicians, and shows her dancing, in an informal setting, with the African American dance duo the Nicolas Brothers.

The most important black star of this period was Sebastião Bernardes Souza Prata, or "Grande Otelo." If artistic prestige were distributed more fairly, Grande Otelo would be as well known as Charlie Chaplin, Buster Keaton, or James Earl Jones. One of Brazil's finest and most versatile actors, Grande Otelo was described by Orson Welles as "the greatest comic actor of the 20th century" and by novelist Jorge Amado as "the epitome of Brazil."[18] As ZeZé Motta put it in her posthumous tribute, "Grande Otelo overcame every obstacle—being poor, black, and without a leading man's physique—through his talent, his pugnacity, his strength, his perseverance, and his modesty."[19] Born in 1915, Otelo reportedly got his name because as a child some adults took him to be a future tenor who "would make a good Othello" in the Verdi opera. Grande Otelo's multiple talents included composing, singing, dancing, acting, and screenwriting. He performed in over 100 Brazilian feature films, participating in virtually all phases of Brazilian Cinema and television, from the *chanchada* through Cinema Novo, the Underground of the 1960s, and the telenovelas of the 1970s and 1980s, working tirelessly up until 1994, when he died just after arriving in Paris for a French retrospective of his work at the Three Continents Festival. In Otelo's luggage at the time of his death was his own screenplay (coauthored with Roberto Moura), entitled *Elite Club,* his attempt to portray the social universe of the *gafieiras* (popular dance halls) of the 1950s, a world Grande Otelo describes as a "place where blacks and whites enjoyed themselves in a spirit of happiness and democracy."[20]

At the time of his first cameo in *Noites Cariocas* (Carioca Nights, 1935), Grande Otelo was already well known as an actor in comic theater and vaudeville. He began work as an artist at the age of eight, in a circus in the provincial town of Uberlândia, in a sketch in which he appeared in drag. After running away from home, Otelo was adopted by a rich white Paulista family, thus gaining access to some of the best schools in São Paulo. The first theatrical company for blacks actors and musicians—the Companhia Negra de Revista (The Black Theatrical Review Company) hired Grande Otelo, then only nine, in 1924. It was during one of the troupe's performances that Otelo met the Brazilian novelist Mário de Andrade, the author of the novel *Macunaíma,* in the adaptation of which Grande Otelo would star over 40 years later. It is fascinating to speculate that watching Otelo in action might have partially inspired the figure of Macunaíma in the mind of Mário de Andrade. It is also ironic that Grande Otelo played the role of Mário de Andrade himself in the Camilla Amado adaptation of *O Banquete* (The Banquet, 1978) and that in *Exu-Piá: Coração de Macunaíma* (Exu-Piá: Heart of Macunaíma, 1984) Grande Otelo, reincarnating his role in the 1969 film, travels through present-day Brazil in search of Mário de Andrade, in the hopes that the author will agree to rewrite the destiny of the "hero without any character."

Grande Otelo was reportedly inspired to work in film by the presence of a black boy (Farina) in the American "Our Gang" series; Otelo wanted to be the black boy in a Brazilian equivalent series. In the early period, Grande Otelo polished his musical and linguistic talents, learning to speak English, French, Italian, and Spanish, even singing *Tosca* and dancing the minuet, and distinguishing himself generally by his improvisatory talents. Grande Otelo became a star in the world of Rio Casinos such as the Urca, where Orson Welles was to see him perform when he went to Brazil to make *It's All True*. At the time, the Urca Casino had a policy of allowing blacks to perform on stage but not be patrons in the casino, a policy analogous to that which allowed African American stars like Lena Horne to sing at New York's Savoy Hotel, for example, but not to stay as guests. Even before having performed in the Welles film, Grande Otelo was famous enough to be invited to Hollywood. Walt Disney expressed interest in having Otelo provide the voice for his cartoon character Zé Carioca, and in 1940, he was invited to join Carmen Miranda in Hollywood. (Otelo ultimately did not go only because he was tied down by an exploitative contract that obliged him to remit 50 percent of his earnings to the Urca Casino.) Otelo also performed together with Josephine Baker during her first visit to Brazil in 1939. (According to her biographers, Baker fell in love with Brazil, planned to incorporate samba into her repertoire, and dreamed of filming in Rio.)[21]

It would be difficult to summarize all of Grande Otelo's innumerable film roles.[22] He began in *Noites Cariocas* (1935) with an extremely minor and subaltern role as a valet for the film's star. After *Noites Cariocas,* Wallace Downey invited Otelo to play a minor role in a dramatic comedy entitled *João Ninguém* (John Nobody, 1937). In 1939, Otelo played a messenger in a comic film called *Futebol em Família* (Family Soccer), a film inspired by the success of two black athletes (Domingos de Guia and Leonidas da Silva) in the 1938 World Cup. In 1941, he played a street kid with artistic ambitions in *Céu Azul* (Blue Sky). In 1943, he played the employee of a pension in *Samba*

18. Grande Otelo at Atlântida

em Berlin. Also in 1943, he starred in *Moleque Tião* (Street Kid Tião), the premiere film of the Rio film studio Atlântida (photo 18). Founded in 1941,
Atlântida hoped to create a socially conscious cinema. Its self-declared goals
were to create a "Carioca cinematic experience," and "to explore social problems which had up to that point been absent from national cinema."[23] The
studio's debut was commemorated by a huge party, transmitted over the radio, featuring filmmaker John Ford and cinematographer Gregg Toland as
honored guests. The DIP (Department of Press and Propaganda) footage recording this banquet reveals both the honors accorded to Grande Otelo as the
star of the film and his isolation as a black person, since Otelo is virtually the
only black face in sight. (One is reminded of Sidney Poitier's "raisin-in-the-
rice" situation in the 1950s as the only black, apart from janitors and servants,
at the Hollywood studios where he worked.)

Directed by José Carlos Burle and scripted by Alinor Azevedo, *Moleque
Tião* offered a fictionalized version of Grande Otelo's own life (see photo 19).
At the time it was considered a very risky enterprise to feature a black actor in
the leading role for a studio's first film, especially since Grande Otelo was not
yet a star. The film tells the tale of a young black man from the back country
of Minas Gerais, who, inspired by newspaper reports about the successes of a

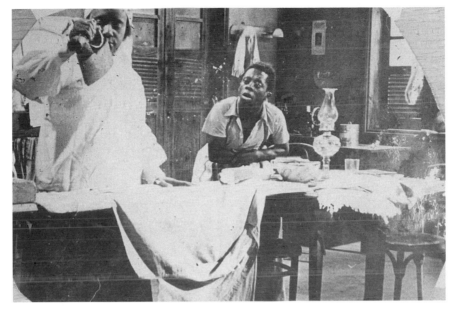

19. Grande Otelo in *Moleque Tião* (1943)

black theatrical company, does all in his power to go to Rio. Once there, he learns that the company is about to break up, but he shows his dramatic talents to the theater director anyway. After getting a job as an errand boy, he is interned in an orphanage, but he manages to escape. Finally he gets his break, and he is a tremendous success. To complete his happiness, his mother arrives from Minas to applaud his theatrical apotheosis. *Moleque Tião* tells the formulaic tale of the artist who suffers setbacks before achieving his goals; in short, a Horatio Alger story, combined with backstage musical, but one with a black accent. *Moleque Tião* innovated by the naturalness of its acting and the location shooting of its impoverished decors, leading later critics to link it to the neorealism of Visconti's *Ossessione* in the same year. Extremely popular with the public, *Moleque Tião* guaranteed Grande Otelo's future as a star performer.

In *Tristezas Não Pagam Dívidas* (Sadness Pays No Debts, 1944) Grande Otelo plays the manager of a *gafieira*. Then Atlântida's reigning star, Otelo also participated in the scripting process and even directed a scene set in a *gafieira* modeled after the Elite Club in Rio.[24] Otelo also plays a minor role in *Berlim na Batucada* (Percussion in Berlin, 1944) — the title has to do with the news arriving from the European front about Brazilian participation in World War II — a film *à clef* that references Orson Welles's 1942 trip to Brazil. The director, Luiz de Barros, had worked with Welles on *It's All True;* his task was to organize the scenes set in the municipal theater. In *Berlim na Batucada,* Welles is portrayed as a heavily accented, cigar-smoking tourist in search of authentic samba; Otelo plays his Brazilian valet. (Reportedly, Luiz de Barros saw Welles as part of a Hollywood conspiracy aimed at destroying the Brazilian film industry, the irony being that it was Welles himself who was largely destroyed by Hollywood.)[25] *Berlim na Batucada* features on-site shooting of samba school performances in the favelas, particularly from the Escola de Samba de Heitor dos Prazeres, as well as a number of songs, for example, "Silenciar a Mangueira Não") coauthored by Otelo and Herivelto Martins. (Grande Otelo wrote at least 30 songs, recorded either by himself or by others.)

Tristezas Não Pagam Dívidas was the first film in which Grande Otelo joined in a duo comprising himself and another famous comic actor— Oscarito. (The two had acted together in earlier films, such as *Noites Cariocas,* but not as a pair.) Like most comic duos—the slender Laurel and the obese Hardy, the elegant Bing Crosby and the clumsy Bob Hope, the smooth-voiced white Jack Benny and the rough-voiced black Rochester—the Oscarito–Grande Otelo pair plays with oxymoronic contrasts. Paired with Oscarito, and later with Ankito, Otelo became the "king of the *chanchadas.*" Unlike the servant-master pattern that prevailed in the black-white friendships in Hollywood films of the same period (e.g., Jack Benny and his valet Rochester), there was a rough equality between Otelo and his white costars, although Otelo was perhaps more likely to suffer from injustice outside of the friendship. Within the friendship, however, Oscarito's characters tended to be more vulnerable. At the same time, a sense of physical ease reigns between Grande Otelo and Oscarito. *Matar ou Correr* (To Kill or to Run, 1954) ends with a parodic "final kiss" between the two actors, a kiss that probably would have provoked paroxysms of racialized homophobia in the Hollywood of the same period.

Otelo's persona was invariably sympathetic. He often played the *malandro,* the urban survivor who got by thanks to his glib tongue and quick imagination, the person who turns not working, or working paralegally, into an art form. The *malandro* circumvents the dull weight of legalistic obligations, performing a deft end-run around systemic constraints. (In the sense that blacks have been required to evade the harsh consequences of the law more than whites have, the role can be seen as black connoted.) Otelo plays the *malandro*

20. Grande Otelo in
De Pernas Prò Ar (1957)

in films like *O Caçula do Barulho* (The Great Youngest Son, 1949) and *Amei um Bicheiro* (I Loved a Bookie, 1952). In *De Pernas Prò Ar* (Upside Down, 1957), he plays an illegal street vendor who sells mechanical dolls and outwits the various plainclothes policemen who try to entrap him (photo 20). Otelo and his friend (fellow *chanchada* star Ankito) work in the theater providing background music for lip-synching singers. In a scene somewhat reminiscent of *Singin' in the Rain,* the pair embarrasses the talentless singer by inadvertently putting on a record of animal noises. Through a subplot involving a bank robbery, Ankito and Otelo end up with the money, while the thieves end up with the mechanical dolls.

According to Sérgio Augusto, Grande Otelo complained of his subordinate status in relation to Oscarito, in the sense that although Oscarito's character was more vulnerable, Otelo's role was always to save him rather than to take the lead in the first place.[26] Otelo also resented earning less than his partner because he thought of himself as a more complete actor,[27] and indeed Otelo did deploy a vast arsenal of postures, faces, and gestures for comic, dramatic, and distancing effects. For Otelo, Oscarito was an "eccentric" whereas Otelo "tried to valorize the dialogue and the interpretation, always looking for the right tone. . . . Oscarito was a 'type,' while . . . [Otelo] was an actor."[28] Otelo's first films were written for him to be the "straight man" for Oscarito, but Otelo subverted that arrangement through his diabolically creative improvisions. His resentment is given narrative form in Carlos Manga's *A Dupla do Barulho* (A Great Pair, 1953), a film that treats, in a displaced semibiographical manner, the lives of the two greatest stars of Atlântida. In this sentimental melodrama, Otelo and Oscarito are both circus artists, who separate when Otelo begins to drink. Otelo is badly treated, both as a black man and as an alcoholic, but in the end he is restored to well-being and applauded in his return to circus performance. In one sequence, a drunken Tião (Otelo) complains about his partner Tônico (Oscarito): "Tônico and Tião! Why not Tião and Tônico? I'm tired of being a ladder to someone else's success." (In Portuguese, *escada* [ladder] means "straight man.") Oscarito himself collaborated with this critical portrayal and even gave some of his better lines to Otelo. The director, meanwhile, a self-described man of the left, had the explicit intention of "questioning the subaltern position of blacks."[29]

Parenthetically, it was this same hatred for racial prejudice that led Carlos Manga to give support to a mulatto artist named José Cajado Filho, who had made a career for himself as a set designer in film and theater. Manga, in one of the rare direct testimonies to the effects of racism in the world of Brazilian cinema, describes Cajado Filho as a resentful person but one who had every reason to be resentful: "Cajado was an eternal victim of racial prejudice. They didn't let him into the School of Fine Arts, even though he won First Prize in the contest they offered. We, the whites of the Atlântida Studio, were highlighted; he wasn't. But all of us directors—myself, Macedo, Burle, Roberto Farias—were paying the price of losing his enormous talent. He knew how to do everything—decor, script, gags, directing. For me, Cajado was the real father of the chanchada."[30]

In another of Manga's films, the western parody *Matar ou Correr*, Cajado Filho constructed a western-style set that was so convincing that many critics were sure the shots were made in Hollywood. Cajado Filho also scripted and designed *O Homen do Sputnik* (Sputnik Man, 1959), the first film, as Sérgio Augusto puts it, "to look at the Cold War from a Third World perspective."[31] The film concerns a rural Brazilian (Oscarito) who discovers a Russian satellite in his backyard and who is consequently courted by the Russians, the Americans, and the French. Although Cajada satirizes Russian authoritarianism, he also lampoons the Americans as gum-chewing cretins. One shot shows the American eagle with a bottle of Coke in its claws, framed by the words "Usa e Abusa," literally "Use and Abuse" but also a pun on "U.S.A."

The opening gag of *E o Mundo se Diverte* (And the World Enjoys Itself, 1949) inadvertently reveals a melancholy underside of Grande Otelo's comic roles. In the film, both Oscarito and Grande Otelo are theater janitors. Working overtime one night, Otelo answers a call from a young woman. When the woman asks about his appearance, the flirtatious and very black Otelo describes himself as "tall, neither fat nor skinny, well-shaped nose, good lips, and more blond than dark." The "gag" is premised on the self-rejection engendered by the "ideology of whitening." Another, later film, *Samba em Brasília* (1960) reverses the situation by making a joke out of blackness and discrimination. In the film, Ivete, the black *sambista* trying to replace Terezinha (played by the white actress Eliana) as the standard-bearer of the samba school, complains that she has never before seen a white person chosen as standard-bearer over "normal people," to which her neighbor responds: "Listen here girl. We live in a democratic society. We aren't prejudiced." The joke, then, is premised on calling blacks "normal people" and on the presumably absurd idea that white people could ever be victims of discrimination.

Vinícius de Moraes, author of the source play for *Black Orpheus,* described Grande Otelo as "an especially rich person in human terms, with a formidable capacity for pathos and an extreme tenderness, all hidden behind irony and verve."[32] Given this emotional range, it is fortunate that not all of Grande Otelo's roles were comic. Apart from his role in *Moleque Tião*, Otelo also played in the first Brazilian film to confront the problem of contemporary racial discrimination—José Carlos Burle's symptomatically titled *Também Somos Irmãos* (We Are Also Brothers, 1949; see photo 21). The film was a Brazilian example of the "problem film" genre then popular in Hollywood, that is, the socially conscious reformist films of the late 1940s that examine specific problems such as antiblack racism (*Pinky* [1949]), or anti-Semitism (*Gentleman's Agreement* [1947]). The film's story concerns a wealthy, childless widower who adopts four children, of whom two are white (Vera Nunes and Agnaldo Rayol) and two are black (Otelo and Aguinaldo Camargo, then involved with the Black Experimental Theater). During childhood everything proceeds peacefully, but with the passage of time the limitations imposed on blacks turn into bitter humiliations. The Camargo character submits to the indignities because he is secretly in love with the Vera Nunes character and hopes to finish his law degree. He composes songs, which the white brother interprets. When the widower discovers Camargo's love for Vera, he bans him from the house. He then goes to live in a favela and ultimately finishes his degree. When he invites Vera to his graduation ceremony, her father prohibits her from attending. Otelo's character, meanwhile, is a *malandro,* who advises his brother to drop law and become a hustler like himself. When Otelo gets arrested, Camargo defends his brother in court, managing to get him acquitted. *Também Somos Irmãos,* from these accounts, seems to have been quite critical of reigning ideologies. In one scene, a white friend suggests that Otelo emulate his brother, lauded as a "black man with a white soul," to which Otelo responds: "For me, a black man with a white soul is a ghost." Although critics were enthusiastic—the Brazilian Critics' Association named it "Best Film of

21. Social-problem film: *Também Somos Irmãos* (1949)

22. Parodying *High Noon: Matar ou Correr* (1954)

the Year"—the public was less receptive since, as the director himself explained, "whites were uncomfortable about being criticized, and blacks at that
time were not sufficiently politicized to appreciate the message."[33]

Grande Otelo also played a key role in the Brazilian *chanchada* parodies of
North American films, a tradition that goes all the way back to *O Babão* (The
Baboon, 1930), a spoof of Roman Novarro's *The Pagan* (1929; in Portuguese,
O Pagão), and which continues as late as a parody of Spielberg's *Jaws* (1975)—
entitled *Bacalhau* (Codfish, 1976).[34] The Brazilian parodies must be set against
the backdrop of the elitism dominating the critical scene in Brazil. In the
1950s a critic from the *Revista Anhembi* denounced the *chanchadas* for "exploiting the bad taste of the masses, feeding its primitive instincts, confusing
and deluding the masses, lowering the cinema for the public rather than raising the public to the level of cinema."[35] For elite critics, then, the *chanchadas*

were distinctly uncivilized, too full of sambas and *baianas*. At times the implicitly anti-African spirit of these critiques becomes explicit. In an article entitled "Nudismo, Macumba, e Malandragem" (Nudism, Macumba, and Hustlerism), one critic deplores the *chanchada*'s evocation of "a race of hustlers, beach thieves, and obnoxious capoeira toughs, giving the impression that our religion consists of low-grade spiritism and African myths."[36]

In Carlos Manga's *Matar ou Correr* (photo 22, a parody of Fred Zinneman's *High Noon* (translated into Portuguese as "To Kill or to Die"), Otelo plays Ciscocada (a punning fusion of Cisco Kid and *cocada*, or cononut candy), the sidekick of Kid Bolha (Kid Bubble), the comic incarnation of the Gary Cooper character of the original. Thanks to the parody, Otelo plays a role as a black actor though the Hollywood original did not include a black. As João Luiz Vieira points out, the parodic element of *Matar ou Correr* is located uniquely in the comic figures of Oscarito and Otelo, who are grotesque caricatures of their North American prototypes. The Otelo character is made ridiculous by his outsized western clothes and by his general incompetence in the codes of the western, this in a film that otherwise respects the aesthetic and characterological norms of the Hollywood western, resulting in what Vieira calls a "comedy of self-denigration."[37]

In José Carlos Burle's *Carnaval Atlântida* (1952; see photo 23), a reflexive film about filmmaking, Brazilian director Cecílio B. de Milho (translates as "Cecil B. of the Corn") wants to make a Hollywood-style epic version of the Helen of Troy story. Grande Otelo and Colé play aspiring screenwriters who are demoted to janitor when de Milho rejects their "carnivalesque" scripts. In a key sequence, de Milho shows them the sets and explains his conception of *Helen*. Grande Otelo gladly informs the director that he knows a mulatta named Helen (Elena) from the Morro da Formiga who would make an excellent Helen of Troy. The director explains condescendingly that he is interested in "universal" beauty and that the role has nothing to do with a *mulata* from a favela. (Just two years before, interestingly, Orson Welles cast an African American performer, Eartha Kitt, as Helen of Troy in a European production of the Marlowe play, precisely because for him she represented "universal beauty" and "all women.")[38] The director then conjures up his vision of the scene. We see a white Helen being fanned by her black servant. The set, a precariously constructed studio garden in the decor of a Greek palace, is artificial, and the actor's gestures are labored and theatrical. Unimpressed, Grande

23. Grande Otelo and Eliana in *Carnaval Atlântida* (1952)

Otelo and Colé insist that the director needs something more lively, with music. They then propose their own version of the epic. In their imagined version, all the performers break out into a carnival samba as the black singer Blecaute (Blackout) sings "Dona Cegonha," a carnival hit from the same year.

The sequence counterpoints a series of contrasts—Europe and Third World, Hollywood and chanchada, USA and Brazil, epic and musical, palace and favela, high culture and popular culture—consistently showing sympathy for the latter rather than the former term. As Vieira points out, the film offers an allegory of inappropriateness: the Hollywood production style (and that of its imitators in Brazil) is as inappropriate for Brazil as Grande Otelo's toga is for samba dancing. The film's sympathies clearly lie with the popular characters. Although the actual director of *Carnaval Atlântida*, José Carlos Burle, himself nourished Hollywood ambitions, he also knew, unlike the filmmaker within the film, that such a cinema was impossible in Brazil. The film also spoofs the Eurocentric idea of ancient Greece as the fount of "universal" culture, not only in this sequence but also in the parodic form of scholar–professor–film consultant Xenofontes (Oscarito). Xenofontes abandons his job at Athens High School—where he lectures on Greek philosophy to an uncomprehending class of adolescents more interested in Eros than in Minerva—to advise Cecílio B. de Milho on the film. Significantly, it is the black subalterns who puncture the colonized pretensions of official Brazilian cinema; it is they who point out that Brazil is not Europe, that its people are different, and that Brazil therefore requires a cinema distinct from the Hollywood model. Interestingly, this comic sequence poses paradigmatically serious questions about multicultural politics and representation: Who is to write the script: Grande Otelo or a studio hack? Who is to perform: a white actress or the mulatta from the favela? The mulatta is ultimately rejected in the name of "universal beauty," and while black male performers do enter this film-about-filmmaking the mulatta is described but never seen, even though the sequence presumably stages Otelo's fantasy, pointing again to the structural absence of black women. It is the director Cecílio B. de Milho, finally, who retains final cut, the power to put a *basta* both to the carnival dance and to Grande Otelo's *chanchada,* reminding us, as a very distant echo, of the historical repression of *candomblé* drums and Africanized carnivals.

Victor Lima's *Os Cosmonautas* (The Cosmonauts, 1963), meanwhile, revolves around a Brazilian scientist who heads a Brazilian center for space studies, called "Cape Carnival" (a linguistic play on Cape Canaveral). After managing to put a monkey into orbit, the scientist aspires to a higher goal: he wants to outdo the Russians and the Americans by putting two Brazilians on the moon. The scientist contracts Zeobio from the FBI (Brazilian Fiscalization of Investigations). Using class and eugenic criteria, the scientist chooses some "unnecessary individuals," specifically some loafers and gamblers from the streets of Rio, with the logic that if these individuals do not reach the moon, nothing will have been lost. Since the original "unnecessary individuals" become frightened by the prospect of the voyage, Grande Otelo is chosen, along with a vacuum cleaner salesman named Gagarino da Silva (a play on the name of the Russian astronaut Gagarin) and a mysterious woman (Myrna Iris) from the planet Korson (photo 24). Before the United States, then, Brazil sent an interracial group into space, even if the voyage was only filmic and carnivalesque. *Os Cosmonautas* satirizes the American and Russian obsession with space competition—an obsession mocked as well in *O Homen do Sputnik* (Sputnik Man)—while also making fun of the Brazilian incapacity to emulate such high-tech feats. Cape Carnaval, in this reflexive allegory, is to Brazilian cinema as Cape Canaveral is to Hollywood. Although the mention

24. Cape Carnaval: *Os Cosmonautas* (1963)

of "eugenic criteria" evokes nineteenth-century "scientific racism," the idea is clearly spoofed and in any case is not directed exclusively at blacks. The use of a black actor merely reinforces a double-edged irony that works both against the American superpower and the Brazilian "underpower."

At least two *chanchadas*—*Carnaval no Fogo* (Carnival on Fire, 1949) and *Um Candango na Belacap* (Northeasterner in Rio, 1961) parodied Shakespeare's *Romeo and Juliet* and both featured Grande Otelo. In *Carnaval em Fogo,* Oscarito and Grande Otelo in drag (looking rather like Flip Wilson's "Geraldine"), perform the balcony scene from *Romeo and Juliet.* Both actors spoof the grand style of hyperarticulated pomposity, as Otelo speaks of the "nocturnal mask that hides my damsel shame" and Oscarito expresses a desire to kiss "the virgin pulp of my beloved's lips." But their passionate declarations of love give way to a boisterous argument about whether a nightingale or a lark is singing in the trees. Romeo finally flees when Juliet warns him that her father, Mr. Capulet, will turn him into "shish kebob" if he catches him. Here the comic inversions are multiple and superimposed. Choosing a Juliet who is both male (thus reprising the Elizabethan theater's custom of having male actors play female roles) and black, shows comic irreverence toward one of the canonical classics of Western theater.

25. Foregrounding whiteness: *Rio Fantasia* (1957)

Speaking generally, what can we say about the role of blacks in the comic musical films of this period? First, given their Brazilian origins, their Rio de Janeiro setting, and their samba subject, the musicals shockingly underrepresent the black presence. Apart from Vera Regina, Colé, Chocolate, Blecaute, Otelo, and occasional singers, dancers, and musicians, blacks are not a strong presence. In fact, when Luiz de Barros made a musical biopic *O Rei do Samba* (King of the Samba, 1952) about the mulatto sambista José Barbosa da Silva, better known as "Sinhô," he cast a white actor (Bene Nunes) for the role. (In 1995, in contrast, Gilberto Gil was cast as "Sinhô" in Júlio Bressane's film *O Mandarim* [Mandarin].)[39] Second, the musicals do manifest the strong presence of black cultural forms, as if Brazilian producers, not unlike their Hollywood counterparts, wanted to have black culture without dealing with the people who produced it. Third, we must note the virtually complete absence of black women as major players. When Grande Otelo dances or sings with women performers, Marie Antoinetta Pons in *Carnaval Atlântida,* for example, they are almost invariably white. Fourth, although we do see musicians and dancers of color in the background of the films, they are there to support the white stars, with blacks serving to visually "set off" the beauty and elegance of the white elite, in a slightly less binaristic version of the racial "foil effect" so well analyzed by James Snead.[10] In films such as *Rio Fantasia* (Rio Fantasy, 1957), the Debbie Reynolds–like white actress Eliana is center stage, while colorful *baianas* dance in the background (see photo 25).[41]

The privileging of the figure of Grande Otelo as the key black actor, and his pairing with white costars, had the effect of isolating him from his black brothers and sisters. As a lone representative of black Brazil, he was made to bear a heavy "burden of representation." At the same time, it would be a mistake to always correlate specific traits of the Otelo character with race, given his extremely variegated roles and the fact that he often plays figures such as the *malandro* who transcend racial definition, constituting archetypes incarnated as well by other, nonblack actors. The Carioca *malandro* was always viewed with a mixture of sincere admiration and class condescension, considered lower-class but also a gifted trickster or shape-shifter loved for his survival skills and for his antiauthoritarian stance. The audience generally laughed with the *malandro* figure rather than at him. As an actor, Otelo tended to incarnate a popularesque type in the grand comic tradition, characterized by broad gestures, exaggerated facial expressions, and acrobatic corporality. At the same time, he was generally treated as comically asexual; his role was to help along the amorous intrigues of his white partners (Oscarito, Zé Trindade) a desexualizing pattern that Donald Bogle has noted about the North American black-white buddy films. Indeed, Otelo's persona has something of the smart child, bright but somehow presexual, infantilized, as if the middle-class white audience might have trouble accepting a sexually assertive black male.

In real life, pressured by the black community and by activists such as Abdias do Nascimento, Otelo progressively came to affirm his blackness. He retroactively described his 1940s persona as that of the *enfant gâté* of Carioca high society, blithely unaware of the racist policies that prevented blacks from entering the Casino da Urca as patrons.[42] Although Otelo was hardly what in North America would be called a "race man," it is nevertheless significant that he repeatedly chose to work in acting companies led by black men like Oduvaldo Viana and Chocolate. Over the years, he showed an increasing identification with his Afro Brazilian roots, attributing his strength as an actor, for example, to an "ancestral heritage very linked with the formation of my race."[43] Grande Otelo had a crucial role in subsequent phases of Brazilian Cinema, and we will return to his work in subsequent chapters. (In 1978 the Império Serrano Samba School chose as its theme the artistry and friendship of Oscarito and Grande Otelo.) Otelo is also the subject of at least one Brazilian documentary: Murilla Salles and Ronaldo Foster's *Sebastião Prata ou Bem Dizendo Grande Otelo* (Sebastion Prata, or Better, Grande Otelo, 1980).

Grande Otelo was not the only black actor who gained fame in the 1940s and 1950s; among the others were Nilo Chagas, Chocolate, Blackout, Príncipe Pretinho (Little Black Prince), and Colé. Interestingly, the names of many of the black performers, like that of Grande Otelo, call attention to their blackness, evidence perhaps of a relatively unembarrassed color-consciousness or perhaps of objectification: they could not simply be seen as actors but rather only as *black* actors. These "comic" names reflect as well, perhaps, a kind of generic glass ceiling, a difficulty in moving beyond comedy, in taking black people seriously, as if by their mere presence blacks connoted instant humor and gratification for white audiences.

Although most of the films featuring blacks in this period were musical comedies, there were a few exceptions. *Pureza* (Purity, 1940), produced by Adhemar Gonzaga, directed by the Portuguese director Chianca de Garcia, and based on a novel by José Lins do Rego, features a dramatic sequence in which the black boy Joca finds himself adrift in a boat in rapids that lead to a waterfall, filmed in such a way that the spectator is led to empathize strongly with the character. Humberto Mauro's *O Despertar da Rendentora* (The Awakening of the Redemptress, 1941) stages, in an idealized manner, the coming to consciousness of Princess Isabel, the signer of the Lei Áurea that abolished slavery in Brazil. The film portrays Isabel as a lively adolescent who enjoys running in the forest. During one of her forays, a black woman kneels at her feet and begins to tell her about the depredations of slavery. A flashback reveals the woman's memories. We are shown men in stocks, torture equipment, slave drivers abusing black men. Deeply moved, the princess promises to do all in her power to end slavery, after which the film flashes forward to the signing of the Lei Áurea, as shots of men being unchained are superimposed on a facsimile of the document itself, giving way to the final title: "Slavery is Abolished in Brazil." A 1945 adaptation of the novel *O Cortiço* (The Tenement) meanwhile, produced by Gonzaga and directed by Luiz de Barros, does at least use a *mulata* actress (Horacina Correa) to play the *mulata* character of Rita Baiana. And *Vendaval Maravilhoso* (Marvelous Storm, 1949) a Luso Brazilian coproduction, finally, adapted Jorge Amado's *ABC de Castro Alves,* his biography of the abolitionist poet Castro Alves and included scenes representing the famous poem "Slave Ship" as well as scenes of *candomblé.*

A newspaper report from February 11, 1942, reveals the nuances of Brazilian-style racism. Entitled "From the Favela to Hollywood," the article concerns two Afro Brazilian radio stars, Henricão and Carmen Costa, who have been contracted by an American impresario to work in Hollywood. Unlike similar reports about Hollywood-bound performers such as Carmen Miranda, the report is framed by a patronizing preface, which speaks of "almost-perfect" white civilizations and the "retardation of black civilizations." The report begrudgingly acknowledges a white debt to blacks for having "aided us when the domination of the aboriginal element became difficult." At the same time, the article speaks of "our great pride" in the "black stars from Brazil."[44] The paternalistic tone conveys a sense of astonishment that Hollywood might be interested in "our" blacks. The article was published, ironically, just three days after the arrival in Brazil of Orson Welles, a director who, it turned out, was very much interested in black Brazil.

CHAPTER 4

Pan-American Interlude:
Orson Welles in
Brazil, 1942

∞

An exception to the tendency to place black Brazilians in the background came, surprisingly, from a North American director. In 1942, Orson Welles went to Brazil (photo 26) to film two episodes of the never-to-be-finished *It's All True,* a semidocumentary aimed at fostering the Good Neighbor Policy and countering Nazi propaganda in Latin America. The first episode, "Carnival," starring Grande Otelo, was to treat the world of samba and specifically the protests against the elimination of the popular Carioca square Praça Onze. The second episode, "Jangadeiros," was to treat the epic voyage of four *jangadeiros* (raftsmen)—Manoel "Jacaré" Olímpio Meira, Raimundo "Tata" Correia Lima, Manuel "Preto" Pereira da Silva, and "Jerónimo" André de Souza—who traveled roughly 1,650 miles without a compass from Fortaleza to Rio to present their social grievances to then president Vargas. Two days after they arrived in Rio, Vargas signed legislation extending social benefits to all Brazilian fishermen and their families.

One of the famous "lost" films of cinema history, *It's All True* was rediscovered in 1985 when Fred Chandler happened upon 150,000 feet of the film in a Paramount Pictures vault. Whatever its beginnings as a project assigned to Welles due to the vicissitudes of international geopolitics, the *It's All True* project ultimately became a passionate cause with Welles, a project close to his heart and even to the wellsprings of his creativity. Although a well-paid celebrity director at the very peak of his career, Welles was willing to continue filming without studio backing, with minimal equipment, and spending his own money. For years, Welles made strenuous efforts to recuperate the Brazilian

26. Welles in Rio in 1942 (Photo: Rogério Sganzerla)

footage and fashion it into a finished film. "Too much effort and real love went into the entire project," Welles wrote to Brazilian friend Fernando Pinto, "for it to fail and come to nothing in the end." Welles wanted to finish the film not in the name of Hollywood executives or his own career, but in the name of the *jangadeiros:* "I cannot remember you with simple pleasure," Welles wrote his friend, "because no thought of you can exist without some feeling of responsibility unfulfilled to you—responsibility to our common respect for the heroes of the beach, and specifically Jacaré's family." (This last reference being to the *jangadeiro* leader who drowned during the filming.)[1] In paying homage to the *jangadeiros,* Welles was honoring both African and indigenous traditions in Brazil since the *jangadas* (rafts) were an Indian invention, examples of the *caboclo* culture that sprung from the intermingling of black slaves with indigenous groups, and since the *jangadeiros* themselves were black and mestiço.[2]

Despite Welles's dedication, the *It's All True* project became hounded by hostile rumors and negative publicity that were to shadow Welles throughout his career. My goal here will not to be to reconstruct all the events surrounding the making of *It's All True* or to counter in detail the tendentious versions proposed by some of Welles's biographers and critics.[3] Rather, I would like to offer a kind of "view from Brazil" of the *It's All True* experience, stressing four interlinked issues: (1) Welles's nonracist approach to Brazilian culture; (2) the audacity of the project in cultural, aesthetic, cinematic, and racial terms; (3) Welles's relation to Afro Brazilian culture and his working relationships with black Brazilians; and (4) the racial subtext to some of the opposition to *It's All True*, a subtext recapitulated, I will argue, in the discourse of many of Welles's critics.

The conventional version of what is often dismissively labeled the *It's All True* "adventure," as presented by such critics as Charles Higham and John Russell Taylor, has generally been hostile to Welles.[4] Higham's account, less a biography than a relentless and morbidly selective indictment, shows us a profligate Welles, swayed by tropical temptations and incapacitated by a pathological terror of completion, himself largely responsible for the film's demise. According to Higham, Welles's incessant partying, his financial extravagances, his unseemly behavior (throwing furniture out of hotel windows), and his irrational reluctance to mold his materials into a conventional story with box-office appeal, climaxed by the accidental death of Jacaré, a death for which Welles was not directly responsible but for which he was blamed, together with the negative reception of the film *The Ambersons* and a change of leadership at RKO, all led to the acrimonious noncompletion of the film. The language and tone of the Higham account is moralistic and at times even prosecutorial. Within the classical "rise and fall" trope that informs Higham's narrative, *It's All True* clearly marks the beginning of Welles's "fall." It is as if for Higham the *It's All True* experience formed a microcosmic exemplum that further confirmed the overriding parable orienting his observations and which is stated in the final paragraph of *Orson Welles: The Rise and Fall of an American Genius:* "Some perverse streak of anti-commercialism drove him; he was the brilliant architect of his own downfall."[5]

Richard Wilson, George Fanto, and other direct participants, along with film scholars such as Heloísa Buarque de Holanda and Catherine Benamou have countered such prejudicial accounts, pointing to the responsibility of others (the new RKO management, the Brazilian Department of Press and Propaganda (DIP), Production Manager Lynn Shores) for the noncompletion of the film.[6] What interests me here, however, is something rather different. For in the case of *It's All True,* the indictment of Welles's personality— projected as reckless, irresponsible, narcissistic—is linked isomorphically to an implicit critique of a Brazilian culture also very much misunderstood and undervalued. A common hostility embraces both Welles and aspects of Brazilian culture, a hostility subtended, I would suggest, by the implicit racial conventions of ethnocentric discourse. The Rio de Janeiro sequence of *It's All True,* for example, was intended to be an enthusiastic tribute to the gregarious spirit and protean energy of Rio's carnival, yet a striking feature of the critical discourse is a pervasive, almost visceral, anticarnivalism. A metonymical "contamination" links Welles's personality and his carnival subject; the bill of particulars against Welles echoes the perennial accusations against carnival itself—both are seen as debauched, dissipated, dissolute. Welles's "tragedy" must entail a tragic flaw, and that flaw has a name: carnival and its attendant vices.

John Russell Taylor's account of *It's All True* fairly reeks with a puritanical distaste for carnival and for Welles's "living it up," all superimposed on implicit homages to the Anglo Saxon work ethic. While Robert Wise and others were "struggling on with *Ambersons* and *Journey into Fear,*" we are told, "their leader, incommunicado, was having the time of his life in Brazil."[7] The censorious and somewhat voyeuristic emphasis on Welles's riotous pleasures conveys the distinct impression that Welles's hedonistic "excesses" were somehow responsible for the final scuttling of the film; its noncompletion was the "punishment" for Welles's self-indulgent immersion in the ludic irresponsibilities of the tropical feast. Here film criticism switches genre and becomes cautionary tale. "Even when he got home," Taylor tells us in the language of the ledger book: "he did not fully realize the harm the Brazilian adventure had done his career."[8] The critics thus play the role of policemen-Malvolios at Welles's carnival, throwing a wet blanket over the filmmaker's Brazilian "party" in the name of conventional storytelling, work ethic efficiency, and the unforgiving bottom line.

To first read the accounts of Welles's critics and then to immerse oneself in the primary documents generated by Welles and his collaborators, or in the accounts published by the Brazilian press or expressed in interviews with Welles's Brazilian interlocutors, is to enter two distinct and largely incompatible worlds. To someone adopting the "view from Brazil," Higham's accounts, for example, sound more like a North American's ethnocentric nightmares than anything that actually transpired. Here, for example, is Higham's description of the filming: "Second units went into villages and jungle areas, capturing the frenzied excitement of a nation afire with violent erotic rhythms, voluptuous and pulsating."[9] Quite apart from the improbability of Welles's ever having filmed in any "jungle areas," what is symptomatic is Higham's manner of seeing Brazil through the deforming grid of the "exotic," specifically as mediated through the caricatural formulas of the "darkest Africa" films, with their Eurocentric orchestration of primitivism, percussion, menace, and eroticism. Or here is the Higham account of Welles filming in the favelas, which Higham describes as those "hideous slums that crawled up the hills over Rio": "Shooting amid piles of garbage, and wading through excrement thrown down the hillside, haunted by vultures overhead and surrounded by rats and roaches, Welles and his crew were jeered and pelted with beer bottles by slum inhabitants who resented having their misery recorded on film."[10]

Interviews with Welles's close collaborators, such as Richard Wilson and George Fanto, as well as with Brazilian participant-witnesses (Alex Viany, Edmar Morel), along with a perusal of contemporaneous Brazilian press accounts from the period, reveal no evidence whatsoever that Welles and his crew were ever "jeered and pelted" by slum inhabitants. Welles was harassed by government thugs, who didn't want Welles to show the favelas to the world, but he was not harassed by *favelados*. Indeed, the evidence suggests that Welles was very well received, and even cheered, in the favelas, and this quite apart from the fact that his presence brought with it jobs, money, and a certain prestige for the *favelados*. And although favelas are indeed in some respects socially degraded places, they are not "seamy"—as Welles himself emphasizes in his *Hello Americans* broadcast from Brazil. Higham's account is more evocative of the social nightmares of the First World bourgeois than of anything experienced by the Welles team. A phenomenon beyond mere reporting, then, seems to be occurring here, something having to do with colonialist fantasies about the "peripheral" world as a dangerous *Heart of Darkness*–style site of contamination where Europeans catch the virus of "savagery," exactly the kind of fantasies that Welles himself hoped to combat.[11]

Welles took seriously his responsibilities as a roving ambassador for Pan-Americanism, a role in perfect accord with his personal sympathies and his left-leaning politics. In lectures, broadcasts, and press conferences, Welles stressed the historical-cultural links between North and South America and was appreciated by Brazilians as someone who understood their perspectives.

Welles was highly conscious of the negative legacy of North American condescension toward the inhabitants of what it contemptuously called its "backyard." In a collective interview shortly after his arrival in Rio, Welles excoriated the "confusion and ignorance" that led many North Americans to
believe, for example, that Brazilians spoke Spanish."[12] The Brazilian press accounts of Welles's visit emphasize his enthusiasm for Brazilian culture, his efforts to learn Portuguese and even the latest colloquialisms. One Rio journalist describes him as "perfectly identified with our language," and aware "of the
most up-to-date slang," which he "attempts to use in all his sentences, in a
demonstration that he is au courant of all the latest popular sayings."[13] By
April 1942, a *Cine-Rádio Jornal* reporter tells us, Welles was getting along in
Portuguese: "Welles insisted on speaking Portuguese, with great effort, but
almost always managing to communicate."[14] This insistence on linguistic reciprocity, a leitmotif of Welles's Latin American radio broadcasts as well, is significant not only because it was so rare among North American visitors—especially celebrities—but also because in Welles's case it was emblematic of a
more pervasive sense of Pan-American equality and confraternity.[15]

A look at the Brazilian materials reveals a powerful, reciprocal sense of affinity between Welles and Brazil. A May 27, 1942, letter from the "Brazilian
Division" to the Coordinator of Inter-American Affairs stressed that the Brazilian press had credited Welles with being "the one visitor who most quickly
understood Brazil, its problems and its people." A February 19 letter from Phil
Reisman to John Hay Whitney of the CIIA adds that Welles "seems to be especially great with the masses; he has mingled with them and danced with
them, and wherever we go in the car, the children yell out his name and applaud." Brazilian journalists, for their part, were almost unanimously enthusiastic about Welles. And although it is true that Brazilian journalists, especially
those associated with entertainment journals such as *Cinearte* and *A Cena
Muda,* were traditionally adulatory toward Hollywood and its stars, in this
case there was an important distinction in that many commentators took the
unprecedented step of symbolically "adopting Welles" as an honorary Brazilian. Calling Welles a "Carioca Citizen Kane," Celestino Silveira wrote that
"this enormously sympathetic big boy who's being seen around the streets of
our metropolis is without a doubt an authentic first-rate Carioca."[16] Victor
José Lima calls Welles "a perfect example of the democratic spirit. . . . He's
like us and he enjoys being like us."[17] Vinícius de Moraes went so far as to call

Welles a "great Brazilian": Watching Welles at work in the Cinédia studios in Rio, de Moraes wrote:

> What energy, what vitality, what ubiquity there is in this great Brazilian! Brazilian, yes; Orson Welles is beginning to know Brazil, or at least an important side of the soul of Brazil, better than many sociologists, novelists, critics, and poets. His vision is at times raw, but he never sins through injustice. Orson Welles has known better than anyone how to understand our character, our foibles, our easy-going ways, our so-to-speak "negative" qualities. . . . Welles has felt Brazil and the character of the Brazilian people in a deeper and richer way than the vast majority of foreigners who have lived among us.[18]

De Moraes trusted Welles to generate "the most impressive propaganda yet created in favor of our national values." And this faith in Welles, as Heloísa Buarque de Holanda points out, has less to do with his technological know-how than with "the transgressive and dialogic profile of his work and personality."[19]

De Moraes's portrait of Welles is especially fascinating given his own artistic affinities with Welles. Fond of describing himself as the "blackest white man in Brazil," de Moraes too became involved in black-related artistic projects. In his contemporaneous chronicle in *A Manhã* concerning Welles's visit, de Moraes speaks of the "high cultural values" of black Brazil, and his own *Orfeu de Conceição,* first staged as a play in 1955 and adopted for the screen in 1959 by Marcel Camus as *Black Orpheus,* can be seen in some ways as a direct descendant of Welles's "Voodoo *Macbeth,*" in that both works superimpose classical culture (Shakespearean tragedy in *Macbeth,* antique myth in *Orpheus*) on black performance. In still another sense, the de Moraes play prolongs and "fulfills" Welles's ambitions in *It's All True,* that is, to create a spectacle centered on Rio's carnival that would treat its black participants and black culture with respect and affection.

Welles's production methods and aesthetic contrast dramatically with the conventional Hollywood approach to Latin America.[20] The heirs of Manifest Destiny and the Monroe Doctrine, Hollywoodean paradigms were premised on the political and cultural nullity of Latin America. Hollywoodean portraiture had committed the most inexcusable gaffes, presenting Mexicans as "greasers" and Latin America generally as an extended border town. When Hollywood, shortly after the advent of sound, made alternative Spanish versions of its films, it offended (and amused) Latin Americans by mingling the most diverse Hispanic accents. Even the Hollywood attempts to implement the Good Neighbor Policy through "positive images," in such films as *Down Argentine Way* (1940), foundered on the shoals of studio ignorance. Welles, for his part, consciously marked off his difference from Hollywood. In an April interview with *A Noite,* he remarked that "If I had wanted to make a carnival film in the way in which Hollywood usually portrays the customs and scenes of strange lands, I wouldn't have even had to leave the U. S."[21] Wanting to paint a more knowing portrait of Rio de Janeiro than that offered by such films as *Flying Down to Rio* and *That Night in Rio* (1941), Welles complained that "Rio de Janeiro has not been given its due" by most motion pictures: "I come here with the intention of showing to the United States and to the world the truth about this city and about Brazil."[22]

Welles's approach in *It's All True* constituted a radical departure from Hollywood modes of production and norms of cultural representation. Welles devoured the most diverse kinds of information: geographical, linguistic, political, economic, musical. Brazilian journalists were impressed by Welles's consuming curiosity about all features of Brazilian history and culture. Celestino Silveira praised Welles's "prodigious memory" and his ability to remember not only the melodies but also the lyrics of countless Brazilian songs.[23] But apart from informal questioning, Welles commissioned research by a number of Brazilian writers such as Alex Viany, Clóvis de Gusmão, Ernani Fornari, Luiz Edmondo, Rui Costa, and Ayres de Andrade Jr. The research commissioned by Welles and the indications of his own reactions to the materials tell us a good deal about Welles, Brazil, and what a completed *It's All True* might have looked like. The research offers a number of striking features. First, Welles enlisted Brazilian rather than Hollywood "experts." Second, the materials range over an astonishing variety of subjects: sugar, coffee, rubber, gauchos, mining, Brazilian heroes, social conditions, slavery, festivals, and political institutions. Third, the discussion is strikingly open, nonfinalized, undogmatic. Welles and his partners sought a multiplicity of viewpoints; the emphasis was on polyphony and debate, on lively differences of opinion that were to enter the film via the commentaries of Welles and others. Fourth, the orientation is toward Brazilian popular culture and more particularly toward popular liberatory movements: the antislavery rebellions, Palmares, Antônio Conselheiro's millennial movement, and so forth. Welles saw the *jangadeiro* episode, for example, as part of an ongoing tradition of popular Brazilian resistance to oppression, since the *jangadeiros* in the past had been instrumental in the struggle against slavery—it was the *jangadeiro* Francisco José do Nascimento, better known as "Dragon of the Sea," who helped bring an end to slavery in Céara in 1884[24]—and even in the present were still articulating popular demands, as in the case of their epic journey to Rio. Jacaré was himself a syndical leader who had been imprisoned in Fortaleza for his activism; his death is said to have been celebrated with champagne toasts by his political enemies, the owners in the fishing industry.[25]

All discussion of *It's All True* spirals around an absent center—the missing text. The evidentiary status of the film obliges us to rely on the scant material now visible, on production stills, production team memoranda, memorabilia, the reminiscences of the participants and witnesses, and such paratextual materials as the research documents and even the concurrent Welles radio shows from Latin America. Indeed, much of the material contemplated for *It's All True* made its way into the radio broadcasts. Radio shows such as "President Vargas's Birthday," "Pan-American Day," and the series of *Hello Americans* shows broadcast from Latin America give us a glimpse of Welles's intentions in *It's All True*. In these shows, Welles transcends his role as a roving ambassador representing the Good Neighbor Policy to become a veritable advocate for Latin America. The broadcasts from Brazil, for example, proliferate in subtle and not-so-subtle critiques of North American ethnocentrism. Welles reminds his listeners that Brazil is the "largest republic in the world" and that "you could put the entire U.S. within the borders of Brazil and still have room for several American republics such as Paraguay, Chile, and Haiti." Welles also repeatedly uses the word "American" in its broad Latin American sense, calling Brazilian diplomat Oswald Aranha, for example, a "great American." Or he warns against stereotypical interpretations, for example, that "Brazilians do nothing but samba" or "that the function of Brazilian music is to translate American hits into Portuguese."

One of the *Hello Americans* shows provides an inkling of Welles's approach toward Brazilian music. Lauding Rio as "the loveliest city in our hemisphere," Welles describes the city in implicitly class terms, contrasting the urbane sophistication of the elite southern beach neighborhoods with "another side" of

Rio, embodied in the throbbing music that "comes rolling down from the hills" [i.e., the favelas] . . . called samba." In the broadcast, Welles recasts the information gathered by his researchers in the typically dialogical form of a debate. Welles's claim that samba came from the hills is immediately followed by a counterclaim that samba did *not* come from the hills. Welles then introduces, in a quasi-didactic manner, all the percussion instruments, placing special emphasis on the notion of polyrhythm and often making cross-cultural comparisons to American instruments and musical traditions. He calls attention to the extraordinary musicality of the Brazilian people. "Brazilian babies can beat out samba rhythms before they can talk," Welles tells us, "and they can dance to the samba rhythm before they can walk." And then he injects a note of skepticism: "At least that's what I've been told."

To deepen his own vision of samba and Brazilian music, Welles commissioned research into its roots. In "The Genealogy of Samba and Other Aspects of an Unquiet Life," Welles's special assistant Robert Meltzer speaks of the pedigree, ancestry, and roots of samba but notes that opinion on the subject is still "in suspension," untouched by the "crystallizing effects of critical prose." (Indeed, Welles was among the first to call for serious erudite studies of samba and popular culture, thus anticipating the 1980s slogan: "Samba também é cultura" [Samba is also culture].)[26] The commissioned essay by Ayres de Andrade Jr. ("The Story of the Rio de Janeiro Carnival") speaks about the gradual Africanization of carnival via such African-derived dances as the maxixe. All in all, the commissioned research covers a wide spectrum of topics linked to Afro Brazilian music and culture: the origins of the *roda* (circle dance); the nature of *capoeira;* and the derivation of carnival's percussion instruments, whether African (e.g., the *cuíca*) or indigenous (e.g., the bead and bean percussion instruments originally used in religious ceremonies). Welles himself acquired a certain intimacy with samba songs and rhythms. One of the *Hello Americans* shows (November 1942) features him singing "Tabuleiro da Baiana" in Portuguese along with Carmen Miranda. Vinícius de Moraes described Welles as a "master of our carnival," familiar with "its mannerisms, rhythms, instruments," and the filmmaker, critic, and researcher Alex Viany claims that Welles mastered samba rhythms "better than any foreigner." A popular magazine tells us that "there is no party, samba, frevo or batucada at which [Welles] doesn't make an appearance . . . here we see him at the Actresses' Ball, sambaing like a connoisseur."[27] At times, when Welles would disappear and people would have to search for him all over Rio, "they would finally find him in the favela, playing the pandeiro and drinking cachaca."[28]

Music was absolutely primordial in the Wellesian conception of *It's All True,* making it virtually impossible to appreciate the film on the basis of musicless rushes. "Music is the very basis of our picture," Welles writes in his script presentation of the film, "and it is our very good luck that our music is samba." The very aesthetic of *It's All True,* Welles writes, "is based on the conception of an illustrated musical constructed of Brazilian popular tunes." The music is not incidental, but of primary importance: "Music had to do more than complement the picture—it must dictate what was to be seen." "In the interests of veracity," Welles goes on, "our picture had to be true to the music. We had to discover what samba was before we found an architecture for our film. Samba, we learned, comes from the hills, so our picture had to be oriented to the hills." (This "preferential option" for the hills and for blacks, as we shall see, got Welles into considerable trouble.)

Although on one level Welles intended to downplay individual talents in favor of the collective phenomenon of carnival itself, on another level he hoped to promote Brazilian performers. Welles was uninterested in the conventional practice of displaying North American stars against "exotic" backdrops; rather, he was seeking local talent. Welles solicited the participation of well-known actress-singers like Linda Batista and Emilinha Borba, along with some of the best carnival orchestras (Chiquinho, Fon-Fon, Dedé), instrumentalists and composers (Pixinguinha, the black flautist and composer of "Carinhoso"). Grande Otelo's role would be to "personalize" the carnival sequence (see photo 27). Welles repeatedly characterized Otelo as one of the world's pre-eminent comic actors and a "multi-talented performer." Interestingly, Welles did not see Otelo's talents as exclusively comic. Welles told de Moraes that "Otelo could be a first-rate tragic actor" and that he lamented not being able to take more advantage of that aspect in his film.[29] In his script presentation, Welles introduced the black actor with the Shakespearean name as follows: "His name is Othello. Remember that name. . . . This is only his first American picture, and he's a big hit in it for sure. Othello likes to be compared to Mickey Rooney, but he's closer to a young Chaplin." It is significant that Welles does not racially categorize Otelo; nor does he feel compelled to compare Otelo only to *other black* actors.[30] According to both their accounts,

27. Welles: Filming Otelo

Welles and Otelo became close friends, and Otelo named one of his children (with Josephine) "Orson," as a tribute to the American director.[31] Welles even wrote a note to Otelo proposing that the Brazilian actor play one of the principal roles in a film about black Americans, although he confided to Otelo that he was afraid racism might prevent the project from taking place.[32]

Again in contrast to Hollywood practice, Welles engaged in a multileveled collaboration with Brazilians themselves. This collaboration took many forms that went beyond on-screen performance: research; scripting (Jacaré's diary was to be the primary source for the Fortaleza episode, and Jacaré was to be the narrator); and preparatory treatments (Edmar Morel was asked to do a treatment for the same episode). One of Welles's collaborators was Herivelto Martins, who apart from being a samba composer and samba pageant organizer was also a union leader and had excellent relations with people in the favelas. His background in the cinema both as actor and composer also facilitated his collaboration with Welles. According to both Otelo and Martins, the twosome would spend nights conversing with Welles about samba and carnival, and in the following days their ideas would be "idealized" by Welles. Martins describes Welles as voracious in his search for information: "He would ask about everything: what people in the favellas did when they weren't doing the samba, what was the 'porta bandeira' like, if there were fights." It was thanks to the information provided by Herivelto and Otelo that Welles reconstructed Praça Onze inside of the Cinédia studios. "He reproduced everything," Herivelto tells us, "exactly as we described it." Welles also gave Herivelto considerable control over all aspects of filming the samba. Thus Herivelto worked both as a kind of coscriptwriter with Welles and as a kind of production director for the samba school scenes. Both Otelo and Herivelto insist that Welles respected Herivelto's word on all filming of the samba. "It had to be done as we wanted. . . . There were grandiose scenes, with three or four hundred extras, with all the Technicolor lights lit, four or five cameras filming, and when he finished shooting, he would ask: 'OK?' and if I said 'no good,' he would do everything all over again."[33]

It is even possible to see the carnival episode of *It's All True* as part of the *chanchada* tradition (photo 28). Welles worked with Cinédia, the studio that first developed the aesthetic formulas of the *chanchada*. Like *It's All True*, the early *chanchadas* based their appeal on the prestige of popular singers and were intimately linked to the carnival universe. One of the functions of the *chanchada* was to disseminate the annual repertory of carnival songs, just as *It's All True* was planning to disseminate "Amélia" and "Nega de Cabelo Duro." And although we do not know for certain that Welles actually saw any *chanchadas*, he did work with collaborators linked to the genre, notably Adhemar Gonzaga, founder and director of Cinédia; Luiz de Barros, *chanchada* director (who helped Welles stage some of the studio scenes); and Rui Costa, commissioned researcher, who had directed *chanchadas* in the years just prior to *It's All True*. George Fanto, Welles's cameraman, had also shot three films at Cinédia prior to his collaboration with Welles. But in racial terms Welles went beyond the *chanchadas*, which tended to treat black performers as tokens, by making Otelo a leader, by surrounding him with other blacks, and by using editing to equalize and interweave his performance with white performers like Linda Batista in the Praça Onze sequence.[34]

Especially impressive in Welles's work in Brazil is his felt responsibility toward the Brazilians themselves. Here we find a clear contrast with another visiting American: Walt Disney in *Saludos Amigos* (1943) and *The Three Caballeros* (1945). Despite its dazzling visualization of Ary Barroso's "Aquarela do Brasil," the former film confuses *cantiga de roda* (circle song) and *chorinho* (ragtimelike instrumental music featuring rapid modulations and improvisation by the lead instrument) with samba, and the latter has the white actress

28. The carnival episode of *It's All True*

Aurora Miranda, Carmen's sister, play the sweet vendor *baiana* Yayá, the kind of figure who in Bahia itself is invariably black and linked to African religions (even the name Yayá has religious connotations). Disney's lily-white Bahia displays the accoutrements of black culture—in the form of African instruments like the *berimbau* and the *cuíca*—but here detached from black bodies; African culture is to be heard but not seen. The cultural expression, furthermore, is severed from any larger cultural environment. Whereas Welles saw samba, like jazz, as the artistic transcendence of pain, Disney and his collaborators saw only exotic excess to be spectacularized, in a predatory approach that explores the world only to suck out its reserves of entertainment.[35]

Welles understood Brazil's ironic, self-mocking humor, its love of irreverent play, characteristics especially amplified and exalted in Rio's carnival. Although Barbara Leaming portrays Welles as not being particularly fond of carnivals, Welles's collaborators in Brazil, such as close associate Richard Wilson and filming coordinator José Sanz, claim that Welles "loved" carnival. In his script presentation, Welles describes carnival very much along Bakhtinian lines, as a privileged moment of "free and familiar contact," when "cariocas think only about dancing, singing and making love to one another" and where individuals "set aside their self-consciousness and timidity and reticence." In a melange of individual and collective *jouissance*, "the city loses its control and each individual loses his."[36] Welles also calls attention to Brazilians' "unaggressive good humor," and the "unpoliced good behavior of carnival mobs." Carnival's "hilarious congestion," Welles writes, "exists in the very hottest latitudes of human hilarity," and is as yet "uncharted and unexplored." Remembering Rio's carnival three years after the fact in his "Orson Welles' Almanac," Welles described carnival as "brighter than a circus, bigger than the World Series, and louder than the Fourth of July. It's all those good times rolled into one. It's New Year's Eve, Halloween Night, and Christmas morning. It's wild and it's gay and it's absolutely sober, because in carnival you don't need liquor to help you forget you're getting old. You're too busy remembering what it was like when you were young."[37] Hollyood, Welles explains, "has never before exploited any part of its color or atmosphere. A dozen carnival pictures may be made this year in North America, but none of them can possibly have anything to do with the real thing." The sheer immensity of Rio's carnival, Welles writes, "defies studio representation" and "is hopelessly beyond the scope of any Hollywood spectacle." The suggestion that any spectacle might be beyond the scope of Hollywood, and indeed that the supposedly underdeveloped Brazilians might put on a better show than Hollywood itself, is typical of Welles's penchant for needling Hollywood pretensions and upending cultural hierarchies.

The research commissioned by Welles would have alerted him, if he were not already aware of it, to the indispensable black contribution to carnival. Alex Viany's commissioned essay "The Samba Goes to Town" describes Praça Onze, whose disappearance was to be memorialized by *It's All True,* as the square closest to the favelas, a kind of "African embassy" whose inimitable feasts were "reminiscent of gigantic Harlem jam sessions." Brazilian whites, Viany explains, had undergone a process of cultural Africanization: "Black slang came down from the hills and took over the city, democracy advanced a hundred years in ten, and the white man's acceptance of his colored brother was easy because he learned to speak the same language and sing the same songs." Viany describes Praça Onze during carnival as the utopian locus of "the most genuine freedom in thinking and speaking," and it is fascinating to speculate on the reactions of Welles, as a fighter against racism from a largely segregated society, on encountering a country, certainly not without prejudice, but where blacks and whites mingled with a celebratory ease relatively unknown at home. Praça Onze was at the center of a region that combined such neighborhoods as Morro da Favela, Morro de São Carlos, Rio Comprido, and Catumbi, in other words the neighborhoods occupied by blacks. For them, the destruction of Praça Onze was traumatic because they were hesitant to move to the more intimidating and aristocratic atmosphere of Avenida Rio Branco.

In his chronicle for *A Manhã* (February 10, 1942), Vinícius de Moraes speaks of Welles's prior involvement with black culture in North America. And the Orson Welles who went to Brazil in 1942 was already well attuned to the power and intelligence of what Robert Farris Thompson calls "black Atlantic civilization" and therefore well prepared to appreciate the black contribution to Brazilian culture. Even before his trip to Brazil, Welles had demonstrated his deep animosity to all that smacked of white supremacy and cultural apartheid. More than a "tolerant liberal," Welles was a passionate antiracist. Indeed, one might regard Welles as a "premature antiracist," much as one speaks of "premature anti-fascists." Retroactively, we see evidence of pro-black attitudes throughout Welles's career: from his impromptu version of *Uncle Tom's Cabin* at Todd School, through his script for *Marchingsong*, a depiction of John Brown as abolitionist prophet and warrior, to the various creative encounters with black performers and themes in the period immediately preceding *It's All True*. In a period of extreme antiblack racism, of Jim Crow laws and even lynchings, of de jure segregation in the South and discrimination in the North, Welles was attracted to black themes and black performers, most notably in his all-black "Voodoo *Macbeth*," set in nineteenth-century Haiti and featuring Caribbean and African drumming, performed in Harlem in 1936.[38] Indeed, in many respects the diasporic intuition of "Voodoo *Macbeth*" prepares the way for *It's All True*. Both treat black themes, one in a tragic, the other in a musical-documentary register, and both projects were called "communist." In both instances, Welles placed his confidence in performers untrained in the classical sense, yet rich in experience, performance smarts, and charisma. In an era when Aryanist race theory saw blacks as ill equipped for dramatic theater since their color prevented them from "demonstrating shame," Welles affirmed black Thespian superiority. Asked in Brazil why he had called on black actors to represent Shakespeare, Welles responded: "In all my years of experience, I have concluded that black actors are more natural, more understanding, and more sure of themselves, even in the most difficult passages, than white actors, and that they perform the roles given them with more facility."[41]

Welles's theatrical adaptation of Richard Wright's *Native Son,* denounced at the time as "communist propaganda," constitutes another major encounter between Welles and blackness. The date, 1940, suggests that racial issues must have been very much on Welles's mind in the period immediately prior to the making of *It's All True.* Here too Welles's willingness to take risks on a black theme, and the Welles-Houseman approach of collaborating with the black community anticipates a similar approach in the case of *It's All True.* The nature of the project suggests that Welles's support for black causes went far beyond a patronizing liberal do-goodism. Welles's language is radical in both cultural and political terms. In his *New York Post* column, for example, he recommended another Richard Wright novel, *Black Boy,* to those "white citizens who claimed to "understand the negro." Such citizens, he said, should be "tied down with banjo strings, gagged with bandannas, their eyes propped open with watermelon seeds, and made to read *Black Boy* word for word."

Welles's other major engagement with black culture, prior to Brazil, was the Duke Ellington "Jazz Story" project originally slated to form the fourth episode of *It's All True.* The jazz episode, to be written by Ellington and Welles, directed by Ellington and Welles, with music written and performed by Ellington, was to tell the story of Louis Armstrong. Along with Ellington and Welles, the film was to feature Bessie Smith, Kid Ory, and Hazel Scott, and shooting was scheduled for December 1941. Both Welles and Ellington were reportedly eager to work on the project, and indeed Welles's initial hesitation about going to South America partially derived from his reluctance to abandon the jazz project. It was when he realized that samba was the Brazilian counterpart to jazz, that both were expressions of the African diaspora in the New World, that Welles chose the story of carnival and the samba. A comparison of the projected jazz episode to what we know of the carnival sequence of *It's All True* reveals a series of paradigmatic substitutions. New Orleans as setting is replaced by another Africanized New World carnival city—Rio de Janeiro. Instead of the Afro American music called jazz, we find the Afro Brazilian music called samba. Songs such as "Didn't He Ramble" give way to Brazilian tunes such as "Bahia" and "Praça Onze," and performer-composers like Duke Ellington and Louis Armstrong make way for Pixinguinha and Grande Otelo.

The Brazilian testimony about the filmmaking tells us a good deal about Welles's relations with black Brazilians. Raul Marques, composer of the samba "Risoleta," who coordinated the participants from the favelas, describes working with Welles as a "holiday," saying "people liked the movement,"[40] an account that directly contradicts the Higham account of enraged *favelados* pelting Welles and his crew with beer bottles. Martins and Otelo describe Welles as extremely democratic, claiming that Welles liked them precisely because they showed "no special servility toward him." Martins describes the communications between the three as follows: "Welles spoke Portuguese badly, I spoke English badly, and Otelo translated badly, but still we understood each other. He was very human, he liked common people, and lived with my son Pery on his lap."[41] As Otelo and Herivelto describe it, there existed both camaraderie and real artistic collaboration between the two of them and Welles. The camaraderie took the form of drinking *cachaça* (rum), of Welles sleeping at Herivelto's house, of frequent visits to the favela, of playing with Herivelto's son Pery, whom Welles liked so much that he gave him a major role in the film. (An older Pery appears in the 1993 documentary about *It's All True*.) We could not be further from the methods and the racial conventions of Hollywood. Here we find not only fraternizing between the director and the "native" actors, but also a strong black creative direction in the film, in the form of performing talent and through a kind of dialogic, conversational coscripting.

Interestingly, Martins offers as an instance of Welles's "tempestuousness" what is in fact an exemplum of Welles's deep feelings about racism. He recounts an incident in which Welles was being honored by a party in the Cassino de Urca, with the presence of the RKO directors. At that time, Martins tells us, "they didn't allow blacks into the casino, and after a while Welles began to ask: 'What happened to my friend Herivelto? Where's my friend Otelo?' In fact, neither I nor Otelo had been invited. When they told Welles that Grande Otelo wasn't allowed to join the party, Welles replied: 'If he can't come, then I can't stay,' and he left to look for us in the local bars. He finally found us, took off his smoking jacket and stayed there drinking with us until the bar closed at three in the morning. Everyone was looking for him, he was the guest of honor, but he stayed with us. 'Today,' he said, 'today we will drink only black beer.'"[42]

The incident reminds us, of course, of other similar incidents in Welles's career, of his *New York Post* open letter to Jack Benny protesting the segregation that prevented Benny from taking Eddie Anderson (Rochester) along on troop shows and of the incident, registered by Barbara Leaming, in which Welles vigorously protested a suggestion, by a production person on "Orson Welles' Almanac," that Duke Ellington be presented not as his "friend" but as his "servant." On Sunday, July 28, 1946, Welles surprised the listeners to his radio show by reading an affidavit by a black veteran, Isaac Woodard Jr., who, shortly after his discharge from the service, had been beaten and left blind by a South Carolina policeman. Directly addressing the unidentified officer responsible, Welles accused the policeman of bringing the "justice of Dachau to Aiken, South Carolina," and promised, in his most resonant "the-Shadow-knows" voice, to haunt him forever. "Officer X— after I have found you out, I'll never lose you. If they try you, I'm going to watch the trial. If they jail you, I'm going to wait for your first day of freedom." Echoing Lady Macbeth, Welles exhorted the officer to "wash [his] hands well. You won't blot out the blood of a blinded war veteran, nor yet the color of your own skin." Welles pursued the case until the Department of Justice brought charges against the officer. Why was the issue important? "Because I was born a white man and until a colored man is a full citizen like me I haven't the leisure to enjoy the freedom that colored man risked his life to maintain for me."[43]

In the case of *It's All True*, Welles paid dearly for choosing black friends over the white elite. Edmar Morel, hired by Welles to research the *jangadeiro* material, describes Welles as an "anti-racist by formation" and attributed much of the hostility directed toward Welles to the fact that he enjoyed the company of blacks and that he became very close to Grande Otelo, who was almost always accompanied by what Morel calls a "black court" of followers.[44] Just as subtly and not-so-subtly racist critics hounded Welles in the United States, so it was in Brazil, and this time the racism came both from the Brazilian elite, from higher-ups in the RKO production hierarchy, and from the Rockefeller Committee of the Coordinator of Inter-American Affairs. A memorandum from the Rockefeller Committee to RKO recommends that the film "avoid any reference to miscegenation" and suggests that the film should "omit sequences of the film in which mulattos or mestiços appear conspicuously."[45] RKO executives, and some members of the *It's All True* production crew, complained that Welles was overemphasizing the black element and showing too much "ordinary social intercourse" between blacks and whites in carnival, a feature that might offend some North American viewers. A July 1942 letter from William Gordon, of the production team of *It's All True,* to an RKO executive, laments Welles's "indiscriminate intermingling of blacks and whites," something that "will be found objectionable south of the Mason Dixon line in the U.S., and in a good many countries of Latin America." Citing Goldwyn's deletion of two close shots of two black members of Gene Krupa's orchestra in *Ball of Fire* (1941), he argues for the deletion of all such shots. Lamenting his inability to control Welles in this matter, he remarks that Brazilians, although "completely lacking in race prejudice," may resent some of the footage "because it will tend to confirm the North American opinion that most South Americans belong to the African race."

The chief ethnic naysayer from within the Welles team was production manager Lynne Shores, an obscure artistic director of B comedies and musicals now appointed as irritable "old hand"—some would say spy—in charge of monitoring what were seen as Welles's irrational tendencies.[46] In his letters and memoranda, Shores demonstrates intense hostility to Welles, to the project, and to Brazil itself.[47] Shores describes himself, in a letter to Walter Daniels back in Hollywood, as the defender of "law, order, morale and progress"—the language, again, is symptomatic—and his conception of "law, order, and progress" gives significant place to white supremacy. Indeed, Shores's letters provide an ongoing document of racism of the most noxious variety. Along with generally patronizing remarks about Brazil and Brazilians, Shores is especially obsessed with Welles's penchant for filming black people. Shores even came to conspire with certain officials of the Brazilian Department of Press and Propaganda. In an April 11 letter to Dr. Alfredo Pessoa, he complains that

> Despite repeated conversations with Mr. Richard Wilson. . . . I still find myself unable to control the tendency of Mr. Welles to utilize our cameras in matters which I do not feel are in accord with the wishes of the Brazilian government and, I am sure, not in harmony with the feelings of our executives in Hollywood. The matter to which I refer to is the continued exploitation of the negro and the low class element in and around Rio, specifically according to yesterday's shooting of films which occurred at these various points as itemized: The original Favela da Saude,

The Cantagallo Favela, the Humayta Favella, the Praia do Pinto Favela. We have on top of these scenes, a schedule which calls for added filming in conjunction with the scenes already filmed at the Teatro República [the theater where blacks celebrate carnival], which I feel are all in very bad taste.

Claiming to represent the feelings of the majority of the working crew, Shores goes so far as to imply the possibility of censorship or even sabotage: "I am holding the negative of this film and not shipping it through for development until I can perhaps have a talk with you on this subject to be sure that I am not unduly alarmed over its possible consequences." On April 14, a Richard Wilson memorandum to Welles tells us, Dr. Pessoa called Wilson to his office to inform him that there had been many complaints about the filming in the favelas.

If Shores was euphemistic in his communications to the DIP, he was more frankly and colloquially racist in his letters to Walter Daniels. In an April 14 letter, the very day that Wilson was called in by the DIP, Shores complains to Daniels that "Last Friday, he [Welles], ordered day and night shots in some very dirty and disreputable nigger neighborhoods throughout the city." And an April 30 letter to Daniels returns to the same racial leitmotif: "we had a very full week as far as shooting goes. However, the stuff itself is just carnival nigger singing and dancing, of which we already have piles." Unappreciative of Afro Brazilian culture and of the nuances that Welles planned to empha-size, Shores sees nothing more than black people jumping around: "We are still pouncing on large groups of colored people doing exactly the same thing that has happened during the February carnival." Racism also affected the Fortaleza sequence (photo 29). In September 1943, when there were still thoughts of recuperating the *It's All True* material, an RKO memorandum from Koerner to William Gordon notes that "the heroes on the raft are re-ferred to as Indians," a perspective that "will be impossible to sell to audi-ences, especially south of the Mason-Dixon line."[48]

When the Brazilian press learned that Welles and Richard Wilson planned to integrate scenes of the Afro Brazilian religion macumba, the Brazilian es-tablishment became quite alarmed. To understand this elite reaction, we must understand its context, not only in terms of a long history of subordination of blacks, but also in terms of a populist-authoritarian Vargas government intol-

29. The raftsmen in
It's All True

erant of black political expression and of Afro Brazilian cultural expression. As an ambiguous figure mingling vague pro-Axis sympathies with populism à la Roosevelt, Vargas was hardly progressive in racial matters. Indeed, it was Vargas who banned the Frente Negra and who presided over the repression of Afro Brazilian religious practice. The Brazilian official placed in charge of working with the Welles team, meanwhile, was Assis Figueiredo, the head of the Department of Tourism and infinitely more interested in disseminating scenic clichés of Sugarloaf and Corcovado than in exploring the social and cultural roots of samba.

Welles and his closest collaborators, in contrast, stressed the origins of samba in the black culture of the hills of Rio, seeing the favelas as analogous to the brothels, back alleys, and streets of New Orleans that spawned North American jazz. "For Welles," Richard Wilson tells us, "the carnival story was essentially a black story."[49] But when the filmmakers put this theory into practice, when they departed from the official program and started to film street carnival, popular balls, and the favelas, RKO, DIP, and some elements in the press unleashed a campaign against Welles. Editorials politely suggested that the filmmakers limit themselves to touristic sites, and leave aside unsavory scenes of squalor. Welles was "accused" of filming blacks, as if one could possibly film the Rio's carnival without filming blacks, who formed the vast majority of the samba schools (at that point roughly 90 percent black or mu-latto) and of the Carioca population as a whole.

The Brazilian elite had never been terribly fond of the black forms of carni-val. A 1942 *Jornal do Brasil* article by Sílvio Moreaux called for a more rigor-ous censorship of unseemly "*macumbas* and *malandragems*" in order to "free our populace from the Africanist ideas imposed by the little maestros and po-ets from the favelas."[50] A perusal of Brazilian press accounts from the period shows elite Brazilians becoming quite concerned with the filming of favelas. Under the punning title of "Carioca Carnival Is Going to Be Very Dark on the Screen," a *Meio Dia* editorialist sneeringly comments on Welles's penchant for hiring black "artists" and "technicians" and "composers" (the words are placed in apologetic quotes) from the hills, and protests the arrogance of two "colored technicians" who had the audacity to claim that "Welles was making a film such as had never been made in Brazil." Welles's informants, the editori-alist complains, are committing an injustice by offering "cinema sequences in which only black people figure, as though Rio were another Harlem."[51] And a May 20, 1942, article by Gatinha Angora in *Ciné-Radio Jornal,* which up to that point had been fairly sympathetic to Welles, expressed uneasiness with Welles's project:

> Each time the robust and handsome fiancé of 'del Rio' points his cameras at the so-called 'picturesque' spots of the city, we feel a slight uneasiness. . . . We should exploit the prestige of Orson Welles to show ourselves to the world as a civilized nation . . . but what do his Brazilian advisors do? Instead of showing him our possibilities, they let him film, to his delight, scenes of no good half-breeds . . . and the filthy favela huts infesting the lovely edge of the lagoon, where there is so much beauty and so many marvelous angles for filming; dances of negroes covered with maracatu feathers, reminiscent of the temples of the African wilds, as though our not always edifying street carnival were not already bad enough.

Angora goes on to regret that the filmmakers, set loose in such a marvelous city, "where there is already the rumble of great capitals," should call on "all the negative elements of our land," choosing as representative of Brazil a "good-for-nothing in a striped shirt, dirty straw hat over his eye, dancing an out-of-joint samba."[52]

In his ingenious low-cost production methods and his interest in the

Northeast, the *cangaceiros* (rebel bandits), millennial cults, popular culture, and rebellions, Welles managed to anticipate many of the themes subsequently taken up by Cinema Novo in the 1960s and after: the Northeast (the theme of *Vidas Secas* [Barren Lives, 1963]), black culture in Bahia (explored in *Barravento* [The Turning Wind, 1962]), *cangaceiros* (treated in Rocha's *Deus e Diabo na Terra do Sol* [literally God and the Devil in the Land of the Sun; Released as Black God, White Devil; 1964]), and the black rebellions of Palmares (the theme of both *Ganga Zumba* [1963] and *Quilombo* [1984]). The *jangadeiro* sequence, from what we know of it, clearly anticipates, in both theme and treatment, the documentary-inflected but formally rigorous lyricism of Glauber Rocha's *Barravento* (1962), released exactly two decades later, another documentary-inflected film about *jangadeiros* and social oppression. By casting the four *jangadeiros,* and by planning to have Jacaré himself narrate the sequence, Welles made an important gesture toward *jangadeiro* self-representation. Both *It's All True* and *Barravento* form odes to Africanized-indigenized mestiço communities surviving in harsh conditions but somehow sustaining energy and optimism. By stressing the work of the fishermen, both films refute the "myth of the lazy native." They stress the communitarian side of *jangadeiro* life, as well as the oppressive role of the fishing industry owners, and they each develop a quasi-Eisensteinian formal lyricism.

More generally, *It's All True* foreshadowed the social and formal audaciousness of Cinema Novo, along with its typical melange of documentary and fiction, pointing not only to what Rogério Sganzerla calls the "beach verismo" of *Barravento* but also to the urban neorealism of dos Santos's *Rio 40 Graus* (Rio 40 Degrees, 1954). Indeed, Brazilian filmmaker Rogério Sganzerla pays homage to Welles in his documentary-fiction feature *Nem Tudo É Verdade* (It's Not All True, 1985), where he re-creates Welles's Brazilian experience through a sound-image collage combining documentary-style material (footage from *It's All True,* footage of Welles in Rio, Brazilian newsreels about Welles, citations of *Citizen Kane* and *The Lady from Shanghai,* newspaper accounts), with staged reconstructions in which an Orson Welles lookalike (Brazilian musician Arrigo Barnabé) encounters Brazilian celebrities and studio executives. Sganzerla portrays Welles as the rebellious victim of the studio system, the press, and North American and Brazilian politicians. Welles's utopian dream of real industrial and artistic collaboration between North and

South America, Sganzerla suggests, violently challenged the neocolonial assumptions of the time. (Sganzerla is currently working on a second feature about Welles in Brazil, entitled *Tudo É Brasil* [All Is Brazil], this time focussing on the role of the Brazilian political elite in sabotaging the film.)

In the same year that *Nem Tudo É Verdade* was released, and shortly before Welles's own death on October 10, 1985, studio executive Fred Chandler inadvertently discovered black and white negatives marked "Bonito," "Carnival," and "Jangadeiros" in film vaults on the lot which had passed from RKO to Desilu to Paramount. Found was a small proportion of "Carnaval" and 80 percent of the "jangadeiro" material. In subsequent years, Richard Wilson, Bill Krohn, Myron Meisel, and Catherine Benamou got access to the material. Supplementing it with present-day interviews and archival material on Welles, they produced a film, *It's All True: Based on an Unfinished Film by Orson Welles,* released in 1993 (photo 30). The first part of the film relates the basic history of Welles's project, including footage of carnival. Grande Otelo and Herivelto Martin's son Pery's singing (in 1993) of the Praça Onze theme song gives way to spectacular footage of Welles's staged carnival. In Fortaleza, there are interviews with the relatives of the *jangadeiros,* Edmar Morel, and Francisca Moreira da Silva, the young woman who played in the film's love story. We see Welles at work, improvising solutions for serious technical problems. The final part of the film provides a glimpse of what the *jangadeiro* episode might have looked like. Diverse blocks of material represent the work of the *jangadeiros,* the everyday life of the community, as well as death and funerals, always moving back and forth between individual and community and between the heroic poetry of the sea and the quotidian prose of onshore life. We see beautifully composed shots, remarkable physiognomies, all accompanied, unfortunately, by banal synthesizer music rather than by the materials Welles intended (e.g., the sea-soaked music of Dorival Caymmi). The makers of the documentary also report that four latter-day *jangadeiros* sailed from Fortaleza to Rio during April through June of 1993, while the film was being edited; then president Collor, unlike Vargas, refused even to meet with them to hear their grievances.

My purpose here has not been to idealize Welles or to ignore the power differentials that made it possible only for a North American director to make a "Pan-American" documentary. But within a highly racist context, *It's All True*

30. Welles in Fortaleza

was animated by a democratic, antiracist spirit. The emphasis was to be not on elite individual history but rather on collective heroism and creativity. Welles wanted to show *Brazilian* heroes, not North American heroes against Brazilian backdrops. The pivotal characters of both episodes were black— Otelo, Tatá, and Manuel Preto, for instance—and mestiço—Gerônimo and Jacaré. The approach in *It's All True* was neither miserabilist nor idealized; his intention was to show people who are poor but dignified, energetic, hard-working, and who transform their lives through art and activism. The conventional critique of Welles projects him as a kind of ethnic renegade, rather like an anthropologist who instead of maintaining the customary distance and superiority has "gone native." Welles in this sense was too good a "neighbor." But that Welles could see a sambista from the favelas and a quartet of mestiço fisherman as authentic popular heroes speaks volumes about the distance that separated him from the ambient racism of his time.

CHAPTER 5
Vera Cruz: Hollywood
in the Tropics,
1949–1954

∞

The post–World War II period in Brazil was a time of relative democratization after the authoritarian Vargas regime. Internationally, the rise and defeat of the Nazi regime led to the discrediting of racism in international politics and the repudiation of "scientific racism" in intellectual discourse. In Brazil, right-wing Integralism was on the defensive and democracy was on the upswing. In São Paulo the First Brazilian Writers' Congress called for free elections as the only legitimate expression of popular sovereignty. In the following year, 1946, Josué de Castro published his *Geografia da Fome* (Geography of Hunger), a classic of social ecology subsequently translated and disseminated around the world. In racial terms, the defeat of Nazism strengthened antiracist currents. In 1951, the Congress passed the Afonso Arinos law prohibiting racial discrimination in Brazil, provoked by an incident in which African American dancer Katherine Dunham was refused entry to a São Paulo hotel, under the pretext that her presence might perturb other Americans staying there. The need for such a law suggested that all was not well in the land of "racial democracy." Two years later, UNESCO, in the erroneous belief that Brazil had found a workable formula for racial togetherness, sponsored a series of studies of race relations in Brazil. Florestan Fernandes, Roger Bastide and Oracy Nogueira were assigned to research black-white relations in São Paulo, Thales de Azevedo and Charles Wagley were assigned to Bahia, and Darcy Ribeiro was to study the assimilation of indigenous people. In all cases, research uncovered a subtle web of prejudice trapping blacks, with "Indians" oppressed even more violently.

In this same period, in 1944, the Afro Brazilian actor, writer, activist, and plastic artist Abdias do Nascimento founded his Black Experimental Theater in order to train black actors and fight against discrimination. Having seen a Lima, Peru, performance of O'Neill's *Emperor Jones* starring a blackfaced white actor (Hugo d'Evieri) as Brutus Jones, do Nascimento resolved to valorize actors of color: "Both on a social and artistic level, the Black Experimental Theater strives to restore, valorize, and exalt the contribution of Africans to the Brazilian formation, unmasking the ideology of whiteness which created a situation such that, as Sartre puts it, 'As soon as he opens his mouth, the negro accuses himself, unless he tries to overthrow the hierarchy represented by the European colonizer and his civilizing process.'"[1] The goals of the Black Experimental Theater, at the moment of its founding at least, were to (1) integrate blacks into Brazilian society; (2) criticize the ideology of whiteness and the sociology and anthropology that promoted it; (3) valorize the African contribution; (4) promote the theater as an ideal medium for these ideas. Apart from plays, the Black Experimental Theater also founded the journal *Quilombo* and organized the National Black Conference (1949) and the First Congress for Black Brazilians (1950). The Black Experimental Theater vigorously defended the theatrical aspects of African culture, citing the continent's religious feasts, its danced liturgies, and the primordial role of song and mimicry. African religions, do Nascimento argued, are no more "folkloric" than are Catholicism or Islam. Through song and dance and pantomime, blacks "capture the divine, configure the gods, humanizing them and cohabiting with them in mystic transe."[2] In 1944, the Black Experimental Theater staged its own version of *Emperor Jones,* together with three poems by Afro-diasporic authors: Langston Hughes, Aladir Custodio, and Regino Pedroso. While encountering resistance from a skeptical white theatrical elite in Brazil, the play won support from Eugene O'Neill himself, who wrote from his sickbed in San Francisco what do Nascimento describes as a "moving letter" in which he waived royalties to facilitate the group's project.[3] Do Nascimento's extraordinary life subsequent to this episode includes teaching at the Yale School of Drama and SUNY, Buffalo; artistic expositions at Harvard and Tulane; and friendly visits with the Black Panthers, Ramsey Clark, Albert Camus (whom do Nascimento describes as unattuned to the "message of the *orixás*"), Aimé Césaire, C. L. R. James, Wole Soyinka, Amiri Baraka, Molefi Asante, and many others.[4]

In this same postwar period, São Paulo had developed immensely, becoming the economic capital or "locomotive" of Brazil. A certain sector of the bourgeoisie enriched by this development resolved to make São Paulo the cultural capital as well. This group founded such institutions as the Art Museum of São Paulo (MASP), the Museum of Modern Art, the Brazilian Comedy Theater, and the Cinematheque, institutions whose fundamental goal was to make European high culture available to the elite. The Brazilian Comedy Theater, for example, was created so that the São Paulo intelligentsia could see the best international drama—Pirandello, Tennessee Williams, Strindberg—without having to go to Paris or New York. In the late 1940s, a group linked to this same bourgeoisie, inspired by the commercial success of the *chanchadas* but scorning what it saw as that genre's "vulgarity," founded the Vera Cruz film company. Giving architectural expression to a Eurocentric paradigm, the studio modeled itself physically on the Metro-Goldwyn-Mayer studios in Hollywood, ironically at a time when the studio system in Hollywood itself was in the kind of precipitous decline registered in films like *Sunset Boulevard*. Vera Cruz set up a luxurious system with well-paid contract stars and directors but without the economic infrastructure on which to base such a system. Vera Cruz was Euro-international in spirit and in personnel, with light technicians from England (Chick Fowle), directors from Italy (Adolfo Celli), editors from Austria (Oswald Haffenrichter). The studio's appointed director, Alberto Cavalcânti, a Brazilian who had worked long years in Europe, did not hire for Vera Cruz any of the old or new talent that had been working in Brazil for decades.

There was little room in Vera Cruz's just-like-Europe classiness for black, mestiço, or indigenous faces. Despite occasional folkloric apparitions—the picturesque Indian who appears just long enough in *O Cangaceiro* (The Cangaceiro, 1953) to offer some trinkets to the heroine, the oddly un-African black *feiticeira* (sorceress) in *Caiçara*, (1950; see photo 31), the occasional mestiço extras in *Tico Tico no Fubá* (1952)—in general the dominating ethnos (and ethos) was that of Euro Brazil. The hallmark of the early Vera Cruz productions, in terms of the physiognomies chosen and the landscapes displayed (not to mention the automobiles driven), was their strict conformity to the aesthetic, industrial, and even topographical norms of Europe and North America. The characters of a film such as *É Proibido Beijar* (It's Forbidden to Kiss, 1952), for example, resemble those of American screwball comedies; they

31. The sorceress in
Caiçara (1951)

drive around in American cars, there is little evidence of tropical vegetation, and there is barely a black or mestiço face in sight.

Vera Cruz's stated goal was to be both Brazilian and "universal," indeed to be universal *by* being Brazilian. Its slogan, "From the Plateau of Piratininga to the Screens of the World" emphasized this double vocation. Franco Zampari, the entrepreneur who helped finance the Brazilian Comedy Theater and Vera Cruz, suggested that Brazilian cinema would interest the world only insofar that it was specifically Brazilian: "Our country forms an extremely rich vein of themes capable of offering the world the vision of a new civilization. . . . This exuberance of themes—while in other countries filmmakers have exhausted the available themes—will help Brazilian Cinema triumph in the world. . . . Our folklore is rich and suggestive, and our music is extremely beautiful."[5] Although Zampari neglects to mention it, black Brazil does have a place in this picture; the folklore of which Zampari speaks was predominantly Afro Brazilian, and Brazilian popular music has from the beginning been completely impregnated with African values.

Vera Cruz subsequently did move toward a more popular cinema, although it did so too late to save itself from bankruptcy. The international success of Lima Barreto's *O Cangaceiro* proved that the more Brazilian the theme the more likely the film was to have international resonance as well. The *Cangaceiro* project itself was animated by a nationalist impulse: "All Brazilians know about Buffalo Bill, Roy Rogers and Fu Manchu," the film's director complained, "but they don't know about our own *cangaceiros*." The film captured a large audience in Brazil and won prizes in Cannes for "Best Adventure Film" and an "Honorary Mention" for music, and was subsequently screened in more than twenty countries.

A kind of Brazilian western, or more accurately "northeastern," as the Brazilian called the genre because of its setting, the film was based on the legendary-historical Robin-Hood-style bandits from the backlands called *cangaceiros*. The black (in Brazilian terms mulatto) actor Milton Ribeiro plays the *cangaceiro* captain Galdino (see photo 32). While there was little historical justification for the notion of a black *cangaceiro*, at least two Brazilian films create the figure: *O Cangaceiro* and much later *Faustão: O Cangaceiro Negro*

32. Milton Ribeiro as Galdino in *O Cangaceiro* (1953)

(Faustão: The Black Cangaceiro, 1975). Milton Ribeiro, who died in 1972, was known for his acute intelligence and his habit of memorizing the parts of all the actors involved in the film. His character is painted as charismatically villainous, hard and even cruel, but also strong and dignified. This portrait, one should add, has less to do with any portrait of black Brazil per se than it has to do with the conventional portrait of the *cangaceiro*, although one might wonder about the color-coded moral schema, reminiscent of "conquest fiction" and the American western, which correlates darkness with villainy and pits a cruel mulatto antagonist against a white actor-hero.

Although many Vera Cruz films feature black maids (usually played by Ruth de Souza), only one film brought black characters and thematics to the foreground: *Sinhá Moça* (The Plantation Owner's Daughter, 1953). A costume drama codirected by Osvaldo Sampaio and the Anglo Argentinean Tom Payne, *Sinhá Moça* is set around the time just prior to abolition (photo 33). At that point in Brazilian history, slaveholders were in a state of panic both about slave revolts on the *fazendas* and about abolitionist support for them. In 1883, the chief of provincial police in São Paulo warned the president about "the continual slave revolts now taking place on the fazendas of this Province and of the increasing arrogance of the slaves."[6] Another panicked telegram reports: "Chaos in the streets. Armed blacks. Threatening to invade the prison and military headquarters. Send cavalry in sufficient numbers to disperse. Urgent."[7] Slave rebellions in the 1880s were especially strong in those regions where slaves formed a majority, and the state of São Paulo, as a result, formed the epicenter of the revolt. Many official telegrams and reports testify to the panic of the slaveholders, who escalated already severe punishments in an attempt to stem the tide of rebellion. The slaves, for their part, formed a number of secret societies, led by such figures as Felipe Santiago and José Furtado, both of whom were *feitores* (slavedrivers) of dubious loyalties. It was said of Felipe Santiago that he "preached subversive doctrines to the slaves, claiming that they were being injustly held in captivity, since the time of slavery was over."[8] The secret societies asked for financial contributions from their members, to pay for the initiation rites and also to buy arms. In these rites, drawn from Nago, Bantu, and Vodou origins (especially in Maranhão), the initiate underwent a kind of spiritual rebirth, receiving a new name and ritual insignia.

Abolitionists, meanwhile, operated mainly in the cities. Many of the aboli-

com
Eliane LAGE
Anselmo DUARTE

Direção
Tom Payne e
Osvaldo Sampaio

SINHÁ MOÇA

Um momento histórico da abolição

HISTÓRIA BASEADA NO ROMANCE DA SNRA. MARIA DEZONNE PACHECO FERNANDES

tionists were free blacks: José de Patrocínio and Luis Gama, for example. José de Patrocínio, using the pen name Proudhon, revised Pierre-Joseph Proudhon's famous maxim about property to read: "Slavery is theft. Every slaveholder is a thief."[9] Other abolitionists came from the white elite; they formed abolitionist political parties and clubs with names like the Gutenberg Abolitionist Association and the Abraham Lincoln Abolitionist Club. (The Americanophile Abolitionists often used pseudonyms reflecting an American influence: Rui Barbosa adopted "Grey"; Nabuco adopted "Garrison.")[10] In the cities, they created support networks to help slaves who had just escaped there. In some cases, members were obliged to demonstrate their commitment by freeing a slave owned by their own family.

Sinhá Moça elicits comparison with *Gone with the Wind*. Both films are based on historical novels by women, the former by Maria Dezonne Pacheco Fernandes, the latter by Margaret Mitchell. Both are studio films, one from MGM, the other from Vera Cruz, the Brazilian imitator of MGM. Both narrate key moments in national history that partially turn on race. But whereas *Gone with the Wind* is about how the Civil War brought tragedy to the South, *Sinhá Moça* concerns the happiness brought to all Brazilians by the abolition

34. The slave quarters in *Sinhá Moça* (1953)

of slavery as the result of struggle. While the credit sequence of *Gone with the Wind* features docile black farmhands working in pastoral landscapes, the credits of *Sinhá Moça* are superimposed on shots of an escaped slave fleeing from slavery. In *Gone with the Wind,* the slaves seem reconciled to their condition and even somewhat anxious about the outside threat to tranquility. The blacks pray for Confederate victory and cheerlead as the Confederate troops parade and march off to fight in the defense of "the spirit of the South" and indirectly for the perpetuation of human bondage. Whereas *Gone with the Wind* idealizes the "Old South," and by implication the institution of slavery, *Sinhá Moça* stresses the actual work (the whippings, the torture, the collective punishments) required to enforce slavery, thus portraying it as an inherently unstable institution (photo 34). Both *Sinhá Moça* and *Gone with the Wind* also feature white female protagonists who are daughters of the plantation owner. They also each contain "auction" scenes, in which the female protagonist is offered for sale to benefit a cause. However, in the American film it is the Confederate cause, in the Brazilian film the abolitionist cause. In the Hollywood film the male lead is a cynical profiteer; in the Brazilian film he is an idealistic abolitionist who secretly sets slaves free. Both films feature dramatic fire scenes: the burning of Atlanta, and the burning of the slave quarters.

While the black characters of *Gone with the Wind* are invariably presented as "in service" to the white characters, the blacks of *Sinhá Moça,* especially those not from the Big House, operate on their own and separate from the whites.

Although comparisons between *Gone with the Wind* and *Sinhá Moça* reveal the latter to have a less idealized vision of slavery, the title *Sinhá Moça* (The Plantation Owner's Daughter) forewarns us that the focus will be on a white protagonist rather than on the black victims of slavery. This impression is reinforced by the film's advertising, which credits the white leads and foregrounds the romance between them, while relegating the black characters to the background (photo 33). The film's story is set in 1886, just two years before the abolition of slavery in Brazil. The male hero Rodolfo, played by Anselmo Duarte, the romantic leading man from both the *chanchadas* and from Vera Cruz, is a white abolitionist who pretends to be proslavery in order to better liberate slaves. The film's *sinhá moça* (Eliane Lage), meanwhile, opposes slavery on moral and political grounds. While attracted to Rodolfo, she is repulsed by what she believes to be his proslavery opinions. Alongside this couple, the film offers a gallery of characters defined by their attitudes toward slavery: Dr. Fontes, Rodolfo's father, active in the abolitionist struggle; Frei José, the abolitionist priest (liberation theologian *avant la lettre*); and Dona Cándida, Sinhá Moça's mother, caught between proslavery husband and abolitionist daughter. Sinhá Moça's Aunt Clara, meanwhile, is a repository of racist clichés. Blacks, for her, "all look alike." She laments the slaves' "selfish" decision to revolt on the day of her gala: "They only think of themselves," she complains, "they could have scheduled their escape for another day."

The black side comprises a parallel gallery of complex personages. Justino and Fulgêncio are the black leaders who plot escape and rebellion. Benedito is the mulatto slavedriver, who incarnates a historical feature of Brazilian (and Caribbean) slavery, the use of mulattos as repressive figures enjoying a modicum of power, who thus serve to divide the black community. (On the eve of abolition, according to Bahian abolitionist Anselmo Fonseca, two-thirds of those who performed three of the central functions of slavery—overseers, slave catchers, and public whippers—were black or mestiço.)[11] Benedito calls slaves "black dogs," doubtless scapegoating and repressing the black man that he also is. Indeed, the elite politician Camargo questions Benedito's ultimate loyalties, asking Coronel Ferreira if Benedito can really be trusted: "His grandmother was a slave, after all, and blood is blood."

Rodolfo and Sinhá Moça first meet on a train taking them from São Paulo to her father's plantation; they accidentally exchange copies of a Portuguese version of *Uncle Tom's Cabin*—one of many references to events in the United States.[12] Rodolfo protects his proslavery reputation by claiming that he was reading the book "only because it was a best-seller in São Paulo." Rodolfo's feigned attitudes are just one of the indications that *Sinhá Moça* offers a fairly complex picture of racialized slavery as an institution. Slavery is shown as a system of production, one that virtually requires repression and abuse as part of its normal functioning. At the same time, the film provides glimpses of black anger and rebellion. The opening image shows us a fleeing slave, whom we later learn to be Fulgêncio; from the outset, we are given signs of black revolt. Throughout, the white plantation owners are anxious, even paranoid, about rebellion; we are made aware of the omnipresent police and army ready to crush all signs of dissidence and hunt down fugitive slaves.

At the same time, the film does not show the slaves as ideologically homogenous. Whereas the slave quarters are seething with incipient rebellion, the servants in the Big House are more acquiescent, a contrast that recalls Malcolm X's distinction between "house" and "field." Socially, the gap between the Big House and the slave quarters is immense, with little social contact or understanding, although the slaves inevitably know their masters better than their masters know them, since their very survival depends on it. (The historical record suggests a more complex picture; house slaves often served as spies for the others and sometimes even led revolts.) The film emphasizes the friendship between Sinhá Moça and Virginia, an elderly slave woman who adores Sinhá Moça and who weeps emotionally at her mistress's return, her face transfigured with joy. When Sinhá Moça explains the meaning of the word "abolition," Virginia asks, "but then who will do all the work?" Sinhá Moça tells Virginia that she dreams of the day when she can present Virginia socially and say: "This is Virginia, who brought me up, and who is now my equal." But if Virginia has trouble imagining freedom, the blacks in the *senzala* (slave quarters) can think of nothing else. More socially segregated and less exposed to the master's ideology, they are less invested in the little perquisites of slavery to be found in the Big House.

The struggle against slavery in *Sinhá Moça* is conducted by blacks and whites. In fact, the spectator, noticing that virtually all the whites seem to be antislavery, might wonder why the institution ever lasted so long. On the white side, Dr. Fontes clandestinely publishes antislavery tracts; Frei José hides runaways; Rodolfo works surreptitiously to free slaves; and women such as Sinhá Moça exert moral pressure on the slaveholders.[13] While the blacks are portrayed as eager for freedom, the film goes against the historical record by suggesting that they were not usually the agents or initiators of their own liberation. Much recent historical research argues against the view relayed by *Sinhá Moça* that it was only beginning in 1887, with the penetration of abolitionism into the *senzalas,* that slave protests took on a coherent political direction. In *Sinhá Moça,* the white liberationists are presented as more rational and responsible than the slaves, less given to spontaneous but ineffective rebellion, and they warn the slaves against what would in another context be called "adventurism." *Sinhá Moça* conveys exactly the view of abolition questioned by historian Maria Helena Machado:

> [The conventional view] has liberation advancing under the leadership of courageous abolitionist actions, consisting of legal as well as illegal actions. But there is little in such accounts that allows the reader to know objectively in what historical period, to what extent, and what sectors embraced a strategy of invading the senzalas and dialoguing *in loco* with the slaves in question. Furthermore, this narrative sins through its style. Occasionally cited, always in romanesque form, the episodes involving abolitionists and slaves, especially the famous mass flights, provoke severe doubts both about the veracity of the facts and about the success in disrupting slave labor.[14]

Yet a romantically direct contact between abolitionist and slave is exactly what *Sinhá Moça* shows, as Rodolfo becomes a kind of caped Zorro, racing from plantation to plantation under cover of night and setting slaves free. The priest Frei José, meanwhile, plays a complex intermediary role. He persuades the fugitive Fulgêncio to return to slave life but feeds him and convinces the master not to punish him. He tells Fulgêncio that slaves will go to heaven for having suffered. When Fulgêncio asks, "You mean only blacks will go to heaven?" Frei José answers that "in heaven, skin color doesn't matter, but only the color of the soul," thus implying the normativity of a "white" soul.

One very powerful sequence orchestrates some of the key motifs in *Sinhá Moça.* When the master interrupts dancing in the *senzala,* Fulgêncio protests that it is St. Benedict's Day and that "we have a right to celebrate." (St. Benedict, patron saint of slaves, was canonized in 1897 and was himself the son of a slave.) The slavedriver, ironically named Benedito and whom we know to have already raped Fulgêncio's wife, Sabina, is eager to punish his rival. But when Benedito moves to strike him, Fulgêncio grabs the whip and breaks it. For this act of insubordination, he is publicly whipped in the town square. (The pillory's location at the very center of the town square suggests the centrality of slavery and the disciplinary spectacle of punishment to the social structure of rural Brazil.) The scene of the whipping is ironically juxtaposed with the celebration of a mass in a church in the same square, so the parishioners overhear the screams provoked by the whipping simultaneous with the religious liturgy. Fulgêncio eventually dies from the beating, as Sabina weepingly embraces his corpse. When Frei José says, "he died," Sinhá Moça corrects him: "No, he was killed."[15]

Based on a novel by a woman, *Sinhá Moça* also suggests a parallel between the heroine's personal revolt against what we now call patriarchy and the abolitionist struggle against slavery; Sinhá Moça struggles for her own liberation and for that of the slaves. She exults in the slave rebellion as the fires of revolt illuminate her face. When her father complains that her activities are besmirching the family's good name, she retorts that holding slaves constitutes a much more serious blot on the family reputation. When her mother warns her not to express her views because "your father might hear you," she retorts: "I have my own ideas. . . . For you Daddy is a God; for me, he's only my father." Sinhá Moça is quite explicit about the slave/woman parallel, telling her father: "My ideas are my own, free, just as your slaves will one day be free," and pan shots take us metonymically from the wooden bedrails in her bedroom to the bars of the slave quarters but metaphorically between two forms of confinement. Thus the film is both anti-slavery and anti-patriarchal. In this sense, *Sinhá Moça* sets up an analogy between sexism and racism, while portraying Sinhá Moça as a strong and dynamic character with great leadership capacity. She takes up the reins of horse-driven carriages, and together with other women she prevents the soldiers from pursuing the fugitive slaves. The film also exposes the sexual exploitation of black women. The slavedriver tries to break up the marriage of Fulgêncio and Sabina in order to take sexual advantage of Sabina. The film thus reveals the seamier side of what Freyre idealized as cheerful, priapic miscegenation. The historical origins of miscegenation, the film suggests, had more to do with the sexual exploitation of black women—even if the film projects this phenomenon onto the ambiguous figure of the mulatto slavedriver—than with any free and equal exchange between racially distinct partners.

Toward the climax of the film, with the slaves in a state of revolt because of the murder of Fulgêncio, Coronel Ferreira awakens one night to discover that the slave quarters are in flames and that the slaves have fled. At this point, *Sinhá Moça* turns into a kind of anti-*Birth of a Nation,* showing community mobilization in a style marked by narrative crosscutting à la Griffith but this time in favor of a black cause. As the cavalry troops gather to put down the rebellion—Rodolfo, still pretending to be proslavery, rides with the troops—the slaves, led by Justino, organize their revolt. In the ensuing battle, Rodolfo is accidently wounded by Justino, and Justino is taken prisoner. Meanwhile, in a telling scene of "people's justice," the rebels try Benedito in an improvised people's court, in effect putting slavery itself on trial. One by one, the former slaves voice their accusations: "He gave me fifty lashes because I had a fever and couldn't work," says one. "He blinded me because I didn't lower my eyes when he looked at me," says another. One witness, Sabina, appears in silent accusation; since everyone knows the story of her rape by Benedito, she is not expected to review the painful details. Despite Benedito's history of cruelty, there is no lynching spirit among his accusers; the former slaves remain cool and fair minded.

Sinhá Moça, meanwhile, rides off with her women abolitionist supporters to stop the troop train, in a manner reminiscent of the Chicana activism of the film *Salt of the Earth* (1954). She approaches the railroad station in hopes of stopping the soldiers from leaving the train to pursue the fugitive blacks. An officer comes around to her point of view: "The army is not the hunter of fugitive slaves." Skillfully manipulating the soldiers' machismo, Sinhá Moça maneuvers them into not fighting women: "I fight with a woman," says one soldier, "only when I'm married to her." We then cut to the trial of Justino, leader of the rebellion and accused of having wounded Rodolfo and killed Benedito. The public is startled when Rodolfo, Justino's "victim" and generally assumed to be proslavery, presents himself as defense counsel (see photo 35). In his dramatic summation, modeled more on Hollywood's cinematic trials than on Brazilian procedures of jurisprudence, Rodolfo marshals every type of argument—political, moral, pragmatic—in defense of Justino. Refer-

35. Rodolfo defends Justino
in *Sinhá Moça*

ring to the whipping death of Fulgêncio, he says that "it is unthinkable, that
at the dawn of the twentieth century, in the public square, in front of the
House of the Lord, and with the complicity of the law, a man, like us, en-
dowed with heart and intelligence, should be whipped and killed." If Justino
had killed Benedito as he intended, Rodolfo argues, it would have been within his rights of self-defense, a law honored by all civilized countries. He then
hails the abolitionist movement as a "generous campaign on behalf of blacks,"
who "in the humility of their color" have "suffered at the whipping post, and
in the suffocation of the senzalas" while "constructing the grandeur of our
civilization." (It is difficult to imagine Hollywood film of the same period reminding white viewers of their material debt to black labor.) Referring to
Justino in particular and blacks in general, Rodolfo then explicitly invokes the
ideology of whitening, calling them "sons of God, who in this generation differ from us only in color, but who in future generations will equal us, even in
terms of color."

At one time, Rodolfo says, "I had to work in the shadows, but now we are
legions working together—the Church, the Army, enterprises, statesmen, the
slaves, and [with a dramatic look in the direction of Sinhá Moça] our
women." But Rodolfo is unable to complete his peroration, for the trial is interrupted by the news that slavery has been abolished. The trial gives way to
pandemonium and mass celebration in the streets.[16] The film's final shots,
pregnant with historic promise and meaning, orchestrate multiple reconcilia-

tions: between Rodolfo and Sinhá Moça, between Sinhá Moça and her now repentant father, and finally between black and white, as Rodolfo and Justino engage in a fraternal embrace. The clear implication is that Brazil, having erased the blot of a shameful institution, will move into an egalitarian, multiracial future. The sound of breaking chains is blended with the celebratory clanging of church bells. Rodolfo and Sinhá Moça, now reconciled, embrace in the foreground, as the festive crowd dances in the background. The film, which began with the image of blacks in flight, ends with the happy face of Justino superimposed on the image of church bells clanging the good news of abolition, encapsulating the overall trajectory from oppression to liberation. But the film itself, and even the final shots, provide inadvertent intimations that things are not quite so simple. The snake in the paradise of racial democracy—social inequality—is figured through the *mise-en-scène*. The elite are in the foreground, the black masses in the background. The elite are well dressed; the former slaves are not. In the final analysis, Brazil has not moved definitively away from the social structure schematically portrayed in the opening sequence: the white elite in the first-class car, Italian immigrants in the second-class car, and blacks running for their very lives outside the train.

Overall, *Sinhá Moça* systematically privileges its white stars and idealizes the abolitionist movement (photo 36). The dramas of the slaves form the background for the amorous involvements and political intrigues of the white elite. The enigma of Rodolfo's attitudes toward slavery becomes a plot gimmick, an obstacle that lends spice and drama to the romance. For him, the triumph of abolition coincides with his winning the affection of Sinhá Moça; political and sexual liberation go hand in hand. The problack message is "sweetened" for a predominately white audience by a stellar romance and the pleasures of spectacle.

The privileging of *Sinhá Moça*'s white stars is especially unfortunate in that the film's black actors do a superior job. A contemporary reviewer specifically praised the black actors as "the great artists of the film": "They felt the subject in their flesh; they lived it in an ancestral fashion. . . . All the black actors performed with dignity, both those with theatrical background like Ruth de Souza, and those just beginning in the cinema, like Henricao, or the admirable figure of Fulgêncio who lives the martyrdom of the whipping post, perhaps the high point of the acting in the film. On the white side, very few achieved the level of the blacks."[17]

36. *Sinhá Moça*

Although the film talks about how abolition wiped out a shameful part of Brazilian history, it does not address the many ways in which abolition served the interests of whites; abolition did not so much free the slaves as it freed the masters from all responsibilities toward the slaves. Furthermore, slavery was no longer viable in economic terms; slave labor had become an anachronistic mode of production. The British were pressuring Brazil to end the slave trade as early as 1827. In many regions, furthermore, slaves did not even form a majority of the *black* population; in the São Paulo of the 1870s, for example, salaried workers already formed the majority. The leaders of the abolitionist movement, such as Joaquim Nabuco, emphasized pragmatic economic as well as humanitarian arguments. Slavery, according to Nabuco, corrupts the character, prevents immigration, degrades manual labor, excites class hatred, and slows down industrialization.[18] The cultivation of salaried laborers would create a market for the products of Brazilian as well as British industry. The elision of the economic motivations for the abolition of slavery in *Sinhá Moça* forms a marked contrast with the Cuban film *El Otro Francisco* (The Other Francisco, 1974), another film based on a sentimental romantic novel about slavery. The Cuban film, by Afro Cuban director Sergio Giral, juxtaposes the sentimentalized story of the original novel, where passion is the motivating force, with its own deconstruction via documentary segments that reveal the British involvement in the abolitionist movement, the sexual exploitation of black women, and the strength of black revolt without white leadership. Whereas *Sinhá Moça* turns slavery into a moral question, *El Otro Francisco* stresses slavery as an integral part of capitalist modernity, a means of perpetrating a specific, if dated, system of exploitation.

Politics, finally, is inseparable from style, and the very style of *Sinhá Moça* carries a political message. In this well-made, well-lit costume drama, the montage is impeccable and the camera movements are fluent and discrete. The opulent Hollywoodean style of the film, reminiscent of *Gone with the Wind*, has the effect of romanticizing and depicting as elegant the old world of slavery. The formalist concern with balanced composition undermines the presentation of historical contradiction. Orchestral European commentative music, moreover, constantly interprets and underlines, as it were, the "meaning" of the scenes, leaving little place for Afro Brazilian music, precisely the music that became the major source of Brazilian popular music. The occasional attempts to reproduce Afro Brazilian percussion, in the *senzala* sequences, for example, are more reminiscent of Hollywood "boogah-boogah" music than of Brazil itself. Even the lighting by Ray Sturgess (the same director of photography who lit Olivier's *Hamlet*) has more to do with England than with Brazil, and it ultimately serves to idealize the white stars, in a foil effect familiar from North American films.[19]

To flash forward briefly, *Sinhá Moça* was adapted in 1986 as a *telenovela* directed by Reynaldo Boury and Jayme Monjardim, with Benedito Ruy Barbosa as screenwriter and Maria Dezonne Fernandes as "adapter." The TV version refuses the romantic vision of the novel, revealing, for example, that Princesa Isabela's Lei Áurea (the law abolishing slavery in 1888) was not a philanthropic gesture but a response to international and domestic pressures. The *telenovela* version was fashioned after and eventually achieved the same success as another black-related *telenovela*—*A Escrava Isaura*—whose formulaic conjunction of slavery, freedom, and romanticism it imitates. Like *A Escrava Isaura*, the televisual *Sinhá Moça* starred Lucélia Santos, and, again like the earlier film, it was ultimately seen in over 90 countries. To adopt the story for TV, Benedito Ruy Barbosa developed 8 of the novel's characters and created 30 more.

In any case, just as Vera Cruz was discovering the formula of popular

37. Cavalcânti's *Canto do Mar* (1954)

themes and relatively low-budget production methods, it was engulfed by the consequences of the overexpenditures of the earlier films and of having surrendered distribution rights to Universal and to Columbia Pictures and went bankrupt. After leaving Vera Cruz, Alberto Cavalcânti made a number of mildly nationalist films, one of which peripherally touches on black themes: *O Canto do Mar* (Song of the Sea, 1954; see photo 37), a film that transferred to Cavalcânti's native Northeast, specifically Recife, the themes already treated in his French film *En Rade* (1927). Within this story about northeasterners who flee the *sertão* (backlands) for the sea, Cavalcânti inserted semidocumentary scenes showing Afro Brazilian cultural practices, specifically *xangô* (a northeastern variant of *candomblé* ceremonies) and *maracatu,* although the scenes sometimes seem more motivated by a desire for picturesqueness than by solidarity with African Brazilian culture. Winner of a prize in Karlovy-Vary, *Canto do Mar* did manage to anticipate some of the themes of the Cinema Novo of the 1960s: the drought-stricken *retirantes* of *Vidas Secas* (Barren Lives, 1963), the role of Afro Brazilian culture in *O Pagador de Promessas* (The Given Word, 1962) and so forth.

Despite the bankruptcy of Vera Cruz, other companies in the same mold quickly grew up in its wake, inspired by the same ideal of thematic dignity and high production values. Oswaldo Censoni's *João Negrinho* (John the Black Boy; shot 1954, released 1958), like *Sinhá Moça*, also treats the subject of slavery and abolition. Directed by Oswaldo Censoni, based on a story by Jacana Altair, and partially filmed in the Vera Cruz studios, the film's narrative is embroidered around the flashback memories of an elderly ex-slave named João Negrinho. The opening images, superimposing the credits over images of the chains and torture instruments of slavery, set the theme. Speaking in the almost caricatural accents of the *preto velho*, the elderly João takes the chains off the wall and shows them to his grandson, announcing that he will explain what slavery was like. The image blurs, ushering us into the story proper and initiating the narrative shuttle between the old man recounting and the life being recounted, which structures the film as a whole.

João Negrinho begins with a portrait of the hard conditions of slavery. On a sugar plantation, a slavedriver extracts the last bit of labor from his wards; lugubrious music underlines the atmosphere of oppression (photo 38). An aristocratic woman with a grating metallic voice has slaves kiss her hand in obligatory obeisance. The master, the narrator-protagonist recounts, was

38. The nature of slavery: *João Negrinho* (1958)

mean to everyone: "for him, blacks were slaves, not people." When a desperately hungry João Negrinho is caught stealing some cakes from the master's table, the mistress shouts that "slaves don't eat cakes" and punishes him by burning his hand, as João Negrinho's mother looks on helplessly. Like *Sinhá Moça*, then, *João Negrinho* undoes the myth of a "benign" Lusitanian form of slavery; slavery is shown to be inherently repressive, sadistic, and ideologically irrational. The master, the quintessential racist, blames blacks for "dying on him," when he has caused their death. He scapegoats the slaves for the economic failure of the plantation, when they have done all the work. The friendship of his son Chiquinho with João Negrinho is for him a sign that blacks are "taking over." João Negrinho, for his part, becomes an escape valve for white aggressivity, a perpetually available punching bag for those who call him a "devil with a human face."

If *João Negrinho* offers a harsh picture of the conditions of slavery, it also paints an idyllic picture of the friendship of João Negrinho and the master's son. Scenes of the prepubertal boys gone fishing provide poetic intimations of interracial intimacy, reminiscent, for the North American viewer, of Huck and Jim on their Mississippi raft, except that *João Negrinho,* unlike the Mark Twain novel, never wrestles with the internal dilemmas of the white boy living within a racist regime. Chiquinho is portrayed as constantly interceding for a João represented as perpetually in need of rescue. When João falls into quicksand, Chiquinho saves his life. Later Chiquinho saves him from disaster in a runaway cart. What we have, then, is a white rescue fantasy, an agenda-driven generosity toward blacks that would oblige them to eternal gratitude. (The original rationale for nonracialized slavery, we are reminded, was that prisoners taken in war owed their very lives to their captors and should therefore be grateful to be condemned to mere slavery rather than to death.)

On the other hand, Joao Negrinho is also portrayed as intellectually talented. When Chiquinho stumbles in his class recitation of the Lord's Prayer, the priest asks João to recite; João recites the prayer letter-perfect, at which point the master becomes enraged at the temerity of a mere slave boy reciting better than his own son. Despite the system's attempt to keep slaves illiterate and uneducated, the sequence suggests that slaves sometimes had a cultural level superior to that of their masters. The film also offers glimpses of black revolt, even while eventually "containing" such revolt. João's warning as narrator that "things couldn't go on that way" segues to the story of an abortive

rebellion. As the slaves plot to kill the master, we hear the conventionally omi-
nous beating of the drums, but the master learns of the revolt and nips it in
the bud. Although the priest intercedes on behalf of the slaves, he also counsels them never to revolt again. The film makes revolt humanly understand-
able, then, but also strategically regrettable and perhaps even ethically reprehensible, in ways that recall the perennial American liberal counsels of
patience to black militants and civil rights activists, symptomatic of a paternalistic attitude that suggests that "they" are not yet ready for freedom and in
perpetual need of white tutelage.

The role of the saintly priest, meanwhile, is especially ambivalent (see
photo 39). A tender-hearted integrationist, for whom all children are God's
children, the priest constantly intercedes on the slaves' behalf. When a slave is
punished for "laziness," the priest tells the slavedriver that it is the "the weight
of those chains that make him lazy." Christlike in his submission to the lot of
the humble, the priest works alongside the slaves and the film seems to glorify
his sacrifice over that of the slaves themselves. In some ways, in fact, his practice denies the equality he asserts. He preaches universal love but applies a
double standard that asks for "understanding" from Chiquinho but demands
"obedience" from João Negrinho. Although the film apparently presents all
events from João's point of view so as to enlist our complete sympathy, what
the film enlists our sympathy *for* is in fact the paternalistic vision inherent in
the dominant racial ideology of the period. Chiquinho goes off to the city to
work as a journalist and legislator for the abolitionist cause, while João prays
for him every night. Once back on the plantation, Chiquinho expresses an
agrarian vision; he excoriates corrupt city life and speaks of his nostalgia for
the good life of the *fazenda*.[20]

João Negrinho, at first glance so "sympathetic" to blacks, is ultimately patronizingly and even "well-intentionedly" racist. The message to blacks is
clear: have faith in well-meaning whites; they will intercede for you. The film
thus displays a crushing form of charity, a nefarious form of benevolence. The
film's saccharine music emotionally manipulates the spectator into sharing in
a moralistic condemnation that fails to illuminate the power arrangements
and historical aftershocks of slavery. With the advent of abolition, Chiquinho
offers a banquet to the newly liberated João Negrinho. Now João becomes
the assimilated, grateful black man who adopts the elite's manners and aspirations; he is accepted in the white world, but on the white world's terms. In a

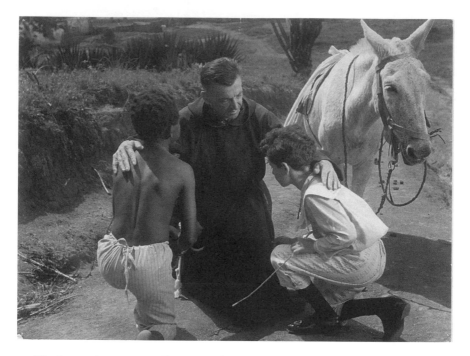

39. The benevolent priest in *João Negrinho*

moving speech, Chiquinho praises João as a fine and faithful friend. Brazil, he announces, "is now freed from the affliction of slavery." But the final sequence of postabolition camaraderie, intended as a celebration of the brave new world of "racial democracy," inadvertently offers clues to the subsequent oppression of blacks in Brazil. A new generation, presumably charitable and egalitarian, has taken over from racist slaveholders like Chico's father. But the final shot shows João driving two white friends from the celebratory banquet in a horse and carriage. Although metaphorically "in the driver's seat," in symbolic terms he has been promoted from slave to servant. The contrast between the sufferings of João Negrinho as a child under slavery and his current status as a proud and dignified old man conveys a completed trajectory of liberation, in which nothing more remains to be done. He tells his story not in order to encourage contemporary struggles, but rather so that the story of slavery will not be consumed by what he calls the "forgetfulness and dust of time."

A 1976 TV commercial, interestingly, offered a very similar message via an almost identical image. An off-screen voice announces: "In the imperial era of Brazil, transport looked like this": The image shows a blond woman carried on a litter by two slaves. Then the voice resumes: "Today, however, it's possible to enjoy the comfort of a Ford LTD Galaxy, thanks to the services of Itapare." We then see the same blond woman, this time in the back seat of a car driven by a black chauffeur, played by the same actor who played the slave in the previous shot. The slave has become the servant, in a movement that recapitulates the overall trajectory of *João Negrinho*.

Apart from one Vera Cruz short, a stylized dance film called *Macumba* (1952; see photo 40), one other 1950s light comedy from São Paulo deserves mention. Maria Basaglia's *Macumba na Alta* (Macumba in High Society, 1958) uses Afro Brazilian religion as a plot gimmick, much as Molière used Turkish culture in *Le Bourgeois Gentilhomme*. The opening credits combine *terreiro* music with high-society imagery. The surprise effect of the title obviously depends on the notion that Afro Brazilian religion is incompatible with upper-class life. The film is largely set among São Paulo socialites, including "the doctor," a charlatan who feigns knowledge of psychoanalysis, and Pinta, a white composer and singer of sambas. The "doctor" speaks about "transference" at the same party where an Afro Brazilian dance group performs. The interesting point, never explored, would be the similarities and differences between fashionable upper-class notions about mediums and psychoanalytic transference and the Africanized mediumship of trance religions, a connection later explored in the 1981 film *A Prova de Fogo* (Trial by Fire), which presents an *umbanda* priest, in consistency with the common view of *umbanda* as the "poor man's couch," that is, as a therapist for the lower classes. A chanchada from the same period as *Macumba na Alta, Samba em Brasília* (1960) also touches on the theme of the infiltration of the popular religion of macumba into the realm of high society, whether "carried" by black characters or not. In the film, Heloísa Helena wants to fire her maid because the maid ruined her party by preparing inedible food. When the maid says that her "saint" (i.e., *orixá*) is very powerful, the mistress exclaims: "so you know macumba!" Instead of firing her, the mistress contracts her services as a *macumbeira*, in hopes that the maid's *despachos* (hexes) will get her cited in the social columns as one of the "ten most elegant." Thus mistress and maid, both white, make common cause around African ritual practices. And, even more surprising, the *despacho* works and the mistress is indeed cited in the social columns.

The late 1950s witnessed other attempts to found a cinematic industry in

40. *Macumba* (1952)

São Paulo. Despite the failure of Vera Cruz, other production companies—Maristela, Multifilmes, Gianelli Films, Brasil Filmes—embarked on the same path of high production values and "international" style. The films of this period reveal an immense effort to demonstrate technical proficiency and to avoid what the filmmakers regarded as the sloppiness of the *chanchada*. This fantasy of "high quality," sustained by the steady prestige of Hollywood films, obsessed the Vera Cruz filmmakers. But in this same period, a group of young filmmakers, formed in the old school but skeptical about the old dogmatisms, began to challenge this colonized vision of what Brazilian cinema and race relations should be, in a movement that prepared the way for the innovations of Cinema Novo.

CHAPTER 6

The Favela: From Rio 40 Graus
to Black Orpheus,

1954–1959

∞

In the late 1950s, left-wing critics like Alex Viany, Carlos Ortiz, Rodolfo Nanni, and Nelson Pereira dos Santos published a series of articles defending a "national" and a "popular" cinema, by which they meant a socially progressive cinema nourished by popular Brazilian traditions. They denounced a pessimistic, demoralizing cinema that flattered the Brazilian upper classes "living in luxury thanks to the exploitation of the overwhelming majority of the Brazilian population."[1] These critics favored production companies that were "100 percent Brazilian," that is, without links to foreign capital, and they criticized the Vera Cruz collaboration with Columbia and Universal. Although they lauded the success of the *chanchadas* they lamented their alienating role. In the first São Paulo Congress for Brazilian Cinema in 1952, dos Santos argued for a popular cinema that could conquer the domestic market. At times these critics called for films made by Brazilians only, as if authenticity were a function of passport and identity card. Their emphasis was on thematic content; they pleaded for more films about drought in the Northeast, poverty in the favelas, and liberatory historical movements. Unlike later adherents of Cinema Novo, these early participants were relatively uninterested in formal questions. They simply wanted a cinema with Brazilian themes, which spoke to the people in their own language. The filmmakers saw themselves as intermediaries, more conscious and informed than the people, perhaps, but capable of representing the people to themselves. They also called for state intervention in the form of protective legislation and the obligatory screening of

Brazilian films as the only way of fighting the foreign domination of the market.

In their search for the national and the popular, the 1950s critics and filmmakers turned to Italian neorealism, then at the height of its worldwide influence. Neorealism provided a model not only for themes but also for production methods, that is, for a low-budget, independently produced, nonindustrial cinema, filmed in the streets, using nonprofessional or little-known actors, and treating contemporary social life. These same critics contrasted the low-budget verism of neorealism with what they regarded as the obscene luxury of Vera Cruz–style superproductions. In a critical essay about *Sinhá Moça* (The Plantation Owner's Daughter, 1953), Benedito J. Duarte anticipated the 1960s notion of an "aesthetic of hunger" by calling for a "cinema of misery." Poverty, he continued, "stimulates the imagination and incites the sensibility, and the creative spirit can only gain. Italian neo-realism was born of hunger."[2] In the mid-1950s these critics began to put their ideas into practice. Alex Viany's *Agulha no Palheiro* (Needle in a Haystack, 1953) exemplified the same neorealist theories that he had defended in his articles: a cinema made in the streets, starring the people themselves, with popular themes, in a language both poetic and realistic.

But it was above all dos Santos who made films within this spirit, and his films constitute the major exception to the general paternalism toward blacks. One of his first experiences in film, as an assistant director was in the São Paulo production of *O Saci* (1951), based on Monteiro Lobato's rendering of folktales concerning Saci Pererê, the one-legged black genie figure, reminiscent of the dwarfs and gnomes of European legend, who smokes a pipe and makes mischief in the forest (see photo 41). In the popular imagination, Saci is black, partially because he was black in the Portuguese tradition but also because the storytellers who spoke of Saci were black nannies. *Saci* is set on an idyllic farm, a utopian space where everyone plays peacefully in a Tom Sawyerish atmosphere. Along with Saci (Paulo Matozinho), the black figures inhabiting this utopia are the corpulent, good-natured nanny figure Nastácia— her name evokes the legendary black woman who helped end slavery—and a *preto velho,* both of whom firmly believe in Saci's existence. (This *preto velho* evokes, for a North American viewer, Mark Twain's Jim and his amiable superstitions.) On the *fazenda* the game is to "catch" Saci, and Saint Bartholemew's Day is rumored to be an ideal day for the catch (Saci's attempts to es-

41a/41b. Paulo Matozinho
as Saci Perere in *Saci* (1955)

cape being "caught" almost inevitably carry overtones of the predicaments of runaway slaves.) The whites are skeptical about Saci's existence, but the black characters believe in him, and the film, by having Saci emerge out of a puff of smoke, seems to support the black belief.

While working in a Rio *chanchada (Balança mas Não Cai)* in 1952, dos

Santos came into contact with Rio's favelas and decided to make a number of films about them. With *Rio 40 Graus* (Rio 40 Degrees, 1954) and *Rio Zona Norte* (Rio's Northern Zone, 1957), dos Santos leaves behind the bucolic innocence of *Saci*. *Rio 40 Graus* (see photo 42)—the title is both a literal reference to Rio's hot climate and a meteorological figure for social tension—treats a typical Carioca Sunday and "stars" the Cariocas themselves. If James Joyce's *Ulysses* portrays a day in the life of Dublin, *Rio 40 Graus* portrays a day in the life of Rio de Janeiro. Indeed, dos Santos was self-consciously mimicking the "holistic construction of *Ulysses,* creating one day in Rio with my characters, with my children, wandering around the city. But I didn't manage to place a level of desired consciousness within them."[3] Nelson especially highlights the black popular life of Rio. The characters who provide the human and rhetorical "glue" linking the diverse episodes are the peanut vendors, largely black, who descend from the favelas and fan out to occupy strategic points of the city—Copacabana Beach, Sugar Loaf, Corcovado, Quinta da Boa Vista, and Maracana—on its day of rest. In each locale a different story emerges.

Breaking with the paternalism of antecedent cinema, *Rio 40 Graus* represents a giant step forward for Brazilian cinema in general and for the representation of blacks in particular. Unlike the *chanchadas,* the film takes the existential dilemmas of its black characters seriously, according them the unpretentious sympathy and solidarity that were to become the hallmark of dos Santos's work. The film treats the oppression of blacks without stridency and in a way that includes blacks as part of a multiracial mass of oppressed Brazilians. Although the film does not formulate its critique in explicitly racial terms, it does show a general pattern of exploitation—of the peanut vendors by their boss (photo 43), of the soccer players by their managers, of the samba school by its sponsor—in which the exploited *tend* to have darker faces than the exploiters. Rather than limit itself to mere denunciation, dos Santos shows people who resist: the peanut vendors outwit the boss; the black athlete refuses to be treated like merchandise. The film proliferates in sharply observed detail. One child beggar offers another some practical advice: "Don't ask for money for yourself. Ask for your sick mother; you'll have better luck." While hardly a Manichean film pitting good black oppressed against white oppressor, *Rio 40 Graus* does satirize the white bourgeoisie in rather schematic terms and even homophobic terms by having effeminate playboys on

EQUIPE MOACYR FENELON apresenta

MODESTO de SOUZA

ANA BEATRIZ

GLANCE ROCHA

ROBERTO BATALIN

CLAUDIA MORENO

JECE VALADÃO

MÚSICAS
A VOZ DO MORRO
RELIQUIAS de um ANTIGO
POETA dos NEGROS
LEVIANA
Com a participação das
ESCOLAS DE SAMBA
PORTELA
UNIDOS de CABUÇU

NELSON PEREIRA DOS SANTOS

RIO, 40 GRAUS

Copacabana beaches speak of life as a "delicious madness" and "delirious adventure." Dos Santos's clear problack sympathies did not go unnoticed: "Never has the black element of our population," wrote Ironides Rodrigues, "been treated with so much sympathy."[4]

Afro Brazilian voices and music permeate the soundtrack of *Rio 40 Graus:* the rumble of the *surdos* (bass drums) from the hills, the yelps of the *cuíca* and the Portela Samba School singing "One voice from North to South heard the cry that slavery has come to an end." Nelson's sympathy extends to specific characters like the young *favelado* who can't afford the entrance fee to the city zoo and the invalid Dona Elvira, desperate for money to buy medicine and worried that her son has died, in a performance Brazilian critics compared to those of Ethel Waters. It was perhaps this undisguised empathy with blacks that led Police Chief Coronel Geraldo de Meneses Cortes, head of censorship in the Federal District of Rio, to ban the film, alleging, among other things, that in Rio it never reached 40 degrees centigrade. (The film was released only after a campaign by Brazilian and international intellectuals.) Why were the custodians of mimesis, so indifferent to the exclusion of blacks from earlier films, so disturbed by *Rio 40 Graus*?

43. Boss and vendor in *Rio 40 Graus* (1954)

The second piece in Nelson's planned Carioca trilogy, *Rio Zona Norte* (1957)—the third part, *Rio Zona Sul,* was never completed—concerns samba musicians and composers. *Rio Zona Norte* begins with images of the Central Train Station and then follows the rail line that takes the urban masses to the *subúrbios* of the Zona Norte. An agreeable city for the wealthy of the Zona Sul, Rio can be a hell for the inhabitants of the Zona Norte, where even the pollution seems to discriminate. Here the means of transportation is less exalted; train-borne shots replace the aerial shots from *Rio 40 Graus,* and we are projected into the lower-class world of the favelas. Whereas *Rio 40 Graus* offers a general "objective" urban tableau, *Rio Zona Norte* offers a subjectivized portrait of a specific black character—Espírito da Luz Cardoso (Grande Otelo)—an uneducated but talented samba composer from the favelas. (The character is partially based on the real-life popular composer Zé Keti, who appears in the film not as himself but as successful singer Alaor Costa, as well as on Grande Otelo, himself a composer of sambas.)

Constructed around a series of flashbacks on the part of Espírito as he lays dying after falling from a train, *Rio Zona Norte* shuttles back and forth via lap dissolve from Espírito's present—his agony—and his flashback memories of his personal struggle for love and family life and his public frustrations and triumphs as a sambista. If *Rio 40 Graus* delved superficially into the world of the samba schools, *Rio Zona Norte* shows the samba as lived by the composers who sell their songs for a pittance in hopes of one day hearing them played in carnival or on the radio. The history of Brazilian music is full of these struggling and often anonymous poets, who helped create the incomparable riches of Brazilian popular music.

Animated by gentle anger, dos Santos here again emphasizes racially inflected forms of class exploitation. Talented but naive, Espírito accepts partners and middlemen who lack his spirit of fairness and who end up appropriating his work. The character Maurício (Jece Valadão) is in this sense typical. While pretending to be Espírito's friend and collaborator, in fact he steals his sambas and sells them to the highest bidder, without ever crediting their author or sharing the profits. When Espírito learns that his samba will be recorded but without his name on it, Maurício tries to placate him by saying "I was going to tell you, but you live so far away," a "far away" that is both literal and metaphorical. Espírito literally lives in the Zona Norte, but figuratively, as a poor uneducated black, he is marginalized, peripheralized, far from the centers of power and decision. Maurício names Ciro as co-lyricist, explaining that Ciro's fame as a disk jockey will guarantee airplay. "I only know that it's my music," Espírito responds, "and my name should be on it." But he accepts 1,000 cruzeiros and is even persuaded to sign away his rights. Maurício displays a "cordial" Brazilian racism in which communicative warmth and camaraderie mask condescension. He constantly hugs Espírito and calls him partner, but his embrace is less a sign of affection than a gesture of contempt, since the core relationship is exploitative.

In later encounters, Espírito actively defends his interests. He refuses to reveal new lyrics to Maurício, and avoids signing away his rights, angrily telling Maurício: "This samba's mine. Only mine. I'm going to record it alone, and it has to be sung by Ângela Maria." Ângela Maria (played by herself) promises to make the song a hit (photo 44).[5] The final sequence shows Espírito on the northbound train, tapping out rhythms and singing his samba to himself. But his pride is not individualistic; rather, he sees samba as a collective creation: "It's my samba, and Brazil's as well."

Rio Zona Norte focalizes a black protagonist as a multidimensional human being. Espírito is no longer the comic figure of the *chanchadas*. He is talented,

44. Grande Otelo and Angela Maria in *Rio Zona Norte* (1957)

dignified, sensitive, generous; he is exploited only because of his inexperience and naive faith that other human beings are as uncalculating as he is. In addition, the entire film is presented as the production of his consciousness. All the cinematic and narrative devices (close-shots, voice-off, commentative music) enforce spectatorial identification with him. The point-of-view shots are largely his, and when he is alone we feel a certain relief at no longer being in the company of phonies. He is also granted a social role often denied blacks in both North American and Brazilian cinema: that of father. With his wife's death, he is left alone to care for his teenage son Norival, for whom the entire favela is a "backyard." Humiliated to find his son in the middle of a robbery— in fact his son is trying to *return* stolen money—Espírito is grief stricken as he sees other *favelados* gun him down.

Rio Zona Norte's natural, offhand treatment of the favela milieu avoids both postcard idealization *(Black Orpheus)* and inadvertent leftist condescension. At the same time, the film clearly denounces the exploitation of black musicians. An interminable parade of "partners," "managers," "disc jockeys," and "executives," most of them lighter skinned than their musician clients, treat blacks

with phony condescension while prospecting for lucrative hits. This exploitation of black musicians—also registered in the Jamaican film *The Harder They
Come* (1972)—reflects a long tradition of appropriation throughout the diaspora.[6] The operative pattern: blacks make the music and whites steal it,
package it, and profit from it, while both blacks and whites consume the music that blacks make. In this sense, dos Santos reveals the financial subtext of
samba, pointing to the shadowy existence of an embryonic "culture industry"
in the form of the mass media (radio) and the largely foreign-dominated record industry. Espírito produces raw material (the songs) but receives few of
the benefits. In this sense, his situation allegorizes that of Brazil, and his ultimate refusal to be exploited constitutes the artistic equivalent of the national-
istic ideology then being advanced by left-wing intellectuals like dos Santos
himself. At the same time, the film questions the role of intellectuals in relation to popular culture. In *Rio Zona Norte,* samba becomes subject to norms
imposed from outside, to be evaluated by people who have little to do with
its milieu of origin. A white musician says of Espírito's music: "I wanted to
write a ballet with his music, but I was afraid it would be too stylized." A
certain Adalberto aspires to compose a popular Brazilian opera, but ends
up with "something that is neither ballet nor popular music." Interestingly, the scenes with these elite characters, unlike the favela scenes, feature more
quickly paced editing, as if positing an stylistic correlative for the characters'
artificiality. Behind this satire of elite dabblers in popular culture, we sense
Nelson's ongoing preoccupation: what is popular culture and what is the
white, middle-class director's relation to it?

Rio Zona Norte shows blacks as economically and socially marginalized. The
whites in the films, especially the rich whites, adopt a condescending tone
with Espírito, as if they were talking to a child. And he is in fact infantilized
through a dependent situation that forces him to rely on untrustworthy partners and managers. Within these relationships there is little reciprocity, a lack
that is linguistically marked: the samba entrepreneur addresses Espírito with
the familiar *você* (you) while Espírito addresses the entrepreneur with the formal *o senhor* (sir). The film also points to a correlation between racism and social position. Although the film is not racially schematic, it does give the impression that the *povo* (i.e., the marginalized mass of Brazilians) is not
racist—the samba rehearsals and performances are multiracial and tension-

free, for example—but those occupying higher social positions are patronizing with blacks like Espírito.

The film exhibits a tension between the "diegetic" sambas—those in which we both see and hear the samba musicians—and the nondiegetic commentative sambas (e.g., those accompanying the credits) not grounded in the image. The commentative sambas tend to be more orchestrated, more Europeanized, reflecting the influence of Hollywood codes and big-band musical styles. The commentative music fosters identification with Espírito, communicating his moods to the spectator through the musical "analogue of feeling." The soundtrack exhibits, ironically, the very process described by the film, that is, the process whereby the samba originates in the *batucadas* (rhythm or chant of the Afro Brazilian *batuque* celebration) of the *morros* and then moves to radio and nightclub, acquiring with each step another patina of sophisticated elaboration.

Ultimately, however, the music comes from the *morros*. The final sequence posits a kind of equation between the morro and the samba and ultimately between the samba and Brazil.

> It's my samba
> And Brazil's too
> They want to make you into
> A despised Nobody
> But the favelas don't forget you
> For the morro, the samba doesn't die

Thus *Rio Zona Norte* gives a socially rooted version of the Orphic theme. The music will live on in the favelas and Brazil, and the people will sing Espírito's music. The music will triumph over death. Espírito sums up in himself the spirit of a community, exemplifying the sambista as described by the samba "The Sambista," as a poet who "sees in rhymes and melodies . . . as the course of life requires."

Just two years after *Rio Zona Norte,* another film about samba and the favelas and the Orphic theme was released, one that was to become internationally famous. Indeed, for many non-Brazilians, the phrase "Brazilian Cinema" instantly elicits the memory of what was in fact a French film: *Black Orpheus* (Black Orpheus, 1959; see photo 45). Directed by Marcel Camus, a director sometimes mistakenly seen as part of the French New Wave, *Black Orpheus* called attention to a highly Africanized cultural phenomenon—Rio's

45. Marcel Camus's *Black Orpheus* (1959)

carnival—combining ecstatic polyrhythmic percussion with the elaborate folk opera of the samba school pageants.[7] Although technically a French film, *Black Orpheus* initiated millions of non-Brazilians into Brazilian culture, forging in the international consciousness a powerful association between three related concepts: Brazilianness, blackness, and carnival. The French filmmakers did their best to familiarize themselves with Brazil; Camus and his screenwriter Viorst reportedly spent five months in the *morros* in order to internalize the atmosphere and learn the social customs. *Black Orpheus* in this sense must be seen in the context of attempts by non-Brazilians to film carnival, and Camus deserves credit mainly for avoiding some of the disastrous gaffes that plagued Hollywood films about Brazil—*It's All True* being the clear exception to the rule—blunders ranging from minor topographical or linguistic errors to racialized slurs against the Brazilian character.

Much that is effective in *Black Orpheus,* at least in comparison to Hollywood films about Brazil, derives from the Brazilian role in the film's process of production. The film is based, first of all, on a Brazilian verse play—*Orfeu da Conceiçao*—first staged in 1956 by the playwright, poet, singer, and diplomat Vinícius de Moraes. De Moraes got the idea for the play during the 1942 carnival, the same one filmed by Orson Welles. De Moraes was reading an eighteenth-century version of the Orpheus story by the Italian Calzabigi, a version later turned into music by the German Christoph Gluck. It tells the story of the famous musician, singer, and poet who sang so seductively that wild animals were tamed and whose most celebrated adventure was his trip to Hades in search of Eurydice, Apollo's daughter. Although de Moraes was one of Welles's hosts in Rio and Welles was perhaps a distant inspiration, it was another North American, Waldo Frank, a literary critic with strong affective links to Latin America, who was the "midwife" for the conception of de Moraes's play. De Moraes had traveled around Brazil with Frank, with the result that both became aware of the "other" Brazil. In Rio, Frank had asked de Moraes to take him to the favelas, where the American was amazed at the beautiful dancing and music-making of the *favelados:* "They look," he told de Moraes, "like Greeks." Later on, after having read the Calzabigi version of Orpheus, de Moraes began to write frenetically, partially inspired by the coincidence of hearing an intense *batucada* while he was writing about Orpheus: "One morning, as I was reading the Orpheus legend . . . a story I always loved for its linking the poet and the musician—I heard a batucada coming from the neighboring favela . . . the two ideas strangely fused in my mind and I had the impression of a strong relation between the two. I began to reflect on the life of blacks in Rio and to Hellenize their experience. Suddenly, I had the idea of making Orpheus a sambista characterized by great interior beauty."[8] In the tradition of European primitivism and of the Negritude movement, which posited Greece as reason and Africa as emotion, de Moraes saw Afro Brazilian performance as bringing a Dionysian dimension to an Appolonian theme, calling the play "a hommage to blacks for their organic contribution to the culture of this country and for their impassioned life style."[9]

After a long gestation process, starting with the original in 1942 (the same year as Orson Welles's visit to Brazil), then proceeding to the writing of the first act (also in 1942), and culminating with the writing of the last two acts many years later (when de Moraes was a diplomat in Los Angeles), the play was first performed in 1956 at the Teatro Municipal in Rio. Many of the actors were from Abdias do Nascimento's Black Experimental Theater. As Charles Perrone points out, the actors faced an ideological conflict in that the play, by a Euro Brazilian, foregrounded their performance skills but not the values of African culture. Nor did it imply any critique of whiteness.[10] Indeed, Abdias do Nascimento became increasingly critical of such works over the years: "Blackfaced white actors, Black Christ, Black Orpheus: in the last analysis they all conspire in the historical rape of my people. African religious culture is rich and alive in our religious communities all over Brazil. We have no need to invoke Greece or the Bible in order to raise it to the status of mythology. On the other hand, Greece and Europe owe to Africa a great deal of what they call 'Western Civilization.'"[11]

Both the play (first performed in 1956) and the film belong to a sixfold intertext: (1) the tradition of updating classical myths and plays, the case, for example, of Eugene O'Neill's *Mourning Becomes Electra* and Jean-Paul Sartre's *Les Mouches;* (2) the more specific tradition of Orphic literature, traceable, as Charles Perrone points out, to symbolist poetry, to Afro Francophone literature, and to Cocteau's Orphic trilogy (*Le Sang d'un Poète* [1930], *Orphée* [1949], and *Le Testament d'Orphée* [1959]); (3) the tradition of black-performed versions of the classics, best exemplified by Orson Welles's "Voodoo *Macbeth*"; (4) the tradition of French fascination with black culture going back to Josephine Baker, *La Revue Nègre,* and even Jean-Paul Sartre's preface to the "Black Orpheus" issue of *Présence Africaine;* (5) the native *negrismo* movement, a kind of subcurrent within Brazilian Modernism; and (6) the tradition of all-black musicals like *Hallelujah* and *Cabin in the Sky.*[12] Whereas the title of de Moraes's play (*Orfeu da Conceição* [Orpheus from Conceição]) made no racial reference, the French and English titles of the film (*Orphée Noir* and *Black Orpheus*) do reference race and echo the title of Jean-Paul Sartre's famous introductory essay to a volume of negritude poetry edited by Senghor. (The Brazilian title of the film was *Orfeu do Carnaval,* again eliding the racial reference.)[13]

The idea of turning *Orfeu da Conceição* into a film also came, indirectly, from a non-Brazilian, in this case the French producer Sacha Gordine, the man who "discovered" Gérard Philippe and Simone Signoret and who happened to have a passion for Brazil. A friend of de Moraes, Gordine was eager to produce a film on a Brazilian theme. The black actor, empresario, and filmmaker Haroldo da Costa, meanwhile, then in Paris with a dance company, offered himself for the title role, provoking instant approval with an impromptu reading of the part. Ultimately, the stage version would feature not only Haroldo da Costa as Orpheus but also many other leading black actors such as Léa Garcia (Mira), Dirce Paiva (Eurydice), and Abdias do Nascimento (Aristeu), along with Cyro Monteiro, Waldir Maia, Pérola Negra, and Ademar Ferreira da Silva (photo 46).[14] The play also featured music coauthored by Antônio Carlos Jobim and de Moraes himself. Sacha Gordine asked the pair to compose new music for the film, partially, it turned out, so that he could monopolize the international rights for himself. Thus the songs from *Black Orpheus,* such as "Manhã de Carnaval" and "O Nosso Amor," some of the most popular ever recorded, brought very little profit to their composers. In any case, de Moraes and Jobim collaborated on "Felicidade," "Frevo," and "O Nosso Amor"; Luiz Bonfá wrote "Manhã de Carnaval" and "Samba de Orfeu." Elizete Cardoso and Agostinho dos Santos dubbed in the voices on the songs.

Despite its French lineage, then, *Black Orpheus* is also Brazilian in that it is based on a Brazilian play; features Brazilian music, Brazilian actors, and Brazilian samba performers; and even used Brazilian film technicians (among the crew, there were only four Frenchmen; the rest were Brazilian). The film combines actual carnival footage from the 1958 carnival with Camus's own staged carnival in 1959. The cast was completely Brazilian, with the single exception of Marpessa Gypsy Dawn, an African American woman formerly from the Katherine Dunham dance troupe, who was cast as Eurydice. The search for actors was long and arduous, involving the screening of thousands of potential participants. In the end, Camus used a mixture of professional actors from the Black Experimental Theater, who worked on the project for the money rather than out of any faith in the film's ideological project, along with professional sambistas and one soccer player—Bruno Mello—as Orpheus.[15]

In play and film, the Orpheus and Eurydice stories underwent a double series of transformations, first between the "original" myth and the play, and then between the play and the film. In the myth, Eurydice's death is unrelated to that of Orpheus; in the film they are fused. Since Gordine found the de Moraes source play somewhat "uncommercial," he asked Jacques Viot to revise it. Marcel Camus and his screenwriter made a number of significant changes from the play. In the play, Orpheus is a bohemian and a sambista; in the film, he is a streetcar conductor. Eurydice is a village girl who comes to the city to visit her cousin and escape from a sinister stranger who wants to kill her. Orpheus and Eurydice fall in love and go to celebrate carnival in the streets, where her enemy, Death, seeks her out and carries her away. Orpheus, heartbroken, goes looking for his lost love at the Bureau of Missing Persons

46. Production still of Léa Garcia for *Black Orpheus*

and then at a macumba rite, where a medium summons up her spirit. In the play, Orpheus's mother is an obstacle to his love for Eurydice; in the film the mother does not even appear as a character. In the play, the women, instigated by Mira, kill Orpheus with knives; in the film, Eurydice falls off the cliff when Mira strikes her with a stone.

At times, the filmmakers even "Brazilianized," or better, "Africanized," the play. In the play, the search for Eurydice in Hades is metaphorized by the name of the samba school in which Orpheus searches for her (Carnival Club from Hell). The film, in contrast, has Orpheus search for Eurydice in a *terreiro* featuring a *caboclo candomblé* with a strong Amerindian element. (The substitution has the unfortunate implication of equating a *terreiro* with hell.) We see a *caboclo pai de santo* puffing on a cigar, wearing a feathered headdress that evokes for the uninitiated Hollywood images of the Indian. (Some scholars posit a Central African Bantu origin for the use of feathers as symbolic of the spirit world.)[16] Hallucinogenic indigenous drugs are evoked after the trance, that is, as a symbol of possession by an Indian spirit rather than as a concrete means to provoke the trance. This use of Afro Brazilian religion provoked a reflex racist reaction on the part of one Brazilian critic, who found the macumba sequence "disagreeable," even though it "does function within a mythic context,"[17] thus exemplifying the prejudices of a colonized elite scornful of Afro Brazilian culture seen as a symptom of "backwardness."

Black Orpheus was diversely received in Brazil. One very interested spectator, Vinícius de Moraes, according to his biographer, was so furious with what was done with his source play that he left the screening room in the middle of the projection. Later, he told friends he found the film full of clichés and superficial notions about Brazil. "Camus missed the pathos of my play," he complained, "He just made an exotic film about Brazil."[18] Many Brazilians were irritated by Marcel Camus's patronizing and uninformed comments. In interviews, Camus described Brazil as a "country without roots, made of transplanted races, without a tradition of expression," where "blacks live in favelas in order to flee from civilization." The Brazilian film critic Walter de Silveira responded that Brazilians were hardly a "people without roots or a tradition of expression. . . . Nor do blacks live in the favelas as an escape from civilization. Blacks live in favelas out of economic necessity. . . . Furthermore, there are many poor and working class whites in the favelas."[19]

Silveira pointed out that although *Black Orpheus* was introduced in Brazil as a "Franco-Brazilian production," in Cannes, where it won the Golden Palm, it was presented as exclusively French. The fascination of the film, he continued, "derives from our national personality, for what is strong and original in our landscape and our people . . . and from the creative work of those persons whose contribution Camus tried to hide: Vinícius de Moraes, Antônio Carlos Jobim, Luiz Bonfá, Antônio Maria, Léa Garcia, Lourdes de Oliveira and other actors."[20] At the same time, Silveira credited Camus with "making a film on Brazilian themes and characters [and] making a film technically superior to Brazilian films," and he praised the film for bringing the beauty of the Portuguese language to the world. The theater critic Sábato Magaldi, in contrast to Moraes, found the film superior to the source play.[21] Similarly, Novais Teixeira praised Camus for capturing the spirit of the play in "an almost miraculous communion of ideas and feeling, especially for a person not from Brazil."[22] Some critics used the film to prod the patriotism of local filmmakers; the success of *Black Orpheus* made Brazilians aware that they had been taking the physical, spiritual, and musical beauty of their country for granted. On a racial level, a number of critics praised the superior "naturalness" of the black actors, scenes that would have been overly sentimentalized by white performers. B. J. Duarte speaks of the blacks performing "with that dramatic and artistic intuition which is uniquely theirs."[23] His essentialist compliments to "natural" talents are of course highly ambiguous: on the one hand they exalt the superior performance of black actors, but on the other they imply that the performance is not the product of art but rather of instinct and intuition.

In the United States, meanwhile, reviewers saw the film through a stereotypical vision of the eroticizing tropics, site of the out-of-control id. Paul V. Beckley wrote of the "sensuous vision" and "noon-hot frenzy" that "strips the skeptical layers of the mind away, suspending the rules of reason and inducing a childlike belief that anything can happen."[24] Bosley Crowther in *The New York Times* raved about "intoxicating samba music, frenzied dancing and violent costumes."[25] In his *New Yorker* review, he spoke of "garishly costumed natives doing the samba with hypnotic fervor to the insistent pulse of multiple brass bands." Apparently unaware that many of the participants (e.g., Lourdes de Oliveira as Mira and Léa Garcia as Serafina) were trained actors from the Black Experimental Theater, or that the female lead was an accomplished dancer, and unaware that members of samba school pageants are highly seasoned performers unintimidated by huge crowds, Crowther praised the "naive quality" emanating from "untrained negro actors."[26]

Some Brazilian critics saw the film as a Frenchman's touristic view of carnival. "The director's camera," Moniz Viana complained, "constantly swerves from its path to point out some touristic curiosity for French audiences."[27] The most acerbic critic was a mysterious journalist named Clauder Rocha—probably a pseudonym for Glauber Rocha—who denounced Camus as an old man who understood nothing about cinema or about Brazil.[28] In the article, entitled "*Orpheus:* Metaphysics in the Favela," Rocha excoriates the Brazilian journalists seduced by Camus's romanticism and by his opportunistic declarations of "love" for Brazil. He censures Brazilian producers for not supporting the many aspiring Brazilian film directors eager to make films but unable even to afford the film stock. The review takes on a biting social edge when Rocha suggests that lyricism is not an appropriate response to the favelas: "A favela is a social disaster, nothing more, nothing less; the question is not of metaphysics but of hunger." For Glauber/Clauder, *Black Orpheus* advanced a mystified vision of carnival and Brazil.[29]

Black Orpheus in many respects constitutes the antithesis of dos Santos's Rio films. Whereas *Rio 40 Graus* was made in quasi-underground conditions and banned by the censors, *Black Orpheus* was pampered with all sorts of advantages. The Kubitschek government cooperated to a degree rarely shown with Brazilian films, receiving Camus personally and offering him many facilities, including the various vehicles and equipment of the Brazilian army. (Orson Welles had also initially benefited from government largesse, although it was subsequently withdrawn.) While *Rio 40 Degrees* was extremely low-budget, *Black Orpheus,* by Brazilian standards, was a superproduction. Camus shot 37,000 meters of film, using only 3,000 meters in the final version. (Brazilian features in this same period generally shot only 6,000 to 10,000 meters for films of comparable length.) Unlike *Rio 40 Graus* and *Rio Zona Norte,* the film depoliticizes carnival by transferring everything to a mythic level; Brazilians, like people everywhere, play out the archetypal patterns furnished by myth. It also depoliticizes samba. In a sophisticated form of "slumming," *Black Orpheus* did for Rio's favelas what *West Side Story,* made not long after, was about to do for the slums of New York (with the important difference that *Black Orpheus* did not ethnically cleanse the slums of black people). The lyrics of Jobim's "Felicidade" tell us that people spend all year working to pay for carnival, but the film itself gives little sense of such hardships. Rather, it offers a highly idealized view of life in the favelas: spacious, cheerfully painted, rustic cabins, complete with colored curtains, metal bed, and menagerie, offering the best views in Rio. Indeed, the film's treatment of the favelas at times resembles a real-estate ad; anyone would love to live there. Indeed, *Black Orpheus* promoted the myth of the *morro* as a mythical space where people are "poor but happy," with samba and carnival playing a major role in that "happiness."

Despite the appeal of its glorious color, *Black Orpheus* is aesthetically conservative; only a chronological coincidence led to the film being seen as part of the nouvelle vague. The film favors horizontal framing, usually in *plan américain,* and the editing lacks both rhythm and a sense of tension and conflict. The camera constantly pans from poor favela to rich city, as if to underline the contrast between the "primitivism" of the *morro* and the modern progress of the city. *Black Orpheus* is framed by Apollonian images of mythological Greek figures portrayed in a frieze, exploded by the entrance of samba musicians. The classical source functions primarily as a legitimating device. A

Western audience recognizes the general myth and the names of some of the characters (Orpheus, Eurydice, Hermes, Cerberus), which thus provide a patina of literary sophistication and "universality" to cover the arbitrary elements of the plot. The possible resonances between Orpheus as shaman and Exu as a figure of mediation and metamorphosis are never explored. Nor is the film ultimately "carnivalesque." The film registers the phenomenal surface of carnival, but Brazilian characters play out the archetypal patterns provided by European myth against a photogenic tropical backdrop. Whereas the carnivalesque proposes a dialectical critique of everyday life, *Black Orpheus* hints at a metaphysical transcendence within an idealized decor. Unlike Vera de Figuereido's later *Samba da Criação do Mundo* (Samba of the Creation of the World, 1979), the film never links carnival to Afro Brazilian mythology. Even though the film includes a macumba ceremony, it never perceives the world of the *orixás* as in some way parallel to the pantheon of the Greeks. Rather than create a synthesis or a counterpoint, it simply superimposes one set of cultural references over another.

What, then, accounts for the manifest and enduring charm of *Black Orpheus*? First, Camus appeals to a myth whose power is rooted in the occidental fascination with love and death: the love that encounters obstacles and which can be fulfilled only beyond the grave (photo 47). As Denis de Rougemont points out in *Love and the Western World,* the Occident has always been fascinated by death-haunted love. The film's masked figure of death in the film betokens this interest as does the penultimate image, the dead lovers cradled in each other's arms. This *Liebestod* theme touches a familiar chord in Western art, the same chord struck by works as diverse as *Romeo and Juliet, Wuthering Heights,* and *Love Story,* just as the final shots of the rising sun suggest the archetype of death and resurrection. Second, the film takes advantage of the spectacular beauty of Rio itself as a kind of tropical Paris set within Yosemite-like granite mountains and placed beside a blue-green Paul Klee sea. The urban topography, in conjunction with colorful carnival costumes, turns the film into a visual paradise, where barefoot Adonises strum enchanting guitars in order to make the sun rise.

Marcel Camus deserves credit for at least transcending conventional Hollywood representations of Latin America and creating a sympathetic portrait of Brazil and of black Brazilians. But what image does *Black Orpheus* offer of black people? The blacks in the film are overwhelmingly likeable, sympathetic,

47. Love and death in Rio: Orpheus and Eurydice in *Black Orpheus*

and creative in their everyday lives. They are not terribly serious, but then why should they be during carnival? On the other hand, we see little of the creative work that goes into a samba school presentation, nor do we see evidence of the high degree of organization required (samba schools are often said to be the best-organized institutions in Brazil). Everything is presented as if spontaneous, giving the European spectator a sense of a carefree tropical "other" playing out a more gratifying life. That life was one to which Europeans were about to gain access, since *Black Orpheus* was made at a time when advances in aeronautics were making tourist travel available on a vast scale. And unlike dos Santos's two Rio films, *Black Orpheus* glosses over such issues as who controls the samba schools and who profits from their performance, issues that might have implications even for *Black Orpheus* itself, a film that made millions around the world and yet brought little to the Brazilian artists who energized the film.

But ultimately the charm of *Black Orpheus* derives from the pulsating energy of carnival itself, with its combination of incomparable percussive force with intensely lyric beauty. The beauty of the film thus lies in what Metz would call the "pro-filmic" elements: the carnival that virtually staged itself before Marcel Camus's cameras. As one of the most gigantic expressions of popular creativity in the world, carnival is a veritable folk opera, mingling various arts such as music, narrative, dance, poetry, and costumes. Camus's image of Brazil is of the tropical carnival, where the pulse of life is expressed in the drums, with the rhythm taking over the soundtrack again and again, driving the actors into a dance forever forming and dissolving and forming again. Setting his mythic fable against such a colorful backdrop provided Camus with a formula for the immense international success the film became.

It was also *Black Orpheus,* more than any other film, that introduced both samba and bossa nova to the world. More accurately, the success of *Black Orpheus* opened doors for the newborn bossa nova, the "modern samba" that the film's soundtrack juxtaposes with traditional samba. "Manhã de Carnaval," with Antônio Maria's lyrics, was recorded over 700 times in the United States alone, and the songs of Tom Jobim and Luiz Bonfá became among the most widely played in the history of world music. After the first samba wave introduced to the world by Carmen Miranda, *Black Orpheus* provoked a second samba wave, thus preparing the way for the explosion of samba and axé music around the world in the 1980s and 1990s. *Black Orpheus* introduced not only street samba but also the *samba canção,* the Zona Sul version of the samba, a kind of "samba lite," more intimist than collective, to be sung by small groups of people in middle-class apartments. Bossa nova was influenced by a wide spectrum of styles, from the 1940s "tunes" of composers like Cole Porter, through the Brazilian music of Dorival Caymmi and Ari Barroso, to the singing styles of Nat King Cole, Frank Sinatra, and Sarah Vaughan and the "cool jazz" of Chet Baker, Gerry Mulligan, and Miles Davis. (In the case of Tom Jobim the influences included Debussy, Ravel, and Villa Lobos.) But musical exchange is always a two-way street: bossa nova, often seen as a whitened samba, can also be seen as a blackened version of the pop crooning of that era.[30] At the same time, *Black Orpheus* did more than any other film to make carnival the symbol of Brazil itself. And Camus should be given credit for emphasizing the blackness not only of Rio's carnival but also of Brazil, something that Brazilian films themselves had tended to shy away from.[31]

The ultimate shallowness and nonrepeatability of Camus's formula—Brazil plus carnival plus literature/myth spells success—becomes obvious in another of his "Brazilian" films, *Otália da Bahia* (Otália from Bahia, 1976), an adaptation of Jorge Amado's *Pastores da Noite* (Shepherds of the Night). Here

48. Mira Fonesca in *Otália da Bahia*

Camus gives free reign to a stereotypical vision that had remained more or less in check in *Black Orpheus. Otália da Bahia* picks up the characters from the source novel—the young prostitute Otália (Mira Fonseca; see photo 48); Massu, son of Ogum (Massu); the *capoeirista* and woman's man Martin (Pitanga); the wise old madman Jesuíno (Jofre Soares)—but bathes them in a chaotic atmosphere of nonstop drinking, passionate laziness, and *malandragem* (street-smart tricksterism). The social protest side of the novel —the favela's resistance against the police—is completely played down. The "joie de vivre" of the Bahians consists of shouting and jumping in and out of the frame. In a life of perpetual parties, every conversation is fueled by *cachaça,* in an atmosphere full of palm oil, spices, sexy mulattas, and golden-hearted prostitutes, as if in demonstration of the "miserably poor but won-derfully happy" cliché that Marcel Camus himself repeated in interviews.[32] In this film, Camus "refolklorizes" the Bahia that was "de-folklorized" in Triguerinho Neto's *Bahia de Todos os Santos* (Bahia of all the Saints, 1960). It is all as if Camus were trying to illustrate the notorious boutade attributed to another French visitor, Charles de Gaulle: "Le Brésil, ce n'est pas un pays sérieux."

CHAPTER 7

Intimations of Blackness,

1960–1962

∞

It is not unreasonable to posit an analogy between the musical movement called bossa nova and the cinematic movement called Cinema Novo. In both movements young people in the late 1950s, especially in Rio de Janeiro, constructed a new art that broke with established patterns. Apart from the common word "new" in their names, the movements were similar in that they rejected "well-made" conventional forms in favor of creative experimentation. Both preferred a difficult, challenging aesthetic, whether expressed in the winding dissonances of the phrasings of João Gilberto or the modernist discontinuities of a Glauber Rocha. Both combined technological minimalism with technical and stylistic maximalism. Just as Antônio Carlos Jobim forged a brilliant synthesis of the erudite and the popular, mingling the influences of Debussy and Ravel with African polyrhythms, so Rocha mingled Sergei Eisenstein and Bertolt Brecht with *cordel* (popular poems sold in pamphlet form) and *candomblé*. The lyrics of one of the bossa nova song-manifestos—"Desafinado"—proudly affirms the right to sing "out of key," that is, in an unconventional way. João Gilberto's guitar style was known as *gago* (stuttering) because it was so haltingly difficult to play. Indeed, this out-of-keyness, the aesthetic of "mistakes" that characterizes both jazz and bossa nova, is itself arguably an Afro-diasporic inheritance. In their essays, and in their films, the Cinema Novo directors claimed a similar right to make "ungrammatical," taboo-breaking films, even if the filmmakers saw this transgressive practice as political, and the *bossa novistas* came to a similar conclusion only later.

Cinema Novo and bossa nova grew out of the same process of cultural renovation that generated the architecture of Brasília (by the Communist Oscar Niemeyer), the "Pedagogy of the Oppressed" theories of Paulo Freire, the "Theater of the Oppressed" strategies of Augusto Boal, and the politicized dramaturgy of Zé Celso's "Oficina" and of Guarnieri's "Teatro de Arena." In social thought, this same period saw the birth of "dependency theory," when André Gunder Frank, then visiting professor in Brasília, revealed that Brazil, contrary to myth, had always been an *exporter* of capital. All cultural areas, in sum, experienced strong currents of critical renovation.

But Cinema Novo was also attuned with international "Third Worldist" currents. As a political coalition, the Third World coalesced around the enthusiasm generated by anticolonial struggles in Vietnam and Algeria, and specifically emerged from the 1955 Bandung Conference of nonaligned African and Asian nations. The cinematic corollary of Third Worldism was "Third Cinema," articulated in such militant manifestos as Solanas and Getino's "Towards a Third Cinema," Rocha's "Aesthetic of Hunger," and Espinosa's "For an Imperfect Cinema." Cinema Novo coalesced as a movement toward the end of the 1950s, when its key directors (Glauber Rocha, Leon Hirszman, Carlos Diegues, Joaquim Pedro de Andrade, Rui Guerra) made their first short films and features. The directors shared an opposition to commercial Brazilian cinema, to the Hollywoodean film aesthetic, and to Brazilian cinema's colonization by American distribution chains. Inspired by the independent production methods and antiestablishment stance of dos Santos's first films, the Cinemanovistas rejected both the tropicalesque conviviality of the *chanchada* and the Europeanized high seriousness of Vera Cruz. Instead, they turned to Italian neorealism and to the French New Wave, the latter less for its thematics than for its reflexive aesthetics and its innovative production strategy of basing independently produced films on the talent of young, auteur-cineastes. These directors saw filmmaking as a political praxis, a contribution to the struggle against neocolonialism and class injustice. They sought out the dark corners of Brazilian life—the favelas and the *sertão*—places where Brazil's social contradictions appeared most dramatically, and places, not coincidentally, where blacks, mulattoes, and mestiços were disproportionally present. Building on dos Santos's pioneering achievements, they thus created the beginnings of a symbolically "black" cinema.

Although not technically a Cinema Novo film, *Bahia de Todos os Santos* (Bahia of all the Saints, 1960) heralded the movement and formed a landmark film both for the history of Brazilian cinema and for the representation of black Brazilians. *Bahia de Todos os Santos* was written, directed, and produced by a Euro-Brazilian director from São Paulo, Triguerinho Neto, then just 29 years of age, who had worked with Alberto Cavalcânti in the early 1950s and who had witnessed the collapse of Vera Cruz. Neto studied filmmaking at the Centro Experimentale in Rome, where his documentary *A Market Is Born* (1958) won first prize from the Italian government. On one level, *Bahia de Todos os Santos* can be seen as an anti–Vera Cruz film, and in this sense it "announces" the Cinema Novo movement. Indeed, its low-budget production methods explain its "roughness": lacking money and film, Neto could not "cover" himself with alternate takes. But the roughness, as occurred with neorealism, also generated the feel of "authenticity"; technical imperfection became the index of experiential authority. Like the neorealists, Neto mingled actors and nonactors. He "discovered" the black actor Antônio Sampaio (Pitanga) who was to become one of the actor-pillars of Cinema Novo as well as one of the first black directors. Sadly, the film's lead actor Jurandir Pimental, who plays the mulatto Tônio, and who was reportedly the director's lover, committed suicide shortly after the film's release. Perhaps as a result, Neto never returned to feature filmmaking.

Although criticized at the time as overly melancholic and disjointed, *Bahia de Todos os Santos* today appears prophetic of the themes and approaches of Cinema Novo. Unlike films such as *Sinhá Moça* (The Plantation Owner's Daughter, 1953) and *João Negrinho* (John the Black Boy; shot 1954, released 1958), the film does not offer a rosy view of "racial democracy"; nor is it set around the safely remote and optimistic period of abolition. More audacious than dos Santos's 1950s films, the film addresses the specifically racial dimension of social oppression. *Bahia de Todos os Santos* is set 20 years before the film's making, during Vargas's Estado Novo (New State), a regime that was especially repressive toward black political movements and such black cultural practices as *candomblé*. The opening shot of a map of Salvador, like the film's title, emphasizes the city itself as protagonist, much as the title and credits of *Rio 40 Graus* (Rio 40 Degrees, 1954) announced that film's urban theme. This highlighting of Salvador forms part of the general rediscovery, in the late 1950s and early 1960s, of the cinematic possibilities opened up by Salvador as the blackest and most Africanized metropolis in Brazil. Yet what is most striking in *Bahia de Todos os Santos* is its distinctly antitouristic bent. Just as dos Santos deromanticized Rio, Neto deromanticized Bahia, which up to that point had always been presented as a nonstop parade of samba dancers, *acarajé* vendors, and *capoeira* performers. Although many Bahians were offended by Neto's downbeat portrayal, fellow Bahian Glauber Rocha saluted the film as the first authentically Bahian film to do without the usual picturesque ingredients. Neto unmasks the misery lurking behind Bahia's potent charms. Rather than display festive, affable people against colonial backdrops, Neto underlines the city's oppressiveness; the mood is heavy rather than euphoric. If Bahia is a paradise for tourists, the film seems to be saying, it can be a hell for its poorer, largely black residents. While Bahia still enjoyed cultural prestige, the film suggests, its economy was obsolete and peripheralized. Indeed, virtually all of the characters are eager to leave what they call a "hole." (Perhaps because of this negative portrayal, the Brazilian government prevented the film from representing Brazil at the Venice Film Festival.)

The film's protagonist Tônio (photo 49) is the Brazilian character who most closely resembles the "tragic mulatto" figure familiar from American films and literature. He is the man "in between": between black mother and white father, between *candomblé* and nightclub, between traditional communitarianism and modern individualism. Eminently rootless, Tônio is the grandson of a *mãe de santo* (priestess), and the son of a black mother and an absent white father. Although scornful of his black parents and grandparents, Tônio also finds little satisfaction in the "fast" world of hustlers and nightclubs. Pimental's beautiful face and graceful movements paradoxically exude an atmosphere of existential anguish. We first encounter Tônio in the port, waiting to pick a rich foreigner's pocket, in the melancholy fetal-like posture he assumes frequently throughout the film. Unhappy but unable to leave, he is as if mummified, a frozen piece of angst on the docks of Salvador. In racial terms, he is seen as quasi-white by black people and as black by white people. A walking contradiction, he rejects his mother and grandmother yet misses them. He hates his father, but gets angry when people say he has no father. Although attracted to a beautiful prostitute (Arassari de Oliveira), he sleeps with an Englishwoman whom he resents. He survives through theft, but uses the loot to help his friends. When the dockworkers go on strike, he supports them, but at a safe distance.

Tônio leads a life of listless hustling along with a multiracial cohort of rest-

49. Tônio (Jurandir Pimental) in *Bahia de Todos os Santos* (1960)

less, unemployed youths, Brazilian versions of the *vitelloni* that inhabit the early films of Fellini and Pasolini. Skeptical about "racial democracy," Tônio tells his white painter friend Crispim that Crispim's life is less difficult because of his whiteness: "They say that everything is easy, that color doesn't matter, but it's just empty words." The indictment of racism in Bahia is especially impressive when one remembers that Bahia had often been portrayed, for example, in Donald Pierson's *Negroes in Bahia: A Study of Race Contact in Bahia,* as the Brazilian region most free from racism.

While the film does show a racially mixed world where black, white, and mulatto hustle together, strike together, and party together without apparent tension, it also points to structural forms of oppression such as the systematic police repression of *candomblé*. When Vargas's soldiers find the priestess Mãe Sabina (Tônio's grandmother, played by the real *mãe de santo* Masu) without a religious permit, which they know she as a priestess cannot obtain, they sweep the *candomblé* statues off the altar, destroying everything they can find. When a soldier lectures her on proper social order—"You portray yourselves

50. Vargas's New State and the *candomblé* priestess

as victims, but you're all just parasites"—Mãe Sabina reacts with proud composure (photo 50). A scene of the *candomblé* faithful scattering before the onslaught of the cassock-like mounted police has a poignancy reminiscent of the portrayal of police repression in Eisenstein's films (see photo 51). The Estado Novo officers are as cruelly impersonal, and as artistically depersonalized, as the cossacks in *Potemkin*. As the officers destroy the objects of worship in a barbarous display of Inquisitionlike violence, the *candomblé* faithful react with dignity: "They think we have to live exactly like them," says Mãe Sabina, "but they can't wipe out what we have in our souls." Glauber Rocha picks up on this theme in his review of the film: "Where is freedom of religion for blacks," he asks, "when police invade macumbas in Rio and blacks in Bahia are exploited as part of the industry of the picturesque?"[1]

Alongside its depiction of religious struggle, *Bahia de Todos os Santos* portrays political struggle, specifically the attempt to form a longshoreman's union. The unionists take advantage of the arrival of an American ship to stage a work stoppage; the strikes are brutally repressed and a docker is killed. The political and religious struggles converge when the fugitive strikers hide

51. The repression of *candomblé: Bahia de Todos os Santos*

in Mãe Sabina's *terreiro* and when a *pai de santo* throws *buzios* (cowrie divination shells) to see if the *orixás* approve of the strike. The fugitive workers, furthermore, are implicitly compared to fugitive slaves. Neither the workers nor the religious community passively accept police aggression. The workers try to seize police guns, while the *candomblé* faithful aid the strikers. The film heightens the repressiveness of the police by having Tônio arrested precisely at a moment when he is literally on the tips of his toes, euphorically dancing a magnificently acrobatic *frevo* (popular syncopated dance from Recife). Seized in mid-dance, Tônio is arrested, it seems, not only for helping the strikers but also as a moving exemplar of Afro-diasporic kinetic culture. Neto further heightens the beauty of the *frevo* by combining the music, played at normal speed, with imaged movement in slow motion, transforming lively popular dance into stylized ballet (see photo 52).

Like many films set in Bahia, *Bahia de Todos os Santos* begins with the sound of the *batuque,* but these African sounds give way to more Europeanized, melancholy, commentative music, music especially associated with Tônio; the muffled weeping of a cello, for example, underlines his sadness. The music

52. Tônio's arrested *frevo* in *Bahia de Todos os Santos*

suggests his distance from the *candomblé* world of his mother and grandmother; at the same time it signals the unorthodox portrayal of Bahia as the
site not of carnivalesque euphoria but rather of economic and even emotional
deprivation. In this sense, the music tears the veil of cliché off the face of Bahia, saturating with sadness and solitude a scene usually presented as festive
and gregarious. The visual style further reinforces this theme. In a kind of
scene usually showered with light, Neto favors a dark tropical expressionism
or baroque neorealism that combines the methods of a Roberto Rossellini
(location shooting, nonprofessional performers) with the passionate dramaturgy of a Luchino Visconti and the critical distance of a Bertolt Brecht. The
acting is understated and convincingly naturalistic, at the opposite pole from
Vera Cruz. The montage refuses spectatorial indulgence; shots (for example
of the slaughtered Pedro lying on the pavement) are cut before they exercise
their full emotional effect. The spectator has to make sense out of a laconic
montage of episodes and emotions.

Bahia de Todos os Santos is remarkably free in its sexual representations. At a
time when *Hiroshima Mon Amour* (1959) was considered scandalous, Neto's
film vibrates with an explosively erotic atmosphere. On a certain level, the

53. Neocolonial allegory: Tônio and Miss Collins

film denounces the sexual exploitation of the black male. Whereas many Hollywood films portrayed the black man as a stereotypical "buck" and a figure of menace, Tônio is depicted as the reluctant sexual object of the white Englishwoman Miss Collins (photo 53). He accuses her of being attracted only to his color; he feels degraded and objectified by her desire. She calls him to bed as if he were a sexual slave. While attracted to him, she also betrays him. Tônio decides to leave her after she insults him and his race, but she takes vengeance by reporting his theft. Tônio is forced into a humiliating dependency; he is constantly prodded toward gratitude: "I did everything for you," Miss Collins upbraids him. Ultimately, he breaks loose, steals her money, and gives it to the strikers.

Miss Collins comes wrapped in the aura of diverse cultural and political associations. In an artful bit of intertextual casting, Neto assigns the role of Miss Collins to Vera Cruz veteran Lola Brah, thus hinting at an association between neocolonial exploitation and colonized cinema and linking her to those the young directors saw as the betrayers of Brazilian cinema. Neto treats Miss Collins in the decadent expressionist style of Vera Cruz dramas, much as Rossellini associated the character Marina in *Rome Open City* (1945) with the decadent aura of the fascist "white telephone" films. Miss Collins evokes both British and American imperialism, the successive exploiters of Brazil's symbolic "body." Tônio's dependency parallels Brazil's; her claim to have "pulled him out of the mud" could have been made by British banks or American multinationals. Yet many Bahians themselves have internalized neo-colonial ideals. "So many people would want her," a friend tells Tônio, "and yet you throw her out."

Not all of the hostility toward Miss Collins has to do with race and nation, however. Some of it derives from misogyny, in this case gay male misogyny. A strong Visconti-like homosexual undercurrent, a kind of gay subtext, energizes the film. The female characters' attraction to Tônio is, one suspects, a projection of the desire of the director, who was in fact sexually involved with the lead actor. On the other hand, the film's sensitivity to racial issues perhaps also derives from the identification felt by a member of one stigmatized group —homosexuals—toward a member of another—blacks. The obverse side of this analogical structure of feeling is the hostility to the woman rival, portrayed as a treacherous exploiter. And even apart from Miss Collins, the film communicates a certain ambivalence about women. The idyllic scenes of male camaraderie, for example, intimate a kind of relief at not being with women. The film suggests a possible alliance between blacks and homosexuals as oppressed groups, unfortunately at the expense of women as objects of mutual hostility.

Bahia de Todos os Santos was diversely received by Brazilian critics. Glauber Rocha saluted the film as a breakthrough auteurist masterpiece, deeply imbued with a spirit of anarchic freedom. If the film had been made in technicolor by foreigners (an obvious allusion to *Black Orpheus,* released the previous year), Rocha suggested provocatively, the critics would have loved it. Walter de Silveira disputed Rocha's claim that the film was avant-garde, arguing that it was merely inept. Others reacted negatively to the harsh portrait of Bahia, and the Brazilian government went to some lengths to prevent the film from being screened in European festivals. But subsequent film history has revealed *Bahia de Todos os Santos* to be a prophetic film that treats many of the themes explored by Brazilian Novo over subsequent decades: Afro Brazilian religion (*Barravento* [The Turning Wind, 1962] and *O Amuleto de Ogum* [Amulet of Ogum, 1974], working-class struggle (*A Queda* and *Eles Não Usam Black Tie* [They Don't Wear Black Tie, 1981]); racial prejudice (*Compasso de Espera* [Marking Time; made 1971, released 1973]), and sexual politics (*Guerra Conjugal* [Conjugal War, 1975] and *Kiss of the Spider Woman*). At the height of developmentalist euphoria, Neto saw developmentalism as a form of neocolonialism. In the optimistically democratic early 1960s, he set his film in a dictatorial period, foreshadowing the coming authoritarianism of the 1964 military coup. In this epoch-making but little-seen film, Neto made the mistake of being ahead of his time. Instead of the Europeanized theatricality of Vera Cruz, he chose an understated yet stylized realism, showing the physically affectionate side of Brazilians along with their gift for ironic repartee. In a period when blacks appeared largely as musicians and entertainers, the film shows blacks as political activists. He also questions the clichéd notion of Brazil as paradise for the mulatto. Rather than subsume black people under the amorphous category of "the people," Neto addresses them in their variegated specificity—as workers, as religious people, as marginals, as policemen.[2]

If in political terms *Bahia de Todos os Santos* gives expression to a kind of anarchist left sensibility, *Cinco Vezes Favela* (Five Times Favela, 1962) is the product of a more orthodox left, that of the Leftist Popular Culture Centers (CPC) of the National Union of Students in Rio from 1961 to 1962. Many of the original members of Cinema Novo were active in the CPC, and many of them participated in *Cinco Vezes Favela*. The CPC consisted largely of radical middle-class students who wanted to use popular culture to push Brazilian society in a progressive direction. Subsidized by the Ministry of Education and Culture prior to the 1964 coup d'état, the CPC tried to connect with the Brazilian masses by staging plays in factories and working-class neighborhoods, producing films and records, and participating in Paulo Freire–style literacy programs.

The CPC had an ambiguous relation to black culture. The CPC's executive director and chief theoretician, Carlos Estevam, outlined the group's official positions in a manifesto called "For a Popular Revolutionary Art." The manifesto combines a rather mechanistic and economistic brand of Marxism with populist voluntarism. It proposes "popular revolutionary art" while dismissing the cultural production of the people as "coarse," "clumsy," and "backwards." Truly revolutionary art, according to this theory, is that produced by middle-class students and intellectuals leading the people to revolution. For black people, the theory is doubly insulting, in that it denies both the validity of black culture and black potential for political leadership, since it is blacks who largely produced the popular culture here dismissed as "clumsy" and "coarse."[3]

Cinco Vezes Favela consists of five short fiction films set in the favelas. To speak of the favelas is automatically to speak of black people, since the favelas are primarily, although not exclusively, inhabited by blacks and mulattoes. All the episodes constitute socially didactic stories. The first, Marcos Farias's "Um Favelado" (A Favelado), revolves around a favela tenant (played by a mulatto actor) beat up by thugs for not paying the rent. The episode portrays hungry *favelados* forced to pick through garbage for food alongside the vultures. Unable to pay, the tenant joins a gang that robs a bus driver, but he is caught while the others escape. The film's didactic messages are quite transparent: (1) *favelados* steal out of necessity; (2) the problem is caused by cruel, high-living landlords; (3) political organizing, not crime, is the solution. Continuing the same theme, Miguel Borgues's "Zé da Cachorra" features the black actor (and future filmmaker) Waldyr Onofre as a worker who defends the *favelados* against exploitative landlords. Carlos Diegues's "Escola de Samba: Alegria de Viver" (Samba School: Joy of Living; photo 54) urges *favelados* to pay less attention to samba parties and more to union organizing. In a didactic bildungsroman, one *favelado* becomes aware of his own alienation and exchanges samba for politics. At the same time, the film respectfully highlights the artistic seriousness and discipline of the samba schools. Joaquim Pedro de Andrade's poetic short "Couro de Gato" (Cat Leather), meanwhile, speaks of the stealing of cats by *favelado* children for the purposes of making tambourines out of the skins. Cats here become a linking device enabling comment on social classes in Brazil: the rich lady with her cats; poor boys stealing cats for tambourines; children, like cats, scrounging for food. The last episode, Leon Hirszman's "Pedreira de São Diogo" (The São Diogo Quarry), has to do with quarry workers and *favelados*. As the quarry face recedes, there is a real danger that the *favelados*' homes, poised on the edge of the cliff, will fall because of the explosions. Although the boss insists they keep working, the *favelados* and the workers cooperate to avert disaster. The challenge is to prevent the explosions but also keep their jobs. The workers therefore tell the *favelados* to appear at the edge of the cliff to dramatize the danger. The message: the working class in conjunction with the marginalized masses can work together to defeat the boss, keep their jobs, and prevent disaster.

Although each episode of *Cinco Vezes Favela* makes a specific point, certain

54. *Cinco Vezes Favela* (1962):
"Escola de Samba: Alegria
de Viver"

themes permeate all the films. Most of the episodes, for example, present landlords and bosses not only as cruel and exploitative, but also as inclined to sexual decadence, signified by sexy molls who smoke and cross their legs while listening to music of a Xavier Cugat variety. One episode ("Zé da Cachorra") even insinuates lesbianism among the molls. Thus the films display a schematic and to some extent puritanical and homophobic sociology derived more from reading orthodox leftist books than from actual contact with the subjects depicted. The social spectrum bifurcates into poor but noble *favelados* on one side and decadent bourgeoisie on the other (photo 55). In what amounts to a microversion of dependency theory, the latter are directly responsible for the misery of the former. There are no industrialists, functionaries, merchants, students, intellectuals, or any other in-between groups. The personal transformations in *Cinco Vezes Favela* are synecdochic: that a character gains consciousness intimates progress for the group as a whole. As Jean-Claude Bernardet points out, the film's episodes illustrate a priori theses; they close off all ambiguity and preempt any interpretations not intended by the authors themselves. Thus although the goal of the films was to politicize and mobilize the audience, the directorial approach encouraged the passive acceptance of prefabricated solutions.[4]

55. Class over race: "Pedreiro de São Diogo"

In racial terms, *Cinco Vezes Favela* portrays the problems of Brazilian blacks as not racial but social, reflecting a fairly standard leftist orthodox position that favored explanations and solutions involving class over those connected to race. Although many of the *favelados* are black, and although their oppressors tend to have lighter skins, the confrontation is not portrayed as racial. People of all colors are shown as oppressed by the same system, defined as capitalist dominated rather than white dominated. The problem is thus one of class oppression, and the solution is revolution, an easy solution for white intellectuals, who might sincerely desire revolution but who rest secure in the knowledge that revolution is not for tomorrow. Nor does a critique of class oppression implicate the white intellectuals in a history of specifically racial privilege and oppression. Blacks, it is implied, should wait for this general revolution and not divide the movement by speaking of racism. For white leftists, class is the answer to the race question. For blacks, as suggested earlier, race remains both a wound in itself and the salt ground into the wounds of class.

One year after *Cinco Vezes Favela* another film about *favelados* was released:

Roberto Farias's *Assalto ao Trem Pagador* (Attack on the Pay Train, 1962). The plot, partially based on actual events, revolves around an attack by six armed men on a Brazilian postal train. During the attack one person is killed and 27 million cruzeiros are stolen. All the thieves—Tião Medonho (Eliezer Gomes), Tonho (Atila Iorio), Edgar, Lino, Cachaça (Grande Otelo), and their leader, Grilo Peru (Reginaldo Faria)—are from the favela. After dividing the money, they begin to spend their take. Grilo Peru slides into a debauched life in the Zona Sul; Tião tries to help his family. After an intense chase, the police capture the criminals, but only after the gang has killed Grilo Peru. What impressed Farias in the real-life story was that few of the thieves had a real vocation for crime; their goals were largely social. One wanted to buy a truck, the other wanted to improve a school, still another hoped for a better life for his children (photo 56).

Assalto ao Trem Pagador was one of the films most screened outside of Brazil in the early 1960s. Audiences in the United States, Canada, and the Soviet Union were surprised to discover a well-made Brazilian thriller exhibiting high technical skills. In generic terms, *Assalto ao Trem Pagador* is a Brazilian film noir. Its subject is crime, and its characters are criminals acting in a

56. Film noir domesticated: Tião in *Assalto ao Trem Pagador* (1962)

treacherous milieu where the solidarity among thieves is in perpetual danger of disintegrating. Even the cinematic style, with its dim lighting and night-time shooting, its careening car-chases around city streets, its venetian blinds casting parallel ribbons of light and shadow, is redolent of film noir. As in film noir, American convertibles serve as cinematic shorthand for the gangsterly good life. Yet the differences are as significant as the similarities. Here there is no femme fatale wrapped in slinky white dresses, and most of the thieves go back to wife and family after the robbery, a domesticity inconceivable in the wifeless, childless, lounge-lizard world of film noir.[5] More important, American film noir of the same period tends not to feature *les noirs,* that is, blacks, while here the band of thieves is interracial: three blacks, three whites, a combination highly unlikely in an equivalent American film of the same period. The tensions in the group, however, are not generally racial; the allegiances and hostilities do not respect racial lines. One of those who betrays the group is black, the other is white; no racial schematism binarizes the discussion. The film does feature one explicitly racial confrontation, however, between Grilo Peru and Tião Medonho. Grilo Peru, a white *favelado* associated with social *arrivisme,* foreign cars, and travel abroad, also happens to be the only character who expresses racist opinions. When Tião learns that Grilo was ready to sell out the group, Grilo taunts Tião: "You're envious of my blue eyes and blonde hair. You thought that money could make you handsome? You're ugly, dirty, sweaty . . . you're destined to live in the favela. All the money in the world won't make you white. I have the face that goes with a beautiful car. You have the face of a monkey!" At this point, Tião shoots him, telling his colleagues: "Throw him in the river so the fish can feed on his beautiful blue eyes." The sequence depicts racism as coming from a socially ascendant white, suggesting a correlation of racism with class opportunism. Although little else in the film suggests the existence of racial prejudice, Grilo's use of a classic racial epithet (blacks as monkeys) is rooted in colonialist and racist discourse. Although the racial confrontation is of a virulence more typically associated with the United States than with Brazil, *Assalto ao Trem Pagador* deserves praise for revealing the subsurface tensions of a country characterized by the "prejudice of no prejudice." Grilo's insult also gives brutal form to the aesthetic valorization of whiteness—a real tendency in Brazilian society reflected as well in the official Brazilian media.

The favela of *Assalto ao Trem Pagador,* like those of *Rio 40 Graus* and *Cinco*

57. Eliezer Gomes and Atila Iorio in *Assalto ao Trem Pagador*

Vezes Favela, though predominantly black, is also multiracial. The presence of poor whites helps obscure the structural aspects of Brazilian racism. If whites are also poor, the reasoning goes, then blacks are not poor simply because they are black. Favela life as portrayed is both oppressively hard but also gentle and human. One eerily prophetic moment, proleptic of the murder of favela children in the 1990s, shows an interracial clutch of children bearing the casket of one of their slaughtered young friends. A drunken Grande Otelo, playing "Cachaça" (Rum), exclaims that people should celebrate the death of a favela child, since one less person is being condemned to a life of misery. (We are reminded of the blind beggar's "One kid less!" response to Jaibo's death in Buñuel's *Los Olvidados* [The Dispossessed, 1950].) But there are also moments of happiness. The appearance of the thieves with their goodies triggers general euphoria, and the community does not inquire too closely into the origins of the "presents."

Within *Assalto em Trem Pagador*'s rich gallery of black characters, Tião Medonho, played by Eliezer Gomes, clearly comes closest to being a hero (photo 57).[6] A postal worker by profession, he steals only in order to improve

58. Wife (Luiza Maranhão) meets mistress (Ruth de Souza)

life for his hard-pressed family. As a slum Robin Hood, he is generous with what he steals. (This situation is not completely unknown in the favelas even today, where some of the top drug dealers support community schools and services, the case of "Escadinha" perhaps being the best-known example.) A domestic hero rather than a flashy gangster or *malandro,* Tião is constantly surrounded by children. Strong, principled, intelligent, he is loving father to two families, and in a larger sense, to the community as a whole. He more than anyone is granted point-of-view shots, and in the end the mise-en-scène transforms him into a Christ figure by visually associating him with crucifixes. He asks his wife not to reveal the whereabouts of the stolen money but only so as to guarantee a better life for his children. While he embraces his child and dies, even the cop who had interrogated him is moved. The impression is not only of a moral giant but also of a proud black man.

Unlike most Brazilian films on black themes, *Assalto ao Trem Pagador* offers especially sympathetic portraits of black women. Tião is involved with two black women, his wife and his mistress, played respectively by Luiza Maranhão and Ruth de Souza(photo 58). Both are portrayed as dignified, loving, responsible. (Indeed they are treated much more sympathetically than the film's white women, largely portrayed as gold diggers.) When the two women

59. Luiza Maranhão in *A Grande Feira* (1962)

meet, Tião tells them: "Now you'll have to be friends." The film's finale focuses on Luiza Maranhão's desperate attempt to keep the secret of the money's whereabouts as the police and the media raid her home. The dismantling of her home is rendered as a violation, a kind of rape. One is left to wonder which is worse, the original assault on the pay train, or this obscene defiling of a family. She finally breaks down and reveals the hiding place, but in such a way that we understand both her initial decision and her ultimate failure to resist such intense pressure. In the treatment of Tião, in the treatment of the two women, and in the general treatment of the favela, the film communicates the quiet dignity and strength of black communitarian culture.

Whereas *Assalto ao Trem Pagador* gives voice to its black characters, Roberto Pires's *A Grande Feira* (Big Market, 1962) merely includes them. The film interweaves two strands of plot. The first plot is amorous, having to do with the love affairs of Roni, a "Swedish" sailor (actually from the South of Brazil) stopping over in Bahia and divided between a decadent upper-class white woman (Ely) and the black woman Maria, the latter herself divided between hopes for a respectable life and the fast life she has been leading (photo 59). The second plot, invoked by the film's title, has to do with a Bahian market ("Feira de Agua de Meninos") threatened by real-estate speculators. The mer-

60. White leftist and black rebel: *A Grande Feira*

chants ask Roni to help them. In the meantime, the "marginal" Chico Diabo (Antônio Sampaio, i.e., Pitanga), outraged by the threat to the fair, plans to take matters into his own hands and blow up the Esso gas tanks next to the market. The police, meanwhile, are after Chico because of some stolen jewelry. A woman named Zazá informs on him; he kills her in revenge. As a pompous politician makes empty promises at the fair, Chico gets ready for his attack on the oil tanks. Maria takes over the microphone to warn people about Chico's plans, but no one believes her except Roni, who rushes to the oil tanks, where he catches Chico just as he is lighting the fuse. Maria tries to put it out, running to the sea with it, but drowns in the attempt. When the people at the fair find out what has happened, they want to lynch Chico, but other people prevent it. Roni, meanwhile, decides to leave town, telling the people of Bahia if they were really ready to make a revolution, he would join them. Ely begs him to stay, but he leaves her.

Although race is downplayed in the film, it is surely no coincidence that it is the black man who is ready to blow things up and the "responsible" white leftist who restrains him (photo 60). In this sense, Chico represents the black man as archetypal rebel-anarchist, a type that Pitanga was often called on to play in the early 1960s. As Jean-Claude Bernardet points out in his critique of the film, *A Grande Feira* presents a schematic view of Brazilian society, bifurcated into lumpen marginals — murderers, beggars, thieves — and decadent bourgeoisie, with the director as intermediary between the two.[7] The white leftist functions as a surrogate for the white, middle-class director. Even his erotic involvements, one with a woman of the people, the other with the decadent, bored socialite, reflect the intellectual artist's ambiguous class situation. The binaristic treatment of Chico Diabo and Roni translates the official left's fear of (1) any revolt not under its leadership, and (2) black revolt and consciousness. The film opts for union organizing as opposed to the adventurist policies pursued by Chico Diabo. At the same time, the Chico Diabo character wins the spectators' sympathy through the passion conveyed by Pitanga's charismatic acting. But Chico's grandstanding gesture backfires, causing the death of an innocent bystander. The film presumably supports union struggle as an alternative but never really outlines what this might mean; the union leader in the film lacks depth and gets lost among the host of secondary characters. In sum, Roni comes to Bahia, gets mildly involved in the struggle, and then leaves, like the spectator who gets involved and then leaves the theater. He seems to throw out a challenge: get serious about revolution and I will join you. But in the end he assumes the attitude of a voyeur and tourist toward the revolution, one who leaves when he gets bored.

The following year brought *Gimba,* an adaptation of a leftist play by Gianfrancesco Guarnieri (author of *They Don't Wear Black Tie*), directed by the well-known theater director Flávio Rangel. Although the film and play share certain themes with Cinema Novo, the aesthetic strategies are completely different. The story concerns a criminal, Gimba (Milton Moraes), who escapes from a São Paulo prison and returns to the Rio favela where he spent his youth. The *favelados* welcome "King Courage" with delirious enthusiasm, but the police are trying to track him down. Gimba is the likeable, resilient, resourceful, and philosophical *malandro,* a figure who is usually black and only rarely white, especially when he—the *malandro* was invariably "he"—comes from the favela. His philosophy is left-wing anarchist; he fantasizes, for example, a scene of naked politicians dancing in the public square. The film's subplots have to do with his relations with his mulatta lover Amélia (Gracinda Freire), and with a young boy admirer named Chiquinho, who feels torn between the attractions of the street and those of respectable life. Gimba kills a cop while rescuing a black *favelada* from police abuse, in a kind of white rescue fantasy that recalls *João Negrinho*. In the heavy-handed ironical ending, the police kill Gimba exactly as he is about to abandon his life of crime. Chiquinho weeps over his dead hero, but it is implied that he will take Gimba's place.

In casting for *Gimba,* Flávio Rangel and his collaborators originally advertised to cast two mulattoes in the principal roles of Gimba and Amélia. Hundreds of persons of color auditioned for the various roles, yet in the end the choice of a white actor for the principal role generated protests on the part of the black artistic community. The Center of Afro-Brazilian culture, along with the Popular Brazilian Theater and the Black Experimental Theater jointly protested the "lack of sensitivity toward black artists" implied by the film's production choices. Key roles, they complained, were not being given to blacks, even though the roles themselves are largely black, noting as well that "We see once again the absurd practice of white actors using makeup to seem darker." The protestors also contrasted the appreciation expressed for Afro Brazilian culture by foreign celebrities—an allusion perhaps both to Orson Welles and Marcel Camus—with the lack of respect shown by Brazilian directors. The letter goes on to list all the black and mulatto performers who could have been used in the film.[8] At least one of the performers mentioned—Ruth de Souza—was cast for the film.

Gimba stresses the solidarity of the favela where virtually no one is ready to denounce the protagonist to the police. Although *Gimba* was filmed in Mangueira (home of one of the most prestigious samba schools), the film's unfortunate choice of a white actor (Milton Moraes) severely compromises the film's integrity from the outset. A similar absurd effect would occur if a white actor, say Tom Cruise, were to star in a black-focalized film about the inner city, though the situations are not strictly parallel, since Brazilian favelas are more racially integrated than American ghettos. *Gimba* suggests a world in which a white *malandro* is adored by black *favelados,* three of whom literally carry him on their back in a spectacular welcome (see photo 61). The privileging of Gimba, whose appearance is that of a Brazilian Sterling Hayden, turns the other actors, many of them black and mulatto, into Thespian subalterns, while turning the favela into a mere decor. Whites, the film inadvertently suggests, have to be superior even in *malandragem*. The seasoned actress Ruth de Souza (photo 62), meanwhile, plays a *macumbeira,* a black Cassandra who is

61. Milton Moraes as king of the *malandros* in *Gimba* (1963)

constantly predicting, and at times producing, disasters. It is she, for example, who arranges a *despacho* against Gimba's lover Amélia. A mere dispenser of hexes, the *macumbeira* is portrayed as an isolated figure rather than a member of a vibrant religious community. While the favela is on one level humanized, domesticated, and normalized, it is also subjected to a dark romanticization in its projection as the titillating site of crime. *Gimba* also suffers from generic indecision, not knowing if it wants to be musical, social drama, film noir, agit-prop, or melodrama. The music, for example, by Carlos Lyra is excellent in its own terms, but does not interface effectively with the image track. Milton Morais's hesitant, tortured imitation of the tics of method acting is also less than convincing. As a white filmmaker's exoticization of popular culture, *Gimba* failed to do justice to its subject. (Other, more successful films will be the subject of our next chapter.)

Paulo César Saraceni's cinema verité documentary feature *Integração Racial* (Racial Integration, 1964), to conclude, treats the same subject as some of the fiction films—Brazil's multiracial reality. The word "racial" in the title is meant in the broadest sense, that is, to apply to all ethnic groups including German and Japanese immigrants. The film opens by foregrounding the black cultural presence, however, by showing an *umbanda* ceremony on a Rio beach. The

62. Ruth de Souza as the *macumbeira* in *Gimba*

filmmakers then interrogate people in the street about their views on racism. Many interviewees, some of them black, exalt "racial democracy." The documented street scenes, with their mix of people of all colors, seem to confirm this impression. "Everyone is treated equally in Brazil," says an elderly white man, and a black man seconds his opinion. But some interviewees also express clearly racist attitudes. "I like all races," says one, "but not blacks." "I would never marry a black or an Indian," says another. A mulatta tells the filmmakers that men find her very sexy, although she doesn't share their opinion. She has had a number of white lovers, she continues, but their mothers did not approve. But against those mothers, she claims, "I love my color." We then go to a *gafieira*, the popular dance halls frequented by black people but recently "discovered" by middle-class whites. In the streets, we see a black man in military uniform, and black women, presumably nannies, taking care of white children. Then we meet two women involved in a "Pudd'n'head Wilson" situation—their babies, one white and the other mulatto—have been exchanged. The black woman explains that although she was surprised by the baby's color, she assumed it was hers and was prepared to love it. The white woman, however, was disappointed with "her" baby. Although her husband told her not to worry since the baby will get lighter later, the white mother didn't like "that color." The filmmakers then play a tape of the black mother's reaction to the white mother, in which the black mother says: "When the other was my child, I loved it as if it were my own." The sequence brings up complex issues. On one level, the black mother was clearly not racist; she accepted the baby no matter what its color, whereas the white mother was intolerant. On the other hand, an ambiguity lingers about the black mother's motivation. Since parents of color often desire a socially useful "whitening" of their children in order to *limpar o sangue* (cleanse the blood) and ease their path in life, it may be that an (imposed) prejudice explains the woman's readiness to accept a surprisingly light baby. The film then goes off to São Paulo for an interview of Italian and Japanese immigrants. A Telephoto lens records soccer games and samba schools, two activities in which people of color predominate, although less today than at the time. At carnival, blacks dressed as aristocrats show unmistakable stylistic flair. The film, in the end, has been inconclusive. While casting doubts about "racial democracy," it has also closed in a hackneyed celebration of blacks during carnival.[9]

CHAPTER 8

Afro Brazilian Religion and the Bahian Renaissance,

1962–1963

∞

Although many Cinema Novo directors at first either ignored African Brazilian religion completely or regarded it as alienated and marginal, something to be tolerated or reformed by well-meaning secular leftists, these attitudes began to change with the "Bahian Renaissance"—the cinematic rediscovery of the cultural riches of Salvador, Bahia, in the early 1960s, a movement that generated such films as Trigueirinho Neto's *Bahia de Todos os Santos* (Bahia of All the Saints, 1960), Anselmo Duarte's *O Pagador de Promessas* (The Given Word, 1962), Glauber Rocha's *Barravento* (The Turning Wind, 1962), and Roberto Pires's *A Grande Feira* (The Big Market, 1962). Bahia's "mystique," as Antônio Risério points out, rests on three "legs": historical antiquity (Bahia as colonial capital), natural and architectural beauty (the ocean, the bay, the old and new city), and cultural originality (the strength of Afro Brazilian culture). A city at once Portuguese, Bantu, and Yoruba, Bahia is the charismatic center both of Catholicism, with hundreds of churches, and *candomblé,* with *terreiros* going back to the Iya Nasso's founding house of worship in 1830. (A 1980 census registered 1,500 *candomblé* centers in Salvador.)[1] Yoruba religion is particularly strong there because the Yoruba arrived constantly during the latter decades of slavery, because they entered into an urbanized lifestyle in many ways reminiscent of that from which they came—Yorubaland also being highly urbanized, with cities like Lagos, Ibadan, and Oio—and also because Bahia maintained close cultural and commercial contact with West Africa.[2]

Given the Afro Brazilian religious themes popular in the Bahian Renaissance films, some further background is indispensable. And since the media generally relay a Eurocentric vision of African spirit religions as superstitious, quasi-demonic cults rather than as legitimate belief-systems, we may begin by clearing away the rubble of some deeply sedimented prejudices. These prejudices are enshrined in the patronizing vocabulary ("animism," "ancestor worship," "magic," "fetishes," "cults") used to speak about African religions. The very phrase "African religions" is on one level a misnomer that purveys the myth of a unitary Africa, since virtually all of the world's religions can be found on the African continent.[3] By the same token, African religions are present in the United States; one finds *candomblé* and *santería* in New York, just as one finds Pentecostalists and Jehovah's Witnesses in Brazil. A set of superimposed hierarchies work to the detriment of African spirit—religions specifically. First, the religions are seen as oral rather than written, and therefore as lacking the scriptural authority and cultural imprimatur of the "religions of the book." In fact, however, the "text" simply takes a distinct semiotic form, whether performative or verbal-musical, as in Yoruba praise songs dedicated to the *orixás*. Second, spirit religions are mistakenly seen as polytheistic rather than monotheistic, a debatable hierarchy in any case and a misrepresentation of most African religions. In Yoruba religion the figure of Olodumare (Supreme Being), also known as Olorum (Master of the Skies), refers to an overarching, nonrepresentable, divine principle or vital force reigning over the specific *orixás* with their anthropomorphic personalities. Third, African spirit religions are seen as superstitious rather than scientific, a view deriving from the positivist genealogy of religion as historically moving from myth to theology to science, itself a secularization of earlier notions of religious providence, now sublimated into the more "scientific" idea of "progress." But religions are not arranged in hierarchies of relative rationality; all religions involve a leap of faith, whether in the form of a belief in the Virgin Birth or the resurrection of Christ, or simply of trust in an invisible yet all-powerful supreme Being. African trance religions might even be said to be more open to scientific thinking in that they insist less on rigid dogmas than on practical questions of *axé*. For Moniz Sodré, African religions are radically "ecological," promoting a spirit of "confraternization" with plants, animals, and minerals.[4] If on one level extremely pragmatic, African religions can be seen on another as theoretical and speculative; Karin Barber of the University of Ife (Nigeria) has discerned commonalities shared by poststructuralist theory and by Yoruba *oriki* praise poetry, specifically indeterminacy, intertextuality, and constant variability.[5] Fourth, African trance religions are belittled as corporeal and ludic (danced) rather than abstractly and austerely theological, a prejudice rooted in Manichean ideas of the flesh as inherently evil and in puritanical hostility to bodily pleasures. Fifth, the African religions are seen as insufficiently sublimated in that they involve literal animal sacrifice rather than symbolic or historically commemorative sacrifice. This hierarchy posits more abstract religions as superior, yet religious theorist René Girard sees the scapegoating mechanism—found in the Jewish Bible's sacrifice (by Abraham) of a ram instead of Isaac, in Christianity's idea of the crucifixion, and in the animal sacrifice of African religions—as central to all religious cultures. Fifth, the trance religions are seen as wildly gregarious, drowning the individual personality in the collective and transpersonal fusions of trance, thus disrespecting the unitary, bounded consciousness. The Christian ideal of the *visio intellectualis* flees in horror from the plural trances and visions of the spirit religions of Africa and of many indigenous peoples.[6] In sum, the occidental habit of hierarchizing religions into "real" religion of the book and false "cults" and "fetishes" is misleading and prejudicial.

Diasporic syncretic religions of African origin are almost invariably caricatured in the dominant media. The affiliation of such Hollywood "voodoo" films as *Voodoo Man* (1944), *Voodoo Woman* (1957), and *Voodoo Island* (1957) with the horror genre betrays a viscerally phobic attitude toward African religion, historically rooted in the association of Vodun with the revolts of Haitian slaves. Moreover, recent films show only minimal progress in this regard. *The Believers* (1986) presents the Afro Caribbean religion *santería* as a cult dominated by ritual child-murderers, in a manner reminiscent of the "unspeakable rites" invoked by colonialist literature. Other films eroticize African religion in a way that betrays ambivalent attraction and repulsion. *Angel Heart* (1987) has Lisa Bonet, as Epiphany Proudfoot, the voodoo priestess, thrash around with Mickey Rourke in a sanguinary love scene. Another Mickey Rourke vehicle, *Wild Orchid* (1989), exploits the religious atmosphere of *candomblé* as an "Afro-dysiac."[7] The Michael Caine comedy *Blame It on Rio* (1984), in the same vein, stages *umbanda* as a frenetic beach orgy in which the *mãe de santo* doles out amorous advice in English to tourists while accelerating rhythms excite the celebrants to take off their clothes and fling themselves in the surf.[8] Nor are prejudicial representations of Afro Brazilian religions completely unknown within Brazilian cinema itself. In *As Noites de Iemanjá*

(Iemanjá's Nights, 1981) a bored housewife (Joana Fomm) witnesses a *candomblé* ceremony, goes into trance, and is transformed into Iemanjá, seducing a series of men into the sea during the act of love. The promotional materials for the film reflect a process of diabolization: "Diabolic! Seductive! . . . Possessed by forbidden rites, she emerges from the waves to destroy men." Iemanjá becomes conflated with a whole series of misogynistic myths: Eve, Pandora, the sirens, the Lorelei, and Iara, the voracious seductress of the Amazon.

A good deal of speculation centers on the historical origins, the social function, and the ongoing power of Brazilian syncretism. Whereas traditional African religions in the United States were subject to systematic devastation, in Brazil the religions were able to survive more or less intact. The religions' survival in the wake of the Middle Passage is usually explained by the fact that slaves from the same ethnic group were kept together to encourage "local" cultural identifications and thus undermine any united Pan-African-Brazilian consciousness. Historians also stress the ongoing influx of Africans into a very late period; the arrival in Bahia of Africans from Yorubaland late in the nineteenth century, for example, facilitated a vigorous communitarian religious expression. The most common and persuasive explanation of syncretism is that since African religions were forbidden during slavery, blacks simply pretended to worship the Christian God and the Catholic saints while internally worshipping their own *orixás*. Syncretism in this sense can be seen as a popular exercise in comparative religion, a search for affinities and correlations on which to base an acceptable religious practice. Another perspective sees syncretism as a means of social ascension; that is, blacks in Brazil sensed the advantages to be gained by assimilating into the religion that exercised social power. Indeed, some analysts contrast the daylight co-optability of *umbanda* with the subversive midnight rituals of Bantu-dominated *quimbanda* (mislabeled "black magic"), viewing the latter as the revolutionary religion that retains the memory of the Middle Passage and the *quilombos*.[9] Although it is hard to imagine *candomblé* fitting neatly into the schemas of psychoanalysis, another common interpretation sees different religious traditions as serving similar psychic needs: the Virgin Mary, like Iemanjá, is rooted in the need for a mother figure; the Exu, like the Christian devil, is a phallic Id kind of figure; the *pomba-gira* (the female persona or wife of Exu) is a metaphor for unbridled sexual desire, and so forth.[10] In any case through religion Afro Brazilians conserved traces of an African cosmovision; they found an alternative to the hegemonic systems that denied dignity to blacks and a way to reconstruct identity in the Americas. If the *quilombos* were a form of political resistance, Afro Brazilian religions were a form of cultural resistance.

The core of most of the west African religions practiced in Brazil is the notion of trance or divine possession, the idea of a spirit that "rides" or takes possession of a human being. The phenomenon of spirit possession, by which the responsibility for a person's ritual behavior is assumed by a spiritual entity, has existed everywhere in the world, including in Europe, but in ecstasy-phobic Western society it has generally come to be seen as aberrant behavior. The substratal memory of such practices is betrayed, however, in such expressions as "what got into you?" or "what possessed you?" and their aura still lingers around words like "charm" and "hex" and "enchantment." In west African religions, the *orixás* manifest themselves in the bodily behavior of the believers. The sacred rhythms of the drums, as Mabille puts it, "reach the depths of their being and make them the playthings of the gods who possess them."[11] Rather than an anguished, guilt-ridden, quasi-private dialogue with God à la Puritanism, African religion is gregarious, based on collective participation in ritualized ecstasies. As a voice-over in David Byrne's film *Ilê Aiyê* (1989) puts it: "They threw a party for the gods, and the gods came."

In contrast with a "high" Christianity that emphasizes humble submission to God in postures of subservience and "looking up," and the effacement of the body within a dualistic metaphysic, African religions see the body as gloriously displaying the divine. In spatial, metaphorical terms, human beings do not painfully "ascend" toward God; rather, the gods "descend" into human beings. Spirit possession is in this sense the supreme religious act expressing the fundamental nature of the relationship between human beings and their deities. The possession of the faithful by spiritual beings is thus an important sacramental expression around the Afro-diaspora. In the United States, as Harold Bloom puts it, African Americans made Jesus black; white southern Baptists "came to worship an essentially black Jesus."[12] The difference between Afro American and Afro Brazilian religious practices is that the personalities of the individual *orixás* have been preserved in Brazil, and not just the general spirit of trance and possession. In Brazil, each dance gives expression to the history and personality of the *orixá*; Ogum mimics the thrusts of his sword, Iansã whirls in windy tempests, and so forth. Originally local culture heroes or deified ancestors, the *orixás* generally incarnate human characteristics: they marry, have children, quarrel, and have distinct preferences in terms of colors, foods, drink, and rhythms, rather like the Greek gods. The site of multiple personality traits, they have pleasant and unpleasant aspects.

In terms of sexual politics, the constitutive bisexuality of the *orixás*, and the fact that men can be possessed by female deities and vice versa, can be considered a "feminist" advance over Judaism and Islam, with their very patriarchal conceptions of the Deity, and over Christianity, with its masculine triad of Father, Son, and a sexually ambiguous Holy Ghost expressed in phallic symbols like birds and tongues of flame. Vera Figueiredo's film *Samba da Criação do Mundo* (Samba of the Creation of the World, 1979; see photo 63) tells the story of the mating of the *orixás* to create the world, while her *Pomba Gira: Deusa do Amor* (Pomba Gira, Goddess of Love) plans to offer a feminist interpretation of a figure in *umbanda,* the *pomba-gira* who embodies female mischievousness and creativity. The *ialorixás* (priestesses) of *candomblé* are very powerful, even venerated, figures; they are *mães* (mothers) not of a nuclear family but of a community.[13] It was no accident that Ruth Landes titled her study of Bahia *The City of Women.*[14] Nor is *candomblé* repressive toward homosexuality. In the 1940s, Ruth Landes noted that although women dominated the traditional *terreiros,* homosexual men dominated the others. Many male priests wear female dress and hairdos, and priests are referred to as "wives" of the *orixás* regardless of gender. Analysts speculate that homosexual men saw *candomblé* as a way of identifying with women, noting that the metaphor of the "divine horsemen" who are "mounted" by the saints easily takes on a sexual resonance of corporeal penetrability. The initiates are called the *iao* (wives) of the saints as well.[15] The film *A Prova de Fogo* (Trial by Fire, 1981) touches on some of these issues, as does Eunice Gutman's *Feminino Sagrado* (Sacred Feminine, 1996), which compares the role of women in Judaism, Christianity, and *candomblé.*

The *jouissance* of Brazilian carnival is often concretely linked to the expression of religious groups. In this sense, one might compare the spiritual and secular relation between gospel and blues in the United States with that of *candomblé* and carnival in Brazil, although the lines are less clearly drawn in Brazil. The Bahian *bloco* (carnival group) "Filhos de Gandhi," founded in 1948, for example, secularized the rhythms of *candomblé* at a time when *candomblé* was officially proscribed. In a religion where "soul claps its hands

63. *Samba da Criação do Mundo* (1979)

and sings," the faithful are also performers; they dance and sing, the mediums above all, but also the witnesses for whose collective benefit the ritual is performed. Like carnival, *candomblé* is a kind of *festa* (celebration) played out in an atmosphere of collective enthusiasm. Bahians even attend "play *candomblés*" uniquely in order to dance and sing. Like carnival, *candomblé* too can be seen as an inspired form of role-playing, an exercise in experiential alterity. In *candomblé,* a black woman in her 30s, whose saint is Ibeji (the sacred twins), can metamorphose into a six-year-old boy with an infantile voice and manner.[16] Physical attitudes and the body itself change. Roger Bastide describes an invariably cheerful woman of his acquaintance becoming "cruel and serious; her lips protrude, full of disdain; her head is firm, her manner that of a monarch; she has become Xangô."[17] Both carnival and *candomblé,* in sum, set in motion a complex play of identities, a dance of positionalities, a creative dialogue, often transgender and transracial, between self and other. Just as carnival transforms a *favelado* into an aristocrat, spirit possession turns a cook or a maid into the ruler of sea or storm, into Iemanjá or Iansã. Just as carnival transforms adults into children and proliferates in infantile imagery, the adult reveler drinking rum from a baby bottle, for example, so in *candomblé* an elderly woman can enact the adolescent ecstacies of young gods, and young people can incarnate the slow, shuffling movements of older *orixás*.

The gregarious mysticism of Afro Brazilian religious expression is symbiotically linked both to carnival and to black performance in general. Performance and the arts, dance and song and spectacle, are at the very kernel of African trance religions. If the drums don't play, the gods don't come. As Robert Farris Thompson points out, art participates in the ritual process not only by honoring the deities but also by calling them into presence and action. Sacred objects incarnate *axé* and ritual efficacy.[18] The arts—costume, dance, poetry, music—create the appropriate atmosphere for worship. Olodumare, as creator of the Universe, can be seen as the greatest artist, and any of the *orixás* are not only artists (Ogum as the patron-deity of metalsmiths and carvers) but they also have artistic tastes. The notion that the classical Greek pantheon is noble and beautiful and at the very roots of Western civilization, while the gods of Africa are merely the vestigial superstitions of a backward and remote people, also belongs in the trash can of Eurocentric prejudices. As poetic figures, the *orixás* now play an artistic role in Africa and the diaspora akin to the role of the classical deities of the Greek pantheon within literature, painting, and sculpture. For Henry Louis Gates, the Yoruba trickster figure Exu-Legba provides the germ of the deconstructive "signifying" aesthetic of African American literary narrative.[19] The *orixás* permeate the sculpture of "Mestre Didi" (Deoscoredes M. dos Santos), the photography of Pierre Verger, the painting of Carybé, the plays of Wole Soyinka, and the music of Olodum, Ilê Aiyê, and Timbalada, not to mention Paul Simon and David Byrne. Indeed, Arturo Lindsay speaks of a "neo-Yoruba" genre of contemporary art.[20]

I do not mean to idealize Afro Brazilian religions. Like all religions, they are susceptible to charlatanism, mundane power struggles, or commercial exploitation. But the world of the *orixás* is not the fossilized or disappearing world that the patronizing vocabulary of "survivals," "vestiges," and "reminiscences" would suggest but rather an evolving and cosmopolitan one. Of the hundreds of *orixás* of which the African tradition speaks, only a small proportion survived slavery and the Middle Passage, and the signification of those who have survived has changed with dislocations in time and space. If Ogum was associated with the spread of iron-making technology in sub-Saharan Africa over two millennia ago, he is now recoded, in films like *Antônio das Mortes* (1969) and *Amuleto de Ogum* (Amulet of Ogum, 1974) as a New World

64. Obaluaye, *orixá* of plagues in *Odo Ya! Life with AIDS*

symbol of the struggle against social oppression. Tania Cypriani is currently finishing a film called *Odo Ya! Life with AIDS,* a video documentary about AIDS education programs that use the language, symbols, and culture of *candomblé*—for example, Obaluaye, the *orixá* of plagues (photo 64)—for purposes of AIDS education and prevention. Under the rubric *Odo Ya,* a salutation to Iemanjá as a symbol of life and hope, these programs have developed manuals, cartoon pamphlets, and a newsletter. The campaigns stress the positive nature of sexuality as a form of *axé* while emphasizing the need to preserve life.

Two 1962 films, *Pagador de Promessas* and *Barravento,* focus on the issue of Afro Brazilian religion. The director of *Pagador de Promessas,* Anselmo Duarte, had been a leading man both in the *chanchadas* and in the Vera Cruz films, and his film exists at the point of convergence of three cinematic currents: it has the humor and popularesque appeal of the *chanchada,* the high production values of Vera Cruz (and thus indirectly of Hollywood), and the typical actors and social preoccupations of Cinema Novo. The combination ultimately seduced the jurors at the Cannes Film Festival, where the film won the Golden Palm in competition with such films as Luis Buñuel's *Exterminating Angel* (1962), Bresson's *Trial of Joan of Arc* (1962), and Richardson's *A Taste of Honey* (1962). Many were skeptical about the film's possibilities. The French novelist Christiane Rochefort, who happened to be one of Duarte's lovers, reportedly told him that as a Brazilian he should not expect to win but should be content simply to be in the competition.[21] But according to Duarte himself and other witnesses, another jury member, Francois Truffaut, was especially sympathetic to the film's rebellious Catholicism.[22] Subsequently, the film won many prizes around the world. Duarte was even invited to the White House to show the film to John F. Kennedy, who reportedly thought the film "a masterpiece." Duarte reports that he took advantage of the encounter to denounce to the American president an asymmetrical cultural situation in which "Brazil bought the distribution rights to 600 American films every year, while the U.S. bought none."[23]

To prepare himself for the filming, Duarte immersed himself in Bahian culture, reading up on the city's history, studying the locations, and learning to play the *berimbau,* which he himself played for the soundtrack. (Duarte reports that when the French composer Darius Milhaud handed him the "Best Music Prize" at Cannes he inquired about that "exquisitely melancholy instrument.")[24] Based on the stage play by Dias Gomes, the rights to which cost the highest amount ever paid in Brazil, *Pagador de Promessas* centers on the vow of its peasant protagonist "Zé-of-the-Donkey" to bring a cross to the Church of Saint Barbara in gratitude for the miraculous cure of his donkey (photo 65). Because the vow was proffered in a *candomblé* shrine, the Catholic priest refuses him entrance. Zé does not give up, however; he remains on the church steps. Inexorably, the whole town becomes involved with his dilemma. Zé becomes the victim of a tragicomedy involving diverse people and institutions. *Cordel* poets write about him, and the press turns him into a political symbol, manipulating his naive words to portray him as a left-wing revolutionary favoring agrarian reform. The official church, meanwhile, denounces him as a heretic, while the common people project him as the incarnation of their hopes and dreams. Zé becomes a kind of Christ figure; he sacrifices himself and resists temptation. The people of Bahia, largely black and mulatto, support his struggle. When he is killed by the police, they solemnly

65. Zé in the *terreiro: Pagador de Promessas*

carry him into the church, borne on the very cross that he carried for such a long distance.

Dias Gomes's source play was popular in subject but classical in manner, scrupulously respecting the three neoclassical "Aristotelian" unities of place (all the action transpires in front of the church), time (the events take place within a 24-hour period), and action (the entire story centers on the consequences of Zé's vow). The film adaptation retains unity of time and action but attempts to "open up" and cinematize the closed space of the play by introducing a dozen sequences set in the *sertão*, in newspaper offices, on the docks, in the *terreiro*, and so forth. In terms of production methods and values, *Pagador de Promessas* follows a middle course between the low-budget aggressivity of Cinema Novo and the glossy production values of Vera Cruz. Indeed, the film's production company, Cinedistri, was one of the São Paulo companies formed in the 1950s in the mold of Vera Cruz, and the film's cinematographer, Chick Fowle, the man who lit Olivier's *Hamlet*, was one of the British technicians that Alberto Cavalcânti brought to Vera Cruz from Europe; Fowle uses Salvador's bright sunlight to good effect to achieve maximum depth of field. Aesthetically, the film represents what Glauber Rocha called "coconut milk in a Coca Cola bottle," that is, it packages Brazilian cultural practices like samba

66. The *roda de capoeira* in *Pagador de Promessas*

and the Afro Brazilian dance/martial art *capoeira* in a form largely derivative of Hollywood (photo 66). Like the Vera Cruz films, *Pagador de Promessas* uses conventional Hollywood devices, including classical framing, elaborate lighting, fluid cutting and camera movement, emotionally manipulative commentative music, and shot-reverse-shot for dialogue, all in the name of fluid, well-conducted entertainment. In his analysis of the film, Ismail Xavier stresses the film's "redundancy," its constant concern with causal and motivational clarity, for example, through the schematic play of low- and high-angle camera during the conversation on the steps between Father Olavo and Zé-of-the-Donkey, or the use of foil characters, with the cynical gigolo "Handsome" played off against the naive and innocent Zé.[25]

Anticlerical rather than anti-Christian, the film contrasts Zé's sincere Christlike faith with the ossified hierarchical Christianity of the priest. Father Olavo "diabolizes" African religions; he sees them as the work of the devil (photo 67). In the background, of course, is the historical repression of African religions in Brazil, of *xangô* in Alagoas in the 1920s and in Pernambuco in the 1930s and of *candomblé* throughout the first half of the twentieth century. On one level, the film satirizes official Catholicism, which led to the film be-

67. The priest versus *macumba* in *Pagador de Promessas*

ing banned by the Catholic Church in both Italy and Spain. Both the *galego* (Galician) barman and the *cordel* poet see the church as chiefly interested in protecting its "business" against its more popular rivals. On another level, the film deploys elements of Christian allegory. Zé-of-the-Donkey is associated with Christ; he rides into down on a donkey, he carries his cross, he is tested by temptation, and he is called a "new Christ" by the media. The monseigneur, meanwhile, is associated with Pontius Pilate; "Bonitão" with Judas; Marli with Mary Magdalene.

Although *candomblé* motivates the plot, in that the entire film flows from the fact that Zé's vow in a *terreiro,* in another sense *candomblé* is peripheral, in that the film never brings us into its world. In the opening sequence, Duarte already underlines Zé's separation from *candomblé* by showing Zé alone, kneeling in a posture of Christian humility before a Catholic-style altar featuring an icon of Saint Barbara, while the collectivity sings and dances. The suggestion, from the outset, is that Zé "is really a Christian at heart," an impression reinforced by his repeated refusals of the *mãe de santo*'s invitations to the *terreiro.* (The film, too, refuses the *mãe de santo*'s invitations.) His discourse, as Ismail Xavier points out, is double and contradictory. To Padre Olavo, he insists that Iansã and Saint Barbara are the same, but to the *mãe de santo* he argues the opposite. In social terms, the film evokes a kind of microcosmic revolution by having the people take over a prestigious institution, yet the "revolution" consists, ultimately, only in gaining entrance to a more ecumenically tolerant Catholic Church, not in adherence to *candomblé,* nor in the inauguration of a revolutionary alternative.[26] Although it portrays the official church as authoritarian, formalistic, and intolerant, the film is, in the end, integrationist. Zé catalyzes a larger struggle whose goals are ultimately apolitical. His sacrifices energize the masses, who come to legitimate a Catholic vow that happened to be made in a *terreiro.* Thus the real choice presented is not between Catholicism and *candomblé,* or even between Catholicism and revolution, but rather between a dogmatic Catholicism and a humane, ecumenical Catholicism. (The film was made in the liberal period of Pope John XXIII and the Ecumenical Council.) In the 1980s, to flash forward, Tizuka Yamasaki directed a TV series based on *Pagador de Promessas,* but it was censored by Roberto Marinho, owner of Globo TV network, for supporting land reform.

The style of Glauber Rocha's *Barravento* is completely antithetical to that of *Pagador de Promessas.* Whereas *Pagador de Promessas* was relatively high budget by Brazilian standards—the director paid $20,000 for the rights to the source play—*Barravento* reportedly cost only $3,000. While *Pagador de Promessas* featured well-known actors from theater, television, and film, *Barravento* featured mainly nonactors or beginning actors. If *Pagador de Promessas* was a quasi-industrial production, *Barravento* was artisanal, improvised, and collaborative, using minimal equipment (one tripod, one Arriflex camera, 6,000 meters of donated film). *Pagador de Promessas* is full of "pretty effects," whereas Rocha in *Barravento* deliberately eschewed picturesqueness, asking Tony Rabatony, his director of photography, to avoid all aestheticism. While *Pagador de Promessas* clarifies spatial and temporal relations at all times, *Barravento* is purposefully ambiguous about such issues. If the structure of *Pagador de Promessas* is unified, with clear causality—everything revolves around the vow and its realization—*Barravento* is characterized by rupture and discontinuity. *Pagador de Promessas'* Hollywoodean, redundant, and conventional style contrasts with that of *Barravento's,* which is elliptical, obscure, discontinuous, and influenced by Sergei Eisenstein and by Bertolt Brecht, whose *Threepenny Opera* opened during the final phase of the filming. While *Pagador de Promessas* uses conventional European-inspired commentative music, guiding our feelings at every turn, *Barravento* uses Afro Brazilian music—ritual chants, work songs, sambas, percussion—in a structural way.

If *Pagador de Promessas* implicitly condemns *candomblé* from the point of view of a renovated Catholicism, *Barravento* would seem to critique *candomblé* from the standpoint of historical materialism. But any evaluation of the film's ideological stance must take into account the film's complex and conflictual production history. The first script was by Luis Paulino dos Santos, a Bahian whose background was largely in documentary filmmaking. Brought up in Pelourinho, the traditional black quarters of the center of Salvador, dos Santos's family was intimately linked to *candomblé*. His initial script was relatively apolitical and uncritical of the religion. When Luis Paulino dos Santos began production, however, he fought with the film's producer, Rex Schindler—whom Glauber Rocha describes as a "Jewish mulatto visionary"—who asked for a more critical stance toward *candomblé*. For diverse reasons, Luis Paulino dos Santos left the film and was replaced by Rocha, then 21 years old.[27] Rocha described the original script disparagingly as a "Mexican love story" and gave the following version of the changes he made in the script: "I reorganized black mythology according to the dialectics of religion/economy. Religion as the opium of the people. Down with the Father! Long live human beings fishing with nets. Down with prayers! Down with mysticism!"[28] Rocha's stated goal in *Barravento* was to show that "underneath the forms of exoticism and decorative beauty of Afro-Brazilian mysticism there dwells a hungry, illiterate, nostalgic and enslaved race."[29] According to actor Antônio Pitanga, Rocha's version was far superior to Luis Paulinho's "merely amorous" script: "*Barravento* was a political-cultural manifesto in favor of the black liberation struggle."[30]

On a first reading, *Barravento* does show the oppression inflicted on poor black fisherman and apparently critiques *candomblé* as a distraction from political struggle (photo 68). The protagonist Firmino (Antônio Pitanga), just back from the city, tells his brothers and sisters to forsake religion and organize to fight oppression. In the village, the fishermen rent a net from an absentee capitalist; *candomblé* seems to legitimate the system in that the fishing *mestre* (master) negotiates with the net's owner, who takes the lion's share of the profits while the fishermen remain poor. Although the *mestre* complains that the fishermen are going hungry, he does not push his demands with sufficient energy.[31] Meanwhile, Firmino confronts Aruã, a young man protected

68. The fishermen in *Barravento* (1962)

by Iemanjá and destined to inherit the *mestre*'s role. Firmino, the self-proclaimed agnostic, paradoxically tries to cast a *despacho* against Aruã, but it is
ineffective. Then Firmino cuts the net as a provocation. But when the boss
comes to take back the damaged net, the fishermen simply return to the old
life-threatening days of the *jangadas*. Firmino decides to demystify Aruã once
and all by having his girlfriend Cota seduce him. Parallel montage juxtaposes
the stages in the ritual preparation of Aruã's girlfriend, Naina, a shy white girl
frightened by her own mediumistic powers, with the story of Cota's seduction of Aruã. The initiatory blood ritual is made to alternate with the sexual
initiation at the beach, while both series of images are underlined by
candomblé drumming. The next day, a *barravento* comes up, leading to the
mysterious deaths of Naina's stepfather and of Cota herself. Firmino and
Aruã fight via *capoeira*, and at the end of the fight Firmino tells the community to follow Aruã as the new leader. The flame of political leadership thus
passes from Firmino to Aruã. Firmino disappears from the scene as magically
as he first came, while Aruã plans to go the city, buy a net, and come back so
as to relieve the community's suffering.

Barravento's prefatory intertitles offer a Marxist perspective on religion as a kind of "opium of the people" that prevents the fishermen from mobilizing for change:

> The seacoast of Bahia is the home of black fishermen whose ancestors came from Africa as slaves. There they still worship the African gods and are dominated by a tragic and fatalistic mysticism. They accept misery, illiteracy, and exploitation with the passivity typical of those who await the coming of the Kingdom of God.
>
> Iemanjá is the queen of the waters, the lady of the sea who loves, pro tects and punishes the fishermen. The barravento is the moment of violence, the moment when land and sea are transformed; when love, life, and the social world undergo sudden exchanges.
>
> None of the characters presented in this film have any relationship to people living or dead, and any resemblance is pure coincidence. The facts portrayed, however, do exist.

The preface, then, clearly casts *candomblé* as an obstacle to social progress.[32] It arbitrarily links *candomblé* to the idea of fatalism and passivity, while the phrase "still worship" implies that the people will some day abandon their obsolescent and historically condemned affection for the gods and inscribe themselves within the telos of modernity. The prefatory titles give voice, in short, to a Eurocentric vision of African religions.

The impression created by the preface is further reinforced not only by Rocha's own statements about his intentions, but also by much of Firmino's dialogue: Firmino repeatedly exhorts the fishermen to leave religion and organize to fight the system. Yet in other ways the film affirms the power and beauty of *candomblé*. This ambiguity doubtless derives partially from the ambivalences of the director himself as a white Protestant, yet who as a Bahian inevitably imbibed the ambient respect for Afro Brazilian religiosity. The ambiguity also derives, as we have seen, from the film's conflictual production history and the fact that the original director, who had partial African ancestry (a black grandfather), was more sympathetic to *candomblé* than the white Marxist Rocha. We are led to ask, then, to what extent this ambiguous sympathy for *candomblé* derives from Rocha's own attitudes and to what extent it represents the "trace" of the earlier work by Luis Paulino dos Santos. A comparison of the completed film and the original script by Paulino dos Santos suggests that Rocha politicized the script by "framing" it with a Marxist cri-

69. Rocha at work on *Barravento*

tique of religion and by introducing the "revolutionary" character Firmino, but without completely discarding the core-thrust of the original (photo 69).

The opening intertitles would seem to close off ambiguities and the "undecidables" of interpretation, and most critics of the film have followed the intertitles' lead in seeing the film as a critique of *candomblé*. Within the logic of "trust the tale, not the teller, however," the surface condemnation of *candomblé* is contradicted by a number of the film's superficial as well as by its deep structural features. First, the film has the "feel" of authenticity, due to the care taken to respect the ceremonies themselves; the woman (Dona Hilda) who plays the *candomblé* priestess, for example, was in fact an important figure in the Gantois *terreiro*. Second, although Firmino speaks a racially inflected materialist discourse—"You're just working to fill white men's bellies! . . . Millions of blacks are suffering in the world; each black who wins freedom frees another million!"—his actions imply that he too believes in the religion (photo 70). As José Gatti points out, Firmino is a liminal, beyond Good and Evil, border-line character sharing many characteristics with Exu: he too is a messenger between two worlds, he too is associated with alcoholic drink, with life on the road, and with the "vital strength of the libido and the

70. Pitanga as Firmino in *Barravento* (1962)

dynamic principle of individuation."[33] The film begins with his appearance, much as *candomblé* ceremonies begin by propitiating Exu. Firmino perfectly fits Abdias do Nascimento's definition of Exu as "the god of dialectical contradiction."[34] At diverse points, Firmino is musically and rhythmically associated with Exu. His spying at Cota's seduction of Aruã, for example, coincides with a chant of exaltation to Exu. We are led to wonder if Firmino proposes the seduction of Aruã in order to demystify him in the eyes of the community or because he himself believes that Aruã's defloration will destroy Aruã's charismatic power: the question is left open. Nor can we be absolutely sure that Firmino's critique of *candomblé* coincides with the director's, although Ismail Xavier speaks of a kind of "syntony" between the convulsive behavior of the character and the eruptive, discontinuous style of the film itself. In fact, like most Rocha protagonists, Firmino is riven by contradictions. His words indiscriminately mingle the discourses of the Civil Rights movement, Brazilian populism, and Marxist dialectics. He is a catalyst for mobilization, yet many of his individual decisions backfire. Like the *barravento* itself, he appears suddenly and brings turmoil in his wake. He cuts the net as a provocation, but the dialectic is not advanced; the fishermen merely return to the old, dangerous ways.

The mise-en-scène of the film, furthermore, as Xavier points out, underlines Firmino's isolation from the community. His oratorical style, his direct address to the camera, even his white suit, seem out of place. When he politicizes the fishermen, the editing places him and his interlocutors in completely different spaces. Although the community is socially oppressed, it is also the locus of art, spirituality, and solidarity. The depiction of the work of the *puxada de rede* (pulling in the net) evokes a utopian world where work is transformed into rhythmic, musical play. The film sacralizes communal labor, finding it expressive of cosmic harmony, and thus conforms to a very African notion of collective labor, evoking a world where art, religion, and everyday life are vitally interwoven, even under conditions of oppression. The spirit of Iemanjá, whose name derives from *yeye omo eja* (the mother whose children are fish) presides over the village, just as the *candomblé* music pervades the acoustic space of the community. The music, the lyrics of which thank Iemanjá for a good catch, surrounds community labor with an aura of the sacred, blurring the material world of the Aiyê and the spiritual world of *orun*. While the film denounces poverty, then, it also portrays a communal style of life in some ways more attractive than that which Firmino proposes.

Moreover, *Barravento* offers an affectionate celebration of the sensuous mise-en-scène of *candomblé;* the imagistic core of the film is thus supportive of the religion (photo 71). While excoriating religious alienation, it paints a beautiful picture of the religiously oriented life. The camera movements, the sound, the drums, highlight the beauty of the rituals—the *ialorixá* (high priestess) wielding her long-handled *adja* (metal bell) over the trembling body of Naina in trance; the *iao* (initiates) with their shaved heads; the *mãe de santo* summoning Ifá by throwing *búzios* (cowrie shells) on a lace cloth on the ground. Rather than resorting to the conventional portrayals that showed such religious practices as a meaningless frenzy, Rocha presents a religion that is dignified, complexly codified, and efficacious for its practitioners. A crucial ambiguity, pointed out by Xavier, also marks the film's system of explanation: all the narrative events can be explained either in the materialist manner *or* as evidence of the truth and efficacy of Afro Brazilian religion. Thus there is no necessary contradiction between the "enlightened," "progressive" plot and the "epidermic" level of images, camera movements, *batuque* sounds, and so forth. Rather, the film is the "irresolvable equation of these two opposing perspectives."[35]

71. Naina in *Barravento*

Barravento is thus open equally to a spiritualist or a materialist reading. The *despacho* against Aruã as Iemanjá's protected son can be seen as ineffective either because *candomblé* has no worldly efficacy or because Firmino does not perform the ceremony correctly; the fishermen die because Aruã, who is supposed to remain virgin, has been profaned through Firmino's machinations, or they die from natural causes.[36] The film's title already evokes some of these ambiguities, since it can refer literally to a tropical storm and figuratively to revolution but can also refer to the moment of the onset of trance in the *candomblé* ritual. The spirit of Iemanjá presides over both the community and the film itself; like the ocean, Iemanjá can be serene and calm, or agitated and devastating. Thus the film itself goes in and out of trance. It performs a distanced, exotopic analysis of the social oppression of a community; at the same time it incorporates into its own structure the religious vision of that community. Xavier points to a very vivid example of this process. The morning after Cota's seduction (photo 72), Aruã wakes up eroticized and flushed with his newly awakened sexuality. The camera moves from his body to a palm tree, and then to the clouds and to the swelling *barravento*. The filmic proposition could be summed up as "Aruã's newly sexualized body is at the root of the

72. The profanation of Aruã in *Barravento*

storm; the profanation of Aruã's body causes the *barravento*."[37]

Barravento made a dramatic rupture with the racial conventions of casting and plotting within Brazilian cinema: Afro Brazilians dominate the film, while the Euro-Brazilians are "visitors" like Naina, or oppressors like the owner of the net, and the film's structure is impregnated by Afro-religious values. Much as writers like Alejo Carpentier were inspired by African religion to create *lo real maravilloso, Barravento* creates a "magic realist" world where characters can call on the *orixás* to conjure up a storm. The film cannot be seen as simply praising or condemning *candomblé;* rather, it sees religion as "a master code in which competing discourses fight it out" (Jameson), presenting, as José Gatti puts it, "an unfinished conversation of diverging discourses just beginning to find grounds for negotiation at the time of the film's release."[38] At the same time, instead of producing an exoticist ode to palm trees and tropical sunsets, Rocha created a hungry poem about oppression, within the spirit of what he later called an "aesthetic of hunger."

Carlos Diegues's *Ganga Zumba* (1963) also features a virtually all-black cast and a fairly radical perspective for its time. The film memorializes the seventeenth-century maroon republic of Palmares, a republic, as we have seen, that lasted almost a century in the face of repeated assaults from both the Dutch and the Portuguese. Based on João Felício dos Santos's novel of the same name, the film focuses on a fugitive black whose odyssey leads him to Palmares. Partially because of lack of funds, Diegues was obliged to emphasize the oppression of slavery rather than the grandeur of Palmares itself. The overture sequence features engravings depicting slavery by Johann Moritz Rugendas, Jean-Baptiste Debret, and Franz Post, as a voice-over narration informs us about colonial Brazil. The action then begins on a sugarcane plantation, as one of the slaves, Antao (Pitanga), sees his mother die at the whipping post. The synecdochic images of shackled hands, shed tears, and sullen resentment, vividly encapsulate the situation. The next day, Aroraba (Eliezer Gomes), the spiritual leader of the slaves, reveals that Antão is the grandson of Zumbi, the king of Palmares.

The slaves, meanwhile, plot revolt (photo 73). The overseers try to terrorize them by showing them the cut-off ears of captured fugitives. Antão and his lover, Cipriani (Léa Garcia), in the meantime, conspire to trick the overseer. Cipriani seduces the overseer as Antão watches; Antão then murders the overseer just when he thinks he has won his erotic prize. Subsequently, Antão,

73. Planning rebellion in *Ganga Zumba* (1963)

Aroraba, and Cipriani escape from the plantation; the *orixá* Oxumare's bracelets help point the way to Palmares. On the road, they hide as they observe a white *capitão de mato* (slave catcher) and his wife, carried by two slaves and followed by the *mulata* servant Dandara (Luiza Maranhão). When Dandara drops a fan, Cipriana crawls over to pick it up, which alerts the whites to the rebels' whereabouts. A fight breaks out, in which two whites and one black are killed, while the rebels take Dandara captive. Despite Dandara's political alienation, Antão falls in love with her. He abandons Cipriani, who in her turn falls in love with a young black prospector. A final confrontation takes place against the backdrop of the giant rocks that mark the approach to Palmares. Whites fire on the fugitives; some are killed, but a remnant is saved by the Palmarinos. In these reversed circumstances, one of the mulatto overseers suddenly discovers that his blackness might save his life and pleads: "Look, I'm black like you." Annoyed by his opportunism, Antão kills him. Finally, Antão is crowned king as he leads his people into the promised land of the black republic.

Ganga Zumba deserves praise for its uncompromising portrait of Brazilian slavery. Enslaved Africans are whipped, raped, murdered, and forced to work to the point of exhaustion, a picture that refutes the Freyrean notion of a more gentle, charitable form of Lusitanian servitude. At the same time, the film does not paper over divisions among the enslaved, between blacks and mulattoes, for example, and between domestic servants and cane-field slaves. An ode to black liberation, *Ganga Zumba* assumes a black perspective throughout, showing blacks not as mere victims but as active historical agents. Although Diegues claims not to have read *The Wretched of the Earth* before making the film, some of the scenes evoke Frantz Fanon's thesis concerning the therapeutic value of revolutionary violence. Echoing Fanon, Glauber Rocha wrote in his "Aesthetic of Hunger" that "only through violence does the colonizer, through horror, understand the strength of the culture he exploits."[39] The scene in which Antão kills the slavedriver is in this sense emblematic (see photo 74). After killing him, Antão rips out his heart. It is not here a question of vindictive sadism, but rather of a demystificatory object lesson: you see, whites are merely human, they can die like us. Gone is the time when a few overseers can lord it over hundreds of blacks. While the colonized Brazil of the coast was economically impoverished and politically

74. Slaying the overseer: *Ganga Zumba*

repressive, the film suggests, blacks were constructing a communitarian republic in the mountains of the interior.

A strong sexual undercurrent energizes, and in some ways perturbs, the discourse of the film. Diegues was criticized for showing Antão and Cipriani making love, to which he responded commonsensically that even enslaved people do not spend 24 hours a day thinking about being slaves; they seize whatever ephemeral happiness they can. (These early 1960s criticisms of Diegues anticipated the later criticisms of *Xica da Silva* [1976] and Diegues's own counterdenunciation of "ideological patrols.") Without ever reproducing the notion of the "happy slave," Diegues demonstrates that one of the features of the black response to slavery was a capacity to transform suffering into survival, and everyday life into pleasure and art. Antão and Cipriani, interestingly, play out the trope of love as a delicious kind of slavery; he calls her *feitor* (slavedriver). At the same time, serious problems plague the film's portrayal of women. The two female characters who join the flight to Palmares are portrayed as frivolous and apolitical, more hindrance than help to the struggle. Dandara sees blacks as inevitably serving whites (photo 75), and Cipriani's desperate seizure of Dandara's fan puts all their lives at risk. As an individual-

75. Luiza Maranhão in *Ganga Zumba*

ist rebel without a larger social vision, she contains the germ of a later Diegues character: Xica da Silva.

In the world of *Ganga Zumba,* certain cultural resources are available to the enslaved. Africa is a recent and positive memory, and many characters still bear their African names. They practice *capoeira* and *candomblé* and see Palmares, in a vision imbued with what Benjamin called "revolutionary nostalgia," as a translocated piece of Africa. Nevertheless, there are questions to be raised about the historicity of *Ganga Zumba.* There is no evidence, for example, of a figure like Antão, that is, a grandson of Zumbi called in to save the threatened nation. Furthermore, Diegues unduly stresses the notion of a Palmarino king surrounded by pomp and circumstance; according to Décio Freitas, the Palmarino leaders were elected by hand vote or acclamation. There is also debate about the film's evocation of polygamy: some suggest that polygamy, in a country with few women, was available only to the leaders; others suggest that Zumbi was monogamous, still others that he was gay.[40] The film's evocations of Yoruba culture (e.g., Oxumare's banners) are inaccurate; Palmares was historically Bantu rather than Yoruba. Even the word *quilombo,* meaning "village," is Bantu. But the source novel, like the film, was written at a time when relatively little was known about Palmares. Edison Carneiro's book was first published in 1946 in Spanish as *La Guerra de los Palmares,* and it was a decade after *Ganga Zumba* was made that Brazilian historian Décio Freitas provided fresh information that was to provide the basis for Diegues's later film *Quilombo* (1984).

As is typical of the early Cinema Novo films, *Ganga Zumba* uses popular revolt as a quasi-allegorical springboard to speak of the need for liberation in contemporary Brazil. (Over a decade later, during the dictatorship, the leftist theatrical group Arena also took up the theme of Zumbi-as-anticolonialist with contemporary allegorical overtones in its *Arena Conta Zumbi* [Arena Tells the Story of Zumbi, 1965].) In any case the film, despite its occasional miscalculations, takes a strong positive step in its approving representation of black characters and black struggle by making a glimpse of the historical reality of Palmares available to a large constituency. Glauber Rocha called *Ganga Zumba* "a slow, sad anti-epic . . . the only film by a white director which did not take a paternalistic attitude toward blacks but rather identified with them."[41] The film's pro-black approach explains, perhaps, its enthusiastic reception by the African delegations at the Third World Congress held in Geneva in 1965. Unlike *Sinhá Moça* (The Plantation Owner's Daughter, 1953) a decade before, the blacks in *Ganga Zumba* do not need the help and encouragement of white abolitionists. Blacks, not white heroes and heroines, are the central focus of attention. And unlike Hollywood films, *Ganga Zumba* addresses taboo issues such as the sexual abuses of slavery and the frequency of rebellion, and it treats the issue of blacks who not only exercise violence against the master but even find some satisfaction in it. (We will return to the subject of Palmares when we discuss *Quilombo.*)

CHAPTER 9

From Auto-Critique to
Anthropophagy,
1964–1971

∞

In the second phase of Cinema Novo, extending roughly from 1964 through the coup-within-the-coup of December 1968, filmmakers turned away from favela and *sertão* to examine themselves and the failure of the left-populist project. With the coup d'état, leftist film production was interrupted: universities and *cineclubs* were raided, copies of Soviet silent classics such as *Mother* and *Potemkin* were seized, and Cinema Novo was forced to face up to a political disaster. The new political conjuncture forced a reconceptualization of goals and strategies. As one response, a number of filmmakers performed tortured autopsies of the debacle, in films whose veiled or explicit theme was the coup itself or the problems of the left, the case of Paulo César Saraceni's *O Desafio* (The Challenge, 1965), Marion Fiorani's *A Derrota* (The Defeat, 1967), Glauber Rocha's *Terra em Transe* (Land in Anguish, 1967), Nelson Pereira dos Santos's *Fome de Amor* (Hunger for Love, 1968), and Gustavo Dahl's *Bravo Guerreiro* (Brave Warrior, 1968). *O Desafio,* for example, satirizes what is known in Brazil as the "festive left," that is, a left more interested in wild parties than effective militancy, and *Fome de Amor* allegorizes the left's isolation, embodied in a revolutionary figure who is blind, out of touch, and confined to an island. Whereas the first-phase films tend to be rural in setting, the second-phase films are predominantly urban, and if the first-phase films were committed to realism as a style, the second-phase films tend toward self-referentiality and anti-illusionism.

This shift in focus carries with it a racial corollary. Since the filmmakers were generally white middle-class intellectuals, this critical look-in-the-mirror tended not to include blacks or mestiços. The military takeover destroyed the illusions of leftists who had imagined themselves a vanguard leading the marginalized masses away from alienation and toward freedom. The coup d'état forced this progressive elite to see both its own powerlessness—since the regime jailed leftists or chased them into exile—*and* to see its own elite status. In this sense, the white left was forced to name itself as white and elite rather than simply as the self-appointed spokesman of the people.

One exception that proves the rule of black absence in this period is the character Calunga (played by Pitanga), the imaginative *malandro* of Carlos Diegues's *A Grande Cidade* (The Big City, 1965). Calunga first appears as our "host" for a cinema verité tour of Rio de Janeiro (photo 76). Magically jumping through discontinuous spaces, he interviews everyday citizens about their daily life, much in the manner of Jean Rouch and Edgar Morin's *Chronique d'un Été* (Chronicle of a Summer, 1961), while also providing ironic statistics as in the voice-over commentary of Chris Marker's *Le Joli Mai* (The Beautiful Month of May, 1962). In a reflexive gesture, Calunga addresses the camera/ spectator and asks us what we are doing at the movies, that "temple of magicians, that dream factory, that source of memory." Pitanga once again incarnates the rebel, the anarchist, the eternally playful and creative *malandro*-artist. At the same time, he is a magister ludi, or master-of-ceremonies, figure standing in for the director himself,[1] reminiscent both of Exu as the "opener of paths" and "coordinator of rituals" and of the harlequin figure familiar from Brazilian comic theater, the servant who pulls the strings of events, giving the impression that the play is being constructed in the spectator's presence.[2]

Although blacks and Indian characters are not usually the protagonists or even the secondary characters of the films of this period, they often form an inferential presence, even in a film like *Terra em Transe,* Glauber Rocha's baroque allegory about the coup d'état and its aftershocks, which largely foregrounds the white political elite. Set in the imaginary country of Eldorado, a name that evokes an archetypal figure within the European and the Latin American imaginary, Terra em Transe animates synthetic characters representing vast historical forces: Diaz the fascist (Paulo Autran), Vieira the populist (José Lewgoy), Sara the Communist (Glauce Rocha). The film deploys clearly allegorical strategies, figuring a modern-day coup d'état, for example, in the form of a Shakespearean coronation. The portrait of the leftist poet-

76. Calunga as magister ludi in *A Grande Cidade* (1965)

intellectual Paulo Martins (Jardel Filho) as a contradictory, often reprehensible figure, given to lapses of skepticism and despair and infinitely less coherent than he imagines himself, forms a critical portrait of a whole generation of (white) leftist intellectuals. The portrait is conveyed by a volcanic effluvium of words, sounds, and images that constitutes a baroque allegory of disenchantment.[3]

Drawing on fragments of the allegorical pageantry of Brazilian carnival, *Terra em Transe* shows Brazil as an unstable amalgam of Afro-indigenous mestiço cultures subject to an overarching European domination. Rocha gives proleptic expression to what came to be called the "crisis of totalizations," that is, the spreading skepticism about historical master-narratives such as Marxism with its faith in inevitable revolution and a history ordered by the progressive laws of dialectical materialism. But this crisis within progressive thinking also has a racial dimension. It is photographs of poor blacks—some of them enchained—that prod Paulo into joining Sara in the fight against injustice. Nor is it an accident that in the few scenes where "the people" appear —for example, in the sequence of the police repression of peasants or in the sequence entitled "Encounter of a Leader with the People"—they tend to have darker faces than the elite. One shot encapsulates this racial populism. We see Vieira, arms upraised, under the central arch of his palace, flanked by his sup-

77. The mise-en-scène of populism: *Terra em Transe* (1967)

porters (priest, senator, reporter, student), while the festive multitude dances
on the margins (see photo 77). The image is flattened not only through a telephoto lens but also through the lack of interposed elements between the camera and the recorded scene. The impression is of a populist "united front" that
includes the black *sambistas* on the edges of the shot. The ensuing sequence,
however, opens up this flattened space, revealing its contradictions. Populism
invites the dark-skinned majority into the palace but represses them once they
are there.[4]

The black presence in *Terra em Transe* is felt on registers other than character and plot. The opening shot of the film, which superimposes aerial shots of
Brazil's tropical coastline on the Afro Brazilian music of *candomblé*, powerfully
evokes the "Black Atlantic" as the conduit for Afro-diasporic culture. The
candomblé praise songs on the soundtrack evoke the world of Afro Brazilian
religion and specifically the idea of trance possession already referenced in the
film's title. Eschewing the conventional use of music as mood setter, *Terra em
Transe* exploits the social connotations of specific musical traditions to evoke
the characters' cultural, political, and racial affiliations: the right-wing dictator

is associated with opera (Verdi and his Brazilian epigone, Carlos Gomes); the populist politician with samba; and the Rocha-like protagonist both with Art Blakey-style jazz and with Heitor Villa-Lobos, a composer who, like Rocha himself, produces erudite elaborations of popular leitmotifs.

Terra em Transe exposes what might be called the "whiteness of whiteness." For example, it criticizes not only white-dominated institutions (political parties, the media) but also white revolutionaries. The film's prorevolutionary white intellectual Paulo Martins supports "the people" rhetorically, yet in moments of crisis he abuses and humiliates the darker-skinned representatives of the people. Paulo's behavior, surprising in a leftist "hero," exemplifies that of the Brazilian elite as described by anthropologists. Roberto da Matta, for example, sees (elite) Brazilians as socially schizophrenic, traversed by two contradictory personalities: one egalitarian, carnivalesque, and utopian, the other hierarchical and authoritarian. The authoritarian demands subservience based on social status, asking in peremptory tones: "Do you know with whom you are speaking?" Brazil, in sum, suffers from the racially inflected stratifications generated by a cruelly inegalitarian system. A character like Paulo, in this sense, oscillates between his leftist egalitarian ideals and the typical behavior of a spoiled, arrogant child of power.

Terra em Transe was a major influence on the tropicalist movement in theater, music, and cinema, and it is only with the third, or "tropicalist," phase that black characters and themes reappear in force, a fact that also has to do with Tropicalism's rediscovery of the implicitly multiracial problematic explored by the modernists. Whereas first-phase Cinema Novo turned for inspiration to the "class-over-race" social realism of the 1930s (Graciliano Ramos, José Lins do Rego, Jorge Amado), second-phase Cinema Novo turned to the modernist writers of the 1920s and especially to Oswald de Andrade's notion of anthropophagy, as metaphorically applied to cultural products. Inverting the binary pair of civilization and barbarism in favor of barbarism, Modernism articulated cannibalism as an anticolonialist metaphor in its "Cannibalist Reviews" and "Anthropophagic Manifestoes" and its famous slogan "Tupi or not Tupi, that is the question"; that is, whether Brazilian intellectuals should "go native" by symbolically imitating the putatively cannibalistic Tupi Guarani tribes or alienate themselves into European domination. The idea was to ingest all foreign techniques and models in order to forge a new synthesis that could be turned against the foreigner.

Cannibalism as metaphor has a long history, deeply embedded in European fantasies and misrecognitions. When Columbus landed in Hispaniola, he mistook the native peoples for Mongols, the people of the Grand Khan, and therefore named them Caniba. Within the Western tradition, cannibalism has often been the very "name of the other," the ultimate marker of difference in a coded opposition of light and dark, rational and irrational, civilized and savage. But even within that tradition, a number of writers have turned the cannibalist trope against Europe. Montaigne, in "Des Cannibales" (based, ironically, on interviews with Brazilian Indians), argued that civilized Europeans were ultimately more barbarous than cannibals, since cannibals ate the flesh of the dead only to appropriate the strength of their enemies, while Europeans tortured and slaughtered in the name of a religion of love. Herman Melville echoed Montaigne by asking: "Which of us is not a cannibal?" With the European avant-garde, the metaphor took on renewed vigor. Alfred Jarry wrote an essay on "Anthropophagie" (1902) and in "L'Almanach du Père Ubu" addressed himself to "amateur cannibals."[5] The Dadaists entitled one of their organs *Cannibale,* and in 1920 Francis Picabia issued the "Manifeste Cannibale Dada." But although cannibalism was a common trope among European avant-gardists, only in Brazil did anthropophagy become a key trope in a cultural movement that was to prolong itself over many decades, ranging from the first "Cannibalistic Review" in the 1920s, with its various "dentitions," through Oswald de Andrade's speculations in the 1950s concerning anthropophagy as "the philosophy of the technicized primitive," to the pop recyclings of the metaphor in the tropicalist movement of the late 1960s. As exploited by the Brazilian modernists, the cannibalist metaphor had a positive and negative pole. The positive pole posited aboriginal matriarchy and communalism as utopian model. Oswald de Andrade saw indigenous society as offering a more adequate model of social behavior, especially in terms of the full enjoyment of leisure. Playing with the Portuguese word *negócio*—"business," but literally "neg-ócio" or the negation of leisure, Andrade offered a proto-Marcusean encomium to leisurely pleasure rooted in his knowledge and theorization of indigenous society.[6] Thus we find a literalization, in Brazil, of the metaphors of the European avant-garde. Whereas the Dadaists called for "progressive unemployment" and André Breton's surrealist "rules" forbade regular work, Brazilian artist-intellectuals could point to existing indigenous societies quite free from both work, in the occidental sense, and from coercive power.[7] The negative pole of the cannibalist metaphor, mean-while, made cannibalism a critical instrument for exposing the exploitative so-cial Darwinism implicit in "savage capitalism" and bourgeois civility. The two poles complement each other, of course, in the sense that the cannibalism-as-critique motif contemplates the melancholy distance separating contemporary society from the imagined ideal *communitas* of the Amerindian. "At the heart of every utopia," Oswald de Andrade wrote, "there is not only a dream but also a protest."[8]

Of the two poles of the cannibalist metaphor, Joaquim Pedro de Andrade's 1969 adaptation of *Macunaíma* clearly emphasizes the negative pole.[9] Fusing what he knew of Oswald de Andrade's anthropophagical movement with the theme of cannibalism that runs through the de Andrade novel, the director turns the theme of cannibalism into the springboard for a critique of repres-sive military rule and of the predatory capitalist model of the short-lived Bra-zilian "economic miracle." In a preface written for the Venice Film Festival, the director offered a kind of cannibalistic hermeneutic to help spectators de-code the Rabelaisian *paroles gelées* of the film: "Cannibalism is an exemplary mode of consumerism adopted by underdeveloped peoples. . . . The tradi-tionally dominant, conservative social classes continue their control of the power structure—and we rediscover cannibalism. . . . The present work rela-tionships, as well as the relationships between people—social, political and economic—are still, basically, cannibalistic. Those who can, 'eat' others through their consumption of products, or even more directly in sexual rela-tionships. Cannibalism has merely institutionalized and cleverly disguised it-self. . . . Meanwhile, voraciously, nations devour their people. *Macunaíma* . . . is the story of a Brazilian devoured by Brazil." The cannibalist theme is treated in all its variations: people so hungry they eat themselves; an ogre who offers Macunaíma a piece of his leg; the urban guerrilla who devours him sexually; the cannibal, giant, and capitalist Pietro Pietra with his anthropophagous soup; the capitalist's wife who wants to eat him alive; and finally the man-eat-ing siren who lures him to his death. We see the rich devouring the poor, and the poor, in desperation, devouring each other. The left, meanwhile, while be-ing devoured by the right, purifies itself by eating itself, a practice Joaquim Pedro de Andrade calls the "cannibalism of the weak."[10]

The very first narrated words (in both film and novel)—"In the depths of the virgin-forest was born Macunaíma, hero of his people"—signal entry into

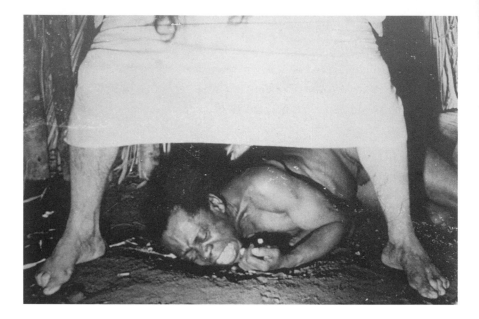

78. The prodigious birth: *Macunaíma*

the carnivalized world of comic epic. An improbably old white woman (actually a man in drag) stands and grunts until she/he deposits a wailing 50-year-old black "baby" on the ground (photo 78). The expression on the "mother's" face recalls Mikhail Bakhtin's description of the grotesque body in Rabelais: "The gaping mouth, the protruding eyes, sweat, trembling, suffocation, the swollen face—all these are typical symptoms of the grotesque life of the body: here they have the meaning of the act of birth."[11] As the "grotesque body of the people," the hero is virtually shat into existence, rather like Gargantua, who was born during a maternal bout of severe diarrhea, his mother having eaten "too much tripe." Here we find as well the "violent contrasts" of the Menippea: the man-woman "mother" (very reminiscent of Bakhtin's favored image of the "pregnant hag"), the adult "baby," the black-white "family." The birth itself, at once prodigious and grotesque, encapsulates a privileged carnival image: the old, near death, giving birth to the new.

The first sequence also performs the mise-en-scène of *mestiçagem*. The names of the family members—Macunaíma, Jigûe, Manaape—are Indian, but the family is at once black, Indian, and European. Interestingly, de Andrade ignores his anthropological source to call the tribe "Tupanhuma" (black). The decor and costumes, meanwhile, are oxymoronic, syncretic, culturally

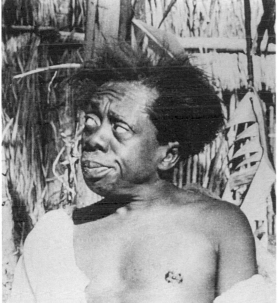

79. Grande Otelo as
Macunaíma

miscegenated. The hut that serves as maternity ward is half backlander and half Indian; the manner of giving birth, in a standing position to take advantage of gravity, is Indian. At the same time, the institution of the family is desentimentalized and comically degraded. Instead of the customary exclamations at the newborn's "cuteness," the family reacts to the hero's birth with "How ugly!" and "He stinks!" The film further underlines the surreal nature of this family by having the same actor (Paulo José) play both the original "mother" of Macunaíma and Macunaíma himself (in his later white incarnation), while another actor (Grande Otelo) plays both the first and the second black Macunaíma (see photo 79). Thus the white Macunaíma gives birth to the black Macunaíma, who is magically transformed into the white Macunaíma and who marries Ci the guerrilla and thus fathers another black Macunaíma.

The logic of carnival is that of the world turned upside down, in which the powerful are mocked and ridiculous kings are enthroned and then dethroned in an atmosphere of gay relativity. The film proliferates in the sexual inversions common in carnivalesque literature and in carnival itself: Paulo José in drag giving birth to the protagonist, Macunaíma costumed as a French divorcée, and the giant himself bathing in a Hollywoodean bubble bath of the kind usually reserved for starlets. The Ubuesque industrial magnate and people-eater Pietro Pietra is the most powerful figure in *Macunaíma,* and he too is dethroned. In his purple smoking jacket and green boxer shorts covering his padded buttocks, he looks very much like the "Rei Momo," the burlesque lord of the revels from Brazil's carnival. Graced with multinational names and an Italian accent, the figure of Pietro Pietra referred in the novel to the Italian nouveaux riches families of the 1920s and in the film to the dependent national bourgeoisie with its second-hand American technology. Pietro lives in the hybrid vulgarity of a kitsch palace, where rococo clocks and breathing mannequins cohabit with Egyptian sphinxes. He struggles with Macunaíma over an amulet with a traditional folkloric role of guaranteeing fishing and hunting (i.e., prosperity). As a millionaire who wants to eat Macunaíma, the hero of his people, Pietro alludes to all the "multinational" economic giants who want to devour Brazil and its resources. But even Macunaíma, although he defeats Pietro and wins the amulet, is enthroned and then dethroned. After feeling the "immense satisfaction" of defeating the giant, he dissipates his advantage by returning to the jungle with the useless electronic bric-a-brac of consumer civilization. Thus the film's carnivalized critique includes the "hero" as well, shown, as Ismail Xavier points out, to be almost as individualist and selfish as his enemy Pietro Pietra, hardly a viable agent of progressive change.[12] Unlike the urban guerrilla Ci, who is at least dynamic in her resistance to established power, Macunaíma has no coherent political project. In the final sequence he incarnates the figure of the "Jeca Tatu," the toothless hillbilly created by Monteiro Lobato.

Macunaíma was predictably censured by some critics for its "bad taste," an irrelevant category for a carnivalesque aesthetic since the category invokes exactly the notion of taste that is being derided. The director himself described the film as intentionally in "execrable taste . . . innocently filthy like the jokes of children."[13] But however grotesque or fantastic, the carnivalesque aesthetic retains a certain realism that addresses everyday life and contemporary events. The film, in this sense, lampoons a host of satiric targets, for example, the political repression triggered by the 1968 "coup-within-the-coup" ("suspicious attitude," explains the plainclothes man as he arrests Macunaíma), as well as the rampant consumerism inherent in the Brazilian economic model, the absurdity of which is emphasized by its uselessness in the Amazon. The film also subtly critiques Brazilian racism, something about which the novel's mulatto

80. The family faces drought: *Macunaíma*

author was personally aware. When the white brother explains why his black brother Jigûe was singled out for arrest, he reminds Jigûe of the Brazilian proverb (reminiscent of the African American "If you're black, stay back"): "a white man running is a champion; a black man running is a thief." At one point the white Macunaíma speaks disparagingly of "that mulatto guy," and Jigûe objects: "So now that you're white you've become a racist?" When Manaape and Jigûe, living in a favela, ask Macunaíma to let them live with him in his roomy new home, he responds: "One is too few, two is great, but three is a mess." In social-allegorical terms, Macunaíma, "whitened" by money and class ascension, turns his back on his poorer *favelado* brothers. Yet even white Macunaíma cannot finally escape his originary blackness; the son born to him and to the equally white Ci, the urban guerrilla, is black (again, Grande Otelo), as if the proverbial "foot in the kitchen" (i.e., the inevitable partial African ancestry of all Brazilians) were reasserting itself through the child.

The macumba sequence in the film weds the magic of trance religions to the magic of montage. A medium "picks up" the cannibal giant's spirit; as Macunaíma beats her up, all the blows are transferred to the giant. In the novel Macunaíma goes to a Rio *terreiro* to ask for the protection of an *orixá*.

He dances and is consecrated son of Exu, a perfectly appropriate *orixá* for a semiotic shape-shifter like Macunaíma. In the novel, interestingly, de Andrade invites a number of Brazilian modernists and European surrealists (Manuel Bandeira, Blaise Cendrars, Raul Bopp) to the *terreiro;* in fact, he calls them all *macumbeiros,* thus positing a link between African religion and the European and Latin American avant-gardes.

The film generally downplays the magical transformations of the novel, where the hero variously transforms himself into a French prostitute, a leaf ant, a drop of water, and several varieties of fish. When Pietro Pietra chops up Macunaíma for his stew, the hero's brothers reassemble his scraps, wrap him in banana leaves and blow smoke on the ensemble to bring him back to life. (Only an animated cartoon, or some high-tech cybernetic morphing, could perhaps do justice to the novel's metamorphoses.) The film does feature two sequences of racial transformation, however, in both of which the black Macunaíma (Grande Otelo) turns into the white Macunaíma (Paulo José). In the first, Macunaíma and Jigûe's girlfriend Sofará (Joanna Fomm) go into the woods to set a trap for a tapir (photo 81). Sofará lights a joint and gives it to Macunaíma; one puff turns him into a handsome prince. They romp in the woods as we hear an old carnival song ("Peri and Ceci"), which references the characters from the Indianist novel *O Guarani,* Peri being the noble savage Indian and Ceci the Euro Brazilian woman with whom he is in love. As Randal Johnson points out in his illuminating study, the sequence, occasionally misread as racist by North American audiences, is in fact a satirical barb directed at the Brazilian "economic miracle" of the late 1960s.[14] Sofará, the European "Ceci" of the allegory, is dressed in an "Alliance for Progress" sack. Her magic cigarette, that is, American intervention, has turned Macunaíma, hero of his people, into a papier-mâché prince, just as the "economic miracle" touted by the military junta supposedly turned Brazil into an apparently prosperous nation. (In fact, the prosperity was short lived, consisting largely of a brutal transfer of wealth from bottom to top, and soon gave way to a record national debt and widespread accusations of official corruption.)

The second sequence of racial transformation can best be read as a sardonic comment on Brazil's putative "racial democracy" and the "ideology of whitening." The sequence illustrates a common folktale about the origin of racial diversity, one in which everyone in the world is born black but where a step into the water filling a footprint left by Saint Thomas turns people white.

81. The allegorical miracle: Sofará and Macunaíma

(One of Joel Chandler Harris's Uncle Remus stories—"Why the Negro is Black"—tells a similar tale.) In the novel, Macunaíma is born black but becomes white after touching the water, but he so muddies the water that Jigûe, who bathes second, becomes a red-skinned Indian; even less water is left for Manaape, who can only lighten his palms and the soles of his feet. The film eliminates the red Indian as intermediate stage. When the black Macunaíma enters a magic fountain that turns him white, the soundtrack plays the Portuguese version of "By a Waterfall," taken from the Lloyd Bacon musical *Footlight Parade* (1933), a film whose musical numbers were directed by Busby Berkeley. The choice seems especially apt when we recall that the original diegetic inspiration for the "By a Waterfall" number was black children playing with the water spurting from a Harlem hydrant, a sight that suggests to the James Cagney character the spectacular possibilities of waterfalls splashing on white bodies. The allusion is richly suggestive, evoking not only a complex play of black and white but also the relation between the American musical comedy and Brazil's carnivalized imitations of them in the *chanchada,* the genre in which Grande Otelo, the actor who plays Macunaíma, was the most famous star. Indeed, *Macunaíma's* renewed contact with the world of carnival and the *chanchada,* and its socially conscious recycling of *chanchada* strategies, enabled the film to realize a goal long accessible to Cinema Novo directors: the reconciliation of political and aesthetic avant-gardism with popular appeal. But the film rejected the implicitly rosy social vision of the *chanchada* by refusing the shallow utopianism of the *chanchada*'s conventional happy endings. In *Macunaíma,* the ideal of the hustler-trickster-hero typical of the chanchada is revealed to be empty, a social dead-end.[15]

Macunaíma, with its raucously Rabelaisian aesthetic, illustrates the pitfalls of a misdirected search for "positive images" or even for conventional realism, in a film that obeys another aesthetic orientation.[16] *Macunaíma* transforms the ultimate negative stereotype—cannibalism—into a positive artistic resource. Indeed, although the North American critic is tempted to find in the lazy Macunaíma, whose favorite expression is "ai que preguiça" (Ai, what laziness), a Brazilian version of Stepin Fetchit, the archetypal "coon" of the 1930s, such an interpretation scarcely does justice to the character or to the film. It forgets that the modernist movement saw "laziness" as a positive quality. Mário de Andrade wrote an "Ode to Laziness," and Oswald de Andrade, as we have seen, portrayed indigenous culture as more attuned to leisure. Macunaíma, furthermore, is a multiple, contradictory character, by turns stupid, brilliant, lazy, and enterprising. These qualities are not correlated with race; the white Macunaíma displays the same diversity of characteristics and the same fondness for the expression "ai que preguiça." Both Mário de Andrade the writer and Joaquim Pedro de Andrade the filmmaker are obviously caricaturing what they see as an occasional Brazilian trait common to all races. A more sophisticated methodology would be aware of the danger of "genre mistakes." A search for "positive images" within the culturally coded carnival of *Macunaíma* would be fundamentally misguided. Both film and novel belong to a carnivalesque parodic genre that animates not rounded three-dimensional characters but rather two-dimensional "grotesques." Virtually all the characters—white, black, and mestiço—exhibit elements of the grotesque. Indeed, the film's two most archly grotesque characters are Pietro Pietra, the white industrialist-cannibal, and his ghoulish spouse. The sequence in which Macunaíma beats up a macumba medium as a way of beating up Pietro Pietra by proxy, similarly, could be misread as simply "a white man beats up a black woman," without seeing the levels of complicity, that both (white) Macunaíma and the (black) priestess are sharing the same cultural code. Such an interpretation misses, furthermore, the link made between the Afro-magic of macumba, which operates across physical distance, and the cinematic "magic" of montage, which creates the simulacrum of magical efficacity. (We will return to the issue of racialized reception of *Macunaíma* in the final chapter.)

The film *Macunaíma* also generated further textual metamorphoses in the form of "after-texts," that is, works that reference or are inspired by both the novel and by Joaquim Pedro de Andrade's film. Paulo Veríssimo's *Exu-Piá: Coração de Macunaíma* (Exu-Piá: Heart of Macunaíma, 1984), has the two most famous incarnations of the Macunaíma character (Grand Otelo from the film, and Carlos Augusto Carvalho from the Antunes Filho theatrical adaptation), go off in search of their creator. The old *caboclo* Macunaíma from the play flees an Amazon forest in the process of being destroyed, while the Macunaíma who became a starry constellation at the end of the novel leaves the heavens for sunny Brazil. The two characters in search of their author travel through contemporary Brazil to see if Mário de Andrade will consent to changing their destinies. The film mingles fiction and documentary, the popular humor of Grande Otelo and the theatrical spectacle of Antunes Filho, along with sequences depicting Mário de Andrade's actual home on the outskirts of São Paulo *Exu-Piá* also invokes the popular rituals referenced by the novel: carnival, *candomblé*, Bumba-Meu-Boi, and even soccer, which Macunaíma, according to the novel at least, invented by kicking a tropical fruit.

The tropicalist allegorical phase of Cinema Novo also resurrects, on a more critical register, the Indianist theme, expressed not only in *Macunaíma* but also in 1970s "allegorical" films such as Arnaldo Jabor's *Pindorama* (1971; see photo 82) and dos Santos's *Como Era Gostoso Meu Francês* (How Tasty Was My Little Frenchman, 1971). "Pindorama," in Tupi, signifies literally "country of the big trees" and metaphorically evokes the golden age of indigenous freedom. But in Jabor's film the arrival of the Europeans brings the plague: calendars, the myth of progress, diseases, slavery, puritanism, the sword, and the cross, as Indians are sucked into the vortex of sixteenth-century political struggle.

Dos Santos's *Como Era Gostoso Meu Francês* (How Tasty Was My Little Frenchman, 1971), meanwhile, performs an "anthropophagic" critique of European colonialism (photos 83a and 83b). On one level, the film reflects on the

82. Arnaldo Jabor's *Pindorama* (1971)

complex historical relationship between the French and the Tupinambá. In the 1550s, at the time that France was trying to found the colony of France Antartique in Rio de Janeiro bay, they brought Tupinambá Indians back to Rouen so that they might play themselves at a kind of French-built theme park built in honor of Henry II and Catherine of Medici. The Tupinambá staged episodes from their daily life—cooking, hunting, fighting—for the delectation of French observers, among them the French philosopher Montaigne. The film is largely based on the diary of Hans Staden, a German gunner captured by the Tupinambá and who wrote a sensational travel tale—*Hans Staden: The True History and Description of a Country of Savages, a Naked and Terrible People, Eaters of Men's Flesh, Who Dwell in the New World Called America*—which set the tone for lurid accounts of cannibals in the New World. (Although some scholars, such as William Arens, are skeptical about claims of Tupinambá cannibalism—dos Santos assumes that such accounts have a basis in truth.)[17]

Como Era Gostoso Meu Francês concerns a Frenchman captured by the Tupinambá and sentenced to death in response to massacres inflicted upon them by Europeans. (Dos Santos presumably transformed the prototype into a Frenchman because the French, unlike the Germans, participated directly in

83a/83b. The allegorical cannibal: *Como Era Gostoso Meu Francês* (1971)

the colonialist enterprise in Brazil.) Before being ritually executed and eaten, however, the Frenchman is given a wife, Sebiopepe (widow of one of the Tupinambá massacred by the Europeans) and is allowed to participate in the tribe's daily activities, while he also initiates them in the use of cannons and gunpowder. He assimilates by joining his "hosts" in war, shaving his head, and decorating his body. In the last shot, the camera zooms into Sebiopepe's face as she devours her Frenchman, with no apparent regret despite her close relationship with him, an image that segues to a quotation from a report on genocide committed by Europeans. Subverting the conventional identification with the European protagonist of the captivity narrative, the film systematically cuts off the conventional escape routes—the "hero" does not escape alone, nor does he escape with his wife, nor does he become a happy "white Indian"—all the while maintaining an ironically neutral attitude toward the protagonist's deglutition. Sebiopepe eats the Frenchman not out of hatred but because her loyalty is to the tribe. He is killed not because he is evil but because his people killed many Tupinambá.

Como Era Gostoso Meu Francês superimposes (at least) two versions of history. The first consists in a historical reconstruction of the life and times of a Tupinambá village. The other version of history is relayed by the intertitles that offer the Eurocentric impressions of various Europeans (Hans Staden, Jean de Lery, Villegaignon, Abby Thevet), who describe the indigenous peoples as "beasts with human faces," lacking all modesty, religion, and morality. The first letter (dated March 31, 1557), from Villegaignon to John Calvin, is read in the manner of a contemporary news report and is accompanied by the baroque music that usually accompanied 1960s French newsreels. At times image and sound enter into direct contradiction. As the voice-over tells us that the Frenchman received a fair trial but "threw himself into the sea and drowned," the image shows him weighted down with stones and being pushed into the sea. (Such tales certainly reminded Brazilian spectators living under the dictatorship of mendacious official reports about leftist prisoners committing suicide in prison.)

Como Era Gostoso Meu Francês offers a didactic lesson in cultural relativism, indirectly posing Montaigne's question: "Qui sont les vrais barbares?" Ironically inverting the homogenizing convention by which Europeans perceive only generic "Indians"—"they are all the same"—here the "Indians" are unable to distinguish between the French and the Portuguese. (Throughout the film the protagonist is misrecognized as a Portuguese enemy rather than a French ally.) The film is almost entirely spoken, furthermore, in Tupi-Guarani. Thus the film, which has to be seen with subtitles even in Brazil, estranges or renders foreign Portuguese-speaking spectators, who find themselves thrust back into the *lingua geral* that dominated Brazil for centuries. The Eurocentic spectator is caught up short as well by the film's nonvoyeuristic "normalization" of male and female nudity. (The film was rejected for the Cannes Festival precisely because of this "normal" nudity.) At the same time, the film subverts narratological norms; here the European is the protagonist, but not the hero, and romantic love is less important than tribal loyalty. The film's title embodies an indigenous perspective: How Tasty was *My* Frenchman. Unfortunately, dos Santos underestimated the dumb inertia of Eurocentric patterns of identification; many spectators identified with the protagonist despite the film's ironic intentions.

At the same time, dos Santos deploys the events of the past to indirectly call attention to the contemporary predicament of indigenous Brazilians: the pressure on their land base, the devastation of the Amazon due to the Trans-Amazonian Highway, the corruption of the authorities. In the best anthropophagic tradition, dos Santos deploys the trope of cannibalism to denounce the economic cannibalism of European colonialism. The Tupinambá appreciate the Frenchman's gift of gunpowder, but they eat him nevertheless. Contemporary Brazilians, the film suggests, should emulate their Tupinambá forebears by devouring European technologies in order to use them against European domination.

Concurrent with the tropicalist phase of Cinema Novo, there emerged a radically different tendency, variously called "Udigrudi" (the Brazilian pronunciation of "Underground"), "Marginal Cinema," "Subterranean Cinema," and "Mouth of Garbage Cinema." Just when Cinema Novo decided to reach out to the popular audience, the Underground decided to slap that audience in the face. As Cinema Novo moved toward technical polish and higher production values, the "Novo Cinema Novo," as it came to be called, demanded a radicalization and urbanization of the aesthetics of hunger, rejecting well-made cinema in favor of a "dirty screen" and "garbage aesthetics." A "garbage style," they argued, was appropriate for a Third World country forced to pick through the leavings of an international system dominated by First World capitalism. The garbage aesthetic represented as well the antithesis of the ideals promoted by the hegemonic ideology of modernization and development then taking over Brazilian Television.[18] The Underground films occasionally treated black characters, but usually as synecdochic tokens evocative of Third World poverty. *Bandido da Luz Vermelha* (Red Light Bandit), for example, begins and ends with images of black *favelado* children dancing around garbage dump fires, to the same *candomblé* music featured in Rocha's *Terra em Transe*. The images and sounds form both a tribute to Rocha and a critique. The apocalyptic energy evokes Rocha at his best, but at the same time Sganzerla suggests that these squalid slum images, and not the stylized allegorical images of Rocha's films, come closer to evoking contemporary Brazil. For filmmakers who self-consciously declared their own marginality in their acts of self-naming, blacks were ideal figures for projection. Thus white directors identified "downward" with rebellious lumpen characters, both black and white, in a kind of updated *nostalgie de la boue*. Thus João Trevisão's *Orgia, ou*

84. Brazil's "only black millionaire": Pitanga in *Al Mulher de Todos* (1969)

O Homen Que Deu a Luz (Orgy, or the Man Who Gave Birth, 1970), features a black transvestite, and Rogério Sganzerla's *A Mulher de Todos* (Everybody's Woman, 1969), features as one of the female protagonist's lovers Pitanga, in the role of "Brazil's only black millionaire," whose wealth paradoxically calls attention to the absence of wealth of the majority of blacks (see photo 84).

Júlio Bressane's perversely structured *O Anjo Nasceu* (The Angel Is Born, 1969) has the facade of a linear tale concerning two bandits: one (Hugo Carvana) white, the other (Pitanga) black. The film is reminiscent of the biracial buddy film from Hollywood, but without that genre's sentimentality. In its very refusal to judge its marginal characters, *O Anjo Nasceu* grants them an understated solidarity. The two criminals in this sense recall the radical criminality evoked by the figure and the work of Jean Genet. Their crime simply exists, without forethought or program, without condemnation or redemption. At one point, the two bandits watch the televised transmission of the first astronauts landing on the moon. Richard Nixon, the earthly representative of hegemonic power, occupying a small rectangle to the left of the screen, congratulates the astronauts with perfunctory clichés about peace and progress. The black bandit comments: "They're really out of it. Why do they go to the moon, when I've already been there for a long time." The bandits, in their lunar solitude, represent the hidden face of the official earth. The film identifies with this hidden face; the film itself embodies a cool criminality, constituting an audiovisual assault and battery. Like the crimes it depicts, it simply exists in its provocative gratuitousness, as an apparently nihilistic gesture against the hypocritical discourse of power. In allegorical terms, however, it shows black-white solidarity within marginality, a yet-to-be-politicized revolt against the system.

Bressane's *Rei do Baralho* (King of the Cards, 1973), meanwhile, forms an ironic tribute to the *chanchada,* and uses the key *chanchada* actor: Grande Otelo. *Rei do Baralho* is a meta*chanchada,* a parody of a parody in the sense that *chanchadas* already parodied American musical comedies. *Rei do Baralho* was filmed in the Cinédia studios in Jacarepaguá (a neighborhood outside of Rio), studios associated with the *chanchada* tradition, and exploits that studio's decor. The film provides a collage of stereotyped scenes, each associated with a specific set—a ship, a casino, a cabaret. The "plot," such as it is, centers on a discrete romance between Grande Otelo and a Jayne Mansfield look-alike. The film weaves between them a ludic-erotic play of promises, delays, detours, and interdictions—a kind of *Last Year in Jacarepaguá.* And despite its numerous frustrations for the spectator, the film's final shot does offer one conventional satisfaction: the two principals, who up to this point have barely touched, exchange a prolonged, very Hollywoodean kiss. Thus Bressane has shuffled his cards in such a way as to deal out this one final frisson. The film plays on the obvious contrasts between the two members of the couple—black and white, short and tall, old and young—but without commenting on race in any obvious way. In the context of the sexual and racial politics of the *chanchada,* however, we can see the film as alluding to the taboo on interracial romance in the *chanchadas,* where the romance was left to the white leads and never to the black supporting players like Grande Otelo or Colé. Grande Otelo, we recall, usually got to dance with white women but not to sleep with them, while black women were allowed neither to dance nor to sleep. When Grande Otelo indulged in final kisses, it was often not with the leading female actress but with his male co-star Oscarito, as in the comic finale of *Matar ou Correr* (To Kill or to Run, 1954).

In 1970, while in exile, Glauber Rocha made a film in Africa on an African subject. Its original title was multilingual *Der Leone Have Sept Cabeças* (The

Lion Has Seven Heads)—reflective of five of the colonizing powers in Africa (Germany, Italy, England, France, and Portugal). For Rocha, *Der Leone Have Sept Cabeças* was a "popular film, produced by popular culture," both "anti-colonialist and revolutionary." Although he himself was Euro Brazilian, he saw the film as a case of "going back to his own roots." The film is set in a generic Africa, where the African resistance, aligned with Latin American revolutionaries, struggled against neocolonialism aligned with the local elite and reinforced by mercenary forces. In Rocha's usual style, influenced by Sergei Eisenstein, Bertolt Brecht, and Shakespeare, *Der Leone Have Sept Cabeças* orchestrates a number of synthetic characters. The colonizers represent the "seven-headed beast," that is, imperialism, whose various heads include a broad-shouldered mercenary who sings Nazi songs (like those who worked on behalf of Rhodesia and pre-Mandela South Africa); a Portuguese administrator; an American businessman (who hedges his bets by supporting all sides); a whore-of-Babylon Hollywoodish figure named Marlene, doubtless after Marlene Dietrich; a false prophet (who claims that the revolution is not yet ripe); and Dr. Xobu, a Mobutu-style black bourgeois puppet president in a white-frock coat. A typical colonial "mimic man," the latter recites Corneille and sings "La Marseillaise" to show off his pathetic patina of occidental education. His goal as a leader is to monopolize the crumbs offered by imperialism. The sequence of his inauguration is portrayed as a neocolonized mimicry orchestrated by Europeans. Xobu wears the outfit of an eighteenth-century European nobleman, a white powdered wig, a three-corner hat and a scepter, attire that for a Brazilian audience evokes samba pageant costumes. The African audience seems uninterested in the inauguration; it is not meant for them. Opposing the colonizers are the young militant Samba (named after the Afro Brazilian cultural phenomenon) and Zumbi (named after the Palmarino leader)—representatives, in sum, of cultural and political resistance, along with the European leftist Pablo and a somewhat eccentric revolutionary priest played by Jean-Pierre Léaud. Zumbi's daughter has been raped, and his wife has died for lack of medicine. All the revolutionary characters together represent a tricontinetal revolution of the black diaspora and the European left.

The prefatory text to *Der Leone Have Sept Cabeças,* in some ways prophetic of Afrocentrism, reads:

2000 years ago the lions and the leopards lived free in the forest. 2000 years ago the gods lived free in the skies and the sea. 500 years ago the whites came and massacred the lions and the leopards, and set the sky and the lands of our gods aflame.

The whites led our kings and our people away to work as slaves in the new lands of the Americas, and our gods accompanied them. In the Americas, our gods witnessed the suffering of our kings and our people. Black slaves enriched white bosses, and their sweat turned into the blood which nourished the tobacco, the cotton, and the sugar cane plantations, along with all the other marvelous riches of the Americas. But one day our gods rebelled, and our people took up arms to win their freedom. We have been struggling for three centuries against the Europeans who never stopped decimating us with unprecedented barbarism. But the whites can never kill me, Zumbi, because I am here to reincarnate all the massacred leaders. My sword will cleave the earth in two, leaving the executioners on one side and a free Africa on the other. Here and every-where, blacks will carry Africa in their hearts. We will no longer confront European arms only with swords and magic.

Against hatred, hatred. Against fire, fire.

Although *Der Leone Have Sept Cabeças* is obviously problack and pro-African, it is not racially dualistic. When the blacks shout "Death to Colonialism!" it is the white Pablo who answers "Resistance," a reference perhaps to the partici-pation of some white revolutionaries in the anticolonial struggles of Mozam-bique and Angola. Later, he forms part of the column of guerillas crossing the savannah. The black puppet leader, meanwhile, collaborates with colonialism.

Although anti-illusionist and stylized, consisting largely of artificial tab-leaux and highly formalized sequences, the aesthetic of *Der Leone Have Sept Cabeças* is also realist in the Brechtian sense of "showing causal relations." The three colonialists address us directly, in the Brechtian fashion; they enter the shot, turn their backs to us, then do an abrupt about-face and recite a speech with their finger raised. The identical presentation underlines their common-ality as colonialists. At the same time, the personages are not coordinated with their accents; the German speaks in a Portuguese accent; the American with a French and so forth. Rather than convince us that "real life" is passing before our eyes, Rocha provokes us to reflect on the politics of colonialism.

CHAPTER 10
Afro/Indigenous Celebration:
The 1970s

∞

Despite continuing dictatorship, the 1970s were a time of increasing black militancy and self-awareness. Inspired both by the American black power movement and by the wave of independence movements in the Portuguese colonies of Africa, many activist cultural organizations, such as the Quilombo alternative samba school, Porto Alegre's Senghor Institute, the Black Consciousness and Unity Group, and the dance troupe Olorum Baba Mim were all founded during that decade. A major political organization, the Unified Negro Movement, was founded in 1978. In Bahia, *afoxé* (songs/rhythms derived from *candomblé* ritual) groups like Ilê Aiyê (founded 1974) and Olodum (founded 1979) worked to organize blacks culturally and politically.[1] It was also in the 1970s that the wave of black pride that had long before washed over the United States began to spread through Rio and other cities. Urban youth, especially in Rio, began to adopt African American emblems of black pride, such as coded handshakes and soul music in a style dubbed *bleque pau* (black power). The popularity of American soul music inspired "black Rio" in Rio, "black samba" in São Paulo, and "black mineiro" in Minas. Afro-diasporic music comes to play a role in the constitution of black identity. Gilberto Freyre himself denounced the movement in 1977 as a North American export that would substitute melancholy and revolt for "happy and fraternal" sambas.[2]

It was also during the decade of the 1970s that blacks came into their own within Brazilian Cinema, the culmination of a slow "fade to Afro." The period witnessed not only many features devoted to Afro Brazilian themes but also the emergence of the first Afro Brazilian directors. Although Haroldo Costa, the black impresario and actor who had played the lead in the stage version of *Black Orpheus,* had made a sophisticated, worldly film, set in an elite Jockey Club and entitled *Um Desconhecido Bate à Porta* (A Stranger Knocks, but alternately titled *Pista de Grama*) in 1958, there were no black actors in the film, nor did the film give emphasis to specifically racial issues (see photo 85). In the 1970s, in contrast, films by black directors did reference black themes. The former Cinema Novo actor Waldyr Onofre directed the urban comedy *As Aventuras Amorosas de um Padeiro* (Amorous Adventures of a Baker, 1975), and the by-now-familiar Antônio Sampaio (Pitanga) made his *Na Boca do Mundo* (In the Mouth of the World, 1977). In Porto Alegre, meanwhile, Odilon Lopes directed and acted in *Um É Pouco, Dois É Bom* (One Is Few, Two Is Great, 1977). And in the following year, the Nigerian director Ola Balogun participated in the first Brazilian Nigerian coproduction, *A Deusa Negra* (The Black Goddess, 1978). (We will return to these films shortly.)

Afro Brazilian themes also come to the forefront in the 1970s. If many Brazilian films from the 1960s make a subtle, indirect critique of racism, Antunes Filho's *Compasso de Espera* (Marking Time; made 1971, released 1973) made a frontal assault by inventorying the racist features of Brazilian society in a brutally direct fashion. The film's courage was "rewarded" by a two-year delay in exhibition, doubtless a consequence of the dictatorship's anxiety about issues of race. Some exhibitors refused the film with the alibi that its black-and-white format was obsolete, somewhat ironic given the film's black-white theme and given that the very same exhibitors were then showing contemporary American black-and-white films like *The Last Picture Show* (1971). The concurrent rise to stardom of one of the film's actresses (Renée de Vilmond) probably nudged the distributors into finally screening the film.

The delaying of *Compasso de Espera*'s release was just one of many signs of nervousness about race during the dictatorship. The authorities harassed the "black soul" movement, which drew inspiration from the black political and cultural movements in the United States. Journalist Sérgio Augusto reports that journalists were forbidden to use the word "black" in a racial sense because of fears of a black power movement in Brazil.[3] Musician Dom Salvador and his all-black musical group "Abolition" were reportedly pressured by police agents to include white musicians, an "obligatory integration" perhaps possible only in Brazil.[4] Government censors also scissored a long black

85. Haroldo Costa's *Um Desconhecido Bate à Porto* (1958)

power speech from Luiz Rosemberg Filho's underground film *América do Sexo* (The America of Sex, 1970) and in 1975 banned Brazilian television from showing *Awakening from a Dream,* an East German documentary about the worldwide impact of the book *Quarto do Despejo* (Child of the Dark), Carolina Mário de Jesus's widely translated best-seller about life in the favelas. In 1978, the government objected to a planned cultural festival aimed at promoting links between Afro Brazilian and African American artists and intellectuals. And a questionnaire distributed by the Federal Police Division of Censorship of Public Diversions as a guideline for censors includes the following questions: "Does [the film] deal with racial problems? With racial discrimination in Brazil? With American Black Power? With problems outside of Brazil that could have a hidden or subliminal connotation in Brazil?" Even right-wing censors, it appears, can be adept at "allegorical readings."[5]

Compasso de Espera's director, Antunes Filho, is a prominent São Paulo theater director, famous for his award-winning staging of plays such as *Peer Gynt* and *Richard III* and whose stage version of *Macunaíma* was also widely praised when it toured the United States in 1979. Filho is known for visual flair, dramaturgical competence, and a quasi-academic perfectionism. His film is set in São Paulo, the cosmopolitan megalopolis whose industrialization led to the tentative beginnings of a black middle class, and the base for the Frente Negra in the late 1930s. Filho's mise-en-scène highlights the abstract modernity of the São Paulo setting, a relatively unexplored decor within Brazilian cinema, both to reproduce the protagonist's world and to convey the city's multiethnic cosmopolitanism. Here there is little trace of favela or *candomblé*, but rather steel-and-glass architecture, pop posters, deluxe apartments, and the impersonal simulacra of consumer culture.

Compasso de Espera focuses on a black poet and advertising agent named Jorge de Oliveira (played by Zózimo Bulbul, who also collaborated on the script; see photo 86). Jorge publishes books of poetry—*Compasso de Espera* is the title of one of his collections—with the help of his sponsor, a childless white millionaire (an allusion to the Brazilian institution of the *padrinho,* the patron "godfather"). The impeccably dressed, dignified, articulate Jorge at first glance resembles a number of Sidney Poitier characters, but he lacks the moral stature of the Poitier persona.[6] Romantically involved with an older white woman (Emma), Jorge feels sorry for her, but also resents his financial dependence on her. (Jorge's professional prestige is "traded," as it were, for Emma's real wealth and for the cultural capital of her whiteness.) Emma's relatives suggest that the couple not appear too much in public, so as to avoid "talk." Jorge's subsequent infatuation with the upper-class Cristina (Renée de Vilmond) leads to confrontations first with Emma and then with Cristina's family. When Cristina's parents encounter the couple in a restaurant, the mother sneeringly tells her daughter: "I never thought you would stoop so low." Later, the couple is harassed by rednecks who seem more imported from a Stanley Kramer film about the American South than authentic in Brazilian terms. He is also flirted with by a brazen blond, in a scene reminiscent of the film version of (then) Leroi Jones's *The Dutchman* (1966). When he rejects the blond's advances, she shrieks at him, and Jorge realizes that he has been a sex object for white women. He decides to have nothing to do with white people, but when he visits his own family in a poor neighborhood on the outskirts of São Paulo, they too reject him as a social-climbing snob and a traitor to his race. In a final sequence, he walks alone in a working-class neighborhood, where blacks assume he must be a musician, since "only musicians dress like that."

Successful but dependent on white benevolence, Jorge is internally rent by

86. Zózimo Bulbul as Jorge in *Compasso de Espera* (1973)

the contradictory roles he is called upon to play. A partisan of Martin Luther King–style nonviolence, Jorge is pressured from the left by his militant separatist friend Assis (Antônio Pitanga). To Assis's Rap Brownish "Burn Baby Burn!" Jorge answers, in English, "Build Baby Build." In any case, Jorge's attempt to be at once distinguished author, defender of black rights, devoted family member, and dedicated lover to two white women ultimately exacts a terrible existential toll (photo 87). His social climb is more a pseudoascension than a real liberation. The partisan of "passive resistance," he is, unlike Martin Luther King, often merely passive. The word *desculpe* (excuse me) is frequently on his lips. When the rednecks attack him, Cristina fights back more than he does. A fledgling cultural amphibian, he doesn't negotiate either world very well; full of understanding for everyone, he has too little for himself. Jorge illustrates the thesis of sociologist Florestan Fernandes (on whose work the film is partially based) about the black middle class in Brazil, a thesis reminiscent of Franklin Frazier's work concerning the American black middle class: that black-middle-class adhesion to an individualistic, competitive, and moralistic ethos, combined with a fascination with the external signs of a high living standard, lead to a flight from identification with the masses of black

87. Zózimo Bulbul and Renée de Vilmond in *Compasso de Espera*

people. Jorge's lack of involvement with black women, furthermore, reproduces a typical syndrome within Brazilian cinema, including within films
made by black Brazilians.

Compasso de Espera exposes the myriad forms of Brazilian racism, from condescending gestures to acts of outright discrimination and even physical violence. Jorge is the object of crude racial humor—a consistent source of irrita-
tion for Brazilian blacks—as when a control booth technician suggests
substituting a close-up of Jorge's face for the usual "fade to black." Those who
discriminate invariably deny any racist intent, insisting that unspecified "others" would object. Often the designated discriminators are themselves people
of color. Afraid to lose his job, a mulatto receptionist reluctantly turns Jorge
away from a hotel, precisely the kind of incident often reported in Brazilian
newspapers as a violation of the Afonso Arinos law against racial discrimination. Jorge himself cites Millor Fernandes's ironic dictum that "there is no racism in Brazil because black people know their place." The film mocks a com-
pendium of racist clichés uttered by "well-meaning" white Brazilians: that the
problem isn't racial but social, that the issue is not one of race but of class,
that the success of black celebrities like Pelé proves the absence of discrimination, that "sleeping together" signifies absence of prejudice. One executive of-

fers as proof of tolerance the fact of having a "fantastic" black mistress.

In his advertising work, Jorge designs ads that project whiteness as aesthetic ideal (a real-life tendency easily confirmed by a quick perusal of Brazilian magazine and TV commercials). Even the "charitable" institution of the *padrinho*-protector can be traced to the period of slavery, when the frequency of white-black sexual involvements (sometimes involving coercion) led well-off whites to adopt and protect their "illegitimate" miscegenated offspring and even at times to purchase their freedom. Such mechanisms are typical of societies in which power is distributed along racial lines, and Roger Bastide cites *apadrinhamento* as an institution meant to smooth over racial tensions, a way of knitting the two communities together both materially and affectively.[7] The institution can provide a kind of material "safety net" during hard times, but blacks ultimately cannot be free, the film implicitly suggests, as long as they are dependent on white "charity" and patron-client relationships that impede black solidarity.

Compasso de Espera was rightly criticized for focusing on a highly unrepresentative character, a Brazilian equivalent to American TV's "Julia" or "Cosby." Living in a luxurious apartment, sipping imported whiskey at cocktail parties, Jorge represents an infinitesimal minority of black Brazilians. In this sense, he is less representative of blacks than of the anguished artist-intellectuals of a particularly repressive period in Brazilian history. Jorge becomes an allegorical exemplar of the passivity and frustration of intellectuals in general. Stylistically, *Compasso de Espera* is a highly Europeanized and Americanized film. The parties recall *La Dolce Vita;* the lighting recalls film noir; the hortatory tone recalls Stanley Kramer. In short, the film does not take advantage of the decolonizing achievements of Cinema Novo. The soundtrack mixes abstract percussion, Erik Satie, and Blood, Sweat and Tears, completely ignoring not only African American music but also the Afro Brazilian musical presence in São Paulo, with its samba schools and its avant-garde performers. In short, the film never intimates the existence of a cultural alternative to the alienated white world in which Jorge is immersed. At the same time, the film's achievement is its descriptive anatomy of Brazilian racism. The film's events could as easily have taken place in New York as in São Paulo: perhaps the achievement of the film is to show that the two realities are not, ultimately, so far apart.

The 1970s films reveal a dramatic transformation in the attitude of Euro

Brazilian directors toward Afro Brazilian culture. Whereas 1960s Cinema Novo films sometimes focused on blacks without highlighting Afro Brazilian culture, many 1970s films make that culture the source of all that is most vital in Brazilian life. While the 1960s films saw Afro Brazilian culture through the grid of "alienation," the 1970s films see it in a spirit of anthropological enthusiasm. Nelson Pereira dos Santos's *O Amuleto de Ogum* (Amulet of Ogum, 1974), for example, celebrates the syncretic Afro Brazilian religion called *umbanda*. Founded in the late 1920s and often called one of Brazil's fastest-growing religions, *umbanda* has a following variously estimated at 20 million to 30 million. São Paulo reportedly has 90,000 *umbanda* temples, Rio 60,000.[8] The term *umbanda* encompasses a wide spectrum of practices that combine African elements—the *orixás,* spirit possession (including the Bantu traditions of receiving spirits of the dead)—with Catholicism, Kaballa, indigenous symbology, and an Alain Kardec variety of spiritism. Although the color breakdown in *umbanda* varies from group to group, Africa still, in Roger Bastide's phrase, "casts its great black shadow over *umbanda.*"[9] *Umbanda* is often said to be *the* Brazilian religion in that it incorporates cultural elements from the major groups constitutive of Brazilian identity. It is above all an open, constantly reinvoiced process. Although some *umbandistas* try to de-Africanize the religion, others try to re-Africanize it. *Umbanda* cosmology has recently incorporated Zumbi as spiritual mentor for the *pretos velhos* (literally, "old black men") and some foresee a similar incorporation for Anastácia, the popular black female figure traditionally credited with putting an end to slavery. By referencing Ogum, the film calls attention to the *orixá* first associated with iron and later, within Afro-diasporic polysemy, with all those whose professions bring them into contact with metal: railroad workers, chauffeurs, pilots, astronauts, and with "the hand that holds the scalpel in modern surgery."[10]

In *O Amuleto de Ogum,* dos Santos strives to be "popular" not only in theme but also in perspective, wholeheartedly affirming the values of the *umbandista* audience, to whom the film hopes to appeal. Taking a cue from Glauber Rocha's *Deus e Diabo na Terra do Sol* (literally God and the Devil in the Land of the Sun; released as Black God, White Devil; 1964) *O Amuleto de Ogum* introduces a frame-story drawn from popular ballads and *cordel* literature, in which the narrator-singer, named Firmino (perhaps after the protagonist of *Barravento* [The Turning Wind, 1962]) introduces, comments, and reflects on the action. As a guitar-slung blind singer (Jards Macalé) walks down the street, three street hoods jump him and force him to sing. Firmino claims that the story he is about to tell "really happened" and, at the same time, that "he just invented it," thus installing the same regime of "truth and imagination" invoked by Rocha in *Black God, White Devil*.

After the frame-song, the singer's tale recounts the trajectory of Gabriel (played by dos Santos's son Ney Sant'anna), a young man from the Northeast whose body has been magically "closed"—that is, made invulnerable to bullets—by an *umbandista*. Ten years later, protected by Ogum's amulet, Gabriel moves to Caxias, a notoriously lawless Rio *subúrbio* known for its vigilante violence, its *bicheiros* (bookies), and its vibrant popular culture. Caxias in linked by train to the center of Rio, and Jards Macalé's soundtrack deploys the train's cadenced rumble as musical punctuation. In Caxias, Gabriel becomes a gunman in the service of his uncle Severiano (Jofre Soares), criminal head of a numbers racket. When the criminal gang discovers Gabriel's closed body during a gun battle, Gabriel becomes extremely famous. But he also annoys Severiano by refusing to kill gratuitously, and especially by taking up with Severiano's lover Eneida (Anecy Rocha).

Severiano begins to set traps for Gabriel. He buys him sports cars and fancy clothes, yet he tricks him into murdering the president of the Red Cross. Subsequently, Gabriel is called upon to lead a rival group against Severiano, a conflict that turns Caxias into a war zone. Severiano kills all of Gabriel's companions, but reserves a secret weapon for Gabriel: the *despachos* of Gogo, a mercenary *pai de santo* who tries to get at the alcohol-loving Gabriel's liver. One night, Gabriel's enemies find him drunk, weigh him down with stones, and throw him into the sea. Nearby, however, Pai Erlei, an *umbanda* priest, is paying homage to Iemanjá. Pai Erlei rescues Gabriel, recognizes his amulet, brings him to the *terreiro* and initiates him into *umbanda* (photo 88).

Severiano then has Pai Erlei sequestered, offering him money in exchange for making Gabriel vulnerable; Pai Erlei refuses and defends the principles of *umbanda*. Next, Severiano bribes Eneida to find Gabriel. She finds him at an *umbanda* children's festival, after which Gabriel tells Eneida the secret of his amulet: that his mother had offered her own life as a guarantee for his closed body. Eneida passes on the information to Severiano, who orders his thugs to kill Gabriel's mother. In a bloody confrontation, Gabriel and Severiano kill each other, but Gabriel falls into Severiano's swimming pool, just as Gabriel's mother arrives at the Rio bus station (Severiano's thugs had killed Gabriel's

88. Ney Sant'Anna and Pai Erlei in *O Amuleto de Ogum* (1974)

mother's maid by mistake). Gabriel is magically resurrected, not in the pool, but in a boat at sea, with six-guns blazing as the frame-story ends. The blind singer finishes his story, but the bandits object to the denouement and decide to kill him. They discover that the singer too has a closed body. "If you don't like my story," Firmino tells the bandits, "then you can go to hell."

The character Gabriel is partially based on a real-life popular hero from Caxias (Tenório Cavalcânti) a local Robin Hood–style mobster-politician (and another migrant from the Northeast) reputed to have a closed body because of his talent for emerging unscathed from attempted assassinations. The equation between prototype and role was so strong that opening-night audiences applauded the real-life Tenório as if he had been the hero of the film.[11] In the film version, dos Santos retains the idea of a popular criminal with a closed body, but he gives the figure a religious base in *umbanda* (Tenório Cavalcânti complained that the director had turned him into a mystic). The film's Gabriel is naive, gullible; he is used by Severiano, betrayed by Eneida, and easily manipulated by gangsters. Hardly great in himself, it is his religion and alliance with Pai Erlei that give him strength. Gabriel learns the mysteries of *umbanda* and discovers his saint Ogum Beiramar (Ogum by the Sea). Having made his offering to Iemanjá, he grows in stature and earns the right to represent the people. In his final incarnation, he has become the warrior Ogum.

O Amuleto de Ogum is not just *about umbanda;* it is impregnated with *umbanda* values. The narrative itself, as the director pointed out, is structured by three *umbanda* cycles.[12] The first concerns the ceremony of closing the body and Gabriel's protection by Ogum. The second concerns the *pomba-gira,* an *umbanda* figure representing woman at her most capricious, here embodied by Eneida. The third cycle belongs to Exu. Here Severiano tries to deploy *umbanda* to make Gabriel an alcoholic. When Severino visits Pai Erlei, he is possessed by Exu, throws himself on the ground, screams and giggles, and commits violence to himself. Pai Erlei receives a *preto velho,* and recommends that Severiano redeem himself by performing a *trabalho,* or duty. At another point, Severiano speaks like an astonished child. He then seems quite disturbed for having allowed the religion to "soften" him. The film is also bathed in the purifying presence of water. Pai Erlei's *terreiro* is near waterfalls; Gabriel's offerings are to Iemanjá, goddess of the sea; Gabriel falls into Severiano's pool and emerges from the sea.

Although not a believer, dos Santos shows respect for *umbanda* as a religion, a respect reflected even in his methods of filming. José de Carvalho, a *pai de santo* and head of the Xangô Spirit Tent, was consulted on all religious aspects. To film the closing of Gabriel's body, the filmmakers had to wait for a week to get the permission of the *pai de santo* who could authorize the out-of-season filming of the Cosme and Damião feast. Many of the participants were believers. Pai Erlei is a real *babalaô;* the dancers celebrating Iemanjá are *umbandistas.* One of the actors, Zé Índio, was an adept who kept a protective eye on the filming process. Furthermore, *O Amuleto de Ogum* virtually *requires* the spectator to become an *umbandista,* at least for the duration of the film, if only to understand the narrated events. The film simply assumes *umbandista* values, without explaining them to the uninitiated. A Catholic audience, the director points out, need only see a priest raising the host to know a mass is being celebrated. An *umbandista* audience, similarly, easily recognizes the ceremony that "closes" the protagonist's body and recognizes his protection by Ogum, the warrior divinity and symbol, in Brazil, of the struggle for social justice. It recognizes Gabriel's amulet as being made of steel—since Ogum is god of metals—and recognizes the sword evoking Ogum and the trident evoking Exu. When Gabriel is shot but does not die, the audience recognizes the song "Ogum É de Lei" (Ogum is the Law) and the image of Saint George visible behind Gabriel. The audience recognizes the hoarse voice of the *preto velho* and the provocative manners of the *pomba-gira*. At the same time, the film does not idealize *umbanda:* one *umbanda* priest in the film works for popular liberation; the other is a greedy charlatan and opportunist.[13] In sum, *O Amuleto de Ogum* does accord nuanced, respectful treatment to an African-ized religion while revealing the multiracial participation in that religion.

Afro Brazilian religions interweave the material world of *aiyê* and the spiri-tual world of *orun* together; the sacred penetrates the quotidian. The symbi-ology of the *orixás,* for example, pervades everyday life; what one eats, what one wears encode references to the *orixás.* And everyone knows that Ogum likes beer, that Exu likes rum, and that Xangô is quick tempered. The Afro-in-formed audience knows of the pantheon's kinship relations, that Ogum is Exu's brother, that both are sons of Iemanjá, and that the *pomba-gira* is Exu's wife, much as the audience at a Greek tragedy would know that Zeus is the son of Cronus. And whereas in Africa the *orixás* were linked to cities and re-gions, in Brazil they become linked to individuals, rather like the "guardian angels" of popular Catholicism.

Iberé Cavalcânti's *A Força de Xangô* (The Power of Xangô, 1979) assumes this popular knowledge to construct a plot that interfaces the *orixás* and their protégés in the everyday world (photo 89). The protagonist Tonho (Geraldo Rosa), son of Xangô, an *orixá* known for his virile, seductive orchestration of multiple romances, and an inveterate drinker, *capoeirista,* and womanizer, falls in love with Zulmira (Ivone Lara), daughter of Iansã, on Ash Wednesday, a day dedicated to both Iansã and Xangô. Tonho promises to be forever faithful and take care of their innumerable children. But time passes, Tonho's enthusi-asm wanes, Zulmira ages and gets fat, and Tonho regresses to his womanizing ways. Enraged, Zulmira invokes Exu, and on the third Friday of the seventh month, the blond gypsy Iaba (Elke Maravilha) arrives on a boat from Ita-parica, along with her assistant Beicinho (Grande Otelo) and a loquacious parrot. Tonho falls in love and begins to work tirelessly to buy her clothes and jewels, ultimately losing all his friends and falling into a sad, lonely life. Then he meets Rosinha de Oxum, as sweet and understanding as Iaba is capricious. He goes to a *terreiro* for an exorcism, since what Exu gives, Exu can also take

89. Cavalcânti's *A Força de Xangô* (1979)

away. Xangô comes to the rescue, and teaches Tonho how to escape from Iabá's clutches.

Based on a Carybé story about Xangô and his three wives—Iansã, Oba, and Oxum—*A Força de Xangô* shows the characters as inseparable from their protective saints. They embody their *orixá*'s myth, and the myth, in turn, catalyzes their behavior. Even their clothes reflect their links to the *orixás:* the red of Xangô and Iansã, the yellow of Oba and Oxum, the black of Exu. While the basic premise is brilliant—only rarely has Afro Brazilian religion been used to emplot films—and although the director's goal was to thoroughly mingle reality and dream, the characters and the *orixás*, the film is only intermittently successful in this goal. The opening sequence, a stylized dance to Xangô complete with Xangô's double-headed ax, gives way to banal magic-free realism, and the acting leaves much to be desired. Elke Maravilha overacts as a *pomba-gira,* diabolizing the role in a way alien to the religion, and there is a tension between the Bahian locale and the Carioca dominant among the actors (photo 90).

A year after the release of *A Força de Xangô,* another film about *umbanda* was released: Marco Altberg's *A Prova de Fogo* ('Trial by Fire, 1981). The film's

90. Elke Maravilha as the *pomba-gira* in *A Força de Xangô*

source is an autobiographical book by Nívio Ramos Sales (played by Pedro Paulo Rangel), a Carioca journalist and *umbanda* priest, renamed Mauro in the film, who leaves the Northeast for Rio. As a precociously spiritual child, Mauro shows rare sensibility and intuition. On the advice of a friend, he visits an *umbanda* center, where his vocation as a medium is confirmed. Becoming completely dedicated to the life of the *terreiro,* he discovers that he can "incorporate" very different *orixás,* for example, the virile *boiadeiro* (herdsman, cowboy) and the very feminine *ciganinha* (little gypsy). A more experienced *pai de santo,* João, takes charge of the *terreiro* and assigns a woman, Sandra, as *mãe pequena* (assistant priestess). João is in love with Sandra, but she is more interested in Mauro, especially when he is possessed by the masculine *boiadeiro*. Sandra shows disappointment, later, when Mauro is possessed by the feminine *ciganinha,* wearing women's clothing and colored skirts. Parallel to his religious activities, Mauro works in a bank and studies business administration. In the end he returns to his native Alagoas, where he becomes a well-reputed *pai de santo,* and, alongside his wife and son, follows his spiritual guide: a *ciganinha*.

Unlike *Amuleto de Ogum, A Prova de Fogo* does not mix religiosity with violence and crime; rather, it concentrates on the religious vocation per se within

91. Mauro as the "Little Gypsy" in *A Prova de Fogo* (1980)

the space of the *terreiro*. The protagonist discovers his spiritual vocation, together with his feminine side, and thus manages to reconcile the diverse facets
of his personality. *Umbanda* in the film is portrayed as an amalgam of religion, psychoanalysis, and art—religion because it involves the sacred and
trance, psychoanalysis because it fosters the personal growth of "clients," and
art because it includes performance and staging. The film illustrates the
conceptualization of *umbanda* as the "poor man's couch," the popular view
that *umbanda* is often effective where psychoanalysis or conventional therapy
fail.[14] In *A Prova de Fogo, umbanda* is pragmatic, quotidian; it is neither exotic
nor purely spiritual. It is more couch than altar, less about African traditions,
although they are present, than about individual cure.

Despite its "magical" side, *A Prova de Fogo* is based on phenomena either
lived by Nívio Ramos Sales or observed by the director during his prepro-
duction research. Altberg himself witnessed the gender bending whereby
men can be possessed by female entities and vice versa. In a form of religious
cross-dressing, Mauro wears feminine clothes (photo 91), while his wife encourages him and herself addresses the female entity as if she were a friend
and neighbor. Nor does the film shy away from the issue of homosexuality. At
one point the *ciganinha* advises a homosexual "client" to place candy in his

lover's anus and then give it to him to eat. The source biography describes a time in the history of *candomblé* when men were just beginning to head *terreiros,* and when "it was expected that the men would be gay; if they were not, there was general disappointment."[15] The film portrays *umbanda* as nurturing of bisexuality and the feminine in men and the masculine in women. African-derived religions, speaking more generally, display a great openness to "undecidabilities" of all kinds, whether sexual, intellectual, or spiritual. One *orixá,* according to the source text, spends half of the year as a woman and half as a man. Mauro is first possessed by a masculine entity, but he gradually becomes more open to his *ciganinha* side. *A Prova de Fogo* highlights the capacity of many Brazilians to live simultaneously in two mental and cultural universes, two socioideological worlds. Involved with the spiritual in one of his lives, Mauro studies in the other the quintessentially modern subject of administration.

The 1970s film that perhaps most outrageously confounds all stereotypes is Antônio Carlos Fontoura's *Rainha Diaba* (Devil Queen, 1975). Charismatically played by Milton Gonçalves, the title character is a black drag queen and underworld chieftan.[16] The character's real-life prototype, a black transvestite hoodlum known as Madame Satan, wielded power in Rio's notorious Lapa district. The name Devil Queen translates the two elements of Madame Satan's name—the feminine and the diabolic.[17] The protagonist's transvestitism is also carnivalesque, in the sense that there was an old tradition of men dressing up as *baianas* during carnival. In any case, Rainha Diaba, from his whorehouse headquarters, lords it over organized crime. To protect Robertinho, his most cherished assistant-lover, from the police Rainha Diaba has the smart-alecky Catitu (Nelson Xavier), one of his head thugs, invent a fictitiously dangerous criminal as a way of taking the heat off Robertinho (photo 92). Catitu chooses as his victim the young, cocky, and ambitious petty criminal Bereco (Stepan Narpessian), who is kept by the cabaret singer Isa (Odete Lara). Catitu tricks Bereco into committing a series of crimes that attract police attention and project him as "armed and dangerous." But Bereco enjoys his new-found role as star criminal, to the point that he finally confronts Rainha Diaba himself. The film ends with a stylized holocaust, reminiscent both of Elizabethan tragedy and of Scorcese's *Taxi Driver,* the screen littered with corpses in a manner at once wrenching and diffusely parodic.

92. Nelson Xavier and Milton Gonçalves in *Rainha Diaba* (1974)

Milton Gonçalves based his portrayal in *Rainha Diaba* on an actual madame who controlled the redlight district in a province of the state of São Paulo; the character is indeed regal, or better, "queenly." A marvelous Thespian creation, the character's walk, according to Gonçalves himself, evokes "something between a gazelle and an elephant."[18] The psychology of his character is highly volatile, at once lordly and vulnerable, inflexible and sensitive. As a black, gay mobster, his role recalls that of the racketeer played by Brock Peters in Sidney Lumet's *The Pawnbroker* (1965). Fontoura defines *Rainha Diaba* as a "pop-gay-black thriller" that melds his favored generic strains: musicals, detective films, film noir. On the other hand, the film also inherits a native Brazilian strain of urban realism going back to films like *Rio 40 Graus* (Rio 40 Degrees, 1954) and *Rio Zona Norte* (Rio's Northern Zone, 1957). Although the formulas are familiar, the generic skeleton is fleshed out with very Brazilian details. The dialogue was written by Plínio Marcos, a São Paulo playwright known for transcribing a rough, angry verbal street style with which he was personally familiar. At once realistic and stylized, the dialogue displays a high coefficient of underworld slang, and mixes the argots of São Paulo and Rio de Janeiro. This same quality of stylized realism characterizes the film as a whole. If the lighting is ambient à la Cinema Novo, the decor is fantastically camp and pastel. The film's violence is so exaggerated that we suspect it is all a fantasy, that the blood is paint, and that it is being exploited as a poetic and plastic resource rather than as an emblem of blood-and-guts realism, perhaps as a way for the director to deal with an unfamiliar milieu. For an outsider, the underworld is a fantasy seen through the idealizing prism of other films. The gangsters, significantly, are not only criminals, they are also artists.

The opening Nat King Cole song laments that "they tried to tell us we're too young," but it is hardly a typical case of "falling in love." The silky elegance of Cole's voice contrasts with the hard-edged world we are about to enter, while the lyrics suggests that the gangsters are merely over-sexed children playing at being hoodlums, imitating, in the manner of *Bande à Part* (Band of Outsiders, 1963), stars they have seen in the movies. The Nat King Cole allusion is just one instance of a highly evocative music track, partly composed and partly "sampled" by Guilherme Vaz. Like the film itself, the soundtrack forms a modernist pop-collage dominated by percussive base, an aggressive rhythmic pulse consisting of amplified bass, distorted guitar, electric piano, and synthesizer. The music track moves from the sweetness of Cole into strident dissonance. Another brilliantly orchestrated moment has Rainha Diaba looking vulnerable, passive, and impotent, slumped in his chair as James Brown's "sex machine," in a perfect wedding of sound and image, exhorts him to "Get on up!"

Rainha Diaba makes remarkably little of the blackness of its protagonist, although his designation as "queen" does recall the trope of black royalty (from Duke Ellington to Lady Day to Prince to Chico Rei) as well as the ennobled characters of classical tragedy. When some hoodlums revolt against his rule, it is because they refuse to be bossed by a drag queen, not because he is black; homophobia is stronger than racism. Eminently black, eminently gay, and eminently macho, Devil Queen himself forms a veritable palimpsest of supposedly irreconcilable characteristics. In this sense, the film suggests, in a completely offhand manner, the existence of analogous situations of oppression: an oppressed sexual minority (homosexuals) converges with an oppressed racial minority (blacks). The legend on his t-shirt—"Freak!"—evokes his constituencies, the community of the marginalized, all those that white male heterosexual power peripheralizes and turns into freaks.

In Eduardo Coutinho's *Faustão: O Cangaceiro Negro* (Big Faust: The Black Cangaceiro, 1975) we reencounter a figure familiar both from 1950s films and from Glauber Rocha's critical allegories of the 1960s: the *cangaceiro*. The Coutinho film casts Eliezer Gomes in the title role of the black *cangaceiro* (see photo 93). (There is apparently little historical prototype for such a figure; some blacks belonged to *cangaceiro* bands, but not as leaders.) Set in the 1930s, the plot begins when Faustão kidnaps Henrique, the son of landlord Coronel Pereira. Faustão at first asks for ransom money, but then decides to adopt Henrique, who is eager to join the *cangaceiros*. The intricacies of *sertão* politics lead them to part ways, however, and they become leaders of rival gangs. Henrique asks Faustão to cease his *cangaceiro* activities, but Faustão responds that he is too old to change profession. Then Henrique tries to buy him off, urging him to give up his "crazy dream." At one point, Faustão asks Henrique to kill him, but later he himself kills Henrique by mistake. Desperate, he picks up Henrique's dead body and screams: "I asked you to kill me, you dog! Get up and kill me, you bastard!"

93. Eliezer Gomes in *Faustão: O Cangaceiro Negro* (1975)

Faustão invokes a quadruple intertext: (1) the *cangaceiro* films, the most famous being Lima Barreto's *O Cangaceiro* (The Cangaceiro, 1953) (2) the Hollywood western; (3) the Faust story, the hypotext as well for Guimaraes Rosa's novel *Grande Sertão: Veredas* (The Devil to Pay in the Backlands, 1956); and (4) Shakespeare's *Henry IV.* In Shakespearean terms, Faustão can be seen as a black Falstaff, and Henrique (Henry in Portuguese) as Prince Hal (Henry IV). Henrique's marriage to the local Baninha woman in this schema parallels the coronation of Henry IV, each a situation in which two former friends are separated when one rises to great worldly power. Friendship between Henrique and Faustão is no longer possible, much as King Henry IV can no longer indulge in pranks with Falstaff as he did when he was Prince Hal. An appealing, almost mythic hero, Faustão has Falstaff's positive qualities, such as exuberance, vitality, and camaraderie, but not his negative ones, since he is honest and courageous rather than mendacious and cowardly. A strong and dynamic leader, he survives by his wits as two successive bands are wiped out. Although *Faustão* centers on a biracial friendship, the film never calls attention to race per se. The gulf between them, in this *l'amitié impossible,* has to do not with race but with social allegiances, and with Henrique's alliance with the *coronéis* (landowners), the traditional enemies of the *cangaceiros.*

A *cangaceiro* film like *Faustão* also recalls the American western (here the "northeastern") in which male camaraderie is more valued than heterosexual love. The film evokes the long literary tradition of friendship between white men and men of color, going as far back as *Robinson Crusoe,* proceeding through Ishmael and Queequeg in *Moby Dick* and Huck and Jim in *Huckleberry Finn,* and continuing on through the many Hollywood biracial buddy films, in all of which some analysts such as Leslie Fiedler detect a homoerotic undercurrent. But unlike some of these other texts, *Faustão* emphasizes the protagonist's heterosexual attractiveness. One white woman dreams of marrying him, bearing his children, and becoming his companion in banditry as Maria Bonita was for Lampião. Faustão defends the poor and oppressed against the ruthless *coronéis.* For the people, he says, in a transparent allusion to the dictatorship, it doesn't matter which coronel wins. In another reading, the phrase suggests that for the people (largely black and mestiço) it doesn't matter what the elite (largely white) decides, since their oppression continues. But Faustão is not given racial specificity; he is not a black man struggling for power, but a popular representative who happens to be black. His "crazy dream" has to do with Robin Hood–like opposition to the rich, rather than with black liberation.

Not all of the black films from the 1970s are as progressive as *Rainha Diaba* or *Faustão*. In this same period of maximum repression, blacks and mulattoes played a significant if ambiguous role in an emerging genre: the *pornochanchadas*. These erotic comedies generally exalted the fast-track good life of the Brazilian "economic miracle," replete with sports cars and wild parties in luxurious nouveau riche surroundings, while serving up shots of breasts and buttocks for the delectation of male voyeurs. Their vulgarity and sexism is reflected in titles such as *Um Soutien para Papai* (A Bra for Daddy, 1972), *As Secretárias que Fazem de Tudo* (The Secretaries Who Do Everything, 1974), and *A Virgem e o Macho* (The Virgin and the Macho, 1975). Ultimately moralistic and even antierotic, the *pornochanchadas* provide an X-ray of the sexual neuroses of the white middle-class male. Rather than deliver on the erotic promise implicit in their titles, the films served up instead minimal nudity and perpetual coitus interruptus. The stereotypical figure of the "mulatta" as the national sex symbol plays an important role in these films. In real life, mulattas wiggle their derrieres during carnival or in shows like "Oba Oba." They are glorified during liminal moments (carnival) and places (nightclubs). But these same mulattas often end up as ordinary prostitutes or gogo dancers for the sex industry. One *pornochanchada* literalizes this trajectory. In Roberto Machado's *Uma Mulata para Todos* (A Mulatta for Everyone, 1975), the mulatta Rosa (Julcilea Telles) leaves the provinces for Rio, defying her mother's warning that she will become a prostitute. She tries to survive as a manicurist, but all her male clients want only to sleep with her, and she ultimately becomes a call girl.

Some *pornochanchadas* even exploit Afro Brazilian religion as an erotic gimmick. *Belinda dos Orixás na Praia dos Desejos* (Belinda of the Orixás on the Beaches of Desire, 1976), according to the press notes, "vacationing university students encounter an *umbanda* ritual on the beach." The press brochure suggests the following as advertising come-ons: "For the first time on our screens, all the marvelous rituals of *umbanda,* its priests and priestesses, its chants and mysticisms, its love and its children who are protected on a spiritual and earthly plane." Nilo Machado's *Tarzão: O Bonitão Sexy* (Tarzan, that Big, Beautiful Sexy Man), finally, rings more interesting changes on issues of sexual and racial identity. The film revolves around a jungle expedition in search of Tarzan. Tarzan's wife, Jane, tells the searchers that her husband is un-available because he is helping other men. When the expedition leader insists, they finally find Tarzan, who turns out to be black . . . and gay.

The 1970s also marked the emergence of the first socially significant Afro Brazilian directors. The spiritual sons of Cinema Novo, these directors made films touching on black themes but not generally dominated by them, thus offering a clear contrast to the Afrocentric or ghettocentric focus of young African American directors like Spike Lee and Julie Dash. Former actor Waldyr Onofre's *As Aventuras Amorosas de um Padeiro* (Amorous Adventures of a Baker, 1975) typifies this tendency (photo 94). As an actor, Onofre was very conscious of the discrimination against black actors: "In the theater as in the cinema, blacks survive taking minor roles—mailman, marginal, janitor—roles which don't allow one to show talent, or which make blackness synonymous with evil and violence."[19] While working as an actor in *O Amuleto de Ogum,* Onofre showed his script to dos Santos, who liked it and suggested that Onofre himself direct it. Onofre's goal was to portray his own Rio neighbor-hood: Campo Grande. Thus the film presents a gallery of quasi-comic charac-ters and types—the bored wife Rita (Maria do Rosário) eager for sexual ad-ventures, the ambitious, neglectful husband (Ivan Setta), and the Portuguese baker Lothário Marques (Paulo Cesar Pereio). This cuckold farce begins with the church wedding of Rita and her husband; the music track during the wed-ding (Brenda Lee's "I'm Sorry") communicates a sense of regret over a hasty decision. Rita first has an affair with the baker, but finds his lovemaking "even worse than her husband's." She then finds the man of her dreams, Saul (Haroldo de Oliveira), a black poet, sculptor, and painter whose real ambi-tion is to play Hamlet on stage. The racist baker, who calls Saul *urubu* (vul-ture), a common racist epithet for blacks, becomes insane with jealousy, but a (black) lawyer advises him that his only chance is to catch her in *flagrant délit* so the husband can sue for divorce. When the baker and the husband's posse finally finds the couple, the twosome are playacting Shakespeare's *Othello.* Un-aware that they are witnessing a theatrical performance, the posse assumes that Saul/Othello has actually slain Rita/Desdemona and that he is about to take his own life. The film ends on a carnivalesque note, as a local samba school parades through town.

For our purposes the most interesting character is Saul, a poet-sculptor-ac-tor-lover, who complains that "they'll never let a black man play Hamlet, I'll

94. Waldyr Onofre directing Maria do Rosaro and Haroldo de Oliveira in *As Aventuras Amorosas de um Padeiro* (1975)

have to spend my life playing Othello." Apart from a punning reference to the largely comic roles of Grande Otelo, Saul's complaint doubtless reflects the black artist-intellectual's frustration at "dreams deferred" because of glass ceilings and restricted opportunities. Saul displays a cool, African pride, underlined by his performance of *capoeira* and by the *berimbau* sound associated with his character. As this plot summary suggests, *As Aventuras Amorosas* does not limit itself to black themes. Indeed, the film demonstrates the artificiality of separating out black characters and issues in a film simply because of the ethnic affiliation of its director. Apart from Saul, the only other black characters are the director himself, who appears in a cameo as a construction worker ogling Rita, and a whiter-than-white-folks lawyer ashamed of his own blackness. (The lawyer fits Onofre's extrafilmic critique of those blacks "who get a degree, rise on the social ladder and become ashamed of their negritude.")[20] In *As Aventuras Amorosas*, blackness is subsumed under the category of the *suburbano*, that is, the working-class resident, of whatever hue, from the Zona Norte of Rio. Instead of a heroicization of black people, we find a "normalization." Thus the film largely succeeds in the director's professed goal of treating black characters simply as ordinary people among others.

AFRO/INDIGENOUS CELEBRATION 279

Another black-directed film, Odilon Lopes's *Um É Pouco, Dois É Bom* (One Is Little, Two Is Great, 1977) also succeeds in this project of "normalizing" blackness. The film tells two stories, one about a black man who loses his job and thus his house, the other about pickpockets lost in a world of dreams of social mobility. Although praised as a "mixture of Chaplin and Fellini" and for "dealing well with the problems of the black middle class," the film was rarely seen outside of its home locale of Porto Alegre.[21]

Nigerian director Ola Balogun's *A Deusa Negra* (The Black Goddess, 1978; see photo 95), the first Brazilian Nigerian coproduction, meanwhile, treats the historically close links between the two countries. (It is not well known, for example, that many freed blacks from Brazil went back to Nigeria and founded influential Afro Brazilian communities in Lagos [the word itself is Portuguese] and other Nigerian cities.)[22] A kind of *Roots* in reverse, the film concerns Babatunde (Zózimo Bulbul)—the protagonist's name in Yoruba means "father returns," possibly a reference to the Yoruba belief that a child born soon after the death of a parent of the same sex reincarnates the deceased—a Nigerian who goes to Brazil to look for long-lost relatives and find out more about Oluyole (Jorge Coutinho), an enslaved ancestor brought to Brazil. At a *candomblé* session, he interrogates a priestess (Léa Garcia) and meets Elisa (Sônia Santos); the latter is possessed by Iemanjá, whose statue Babatunde had been carrying. Babatunde discovers that Elisa is the same person as Amanda, with whom Oluyole had fallen in love centuries before. Elisa suggests that Babatunde go to Vila Esmeralda, in Bahia; he agrees and invites her to accompany him. In Bahia, he gives his Iemanjá statue to a *terreiro* and discovers that Elisa is the relative whom he was seeking all the time. Although *A Deusa Negra* shows a superficial understanding of Brazil and is marred by a mediocre music track featuring bland African jazz, the film does call attention to the *nagô* Yoruba culture common to both Nigeria and Brazil. In a sense an African film that happens to have been made in Brazil, *A Deusa Negra* continues the Yoruba cultural strain already marking Balogun's earlier films (photo 95).

Of all the films by Afro Brazilian directors, Antônio Sampaio's (Pitanga) *Na Boca do Mundo* (In the World's Mouth, 1977) is the most provocative. Pitanga, who got his nickname from his role in *Bahia de Todos os Santos* (Bahia of All the Saints, 1960), is a veteran actor who has played over 50 roles in the cinema. A key figure in Cinema Novo *(Barravento)*, in the Underground *(A*

95. Ola Balogun's *A Deusa Negra* (1978)

Mulher de Todos [Everybody's Woman, 1969]), and more recently in the *tele-novela (A Próxima Vítima)*, Pitanga modeled a generation of actors into a new form of performance, seen previously in alternative theater (e.g., Teatro de Arena) but never before in Brazilian cinema. In Cinema Novo, Pitanga was always cast as a rebel, whether as revolutionary *(Barravento)*, strike leader *(Bahia de Todos os Santos)*, capoerista *(Pagador de Promessas* [The Given Word, 1962]), anarchist *(A Grande Feira* [Big Market, 1962]), rebel slave *(Ganga Zumba* [1963]) or bohemian *malandro (A Grande Cidade* [The Big City, 1965]) — the common denominator being a restless, critical energy with political overtones.[23]

Pitanga learned directing by paying attention to all the stages of film production. *Na Boca do Mundo* was originally coscripted with Carlos Diegues, but Diegues preferred to emphasize the misery of the fishermen while Pitanga preferred a broader theme. The story is set in Atafona, an impoverished fishing village north of Rio, where improvised shacks are threatened by an encroaching sea. Pitanga plays Antônio, an ex-fisherman now working as a gas station attendant while taking a correspondence course in auto mechanics.

96. Antonio Pitanga and Sibele Rubia in *Na Boca do Mundo* (1977)

The self-casting reflects a certain modesty, in that Pitanga had usually played somewhat heroic roles, but also perhaps a deexoticization of the black actor. (Pitanga claimed in interviews that he put in the film everything that was left out of other films.) Antônio loves a mulatta named Terezinha (Sibele Rúbia), who sells crabs along the roadside but whose real ambition is to move to the city (photo 96). At this point of relative equilibrium, the wealthy, disenchanted socialite Clarice (Norma Bengell) arrives from Rio. The same life that the lower-class characters want to escape from represents for her escape, nature, healing. Saved from suicide by the sight of a child playing in the sand, she meets Antônio when she stops at his gas station, and slowly falls in love with his passion for life, a relief from her own lassitude. Terezinha, meanwhile, is not jealous of their affair but rather encourages it as a means of social advancement for both herself and Antônio, even proposing that he get her pregnant and then blackmail her (the assumption being that a love child with a black man would be embarrassing to an upper-class Carioca). Antônio vacillates, but ultimately refuses to be Clarice's *bon sauvage* and declares his love for Terezinha. But Terezinha rejects him, and even beats him as he declares his love. In the end, Clarice, the "woman scorned," poisons Antônio and then burns the hut where they had been living. His death is regarded as an accident, and in a surprise finale, Terezinha runs off with Clarice.

On first glance, *Na Boca do Mundo* reflects a strong dose of masochism on the director's part. His character is generous but weak, and he ends up being abused by two women. For Clarice, Antônio is a noble savage who "sleeps when he is tired, eats when he is hungry, and laughs when he is happy," which she finds refreshing after all the soulless men she has known. On second glance, however, the film is suggestive and critical. Through a conventional triangle with racial overtones, Pitanga manages to say a good deal about the subtle interactions of sex, race, and class in Brazil. The triangle clearly implies a racial schema involving black, white, and mulatto. The white woman loves the black man, but only as part of a search for a gratifying injection of new energy within a dissipated love. The film shows white society killing blacks in the name of love, an apt image for the kind of paternalistic affection, the "cordial racism," with which elite Brazil treats its black citizens. The evidence of the crime is hidden, however: Clarice burns Antônio's hut the way Rui Barbosa, as Rocha put it, burned the archive of slavery.[24] The murder is seen as an "accident," an appropriate metaphor for a society where racism is widely disavowed, never acknowledged as intentional. Since history is written by the winners, the white murderer goes free. As played by Norma Bengell, a kind of Brazilian Jeanne Moreau known for mature, free, complex roles, Clarice seems to recharge her spiritual batteries in a vampirish gesture that kills Antônio. For her to live, Antônio has to die. Clarice, whose very name means "light" and "clear," is respectable by definition; she wields social and economic power. She destroys the black man and steals the mulatta, who takes advantage of what Degler calls the "mulatto escape hatch." Thus Pitanga offers some difficult, structural insights into the operations of Brazilian racism. For Pitanga, "the enemy of the black is mulatto. The black man gets pushed aside because he doesn't conquer the mulatto. The mulatto isn't white, but he identifies with white values."[25] The film's plot has the unfortunate side effect of scapegoating the white woman for what is primarily the responsibility of the white man, while scapegoating mulattoes for a situation not of their devising, in which they too are victims.[26] But the film does at least point to the divide-and-conquer mechanism that disempowers people of color in Brazil.

At the same time, the film shows all three major characters to be oppressed.

97. Pitanga: *Na Boca do Mundo*

From a womanist angle, the film evokes the solidarities of women. Clarice, within this perspective, loves Antônio but is disappointed to find him as sexist and dishonest as her other lovers, and therefore chooses Terezinha. In this sense, the alliance is not between white and mulatta, but between two women. The film focalizes Clarice at least as much as Antônio; it probes her subjectivity even more than it does his. We hear her interior monologue even before we see her, as she speaks her intimate diary into a tape recorder. *Na Boca do Mundo* anatomizes the intersection of sex and race in Brazil. Despite the myth of easygoing sexuality, the film suggests, whites can be very much hung up about love between black men and white women. Antônio has to protect Clarice from "what people might think," and, as if extending this protection to the film itself, the film shows more lovemaking between Antônio and Terezinha than between Antônio and Clarice. Antônio's white boss personifies the eyes of social repression: he also desires Clarice, but he loses in the erotic competition. Clarice tells Antônio that she has had "two husbands and twenty lovers" but that only Antônio has made her happy." (Here again we find the double play of social compensation; Antônio's youth and romantic flair "compensate" for his color, as Clarice's wealth and social prestige make up for her age.) But for Antônio the real test is whether she is ready to have a child by him. At the same time, the film is about class as much as about race. Antônio's final words, "a senhora me matou" (you murdered me), are particularly revealing. Using the polite form *a senhora* rather than the familiar *você*, he returns, after the democratic interlude of lovemaking, to the linguistic tokens of class respect. Indeed, the lovemaking takes place on the auspiciously named Ilha de Convivência (isle of cohabitation), an island that was literally threatened by tides, an apt emblem for the precariousness of love between different races and classes (photo 97).

Na Boca do Mundo is stylistically self-effacing in the manner of a John Ford or King Vidor. Everything is said through the acting, gestures, intonation, dialogue. The light is autumnal, with saturated colors. A dreamlike luminosity underlines the tenderness between Antônio and Terezinha, a luminosity absent in the scenes with Clarice, where backlighting transforms the couple into silhouettes. At one point, Antônio's sand-covered face looks white, as if literalizing Frantz Fanon's concept of "black skin, white masks."

Finally, although *Na Boca do Mundo* suggests that the anomalies of Brazilian racism make mulattoes the enemies of blacks, other black-directed films, such as those of Onofre and Lopes, evoke a possible alliance between black men and women as being analogously oppressed, an alliance that remains problematic to the extent that in these films "women" tends to mean "white women," while black women are left off-screen, on the margins, doubly oppressed as blacks and as women, with no allies at all.

CHAPTER II
Toward the Present: Cultural Victories/Political Defeats

∞

The period of the 1970s and 1980s brings a return to historical themes concerning Afro Brazilians and Indians. A number of films—Gustavo Dahl's *Uirá: Um Índio à Procura de Deus* (Uirá: Indian in Search of God, 1974), André Luiz de Oliveira's *Ubirajara: O Senhor da Lança* (Ubirijara: Lord of the Spear, 1975), Oswaldo Caldeira's *Auke* (1976) and *Ajuricaba: O Rebelde da Amazônia* (Ubirijara: Rebel of the Amazon, 1977), Paulo Saraceni's *Anchieta, José do Brasil* (1978)—critically recycled the Indianist theme. Other films were romanticized adaptations of Indianist novels such as Carlos Coimbra's *Iracema* (1979) and Fauzi Mansur's *O Guarani* (The Guarani, 1979). While the last two exploit the Indian theme largely as an excuse for displaying female nudity, most of the films are more politicized than earlier Indianist films. This politicization partially derives from the discovery, in the late 1960s, that Indian agents, land speculators, and squatters were systematically slaughtering Indians, using everything from bacteriological warfare to aerial bombardment. In *Uirá*, an Indian's search for paradise turns into a disappointment provoked by encounters with white men (photo 98). The title of Jorge Bodansky and Orlando Senna's *Iracema* (1975) explicitly references the Indianist classic by Alencar but only in order to turn its idealism inside out. The novel's Pocahantas-like story of romance between the virginal Indian and the Portuguese nobleman here becomes a brutal encounter on the Trans-Amazonian Highway between a cynical white trucker and an Indian adolescent forced into prostitution. In the novel, Iracema dies but her child with the Portuguese noble lives; in the film, however, there is neither child nor love. The

98. *Uirá: Um Índio à Procura de Deus* (1974)

characters do not generate the "seed" of the nation. Other films stress the links between past and present. *Ajuricaba* stresses historical continuities by shuttling between Indian resistance in the eighteenth century and resistance to multinational companies in the present. It tells the story of Ajuricaba, an eighteenth-century chief of the Manau tribe who fought against his people's enslavement and finally leaped to his death rather than be captured.

In *A Marcha* (The March, 1970), Oswaldo Sampaio, codirector and writer of *Sinhá Moça* (The Plantation Owner's Daughter, 1953), returns to the subject of the abolitionist struggle against slavery. An adaptation of the novel by Afonso Schmidt, *A Marcha* is set, like *Sinhá Moça,* in the final years of slavery: November 1887 to March 1888. The film relates the struggles of two (historical) abolitionists, one white, named Boaventura (Paulo Goulart) and the other black, named Chico-Bondade (played by Édson Arantes do Nascimento, otherwise known as Pelé). Boaventua is a shape-shifter, a Scarlet Pimpernel who infiltrates various Paulista *fazendas* in order to free the slaves. He shuttles between São Paulo, where he struggles against slavery while courting fellow abolitionist Lucila (Nicete Bruno), and the *fazendas.* Chico-Bondade, meanwhile, is a black freedman who astonishes both blacks and whites with his extravagant clothes ("just like white people's") and who tries to free still-enslaved blacks by gathering funds and fomenting revolt (photo 99). Chico-Bondade leads the film's climactic action, the historical march of thousands of slaves away from the *fazendas* toward Jabaquara, the *quilombo* located in the mountains of Santos, a refuge for the slaves who were then abandoning en masse the coffee plantations of the state of São Paulo. As Chico-Bondade watches the final kiss between Boaventura and Lucila, a lap-dissolve takes us to Princess Isabel signing the Lei Áurea ending the slave re-gime. The film portrays abolition as a product of black and white collabora-tion. As in *Sinhá Moça*, there are strong gestures of black revolt, but ultimately the film seems ideologically dated in the era of black liberation.

Another film, also set on a plantation but this time a postslavery one, is Carlos Diegues's *Joana Francesa* (Joanne the Frenchwoman, 1973). Set in the northeastern state of Alagoas in the 1930s, the film chronicles the inexorable decomposition of an aristocratic, landowning family. The story is told in the first person by Jeanne (Jeanne Moreau), the Frenchwoman of the title, former madame of a São Paulo bordello. Jeanne lives with, but refuses to marry, one of her former clients, Aureliano (Carlos Kroeber), a rich sugarcane proprietor. In the background looms the 1930 revolution, an event that transformed the

99. Pelé in *A Marcha* (1970)

social landscape of Brazil, indirectly leading to the takeover of old farms by new money. Made at a time of extreme governmental repression, *Joana Francesa* proposes to dig the grave of what Diegues calls "an old civilization without a future," where the dead "lord it over the living." One of the few characters who demonstrates any consistency, along with Joana herself, is the black servant Gismundo (Eliezer Gomes). When Joana travels to survey the family property, she goes not on foot but rather on her servant's shoulders, "DeGaulle riding Zumbi's back," in Glauber's apt phrase. Rocha compares Joana to Scarlett O'Hara as "fascist matriarchs."[1] Gismundo's apparent servility and affection for Joana is subsequently revealed to be a self-protective mask, for when Joana dies, Gismondo merely shrugs. Gismondo is rather like certain black characters in Faulkner, those who are cast as servants but who ultimately "endure."

Diegues's *Xica da Silva* (1976), meanwhile, memorializes an eighteenth-century black woman, Xica da Silva, who became extremely powerful through her liaison with the richest man in the wealthy region of Minas Gerais, João Fernandes de Oliveira, the official sent by the Crown, beginning in 1737, to preside over the extraction and sale of precious stones. Between 1700 and 1770, Brazil produced half of the mineral wealth generated in the entire world during the seventeenth and eighteenth centuries.[2] The couple reportedly spent 43 years together and produced 13 children, all legitimized by their father. Since the elite of Minas Gerais burned the historical record concerning Xica, her story is textually available only through legend and other fictionalizations. Diegues's sources were both erudite (Cecília Meireles's *Romanceiro da Inconfidência*) and popular, specifically carnival and the samba pageant. Diegues asked João Felício dos Santos, the same historical novelist who wrote *Ganga Zumba,* to devise a script based on popular legends about Xica da Silva. *Xica da Silva* makes excellent use of the baroque architecture of Diamantina, the Minas town restored simultaneously for the film and for the touristic recuperation of the national architectural patrimony. The Minas baroque style, it is important to recall, was also a black product, the work of the blacks who mined the gold, silver, and diamonds that made the region rich; the black workers who built the churches; the blacks who composed classical music in the baroque style (subject of Arthur Omar's *Música Barroca Mineira*), and the blacks like the sculptor known as "Aleijadinho" (the cripple), subject of numerous Brazilian documentaries. Aleijadinho suffered from lep-

100. Xica (Zezé Motta) and João Fernando (Walmor Chagas) in *Xica da Silva* (1976)

rosy, yet he managed to sculpt the intricate sandstone statues that grace the gardens of numerous Minas churches.

In the film, João Fernandes (Walmor Chagas) falls in love with Xica da Silva (Zezé Motta), frees her, and indulges her every whim, making her one of the most powerful people in one of the wealthiest regions in the world (photo 100). João prospers by following smugglers to the best diamond extraction sites and then taking them over. As he prospers, Xica becomes the "power behind the throne" and a dominant force in the politics and fashion of the region. She lives like a pampered princess, with her own palace and servants, and even her own lake with her own ship, which only blacks can use; whites enter only as musicians and servants. While using her new-found power to avenge slights suffered as a slave, she is often as ruthless with other blacks as well. Indeed, she is indifferent to the brutality suffered by the slaves under João Fernandes's control.[3] As João Fernandes becomes richer and more infatuated, the Portuguese Crown sends a pompous inspector (José Wilker) to check into his financial dealings and into his relation with Xica. In order to dissuade the inspector from arresting João Fernandes, Xica stages a banquet-pageant featuring Afro Brazilian dance and cuisine. But Xica's charms, too strong for the effete inspector, ultimately backfire. The inspector calls João

Fernandes back to Lisbon, thus ending Xica's 13-year reign. Having lost her link to power, Xica falls into disgrace and is even mocked by local children.

This plot summary leaves out two important characters—Teodoro (Marcus Vinícius) a black independent smuggler, and José (Stepan Nercessian), the son of the sergeant and a political rebel linked to the Inconfidência Mineira (the abortive Minas revolt against Portuguese rule). The two characters evoke two political alternatives to Xica's individualistic opportunism. Teodoro, as a free black who competes with João Fernandes in the extraction of diamonds, represents black independence and economic autonomy. José, meanwhile, represents political resistance, and in the contemporary period evokes a kind of good-natured anarchist left. In Diegues's own words, the "revolutionary popular Unconscious of Xica meets the intellectual from Vila Rica."[4] But Xica never really aligns with either of them, nor does the film clarify the alternatives. Xica tries to enlist Teodoro in an effort to organize an army to protect João Fernandes, but she inadvertently leads Teodoro's enemies to Teodoro's hiding place, with the result that Teodoro is captured and tortured (photo 101). When João Fernandes tries to intervene, the count tells him to choose sides; João Fernandes chooses to stay loyal to the colonial regime. Teodoro is not clearly drawn as exemplifying an alternative black-led autonomy, while José seems like a frivolous countercultural leftie who dispenses advice. The division of political labor—Xica as the intuitive, capricious rebel, José as the "brains" who sees the larger picture—reproduces a common pattern in Brazilian cinema whereby the whites (the abolitionists of *Sinhá Moça,* the leftist in *A Grande Feira*) ultimately guide and orient the overly impulsive blacks. The black side is granted vitality, the white side political intelligence. Against this view, we have not only the historical record of black rebellions throughout the diaspora, including those registered by Diegues himself in his other films, but also Henry Louis Gates's theory of blacks as the "first deconstructionists," those who "saw through" the system that abused them.

Given the dearth of historical record and the problematic nature of establishing absolute historical truths, we can be skeptical about any approach that stresses strict fidelity to historical fact. What we see in *Xica da Silva* depends very much on the grids through which we look; each reveals a dimension of the film. As a partisan and fellow practitioner of Cinema Novo, Glauber Rocha called *Xica da Silva* an "Afro-feminist, pan-sexualist, libertarian, nationalist, radical and humanist . . . tropical baroque."[5] Looking at the film

101. Teodoro (Marcus
Vinícius) and Zezé Motta
in *Xica da Silva*

through a Bakhtinian grid, Randal Johnson sees *Xica da Silva* as a festive in-
terrogation of social hierarchies, an exercise in "gay relativity," where the "material bodily principle" and the "lower stratum" become a positive force, and
the "culture of laughter" triumphs over all that represses and restricts. The
tropical feast Xica offers for the Count, in this sense, represents the Bakhtinian banquet as the scene of parodic critique of the stodginess of European
high-class culture.[6] (Interestingly, a few years after the film was released, Antunes Filho did a theatrical version of *Xica da Silva* explicitly inspired by the
theories of Bakhtin.)

Certain feminist and black analyses highlight other, less progressive, aspects
of the film.[7] They point out that Xica's power is very much corporeal—consisting of her body itself and unspecified sexual maneuvers—rather than
moral or intellectual. An object of desire for the diverse representatives of political, military, and social power, Xica assumes a role that on one level points
to the hypocrisy of a society that enslaved black people and yet desired and exploited black women. On another level, however, she embodies the fantasy of
the sexually available slave. She is used sexually by a variety of white men—

the sergeant, his son, João Fernandes (all of whom at one point "own" her) —
and seems to enjoy it thoroughly; she aspires only to find a better class of
owner-lover. Even the theme song sexualizes her; Jorge Ben Jor's punning
and stressed repetition ("Xica dá, Xica dá, Xica dá") suggests in Portuguese
that "Xica gives out," that is, fucks. Furthermore, Xica is "in bed" with people
all over the political and social spectrum, and her desire seems to cloud her
judgment; her "dizziness," which afflicts her whenever she is sexually excited,
in this sense, is symptomatic of her political incapacity.

For Beatriz Nascimento, *Xica da Silva*'s representation of cheerful miscegenation in the tropics prolongs Gilberto Freyre's rose-colored vision of Brazilian slavery, showing the "slave quarters seen from the perspective of the Big
House."[8] The film scapegoats the socially subaltern for racism—the children
who throw stones at Xica, a low-level priest, the intendant's frustrated wife—
rather than seeing racism as integral to the entire system. The portrayal of the
black woman, for Nascimento, is highly negative. Xica's reaction to discrimination by the church, for example, is infantile. Her character "reinforces the
stereotype of the passive, docile, and intellectually debilitated black, who depends on whites in order to think."[9]

Although there is much truth in this account, it forgets that the film also
depicts racism and the cruelty of slavery and that its sympathies are fundamentally on the side of blacks and against the white elite of Minas Gerais,
who are caricatured even more than the blacks. And Xica on many levels is
also an engaging character. While opportunistic, she does skillfully exploit
one of her few resources as a slave—her body—with singular imagination.
Within a feminist-inflected variation of the carnivalesque perspective, Xica can
be seen as the "disorderly woman" or the "woman on top" who upends conventional social hierarchies and whose corporeal dynamism undercuts the
staid, closed, classical body of Greco Roman antiquity. Nor can we ignore the
way Zezé Motta's vibrant performance communicates a strong sense of "black
is beautiful" pride.[10]

Xica da Silva disconcerts partially because it constitutes that oxymoronic
entity called a "comedy about slavery." Only someone whose perspective is
that of the Big House, the reasoning goes, would possibly find slavery comic.
Slavery might inspire satire, for example that of George Wolfe's *Colored Museum,* but not comedy. But this "genre critique" misfires, on several levels.
First of all, *Xica da Silva* is not really a comedy. Its ending, Xica's downfall and

102. Samba-pageant aesthetics: *Xica da Silva*

humiliation, is tragic. It would be more accurate to say that the film has elements of farce, largely devoted to demystifying the pretensions and hypocrisies of the Minas elite, and that it is festive. And this festivity has more to do
with carnival than with comedy per se. Indeed, one of the sources for *Xica da
Silva* was the 1962 carnival pageant devoted to Xica da Silva by the Aca-
dêmicos de Salgeiro samba group, a pageant Diegues described as "extremely
beautiful."[11] The samba school pageant, like the film, presented Xica as a
woman who "used her sensuality" to "break the color barrier." Indeed,
Diegues called the film itself a *samba enredo;* that is, a work analogous to the
collection of songs, dances, costumes, and lyrics that form part of that folk
opera called a samba pageant (see photo 102). The low-cost luxury of the
samba schools, ironically, provided an alibi for abandoning the "aesthetic of
hunger." At its best, in such sequences as that where an overjoyed Xica, to the
accompaniment of Jorge Ben Jor's exuberant title song, parades at the head of
her black entourage holding the papers guaranteeing her freedom, the film
weds carnivalesque effervescence to a historically shaped sense of liberation. It
is this combination that popular audiences in Brazil seem to have understood.
A huge success, the film was seen by 8 million spectators in its first two and a

half months of exhibition.[12] In the multiracial working-class district of Madureira, Diegues reports, the spectators danced in the aisles.[13]

Even the color scheme of the film translates this theme of freedom; the film's colors wax and wane with the oscillations of her power. Yet all this affirmation is compromised by ambiguity. All the homages to Afro Brazilian culture—the samba, the dance, the feijoada that overpower the effete Portuguese aristocrat—suggest that Afro Brazilian culture is hegemonic in Brazil. Even under slavery, the slaves dominate through their music, their cuisine, their style of life. The pitfall in all this is what Michael Hanchard calls "culturalism," the reliance on culture alone to effect social change. Xica da Silva briefly lives like a fantasy princess, but she is ultimately divested of her power. The Afro Brazilian culture she intermittently embodies wins consistent victories: samba overpowers European classical music, spicy Afro Brazilian cuisine undoes the pallid representative of Portuguese colonialism, Afro Brazilian dance and energy far outshine Portuguese cultural expression (photo 103), and Xica is seen as more beautiful and vital than João Fernandes's "pale, cold, morbid wife." Yet the carnivalesque inversions of *Xica da Silva* simultaneously reveal and hide a problem. If Brazil's soul is black, its power structure is white. More important, the many instances of appreciation for Afro Brazilian culture are projected into a social conjuncture in which blacks are excluded from the centers of political and economic decision-making. Cultural victories mask political defeats. And this situation will change only when the respect often according Afro Brazilian *culture* is matched by a real change in the social situation of Afro Brazilian *citizens,* a change that would necessarily involve a radical redistribution of that substance vital to the life of any community—political power. (To flash forward to the 1990s, *Xica da Silva* became a TV miniseries in 1996, featuring an older Zezé Motta as the mother of the Xica character played by Taís Araújo.)

Fernando Cony Campos's *Ladrões de Cinema* (Cinema Thieves, 1977)—the title obviously alludes to *Bicycle Thieves*—also refers to eighteenth-century Minas Gerais and also stages the same analogy between film and *samba enredo.* The film begins when some *favelados,* the majority black and mulatto, dressed up as carnival "Indians," steal filmmaking equipment from American filmmakers documenting carnival. Back in the favela (Morro do Pavãozinho), the thieves discuss what to do with the equipment, ultimately deciding to make a film in the favela itself (photo 104). A visiting French ethnographer, Jean-

103. Cultural victories in *Xica da Silva*

Claude Rouch (played by critic Jean-Claude Bernardet) provides them with film stock and a brief technical initiation. The *favelados* conceive the film as a samba school narration, involving choices of theme, costumes, rehearsals, and music. Gradually, the film project energizes the favela and its inhabitants, who lavish on the film the kind of creativity usually devoted to the samba pageant. As in the pageants devoted to historical themes, the *favelados* choose as subject the same abortive revolt against Portuguese rule (the Inconfidênca Mineira), led by the man popularly known as "Tiradentes," that lurks in the background of *Xica da Silva*. Inspired by the theme of freedom, they opt for the actual poetry of the conspirators. The French ethnographer hails the film as that rare work "by the people, about the people, and for the people." (Furthermore, he adds, the film provides useful material for his dissertation.)

Just when they have achieved their goals, the man in the film-within-the-film who plays Tiradentes's historical betrayer (Joaquim Silvério dos Reis, played by Lutero Luis) also betrays the *favelados* themselves by fingering the thieves during a live TV program. The film is seized, the *favelados* are arrested, and the Americans (specifically the Cultural Interests Corporation) market the film with the title *Sweet Thieves*. The *favelados,* arriving at the movie theater in a paddy wagon, attend the gala premiere in handcuffs. They are left con-

104. Favelado filmmakers in *Ladrões de Cinema* (1977)

templating, perhaps, the question of how Brazil might collectively retrieve
the film market stolen from them subsequent to World War I. Those who
steal from thieves, runs a Brazilian proverb, are automatically forgiven. Thus
the film draws parallels between the past, when Brazil was dominated by Portugal, and the present, when Brazil is dominated by the United States. *Ladrões
de Cinema* points to the need for cinematic anthropophagy: the devouring of
the colonizer's know-how for anticolonial purposes; it is hardly accidental,
again, that the cinema thieves are dressed up as Indians.[14]

As its title suggests, *Ladrões de Cinema* is a reflexive film, a Brazilian *Day for
Night,* proliferating in allusions to Brazilian and international cinema. The
filmmaking function is bifurcated between Luquinho (Milton Gonçalves),
the more cerebral of the two, and Fuleiro (Pitanga), the more instinctive and
visceral; their names reference, respectively, Jean-Luc Godard and Samuel
Fuller. Grande Otelo, meanwhile, plays the scriptwriter Rui Zebra, who always carries his screenplay *(O Homem do Surdo)* in hopes of finding a producer. The climate is that of "imperfect cinema" and the "aesthetic of hunger,"
a cinema that is frustrated, underfinanced, forced to improvise, making up in
creativity for what is lacking in material advantages; a situation, in short,
where it is miraculous that films are made at all. And *Ladrões de Cinema* bears

the marks of this situation; the conceptualization, with its interwoven historical analogies, is brilliant, yet the realization is often less than satisfactory. Its most suggestive feature, perhaps, is its samba pageant aesthetic. Since Tiradentes and the Inconfidência Mineira had already been a theme for a samba school (Império Serrano in 1949), the filmmakers themselves asked Mano Décio da Viola, author of "Exaltation of Tiradentes," to compose new themes on the subject. But more important than the mere inclusion of samba in the film is that the film's very process of elaboration parallels that of a *samba enredo*. Thus the film speaks not only *of* popular culture but also *through* popular culture.

Nelson Pereira dos Santos returned to Afro Brazilian culture in another 1970s film, *Tenda dos Milagres* (Tent of Miracles, 1977), based on the Jorge Amado novel of the same name. An ambitious film, *Tenda dos Milagres* was made on a shoestring budget of $300,000, partially facilitated by the fact that dos Santos paid his friend Jorge Amado a paltry 50,000 cruzeiros for the rights.[15] The film offers a broad panorama of life in Bahia, the area of Brazil most imbued with the spirit of African culture. The story unfolds in two alternating time frames. The core story, set in the past and presented as a filmwithin-the film—fragments emerge from the Moviola of poet-filmmaker Fausto Pena (Hugo Carvana)—concerns Afro Brazilian culture hero Pedro Arcanjo (as incarnated by two nonactor culture heroes, popular composersinger Jards Macalé and Bahian plastic artist Juarez Paraíso) and the *Citizen Kane*–like search for the truth about his life (photo 105). This core story is framed by the contemporary story of the making, and later the editing, of Fausto Pena's film (in the source novel, Fausto Pena is a writer; dos Santos makes him a filmmaker). In this frame, interest in Pedro Arcanjo is sparked by a visiting American Nobel prize winning anthropologist, symptomatically named Dr. Livingston, who proclaims Arcanjo, then virtually unknown, one of the world's greatest scientists. Inspired by the anthropologists' tribute, local intellectuals and media set out to piece together the biography of their newly discovered luminary.

Of the two stories, the one concerning Pedro Arcanjo's life is by far the more compelling and cinematically polished. Arcanjo, the poet-filmmaker discovers, led a double existence. While employed in the white world as a lowly functionary at the School of Medicine, at the time the Center of Social Studies in Brazil, he was also a musician, dancer, lover of women of all complex-

105. Juarez Paraíso as (the older) Pedro Arcanjo in *Tenda dos Milagres* (1977)

ions, and, most crucially, a tireless researcher into Afro Brazilian culture. Among his own people, he is called Ojuobá, or the Eyes of Xangô. Scouring Bahia for Africanist survivals, Arcanjo publishes his findings with the help of his typesetter friend Lídio Corró. They work, and play, in the "Tent of Miracles," a meeting place for black artists, craftsmen, musicians, and white bohemians—in short, for all those deemed marginal by the town's status-obsessed elite.

Pedro Arcanjo melds the features of diverse historical figures from Bahia: first, labor activist and Africanist scholar Manuel Querino (author of *A Raça Africana,* 1910), who once proclaimed Brazil's two major advantages to be "the generosity of its soul and the talent of its *mestiços*" and who argued that the black "was the principal producer of the nation's wealth . . . it was the black who developed Brazil";[16] second, Luiz Luna, founder of the Pernambuco Black Front; and third, literacy crusader Major Cosme da Faria, who distributed "ABC" pamphlets to the poor.

Arcanjo begins as the ardent apostle of miscegenation whose self-proclaimed mission is to produce mulatto children and exalt mestiço culture. His theory and practice of "racial democracy" trigger the enmity of those with a vested interest in maintaining white privilege. Arcanjo defends the black spiritual inheritance against the fashionably racist theories of Professor Nilo Argilo (another composite figure) and then against the clubs and guns of the police. Gradually, Arcanjo becomes less preoccupied with siring mulatto children and more with fighting for political causes such as antifascism, but he never stops asserting the dignity of his people or the strength of religion as a source of cultural cohesion and community solidarity. He himself is the hypothetical person whom he describes: the one who "masters despair and misery by being creative in daily life." As a decolonized black Brazilian, he constitutes an "organic intellectual" *avant la lettre*. In his strength, dignity, subtle humor and, above all, in the reciprocated tenderness he bears his community, Pedro Arcanjo embodies cultural integrity and intellectual power (photo 106).

Pedro Arcanjo's ideological antagonist Professor Nilo Argilo is also a synthetic figure, melding the features of a number of racist Brazilian intellectuals such as Sílvio Romero, Oliveira Viana, Estáquio de Lima, and Nina Rodrigues, all of whom espoused white supremacist theories. As we have seen, these intellectuals largely recycled the racist and social Darwinist theories then in vogue in Europe, theories that associated racial mixing with "degeneracy." During his visit to Brazil in 1869, the racist thinker Count de Gobineau pro-

106. Jards Macalé as (the younger) Pedro Arcanjo in *Tenda dos Milagres*

claimed black inferiority, comparing Brazilians to monkeys and prophesying complete racial degeneracy within two centuries, since "not even one Brazilian is pure-blooded, since marriage between Whites, Indians, and Blacks is so common that the nuances of color are infinite, causing a most depressing degeneracy in the upper as well as the lower classes."[17]

Tenda dos Milagres, in contrast, celebrates Afro Brazilian culture without reservation. The film's theme song by Gilberto Gil opens up from the start the question of the black roots of Brazil:

> The son asked the father
> where is my grandfather
> my grandfather where is he?
> The father asked the grandfather
> Where is great grandfather
> great grandfather where is he?

The film pursues these genealogical lines, affirming the Afro Brazilian roots not only of black Brazilians but of Brazilian culture in general. Arcanjo writes tracts praising the aesthetic qualities of black music, art, and dance, citing evidence of the resilience of African culture despite four centuries of oppression. Against white racist scholars, he demonstrates the persistence of "Africanisms" such as the "cult of the serpent" found in places as diverse as Haiti and Dahomey. Arcanjo as a character also undoes the spurious division between science and religion, in that he is both *pai de santo* and social scientist; he is himself a leader in both realms. The film makes clear that *candomblé* is not an atavistic throwback to a "savage" past but rather a beautifully realized cosmology with its own choreography, mise-en-scène, and pragmatic efficacity. At the same time, *candomblé* is shown as a vital source of cultural continuity, community solidarity, and political organization.

Dos Santos evolved over decades from a Marxist-inflected disinterest in Afro Brazilian religion to a more sympathetic attitude. At the time of *Rio 40 Graus* (Rio 40 Degrees, 1954) and *Rio Zona Norte* (Rio's Northern Zone, 1957), as the director himself acknowledges, he never regarded Afro Brazilian religious practices a worthy subject for film.[18] In later films such as *O Amuleto de Ogum* and *Tenda dos Milagres,* he is more knowledgeable about such practices. In *Tenda dos Milagres,* dos Santos was also substantially aided by Jorge Amado himself, as a man respected by many in *candomblé* circles as an initiate,

popularizer, and political advocate.[19] The musician Jards Macalé, who plays
Pedro Arcanjo as a young man and who worked on the soundtrack along with
Gilberto Gil, also researched *candomblé* practices. At the same time, the film
never pretends to know all the secrets of *candomblé*; the film respects the
community's right to protect its secrets and maintain its security. The session
Dr. Livingston attends, for example, is of the kind open to tourists. Dos
Santos expresses his respect for *candomblé* by including magical moments of a
type only explicable through *candomblé*, although there is a lower coefficient
of "magic" in the film than in the novel. When Pedro Arcanjo refuses Rosa,
who loves both Lídio and Pedro, for example, she comes back to haunt him
in another form. The black policeman who comes to repress *candomblé*, similarly, is magically possessed and made to turn against the police.

The portrayal of the official repression of *candomblé*, meanwhile, points to a
real history of subjugation. Largely driven underground during slavery,
candomblé emerged into the light of day after abolition. *Candomblé* temples
became havens of solidarity for struggling blacks, although they were still under police surveillance. For much of the twentieth century, Afro Brazilian religions were required to register with the police. (In fact, the most extensive
collections of *candomblé* objects of worship are to be found in police muse-
ums, e.g., in the Police Museum of Rio de Janeiro.) It was only in the 1970s
that Bahia, with its majority black population, suspended this compulsory
registration. As occurred with the carnival pageant, *candomblé* too looked to
white patrons for protection and financial support, creating the position of
the *ogan,* or honorary patron, usually an influential figure (like Jorge Amado)
who protected the temple and its faithful from outside attack, as a new office
within the religion.

The contemporary frame-story about the posthumous celebrity, cinematic
rehabilitation, and commercial exploitation of Pedro Arcanjo, although
equally fascinating, is flawed in its cinematic realization. Here dos Santos de-
bunks a number of targets, not all of them "readable" for non-Brazilian viewers. Through Dr. Livingston's visit, dos Santos mocks those Brazilians who
recognize their own heroes only when they are "blessed" from abroad.
Livingston himself, appropriately named after his colonizing forebear, is a
spoof on "Brazilianists," international scholars (usually American), especially
in the social sciences, who do research on Brazil.[20] The film credits Livingston
with the "discovery" of Pedro Arcanjo, but scores him for his naive presump-

tuousness. He photographs his Brazilian companion Ana Mercedes (Sônia Dias), whose mestiço beauty he praises, in exotic and animalesque poses. Despite his loudly proclaimed anticolonialism, Livingston acts like a typical gringo, exploiting the Brazilians he claims to admire. For an American audience, unfortunately, this calculatedly two-dimensional figure rings excruciatingly false; his manner is more suggestive of a pompous ass than of the Nobel prize winner he is presumed to be.

The media magnate Dr. Zezinho is more adroitly drawn. In him dos Santos lampoons the colonized mentality of the dominant (white) Brazilian media. Capitalizing on Arcanjo's sudden prestige, Zezinho makes him the pretext for vacuous cultural events and advertising campaigns. His money-making schemes include a "Fresh Black" deodorant, a "Pedro Arcanjo Shopping Center," and a televised essay contest for children on "Why Pedro Arcanjo is a great man." Thus Arcanjo the freedom fighter is sanitized and whitened, transformed into a marketable model of conformism. Immortalized in formal portraits, clothed in academic robes, he is grotesquely metamorphosized into the likeness of his own worst enemy—the pompous Dr. Argilo.

Zezinho's antagonist, Professor Edelweiss (Anecy Rocha), melds the features of four characters in the novel (her own plus three male academics). Dr. Edelweiss is hired by the Pedro Arcanjo Celebration Committee as an attractive figurehead, but she proposes a seminar on racism in a comparative perspective (Brazil, the United States, South Africa). Afraid that radical students might use the seminar to protest racism and dictatorship, the men on the committee react to her proposal by flirting with her while refusing the seminar, proposing instead an innocuous civic celebration for school children.

If *Tenda dos Milagres* celebrates Brazilian popular culture, it just as certainly demystifies the Brazilian elite, including the leftist elite. Arcanjo is at times foiled by a young Marxist professor who espouses progressive ideas but whose life contributes little to the transformation of society. Skeptical about religion in general and *candomblé* in particular, the Marxist cannot fathom that an intelligent man like Pedro Arcanjo could possibly believe in such "superstitions." Arcanjo responds that he too is a "materialist" but that African religion is part of his soul. He warns the Marxist that his materialism runs the risk of turning him into an accomplice of the police; the point is to love the people, not the dogma. Here dos Santos is obviously attacking those on the Marxist-inflected left who love the people in the abstract but who despise the

107. *Tenda dos Milagres*

concrete manifestations of popular culture. However heavy-handed the portrayal of the Marxist—dos Santos slants the issues by portraying the Marxist
as a drunk—the film does at least point to the Eurocentric aspects of Marxist
thought, suggesting that however liberating Marxism has been for Western
thought in its profound critique of capitalism, it has been colonialist in its
"progressive" scorn for non-European cultures.

Tenda dos Milagres both supports and exposes the myth of "racial democracy." It critiques the myth by portraying a closet racist who unmasks himself
when his daughter wants to marry one of "them." More importantly, the film
suggests that the ideologically explicit and politically violent racism of the
past has merely transmuted itself into the subtler mass-mediated racism of
today. At the same time, the film's apparently uncritical advocacy of miscegenation as a solution to Brazil's racial problems echoes a tendency not only
within Gilberto Freyre's work but also within Jorge Amado's: the notion that
structural political problems can be solved in bed (or in the hammock as the
case may be). "There is only one solution for the racial problem," Jorge
Amado has written, "the mixture of blood. No other solution exists, only this
one which is born from love."[21] Although a powerful solvent, Eros alone can-

not dissolve power hierarchies hardened over centuries of colonialism (photo 108). The very idea of miscegenation as solution has colonialist roots. In colonial times, the Marquis de Pombal urged the Portuguese to mate with Indians and blacks in order to populate the subcontinent. In the wake of the slave revolts in Haiti and Santo Domingo, the white elite saw miscegenation as a way of saving white dominance.

In Brazilian ideology, miscegenation has been linked inextricably to "whitening," as the film itself suggests in the almost subliminal "progression" that takes us from Arcanjo, a mulatto, to his child by a white Scandinavian woman (Kirsi), to the marriage of another lighter-skinned son, Tadeu, to a rich white woman. The newlywed couples' move from Bahia to Tadeu's promised position in Rio reinforces this link between "whitening" and social success. The "epidermic meliorism" of the plot thus comes perilously close to the official ideology, by which blacks rise socially when they marry mulattoes, and mulattoes gain status when they infiltrate white families, precisely the formula that continually relegates blacks to the bottom of the hierarchy. Thus "racial democracy" becomes a perpetuum mobile that endlessly generates black inferiority. Interesting too is the film's treatment of the mulatta Ana Mercedes. While critiquing Livingston's animalization of her, the film itself participates in her objectification and thus reproduces a tendency within Jorge Amado's work to "physically exalt mulattas without ever granting them respectability or marriageability."[22] Although the mulatto is the key to progress, the proof that money and success can "whiten," the mulatta is both sexualized and barren, her function being not to bear children but to fulfill the fantasies of the white man. (To dos Santos's credit, he did make the Ana Mercedes character more serious and artistically ambitious than her prototype in the source novel.)

The basic contradiction within *Tenda,* then, is that it supports the values of Afro-culture against its racist enemies, while indirectly supporting a theory that would lead to the disappearance of the people who actually "carry" the culture: black people themselves.[23] The film ends, however, on a note of popular revolt, in the form of a Bahian pageant that encapsulates an insurrectionary spirit. The final credits unfold over images of an Independence Day celebration, not the conventional September 7 commemoration of the day in 1822 when the Portuguese Prince Dom Pedro decided to stay in Brazil and proclaim Brazilian independence, but rather a celebration of July 2, 1823, the

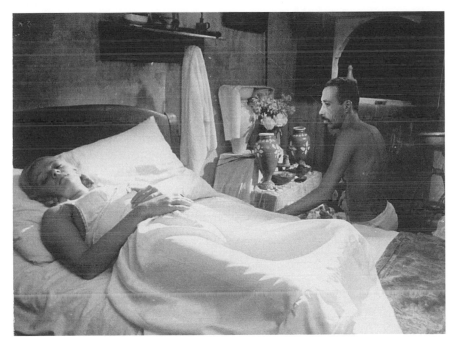

108. Miscegenation as panacea: *Tenda dos Milagres*

day on which Bahians themselves, black, Indian, mestiço, and poor white, expelled the Portuguese, a historical moment in which independence was won from below rather than merely proclaimed from above. The pageant itself evokes black-red collaboration and syncretism, in that blacks sport Indian headdresses as a tribute to native Brazilians.[24]

Overall, *Tenda dos Milagres* manages to be at once festive and critical, celebral and sensuous, celebratory and ironic, a singularly lively cinematic pageant, whose style is as confidently and cheerfully syncretic as the culture portrayed in the film. The film wanders amiably from a television aesthetic to cinema verité; farce cohabits with costume drama and period piece. The result is a raucous, unkempt, animated fresco as colorful and as variegated as Bahia itself. But a dialectic informs this variety, a dialectic announced by the film's opening photos, which contrast Bahia's European masters with the African slaves. Thus the film sets in motion a cultural battle of opera and samba, Catholicism and *candomblé*, ruling-class science and popular mythology, uptight elite banquets and popular feasts. (Incidentally, in 1985, *Tenda dos Milagres* became a TV miniseries, directed by Paulo Afonso Griselli and featuring Nelson

Xavier as Pedro Arcanjo, Milton Gonçalves as Lídio Corró, and Tânia Alves as Ana Mercedes.)

The late 1970s proliferate in homages to Afro Brazilian culture. Antônio Carlos Fontoura's *Cordão de Ouro* (Gold Belt, 1977) pays tribute to *capoeira*, a centuries-old melange of martial art, dance, and ritual whose roots trace back to Angola and to the experience of slavery. *Capoeira* appears in both *Pagador de Promessas* (The Given Word, 1962) and *Barravento* (The Turning Wind, 1962), the latter featuring a highly stylized combat filmed as abstract patterns of moving feet. (*Capoeira* is also the subject of two American features: *Rooftops* [1989] and *Only the Strong* [1993]) *Capoeira* was born out of the desire of slaves to defend themselves against better-armed captors. Since slaves used it against the *capitões de mato, capoeira* was forbidden by colonial authorities. So slaves camouflaged it by practicing it with drums and music, as if it were "merely" a samba. It was prohibited again after the abolition of slavery, as work-starved blacks turned to crime or defended themselves against the police. At once ludic, combative, and spiritual, *capoeira* consists of beautifully orchestrated rhythmic movements, somersaults, handstands, leaps, and tumbles and kicks, as part of a dialogic ritualized play of two partners surrounded by a *roda,* or circle, and accompanied by the music of the *berimbau,* a one-string African instrument that lays down the fundamental rhythms of the art (drums and tambourines can also be used). The *roda* sings in a call-and-response pattern; the leader sings the words of the song, and the rest sing the refrain. The songs tell of life, love, and adventure, and occasionally retain African words. The public image of *capoeira* began to improve in the 1920s, and at present, *capoeira* has become an international form, taught in Brazil by a legion of *mestres* (masters) as well as by Jelon Vieira, Eusébio da Silva, João Grande, and Borracha in the United States. The *capoeira* in *Cordão de Ouro* is performed by well-known *capoeiristas,* not only Nestor Capoeira (who plays the lead) but also Mestre Leopoldino of the Grupo Senzala in Rio.

Like *Tenda dos Milagres, Cordão de Ouro* operates in a multiple time-frame. In a magical and fantastical style, the film tells the story of a modern-day slave, Jorge (Nestor Capoeira) who deploys *capoeira* as part of a struggle for freedom. A slave in a selenium mine in the mythical land of Eldorado (a transparent allusion to Rocha's *Terra em Transe* [Land in Anguish, 1967]), Jorge escapes thanks to *capoeira* but is chased down by a modern-day slave catcher in a helicopter. He throws himself into a waterfall, where he is saved by a *caboclo*

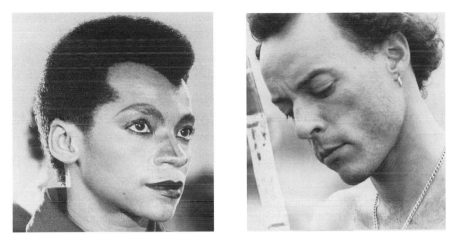

109a/109b. Zezé Motta and Nestor Capoeira (with *berimbau*) in *Cardão de Ouro* (1977)

(an idealized figure of indigenous resistance). The *caboclo* takes him to Aru-anda (a reference to a famous maroon community and the subject of a 1960 film). There he is received by his *orixá,* Ogum, who teaches him the deeper mysteries of *capoeira*. Ogum gives him a gold belt and a mission: to free his body from slavery. Returning to Eldorado, Jorge teaches *capoeira* to other rebels. But they are defeated and he is sent to the slave market of the Progress Company, whose CEO is Pedro Cem (Jofre Soares). He is bought by Dandara (Zezé Motta), ex-slave and now mistress of the CEO, whose personal bodyguard Jorge becomes at a *fazenda* (photos 109a and 109b). He leads a new slave rebellion at the *fazenda,* but is captured again and condemned to being buried alive. But as he is digging his own grave he receives from Ogum himself the secret of ending slavery and the reign of Pedro Cem.

Cordão de Ouro began as a comic strip and as the plot summary suggests, retains some of the attributes of the genre: schematism, irreality, anachronism, heroism. The allusion to the Eldorado of *Terra em Transe* suggests an "allegory of underdevelopment" (Ismail Xavier), but in this case we are confronted with an underdeveloped allegory, in which historical analogies are confused rather than clarified. The fundamental analogy is between classical racialized slavery and contemporary economic slavery of workers for huge corporations, led by a populist manager who congratulates the well-behaved modern slaves. While suggestive, the comparison misleadingly equates race with class and plays down the racialized element of slavery, a problem exacerbated by the casting of what in Brazilian terms would be a "white" *capoeirista*.

The allegory further suggests that a white man liberates the slaves, a choice that evokes unfortunate textual memories of the idealized abolitionists from *Sinhá Moça*. The countercultural emphasis on "getting in touch with the body" detracts from the historical discussion of the roots of *capoeira*. Body politics à la Wilhelm Reich is conflated with racial politics à la Zumbi, all mixed with allegorical denunciations of present-day oppression (multinationals, low wages). Anachronistic mixing of time periods to evoke the continuities of oppression is often a valid strategy, but it is not successfully achieved here.

Two early 1980s films explore the subject of the history of slavery. Like *Xica da Silva*, Walter Lima Jr.'s *Chico Rei* (1982) addresses a black figure, at once historical and legendary, from eighteenth-century Minas Gerais, against the backdrop, once again, of the *Inconfidência Mineira*. Less well known than Zumbi or Xica da Silva, Chico Rei, whose African name was Galanga, was a Congo king kidnapped along with his family and forced to work in the mines and whose real life became embroidered with legend after his death (photo 110). If slavery was treated in a political, serious manner in *Ganga Zumba* (1963) and in a carnivalesque manner in *Xica da Silva*, it is treated in a historical-didactical manner in *Chico Rei*. Chico Rei stands in for the countless Africans who brought royal prestige or artisanal talent to the Americas. His story, much like Xica da Silva's, was first presented as a *samba enredo* before becoming a film. The *samba enredo* from the mid-1960s described a mythical utopia of freedom:

> Once on the African seacoast
> There lived a regal, orderly tribe.
> Whose king was the symbol
> Of a hardworking and hospitable land.
> One day this tranquility succumbed
> To Portuguese invasion.
> They captured men
> And enslaved them in Brazil.[25]

Apart from the samba school presentation about Chico, Walter Lima Jr. drew on other sources, notably from Agripa de Vasconcelos's historical novel *Chico Rei*, from Cecília Meireles's poetry *(O Romanceiro da Inconfidência)*, and from the oral traditions of Minas Gerais.

110. Walter Lima Jr.'s *Chico Rei* (1982)

Chico Rei is framed by the words of a griot-style storyteller (Mário
Gusman), another African who arrives with the same ship and who survives
to tell Chico's story. The tale of Chico's life that forms the film's core takes us
from Africa, where Chico/Galanga was the chief of a small but prosperous
Congolese tribe, to the capture with his family, to the slave ships of the
Middle Passage, where Chico loses his wife when she is thrown overboard as
excess baggage. The film shows the process whereby Africans were separated
from their families, stripped of their names (Calanga becomes Francisco, or
"Chico"), and forced to abandon their religions. It examines, in short, a taboo
moment in Eurocentric historiography—the originary moment of historical
trauma that generated the black diaspora in the Americas—and much of the
film's poignancy has to do with the memory of all the ways that slavery tried
to destroy the black family. Arriving in Brazil, Chico is bought by Seixas, the
owner of the Encardadeira Gold Mine, near Vila Rica (now Ouro Preto) in
Minas Gerais. At that time, slavery in Minas had an elasticity rarely encountered elsewhere in the Americas, as enslaved African miners mingled with
white workers and free blacks. It is also worth remembering that Africans invented the process of iron smelting and that black foremen in the mines often
knew more about the technological procedures of mining than the Portuguese owners.[26] Some blacks worked on their own, merely paying a tax to the

mine's owner. Most were allowed to work one day a week for their own account. Blacks also stole gold dust and precious stones, hiding them in the orifices of their bodies, to the point that the authorities, in a painful and humiliating purge, used hot peppers to expel them.[27]

In *Chico Rei,* the owner Seixas leads Chico into the mine and makes a promise: "Get gold out of this mine and I'll set you free." Chico proposes a more collective solution—"Set me free together with all my relatives"—but Seixas limits his offer to Chico. Chico discovers a rich vein of ore, but hides its whereabouts from the mine's owner. When he and his companion discover the gold, significantly, they do not shout, "Gold!" but "Freedom!" Gold, in other words, is not a value in itself but merely a means to an end: the freedom of the entire clan.[28] They trick Seixas by using drums and music to hide the sounds of their mining in the hidden vein of ore. At one point on the soundtrack, Milton Nascimento, a singer-composer associated with Minas Gerais, whose longing falsetto forms a perfect vehicle for the desire for freedom, sings:

> Gold in the bowels of the earth.
> Sacred is the gold
> Of those who covet freedom.
> My Black Saint
> My black woman
> Ifigênia.

The film shows the official surveillance of slaves, who hid gold and precious metals wherever they could in order to buy their freedom. When Seixas becomes deeply indebted, he sells the mine to Chico, who becomes the first black mine-owner, much to the indignation of the governor. He joins the "Our Lady of the Rosary Brotherhood," an association for freeing slaves, and ultimately gathers sufficient gold to buy the freedom of his entire clan, who become the collective owner of the Encardideira, which they work on a cooperative basis. Together they found a kind of black nation, a ministate within the state. They also construct a church in honor of Saint Ifigênia, one of the patron saints of slaves. But whereas Chico uses his mining skills to buy his own freedom, his son goes off to a *quilombo,* suggesting another possible path to liberation. The film ends with the annual January 6 Festival of the "Reisada do Rosário," which Chico Rei is supposed to have created and which gave birth to the regal ritual of the *congados*. During the *congado* ceremony Chico Rei and his queen were carried around on a throne, in front of which musicians played African instruments. The *congado* involved the crowning of the king of the Congo, rather like negro coronation days in the United States, and involved processions, the display of martial arts, fancy dress and jewels, sword dancing, and the celebration of Ifigênia. "A true king / will stay a king," Milton Nascimento's lyrics tell us, "if his reign is planted / in the hearts of the people."

Chico Rei offers a mediating figure of black heroism, less aggressive than Zumbi but more assertive than João Negrinho. Chico juggles the cunning, tricksterlike *malandragem* of hiding the gold with the respectability of becoming the mine's owner. He converts to Catholicism, but also preserves the African traditions. His solution is at once individual and collective; having become personally rich, he uses his wealth to free other slaves. He moves from the individual and familial to the collective and the political, and thus he regains his stolen crown.

A coproduction with Germany, *Chico Rei* was originally intended to be a 13-episode television series, but after a disagreement with the Germans, Walter Lima Jr. resolved to turn a 17-hour workprint into a 2-hour film. Carlos Diegues's *Quilombo* (1984) passed through a similar metamorphosis. Originally planned as a TV series, it too became a film. *Quilombo* (1984) returns to the theme of his first feature, *Ganga Zumba:* black resistance against slavery. Both films celebrate the historical reality of Palmares, the most spectacular and long-lived of the free communities founded by runaway Africans in Brazil (photo 111). If *Ganga Zumba* brought its characters to the threshold of freedom, *Quilombo* brings them into the promised land itself. The narrative of *Quilombo* sweeps over a historical period from 1650 to 1695, moving through three distinct phases. In the first, a rebel group led by Ganga Zumba flees from a sugar plantation and makes its way to Palmares. In the second phase, Palmares, under Ganga Zumba, has become a prosperous and independent community. In the third phase, another leader, Zumbi, is forced to lead the struggle in an atmosphere dominated by internal tensions and external aggressions. The Palmarinos are ultimately massacred and Zumbi himself is killed, but outbreaks of resistance, as the final intertitles inform us, go on for another century. The overall movement of the film, then, is from spontaneous revolt to the construction of a community, to the violent destruction of

III. Toni Tornado and Jorge Coutinho in *Quilombo* (1984)

that community, with a final coda pointing to ongoing struggle.

Brazilian films about the history of slavery present various alternative roads to freedom—the *quilombismo* of Zumbi in *Ganga Zumba,* the smuggling of Teodoro in *Xica da Silva,* and the economic autonomy or black capitalism *avant la lettre* of Chico Rei. *Quilombo*'s gallery of characters includes Ganga Zumba (Toni Tornado), the African prince who leads the enslaved out of bondage into the promised land of Palmares; Acotirene, a symbolic figure associated with African strength and spirituality; and Dandara (Zezé Motta), associated with the African spirit Iansã and whose performance of religious rituals saves Ganga Zumba (photo 112). The Jewish character Samuel (Jonas Bloch), meanwhile, represents the many Sephardic Jews and *marranos* (forced converts) who fled the Inquisition and took refuge in Brazil; his dialogue in the film brings to the flight of the slaves Biblical echoes of the Exodus, the parting of the Red Sea, and the Promised Land. The film valorizes African culture by associating its characters with the *orixás* of *candomblé:* Ganga Zumba is linked to Xangô; Zumbi to Ogum (the *orixá* of metal, agriculture, and war). At one point, a venerable figure refuses last rites in Latin and insists on singing in Yoruba. After his death, Ganga Zumba appears magically with Xangô's ax in hand. Unfortunately, the film repeats the error of *Ganga*

112. Zezé Motta as Dandara in *Quilombo*

Zumba; Palmares was Bantu rather than Yoruba, the latter group not yet having arrived in Brazil. Diegues is thus guilty of what Antônio Risério calls "Nagôcentrism," the collapsing of the variety of African religions into a single Yoruba practice. But in any case Diegues foregrounds the symbolic value of African culture, while also insisting on the need for struggle.

A didactic saga based on fact, legend, and imaginative extrapolation, *Quilombo* is part historical reconstruction and part musical comedy, partially drawing its style, like *Xica da Silva,* from Rio's carnival pageants, whose spectacles also involve the fanciful recreation of historic events. At the same time, the film is self-designated "science fiction" in that it projects a utopian future.[29] Diegues aims at poetic synthesis rather than naturalistic reproduction, constructing a plausible historical hypothesis that is above all *poetically* correct. The challenge of conveying the historical grandeur of Palmares while retaining a sense of magic and surreality is not, unfortunately, always successfully met. The ritual costumes and the turbans, body paint, and hairstyles, along with the quasi-theatrical lighting, at times suggest a kind of Afro Brazilian Disney World. The hyperauthenticity of the ceramics produced by the "Barravento Factory"—in which Luiz Carlos Ripper managed 300 people making all the ceramics and armor—has the paradoxical effect of provoking a sense of artificiality, of a boutique full of shiny items. At its best moments, however, the film, with the help of the Gilberto Gil's pulsing and deliberately anachronistic soundtrack music, electronic Afro-derived samba-rock, not only evokes a historical utopia but also communicates a sense of what that utopia might have felt like.

If the 1970s and the early 1980s were the period of exaltation of African culture, the 1990s are a period of the normalization of the presence of black characters in the fiction film. Some of the most internationally successful Brazilian films feature important black characters in films not primarily focused on blacks. Babenco's *Pixote* (1980), for example, although not strictly a film on a black theme, does feature important black characters, and a situation—homeless children and violence against street children—which disproportionately affects blacks. The film forms part of an international genre (the street urchin film) that includes not only de Sica's *Shoeshine* (1946) but also Luis Buñuel's *Los Olvidados* (The Dispossessed, 1950) and Mira Nair's *Salaam Bombay* (1988). *Pixote* shares with the Buñuel film its topic (delinquent children), its source (sociological documentation), its setting (the Third World metropolis), its style (documentary-inflected), its casting strategies (a mix of professional and nonprofessional performers), its focalization (the children themselves), and even its episodic structure. The film follows some Brazilian slum kids, synecdochic samples of that country's 3 million homeless children, from police roundup to reform school to a life-endangering "freedom" on the streets (see photo 113). That both the young actor Fernando Ramos da Silva, who plays Pixote, and his brother were themselves subsequently killed by the police in dubious circumstances sadly attests to the film's veracity. Indeed, the film was prescient in foreseeing a situation in which over 1,000 children would be slain every year between 1989 and 1991, usually by police (on- or off-duty) or by death squads.[30] José Joffily's *Quem Matou Pixote?* (Who Killed Pixote?, 1996) addresses the Pixote case specifically and police violence against children generally.[31]

Although the Cinema Novo of the 1960s, despite its revolutionary concerns, had largely ignored the working class,[32] certain late 1970s films register the impact of workers' struggles, partly as a result of the immense coming-to-consciousness and political mobilization of the workers in São Paulo culminating in the strikes that paralyzed the city in 1978. In these events, blacks too played a role. A film that features working-class militancy, and the black role

113. Fernando Ramos da Silva as *Pixote* (1980)

within it, is Leon Hirszman's *Eles Não Usam Black Tie* (They Don't Wear Black Tie, 1981). The film updates Gianfrancesco Gurnieri's 1950s play of the same title, which fostered the emergence of a politicized theater in the middle of that decade. The film offers an impressive gallery of proletarian characters, ranging from the old leftist Otávio (played by Guarnieri himself) and his wife Romana (Fernanda Montenegro), to the wavering but never completely despicable son Tião (Carlos Alberto Ricelli) and his resourceful and courageous wife, Maria (Bete Mendes), and, most germane for our purposes, the courageous black unionist Bráulio (Milton Gonçalves; see photo 114).

Eles Não Usam Black Tie mingles a family story, which contrasts the militant father's lucidity with the son's confused opportunism, and the story of a strike. In political terms, the film supports a cautious nonadventurist militancy, a disciplined struggle for small local victories while condemning the "irrational excesses" of the radicals. Subtextually, the veteran militant filmmaker criticizes the presumably lost generation of the dictatorship and in this sense distorts history. For, in fact, the São Paulo strikes were the product of a new generation typified by Luis Inácio da Silva ("Lula") and his Workers' Party, rather than of the traditional left. Indeed, the real-life prototype for the black character Bráulio, who is killed by a police agent and whose death is commemorated by a massive funeral procession at the end of the film, was

114. Milton Gonçalves as Bráulio in *Eles Não Usam Black Tie* (1981)

Santos Dias, a militant within the Workers' Party. *Eles Não Usam Black Tie* excoriates police violence, a subject that would have been taboo only a few years before. The film shows a world where the working class is not racist but the police are: "Get the black guy," the informer tells the policeman just before the latter kills Bráulio. The murder is shown as both political and racial. Here, too, the film breaks new ground. Black characters in earlier Cinema Novo films tended to be anarchist free spirits like Firmino in *Barravento* or Calunga in *A Grande Cidade* (The Big City, 1965) but Hirszman presents Bráulio, a character not featured in the original play, as a courageous leader and martyr. Indeed, the scene of his funeral, which turns into a huge political rally, is the climactic event of the film.

White Brazilian directors often make black and Indian characters and situations bear the burden of national allegory; they become "carriers" of signs meant to point to something other than themselves. The *quilombos,* for example, at times become the sign for national liberation. Early Indianist allegories had the Indian represent Brazil as a whole; later allegories have the black stand in for the "people." In other instances, general national or social allegories have racial overtones. Two films, one from the late 1970s, the other from the mid-1990s, use the same trope of an invaded bourgeois home to invoke racialized class divisions in Brazil as a reminiscence of slavery. Arnaldo Jabor's *Tudo Bem* (Everything's Fine, 1978), for example, crowds all of Brazil's social and racial contradictions into the apartment of a middle-class Carioca family. When the family invites construction workers to remodel their home, the workers and maids slowly take over. The apartment becomes the site of an irreverent carnival, popular mysticism, and other cultural manifestations detested by the bourgeoisie. The "slave quarters," in Glauber Rocha's felicitous phrase, "invade the Big House."

A similar allegory is posited by the Mainardi brothers film *Sixteen, Oh Sixty* (1995; see photo 115). In the film, a wealthy businessman, Vittório (Antônio Calloni), foils a robbery by stabbing Jackson, a petty thief who breaks into his São Paulo villa. Worried about the thief's threats against his family, Vittório orders him killed but the hired assassins kill Jackson's cellmate Franklin by mistake (many of the characters are named after American presidents and public figures, a reminder, perhaps, that the allegory does not apply only to Brazil). Feeling guilty about the miscalculation, Vittório takes in Franklin's widow and her three children as live-in objects of charity. The forced cohabitation leads to a socially pathological situation in which Vittório's bored wife, Eleanor (Maite Proença) enjoys the children as objects of an eroticized charity, while Vittório's fascist son tortures the children (and seduces Vittório's wife). At one point, Vittório himself invokes the slavery analogy by calling for domestic segregation: "We have to be kept separate. The Big House here, the

115. The *favelados* in *Sixteen, Oh Sixty* (1995)

Slave Quarters over there." The sequels of slavery, the film suggests, are still with us.

A number of films deal with hip-hop and funk culture in Brazil, movements that are primarily black. Muilo Salles's *Como as Anjos Nascem* (How Angels Are Born, 1995) features a young black *favelado* who is caught up in a kidnapping incident and who uses the glare of police and media lights to exhibit his talents as a break-dancer. Francisco César Filho's *Rota ABC* (1991) explores the lives of people living in the industrial periphery of São Paulo. The film begins with a clip from the opening sequence of Luis Sérgio Person's *São Paulo S.A.* (1965), a classic film about industrialization and specifically the automobile industry. *Rota ABC* contrasts the optimistic pronouncements of characters in the earlier film with a description of the mentality and style of life of young people, many of them with little hope for jobs, now living in the same area. The film features hip-hop groups like the Garotos Podres (The Rotten Boys) and the Mulheres Negras (Black Women) who articulate critique and disillusionment. (The director had already explored the social role of music, specifically rap and punk, in *Hip Hop São Paulo* [1990; see photo 116].) Sérgio Goldemberg's *Funk Rio* (1995) portrays pop music and youth culture. Another hip-hop short, Tata Amaral's *Viver a Vida* (Just Livin', 1992) offers a Brazilian reaccentuation of American popular culture. The film chron-

116. *Hip Hop São Paulo* (1990)

icles the life of young black office-boy during a day in São Paulo. Proud of his new sneakers, he moves from overcrowded busses to long lines in banks, has encounters with nonworking phones, and experiences other urban frustrations, all presented as if in illustration of the lyrics of a rap song. In the end his sneakers are stolen, and in the coda he dances in front of a graffiti-covered wall reminiscent of the opening and closing shots of *Do the Right Thing* (1989). And Tania Savieta's *Cães* (Dogs, 1995), finally, allegorizes racism through an allegorical fable about dog training, somewhat in the manner of Samuel Fuller's *White Dog* (1982).

The Emergence of "Indigenous Media"

Some 1980s and 1990s films treat indigenous themes. After the idealized Indian of silent era romanticism, the objectified positivist Indian of the 1920s documentaries, the allegorical cannibal of the modernists and tropicalists, the 1980s and 1990s bring the rebel Indian of the fiction film, the reflexive Indian of the anthropologists, and the activist Indian of "indigenous media." Sílvio Back's feature documentary *República Guarani* (1981) treats the same subject as Roland Jaffe's *The Mission* (1986), the Jesuit missions between 1610 and 1767 among the Guarani Indians. But instead of idealizing the Jesuits à la Jaffe, Back shows that the priests did not ultimately renounce the Christian colonization of the native soul or the colonial enterprise in general; their denunciation was limited to physically genocidal practices. For Back, the Jesuits were the "first ideological multinationals, transmitting the Gospel to Africans, Asians, and Amerindians, superimposing over the mythical universes of each nation and tribe the spiritual imperialism of modernity."[33] Zelito Viana's *Avaeté. Semente de Vingança* (Avaeté: Seeds of Vengeance, 1985), for its part, restages a more recent incident, the 1963 extermination of the Avaeté tribe by dynamite and machine gun, a decimation that left only two survivors. Viana uses the story, originally related in Darcy Ribeiro's book *Os Índios e a Civilização,* as the prologue to a story about how Ava (Macsuara Kadiweu), one of the survivors, seeks vengeance. Befriending the expedition's cook, Ramiro (Hugo Carvana), who is repentant about his role in the massacre, Ava finds out that a rapacious landowner-businessman was behind the massacre. In the climactic sequence, Ava, dressed and painted as an Indian warrior, invades the businessman's home and does justice with his own hands. Another

1980s film, Ruy Guerra's *Kuarup* (1989), adopts the 1967 Antônio Callado novel of the same name ("Quarup" refers to an Indian ritual of homage to dead ancestors). The film, like the novel, portrays Brazilian history from the period of Getúlio Vargas up through the 1964 coup d'état, all focalized through the Jesuit priest Padre Nando (Taumaturgo Ferreira), who moves from religious faith to social idealism to armed struggle. He is encouraged by politicized friends to work with Indians on the Xingu reservation, where he tries to reconstruct a utopian society in the jungle. In the end, he realizes that his real vocation is to struggle against the military dictatorship. Unfortunately, this well-meant story is told ineptly, with vertiginous leaps over space (Rio, Recife, the Xingu Reservation) and time.

In this same period, "ethnographic films" attempt to divest themselves of vestigial colonialist attitudes. Whereas in the old ethnographic films self-confident "scientific" voice-overs delivered the "truth" about subject peoples unable to answer back (while sometimes prodding the "natives" to perform practices long abandoned), the new ethnographic films strive for "shared film-making," "participatory filmmaking," "dialogical anthropology," "reflexive distance," and "interactive filmmaking."[34] Documentary and experimental films discard the covert elitism of the pedagogical or ethnographic model in favor of an acquiescence in the relative, the plural, and the contingent, as artists experience a salutary self-doubt about their own capacity to speak "for" the other. Some Brazilian films from the 1970s, such as Artur Omar's *Congo* (1977), had already mocked the very idea of white filmmakers saying anything of value about indigenous or Afro-Brazilian culture. Other filmmakers, such as Andrea Tonacci, simply handed over the camera to the "other" in order to facilitate a two-way "conversation" between urban Brazilians and indigenous groups. At times the dialogue turned against the filmmakers themselves. In *Raoni* (1978), the Indians ponder the advisability of killing the filmmakers — for them just another group of potentially murderous white men — ultimately deciding to spare them so "they can bring our message to other whites." Thus the filmmaker assumes some of the risks of a real dialogue, of potential challenge from interlocutors. The question changes from how one represents the other to how one collaborates with the other in a shared space. The ideal, rarely realized, becomes the effective participation of the interlocutory "other" in all phases of production.

Sérgio Bianchi's documentary *Mato Eles?* (Should I Kill Them?, 1983) takes a more ironic approach. The film focuses on relations between a tribe in Paraná and the FUNAI (The Brazilian Bureau of Indian Affairs). The Indians work at a FUNAI-backed sawmill constructed on a reservation, where they are forced to cut down their own forests. In exchange, they are promised houses and churches. The film's subject of oppression does not at first glance seem amenable to parodic treatment. Yet the film completely deconstructs the conventional approach (in Brazil and elsewhere) to this kind of topic. Instead of the customary realist depiction of the local habitat, interspersed with talking heads and disembodied voice-over expressing the enlightened consciousness of non-Indian filmmakers, Bianchi satirically undermines not only the official discourse concerning the Indian but also the traditional *bonne conscience* of the "denunciation documentary." Indeed, the film constitutes a relentless assault on the assumptions and sensibility of the middle-class spectator accustomed to documentaries that flatter his/her narcissistic sense of humanist compassion.

Mato Eles? is structured around a series of apparently whimsical multiple-choice quizzes addressed to the spectator. The Brechtianism of these quizzes, in their implicit call for spectatorial collaboration and the "rendering of a verdict," is tinged here with bitter irony, for both question and answer tend to the mutually contradictory and the absurd. One question reads: "Very few Indians remain from the once numerous Xeta tribe. What happened to the others? Choose one of the following: (1) They all intermarried with the white population and are now living in the cities; (2) They all died due to infectious diseases and litigation concerning land rights; (3) They are all on vacation in Europe; (4) The Xeta Indians never existed. This documentary is false; (5) All the above are correct." To the question "what happened to the money generated by the sawmill, one answer choice is "B) FUNAI keeps the money until the Indians grow up." Another quiz poses three unpalatable alternatives: "The extermination of the Indians should be a) immediate; b) slow; c) gradual." The questions and answers leave no comfortable space for the "progressive" spectator; rather, they confront the audience with the reality of extermination, in a manner that initially provokes laughter but subsequently elicits reflection and self-doubt.

Mato Eles? also deconstructs the official "Indianist" discourse predominant in Brazil since the time of the nineteenth-century romantics, for whom the Indian was the idealized symbol of national difference. But the descendants of the *bravos guerreiros* (heroic fighters) celebrated in countless songs, poems, and novels, *Mato Eles?* suggests, are now trapped in a dreary cycle of disease and powerlessness. Bianchi mocks the heroicizing vision of the Indian by announcing a film-within-the-film, an Indianist epic entitled, in transparent homage to James Fenimore Cooper, The Last of the Xetas. The lush strains of *O Guarani,* from the equally Indianist opera by Brazilian composer Carlos Gomes, further swells our expectations for an epic spectacle. Instead, Bianchi shows us the sole-surviving, literally "last" member of the tribe, presented in a series of photographs strongly reminiscent of police mug shots. The "brave warrior" of romanticism has become the despised object of the official discourse of police photos coldly registering the reality of genocide.

Nor does Bianchi exempt himself from criticism. At one point, a venerable Guarani Indian surprises the filmmaker by asking exactly how much money he will make on the film. This inconvenient question, which normally would have found its way into the editing-room trash can, segues to an authorial voice-over in which Bianchi speculates about other avenues for financially exploiting the Indian—anthropological scholarships, photograph albums, arts and crafts shops, showing films in Europe. Thus the "Voice-of-God" off-screen narration is used, against the grain of conventional practice, to mock the filmmaker himself. The condescending voice of monologic Truth here deconstructs itself, thus closing the film's circle of multiple ironies directed at the power structure, at the filmmaker, and at the canonized formulas of the liberal documentary.

The most remarkable recent development has been the emergence of "indigenous media," that is, the use by audiovisual technology (camcorders, VCRs) for the cultural and political purposes of indigenous peoples. (One is reminded of Oswald de Andrade's call in the 1950s for the *barbaro tecnizado,* the "technicized Indian" as artistic ideal; see photo 117.) The phrase "indigenous media," as Faye Ginsburg points out, is oxymoronic, evoking both the self-understanding of aboriginal groups and the vast institutional structures of TV and cinema.[35] Within "indigenous media," the producers are themselves the receivers, along with neighboring communities and, occasionally, distant cultural institutions or festivals such as the Native American film festivals held in New York and San Francisco.

In Brazil, the Centro de Trabalho Indigenista (Center for Work with Indigenous Peoples) has been collaborating with indigenous groups since 1979,

117. The "technicized Indian"

teaching video-making and -editing and offering technologies and facilities in order to protect indigenous land and consolidate resistance. In Vincent Carelli's *O Espírito da TV* (The Spirit of TV, 1991), the members of the Waiapi tribe, newly introduced to TV, reflect on the uses of video for contacting other tribes and defending themselves against the encroachments of federal agents, gold miners, and loggers (photo 118). Taking an eminently pragmatic approach, the Waiapi ask the filmmakers to hide their weakness to the outside world; "exaggerate our strength," they say, "so they won't occupy our land." In *Arco de Zo'é* (Meeting Ancestors, 1993), Chief Wai-Wai recounts his visit to the Zo'e, a recently contacted group known to the Waiapi only through video images. The two groups compare hunting and weaving techniques, food, rituals, myths, and history. The film communicates the diversity of indigenous cultures; Chief Wai-Wai has difficulty adjusting to the total nudity of his hosts, for example. *Como Irmãos* (Like Brothers, 1993), finally, recounts the cultural exchange between the Parakateje of Para and their relatives the Kraho of Tocantins. The two groups compare strategies for maintaining their language and identity and for resisting Euro Brazilian domination. In all the films, the "outside" spectator is no longer the privileged interlocutor; video is primarily a facilitator for exchange between indigenous groups. On a secondary level, "outsiders" are welcome to view these exchanges and even support the cause in financial or other ways, but there is no romantic narrative of redemption whereby the raising of spectatorial consciousness will somehow "save the world."

Video Cannibalism (1995), finally, introduces the Enauene, an extremely isolated group that skipped the pen-and-pencil literacy stage to join the age of electronic media. Like the 1920 modernists, the filmmakers emphasize the group's playfulness and their sexual freedom, where nudity is the norm and where men play act at making love together while their compatriots laugh. The Enauene also enact a meeting between themselves and gold prospectors, resulting in a film-within-the-film—*The Invaders*—which the tribe watches with great pleasure on a VCR. Here video becomes a catalyst for cultural identity, exercising a power that is literally "tribalizing," potentially increasing a community's *axé*.

Among the most media-savvy of the indigenous groups are the Kayapó, a Go-speaking people of central Brazil who live in 14 communities scattered over an area roughly the size of Great Britain. When a documentary crew from Granada Television went to Brazil to film the Kayapó in 1987, the Kayapó demanded video cameras, VCR, monitor, and videotapes as the quid pro quo for their cooperation. They have subsequently used video to record their own traditional ceremonies, demonstrations, and encounters with whites (so as to have the equivalent of a legal transcript). They have documented their traditional knowledge of the forest environment, and they plan to record the transmission of myths and oral history. The Kayapó not only sent a delegation to the Brazilian Constitutional Convention to lobby delegates debating indigenous rights, but also videotaped themselves in the process, winning international attention for their cause. Widely disseminated images of the Kayapó wielding video-cameras, appearing in *Time* and *The New York Times Magazine,* derive their power to shock from the premise that "natives" must be quaint and allochronic, that "real" Indians don't carry camcorders.

In the Granada Television documentary *Kayapó: Out of the Forest* (1989), we see the Kayapó and other native peoples stage a mass ritual performance to protest the planned construction of a hydroelectric dam. One of the leaders, Chief Pombo, points out that the dam's name *(Kararao)* is taken from a Kayapó war cry. Another, Chief Raoni, appears with the rock star Sting in a successful attempt to capture international media attention. At one point a

118. *The Spirit of TV* (1990)

woman presses a machete against the company spokesman's face as she scolds him in Kayapó. Another woman, in a remarkable reversal of colonialist *écriture,* tells the spokesman to write down her name, reminding him that she is among those who will die because of the dam. The spectator enamored of "modernity" comes to question the reflex association of hydroelectric dams with an axiomatically good "progress."

Hector Babenco's feature film *At Play in the Fields of the Lord* (1991) also questions ethnocentric notions of "progress" (photo 119). The plot revolves around diverse groups—adventure pilots (Tom Waits, Tom Berenger), Protestant missionaries (John Lithgow, Daryl Hannah) and local officials (Jose Dumont)—implicated in the fate of the Niaruna, a fictitious tribe reminiscent of the Yanomami. (The group's fictitious language is an amalgam of words from various indigenous languages such as Karajá, Ge, and Tupi.) The film portrays Protestant missionaries specifically, and Europeans and Euro Americans in the Amazon generally, as neurotic, arrogant, puritanical, insensitive, and ultimately dangerous to the general welfare. The missionaries never really succeed, furthermore, in their project of converting Indians to Christianity.

119. *At Play in the Fields of the Lord* (1991)

Contact with whites, the film suggests, always means death for the Indians. The pilots and the missionaries are symbolically linked in their mission; as they fly over the Amazon, the plane casts its reflection on the water in the form of a cross. The Brazilian policeman tells the two aviators to bomb the Niaruna village "just to scare them."

Even the well-intentioned can provoke calamity. Lewis Moon, the half-Cherokee character played by Tom Berenger, ultimately refuses to bomb the Niaruna and even defects to the Indian side, but he provokes genocide when he chooses to be intimate both with Andy (Daryl Hannah) and his native wife, thus spreading a disease that is fatal for the Indians. Although he is from another continent, he calls the Niaruna "his" people, but they answer that he is not Kisu, the god they imagined him to be, but "just a white man." The American identity politics of self-realization cannot be exported to the Amazon. Martin Quarrier (Aidan Quinn) tells Lewis Moon that "as an American he would be proud to have Indian blood," to which Lewis responds sardonically "And just how much Indian blood would an American be proud to have?" Everyone projects their own ethnocentric vision onto the Indians; even the Jewish character Wolf sees them as "the lost tribe of Israel, Jewish just like me." At the same time, the Indians are not noble savages but rather ordinary people faced by a devastating challenge.

The Potentials of Polyphony:
Reflections on Race and
Representation

∞

Having completed our filmic journey, what have we learned about issues of racial representation in Brazilian cinema? What theoretical and methodological conclusions can be drawn? To what extent have Afro Brazilians and indigenous Brazilians been able to represent themselves? How does Brazilian cinema "stage" its racial representations? How useful are such notions as "stereotypes," "positive" images, "realism"? What is the role of cultural difference within the spectatorship of reading films? What voices have *not* been heard in Brazilian cinema? What strategies have *not* been tried?

Brazilian films inevitably reflect, or better reflect on (since the "reflection" is never a question of direct correspondence), the ambient realities as filtered through the competing ideologies and discourses circulating within the social atmosphere. The lack of rigid racial segregation, the fact of a mestiço population, and the ubiquity of Afro Brazilian cultural expression, combined with the equally undeniable reality of the social powerlessness of people of color, all leave traces in the films. The challenge is to discern the structuring patterns within these traces, for films do not merely reflect social reality in an unmediated way; they inflect, stylize, caricature, allegorize. Although poststructuralist theory reminds us that we live and dwell within language and representation, that we have no direct access to the "real," nevertheless the constructed, coded nature of artistic discourse hardly precludes all reference to a common social life. Human consciousness, and artistic practice, Bakhtin argues, do not come into contact with the "real" directly, but rather through the medium of the surrounding ideological world. Literature and, by extension, cinema do not so much refer to or call up the world as represent its languages and discourses. Rather than directly "reflecting" the real, or even "refracting" the real, artistic discourse constitutes a refraction of a refraction, that is, a mediated version of an already textualized and "discursivized" socioideological world.[1] The issue is less one of fidelity to a preexisting truth or reality, then, than one of a specific orchestration of ideological discourses and communitarian perspectives.

One important socioideological grid through which films "see," and through which they are "seen," is that of the stereotype, an issue that exists at the disciplinary boundaries of literary study, psychology, sociology, and anthropology. As a kind of mental shorthand, stereotypes constitute a device whereby people characterize, in a necessarily schematic manner, another group with which they are only partially familiar. Within a situation of racial domination, however, stereotypes have a clear function of social control; they indirectly rationalize and justify the advantages of the socially empowered. Much of the literature on blacks and Indians in North American cinema revolves around the issue of specific stereotypes, classically summarized, at least as far as blacks are concerned, in Donald Bogle's title *Toms, Coons, Mulattoes, Mammies and Bucks*. To what extent, we might ask, are stereotypes congruent in the United States and Brazil? Given the status of Brazil and the United States as two white-dominated New World societies, certain congruencies are virtually inevitable. The art of both countries features the indigenous "noble savage," although there is no equivalent in Brazil to his negative counterpart, the war-whooping savage of the Hollywood frontier western. Indeed, in Brazil there is no conquest narrative in which the "Indian" is the explicit or implicit "enemy." Instead, we have found innumerable adaptations of romantic Indianist novels, a few comedies about urban white Brazilians going to live happily with largely female "Indians" (e.g., *Casei-me com um Xavante* [I Married a Xavante, 1957]), alongside many politically engaged features such as *Como Era Gostoso Meu Francês* (How Tasty Was My Little Frenchman, 1971), *Avaeté: Semente de Vingança* (Avaeté: Seeds of Vengeance, 1985), and *Capitalismo Selvagem* (1993) and documentaries such as *Mato Eles?* (Should I Kill Them?, 1983), *Terra dos Índios* (1987), and many others. At times Indians have been forced to carry a heavy "burden" of allegory. For the romantic poets, the Indian symbolized Brazil, yet that same Brazil was subjugating real Indians. And within Brazilian cinema, blacks too have sometimes been used as allegorical shorthand for the "poor" or "the oppressed," a conflation that mimics the class-over-race discourse typical of a certain Brazilian sociology.

Both Brazilian and American film history also offer the figure of the noble, faithful slave, the honest, devoted subaltern: in the United States the Uncle Tom and the Uncle Remus, in Brazil the "Pai João." As the products of the narcissistic projections of whites, these emblems of happy servility represent the slaves as the masters desired them to be. Both societies also display the Tom's female counterpart, the devoted woman slave or servant; in the United States the "mammy," and in Brazil the *mãe preta* (black mother), both products of slave societies in which the children of the master were nursed at the black woman's breast. The *mãe preta* was celebrated in sentimental poetry as patient and self-sacrificing for the good of the whites in her care. Aunt Nastácia, in Monteiro Lobato's children's story *Viagem ao Céu* (1934) represents the type: obese, with thick lips, large eyes, and a kerchiefed head, reminiscent of Aunt Jemima.[2] Both societies, similarly, generated a "splitting" between the "good black" and the "bad nigger," a splitting superficially about "virtue" but really about the question of black refusal or acceptance of white domination. The black who accepts domination, within white racist discourse, is by definition "good"; the black who refuses is by definition "bad." In Brazil, the question of the "bad nigger" becomes linked to the history of black revolt and resistance, and in most cases, in the cinema at least, this figure is shown to have positive valence.

With other stereotypes, the question of crosscultural equivalencies becomes more complicated. Certain characters in Brazilian films (Tônio in *Bahia de Todos os Santos* [Bahia of All the Saints, 1960], Jorge in *Compasso de Espera* [Marking Time; made 1971, released 1973]) at first glance seems to recall the "tragic mulatto" figure common in North American cinema and literature (see photo 120). The context, however, is radically different. The notion of passing for white, so crucial to American films such as *Pinky* (1949) and *Imitation of Life* (1959) has little relevance in Brazil, which has never been a strictly segregated society and where it is often said that all Brazilian families have a "foot in the kitchen," that is, that they all have partial black ancestry. In Brazil, "passing" is irrelevant, since once the person is light enough to pass, that is the end of the question, even if the person is known to have black ancestry; it is appearance and not ancestry that matters.

In Brazil, the mulatto is often seen as pretentious and vaguely ridiculous, a

120. The "tragic mulatto" in *Bahia de Todos os Santos* (1960)

constellation of associations not entirely foreign to the United States; D. W. Griffith's *Birth of a Nation* (1914–1915), for example, constantly foregrounds mixed-race mulattoes as the most "uppity," the most treacherous and danger-ous to the system. The Brazilian constellation of stereotypes also features the "sexy mulatta," the presumably lascivious, sensuous product of racial mixing and disturber of erotic peace. According to the reigning mythologies, the adoration of the mulatta can be traced back to the Portuguese idolatry of dark-skinned Moorish princesses. Although white North American society also projected blacks as lascivious, this quality was not so exclusively focused on the mulatta as in Brazil. In Brazil, the sexy mulatta figure proliferates not only in literature, for example, Vidinha in *Memórias de um Sargento de Milícias* and Rita Baiana in *O Cortiço,* but also in many sambas, in theatrical reviews ("Oba Oba" in Rio), in advertising, and in film.[3] The mulatta was especially popular in the *pornochanchadas* of the 1970s, as reflected in such titles as *Uma Mulata para Todos* (A Mulatta for Everyone, 1975) and *A Mulata Que Queria Pecar* (The Mulatta Who Wanted to Sin, 1978; photo 121). The mulatta is seen more as mistress than as wife, as in the well-known rhyme "branca para casar, mulata para fornicar, e negra para trabalhar" (white woman to marry, mulatta to fornicate, and black woman to work). The black woman could choose, in other words, between sexual and economic exploitation. White men draw the line of their desire at marriage, a sacramental gesture that might compromise the family prestige and inheritance. Literary mulattas like Rita Baiana in *O Cortiço* or Ana Mercedes in *Tenda dos Milagres* (Tent of Miracles, 1977), moreover, tend not to be constructed as mothers.[4] For Lélia Gonzales, the "mulatta" is a "sophisticated form of reification, an export product to be consumed by tourists and the Brazilian bourgeoisie."[5] The adoration of the mulatta as cultural icon, then, though apparently providing symbolic "compensation" for quotidian oppression, in fact forms part of that very oppression.

Whereas Donald Bogle posits five distinct stereotypes in relation to blacks in American cinema, João Carlos Rodrigues, the author of the sole book-length study devoted to blacks in Brazilian Cinema *(O Negro Brasileiro e o Cinema),* posits twelve stereotypes in relation to black Brazilians. (1) The *preto velho* is the humble subaltern, reminiscent of the Uncle Tom or Uncle Remus

121. *A Mulata Que Queria Pecar* (1978)

figure in the United States, which Rodrigues finds more typical of São Paulo films such as *Caiçara* (1950), *Sinhá Moça* (The Plantation Owner's Daughter, 1953) and *O Saci* (1951). In *umbanda,* the *preto velho* smokes a pipe, walks with a cane, and speaks incorrect Portuguese, but he is also the repository of deep wisdom. (2) The *mãe preta* (black mother) corresponds to the "mammy" of North American tradition, and is found in theater (José de Alencar's *Mãe*) and in the cinema, for example, in *João Negrinho* (John the Black Boy; shot 1954, released 1958). (3) The *martyr,* a classic figure in literature, was subsequently adapted for the screen by Augusto da Silva Fagundes in 1973 in *O Negrinho do Pastoreio* (Black Boy from the Pasture) the story about an innocent black shepherd cruelly abused by his master and devoured alive by ants before his miraculous resurrection (photo 122). (4) The *black with a white soul* in its "positive" version represents the good-hearted negro who knows his place and in its negative variant the uppity mulatto who thinks he's white. Rodrigues cites as "positive" examples the protagonist of *João Negrinho* and Repo in *Alelulia, Gretchen* (1976).

The Noble Savage stereotype (5) has literary origins, for example, in Lope de Vega's *El Santo Negro,* and is more typically associated with the Indian. The noble savage in the form of the (6) *black rebel* is capable of resistance. Rodrigues finds traces of this figure in the *quilombeiros* of *Ganga Zumba* (1963) and *Quilombo* (1984). The most positive example, for Rodrigues, is the title character of *Chico Rei* (1985), the Afro Brazilian who buys his own freedom and that of his family. The black rebel figure is also familiar from literature, going back to Victor Hugo's *Bugh-Jargal* (1883), partially inspired by the black Jacobins from Haiti, which, in 1804, was the first black country to claim its independence. The black rebel appears both in Vera Cruz costume dramas such as *Sinhá Moça,* in commercial superproductions such as *A Marcha* (The March, 1970), and in more politicized films such as *Barravento* (The Turning Wind, 1962), *Ganga Zumba,* and *Quilombo. Compasso de Espera* features two kinds of black rebels: American-style militants who say, in English, "Burn Baby Burn," and their pacifist brothers who respond "Build, Baby, Build." (7) *O negão* (literally, big black) is more or less assimilable to the North American figure of the "buck," that is, a black man notable for brute strength and hyperbolic sexuality. The novel *O Bom Crioulo* features a gay *negão*. At times the *negão* is bracketed as part of a dream or fantasy sequence, for example, in the sexual fantasies of the white woman protagonist of the film adaptation of

Nelson Rodrigues's play *Bonita mas Ordinaria* (Pretty but Ordinary, 1981). In the *pornochanchada A Viagem ao Céu da Boca* (1981), similarly, a perverted black man cruelly violates two women and a transvestite, yet the whole episode is subsequently revealed as merely the dream of a sleeping burglar. In *A Menina e O Estuprador* (The Girl and the Rapist, 1983), a black man is accused of sexual crimes before he is proven innocent. (8) The *malandro*, or "street-smart hustler," is a trickster figure who gets by on his wits. The *malandro* is perhaps more positively connoted in Brazil than a "hustler" would be in North America (Sammy Davis Jr.'s "Sportin' Life" in *Porgy and Bess* would be a *malandro*, and Blaxploitation films played to some extent on the ambivalences of the *malandro* figure). In literature, the *malandro* is seen in Chico Juca of *Memórias de um Sargento de Milícias* and in Firmino of *O Cortiço*, and was crystallized in popular music in the sambas of Wilson Batista and Zé Keti. In film, we encounter the *malandro* as early as 1908, in Antônio Leal's *Os Cupuldrios da Cidade Nova* (New York Imposters), which, according to the marketing brochures, included "capoeiras e malandros." Grande Otelo often played the role of the naive *malandro,* as in *O Caçula do Barulho* (1949) and *Amei um Bicheiro* (I Loved a Bookie, 1952). The adolescents of *Bahia de Todos os Santos,* as Rodrigues points out, also qualify as *malandros* in that they survive through small-time theft, gigolo-like activities, and contraband. A number of 1960s plays, such as Antônio Callado's *Pedro Mico,* Gianfrancesco Guarnieri's *Gimba,* and Nelson Rodrigues's *Boca de Ouro,* revolved around the *malandro* figure. All three, as it happens, were adopted for the cinema, but in only one, *Pedro Mico,* was the part played by a black actor (Pelé). The juvenile delinquents of *Pixote* (1980) are distant cousins of the *malandro,* as is the socially conscious drug-dealer Bira in *Rio Bahilônia* (1982).

The *favelado* (9) was first portrayed cinematically in Humberto Mauro's *Favela dos Meus Amores* (Favela of My Loves, 1935), as well as in dos Santos's socially conscious 1950s films about Rio. (10) The *crioulo doido* (crazy black) combines comedy with childish naïveté and harkens back to folkloric figures like Saci, the one-legged black man who smokes a pipe and performs devilish tricks, and to specifically white traditions such as the Harlequin of Commedia dell'Arte. Its feminine equivalent is the *nega maluca* (crazy black woman) figure from the Rio carnival. The *crioulo doido* conveys an infantilizing impression of blacks as mischievous "eternal children," a portrayal that indirectly justifies control by the more "mature" elements of the population. Some Grande

122. *O Negrinho do Pastoreio* (1973)

Otelo roles have aspects of the *crioulo doido,* as does the black character Mussum in the comic quartet called the Trapalhões (a kind of Brazilian Three Stooges). The most sustained treatment of this archetype is to be found in Carlos Prates Correia's *O Crioulo Doido* (1971). (11) The *mulatta* is largely defined in sexual terms; she is adored during carnival but exploited (as maid, as prostitute) during the rest of the year. Although the "sexy mulatta" is typically Brazilian, one detects a kind of convergence of sexual-racial imaginaries in the erotic valorization of the mulatta within present-day American music videos, including within rap-music video. (12) The *Musa* is encountered in poetry by black poets such as Luis Gama (who speaks of his "musa de Guiné"), the black symbolist poet Cruz e Sousa, and the mulatto novelist Lima Barreto. The figure is more or less absent, as Rodrigues points out, in Brazilian films.

Rodrigues's typology is enormously informative, useful, and suggestive. He traces stereotypes back to literary antecedents, and he imaginatively links the diverse figures to the attributes of the diverse *orixás* in Afro Brazilian religion. Some of his categories, such as *crioulo doido,* had not been noted before. The typology suffers, however, from blurring and redundancy. In practice, it is often difficult to distinguish the "noble savage" from the "black with a white soul," while the *malandro,* the *favelado,* and the *crioulo doido* often blur together. The typology is strikingly heterogenous, furthermore; some of the categories *(negão, pai joão)* constitute stereotypes in the classical sense, others ("the muse") are literary archetypes, others *(favelado)* have to do with place of social origin, and still others ("the martyr") have to do with narrative function. Some of the types are not race specific; the *malandro,* for example, can be white as well as black. And although the schema has a place for the female mulatta, it has no place for the male mulatto.

Apart from the technical "bugs" in such a schema, however, it seems necessary to go beyond the concept of stereotypes and the corollary notions of "positive" and "negative" images. The analysis of stereotypes has been immensely useful, allowing us to detect structural patterns of prejudice in what had formerly seemed random phenomena. But the exclusive preoccupation with images, whether positive or negative, can lead to a kind of essentialism, as the critic reduces a complex diversity of portrayals to a limited set of reified stereotypes. Stereotypes, when seen reductively, run the risk of reproducing the very racism they were initially designed to combat. The notion of positive image, for example, is fraught with methodological pitfalls. The nature of "positive" is relative; one must ask, "positive for whom?" Black incarnations of patience and gradualism, for example, have always been more attractive to whites than to blacks. Even among blacks, one must ask: positive for middle-class blacks, or for the black dispossessed, the wretched of the earth? Oppressed people might have not only a *different* vision of morality, but even an *opposite* vision. (The black slang use of "bad" to mean "good" merely dramatizes this social relativity of moral evaluation.) Within slavery, as *Ganga Zumba* implies, it might be admirable and therefore "good" to deceive, manipulate, and even murder a slavedriver. Since the slave's status as property was itself the result of theft, the normal definitions of crime were necessarily open to revision. The emphasis on moral character rather than social structure places the burden on oppressed people to be "good" rather than on the privileged to change the system. The oppressed, in order to be equal, are asked to be better.

As Frantz Fanon initially and Homi Bhabha later have pointed out, stereotypes can also be ambivalent, hiding guilty attraction under a mask of rejection. Likewise, many apparently positive "compliments" to blacks have historically contained hidden "insults." The exaltation of Indian "innocence" had as its corollary their powerlessness. The lauding of blacks' "natural" ability in sports or music or theater had as its tacit corollary the suggestion that their achievements had nothing to do with work or intelligence. A cinema dominated by positive images, furthermore, in which filmmakers refuse to allow the slightest hint of negativity to enter into a racial portrait, would be as suspect as one conveying only negative images, betraying a neurotic lack of confidence in the group portrayed, which usually entertains few illusions concerning its own perfection. More important than that characters be heroes is that they be subjects.

Primitivism, exoticism, and folklorization, meanwhile, use the colonized other as an erotic fiction in order to reenchant the world. In Brazil, it is largely the Indian who is exoticized in this way, but Afro Brazilian culture has also been "folklorized," rendered as charmingly picturesque but ultimately premodern, allochronic, inconsequential. Folklorization characterizes texts as diverse as Varig Airlines promotional films—where we see the "public relations" deployment of diversified physiognomies—TV News visual logos, and films like *Pagador de Promessas* (The Given Word, 1962). When black culture is reduced to "a generating source of sensuality, a plethora of genital tricks, and an eternal fountain of recipes," as Muniz Sodré puts it, "then prejudice and ethnocentrism persist."[6] Such "affectionate" tributes depoliticize the black contribution, recapitulating the romantic-essentialism to be found within writers like Jorge Amado but also even within the negritude movement à la Leopold Senghor, which posited Greco Europe as Reason and Africa as Emotion. Thus, "boomerang" compliments become minuscule compensations for powerlessness. "Folklorization" also works against "domestication," that is, portrayals of people in their routine, daily lives. Thus, scores of Brazilian films show black people participating in *candomblé* and carnival and *quilombos,* yet few films show the everyday struggles of ordinary black Brazilians. Although many films depict racism under slavery, few depict contemporary racism. If some cinemas are guilty of a flight *from* history, Brazilian cinema has occasionally been guilty of a flight *into* history, opting for gloriously remote triumphs while shying away from contemporary struggles.

As Ella Shohat and I have argued elsewhere, the positive/negative image approach entails more general methodological and theoretical problems, which could be summed up as *essentialism* (a complex diversity of portrayals is reduced to a limited set of reified stereotypes), *verism* (characters are discussed as if they were real), *ahistoricism* (a static analysis ignores mutations, metamorphoses, altered contexts, changes of valence), *moralism* (social and political issues are treated as if they were matters of individual ethics), and *individualism* (the individual character, rather than larger social categories, is the point of reference).[7] As a portrait of a gay black mafioso transvestite, *Rainha Diaba* (Devil Queen, 1975), for example, completely scrambles any notion of "positive" and "negative" image. Is it positive that a talented black actor gets to play title roles? Milton Gonçalves's acting is an artistic tour de force, and that is important for other black performers. Moreover, his character is portrayed as a powerful leader, in a country where blacks are treated affectionately even as they are shorn of power. *Rainha Diaba* poses the question of power indirectly by positing a black leader of indisputable energy and charisma, playing provocatively with a whole series of spectatorial stereotypes. With a drag queen black mafioso as hero, one can hardly accuse the film of being either merely positive or of being merely stereotypical. Although the *Rainha Diaba* character was based on a real-life historical prototype, a literal-minded sociological approach would point out the demographic improbability of such a character; only a tiny percentage of black Brazilians are actually transvestite mafiosos (photo 123). But in fact the film's truth transcends demographics. Anyone who thinks that blacks cannot be homosexual, or that homosexuals cannot be macho, or that blacks cannot be mafia godfathers, is being prodded to think again. By mixing gayness with tongue-in-cheek machismo, the film suggests that the macho world might have unconfessed and subterranean feminine and homoerotic tendencies (expressed, for example, in the "homosociality" of the biracial male buddy films). In this sense, the film elaborates an insight into the repressed gay underside of exaggeratedly masculine behavior.

A comprehensive methodology must also pay attention to the mediations that intervene between social "reality" and its artistic representation as much as to fidelity of representation to a posited "real" model or prototype. We must also beware of "genre mistakes," that is, the mistaken extrapolation of criteria appropriate to one genre to another genre. A search for positive images in the coded carnival of *Macunaíma* (1969), for example, would be fundamentally misguided because that film belongs to a carnivalesque genre favoring what Bakhtin calls "grotesque realism." Cultural difference also plays a role. Indeed, the pedagogical experience of presenting *Macunaíma* in both Brazilian and North American contexts provides an object lesson in the differ-

123. Milton Gonçalves in *Rainha Diaba* (1975)

ential nature of spectatorship. Whereas some American viewers find the film racist, in Brazil a number of factors militate against such a reading: (1) Brazilians of all races see the character Macunaíma as parodically representing themselves and their national personality rather than some racial "other"; they tend to see both the black and white Macunaímas as a national rather than a specifically black archetype. Brazilians regard Macunaíma as a figure for the chameleonic national personality, reflecting a mixture of affection and, perhaps, a colonized self-depreciation. (2) Brazil has a long tradition of self-mocking humor, and jokes by an ethnic insider are always experienced differently from those of an outsider. (3) Most Brazilians, even without having read the novel, are aware of its status as a national classic by a Brazilian of mixed race; the novel had never been accused of being racist. (4) The complexity of the Brazilian racial situation makes Brazilians less likely to racially allegorize their own films. Since the whole issue of racial portrayal is somewhat less "touchy" in Brazil—an ambiguous fact in itself—the films carry less of a synecdochic burden. (5) In Brazil, the consciousness of Grande Otelo as a veritable national institution, a multitalented presence in the media since the

1930s, precludes a racially binary reading by Brazilian spectators, who see his role in *Macunaíma* as just one more role in a variegated career, not as emblematic of the black race. (6) Brazilians, at least at the time of the film's release in 1969, were likely to be more sympathetic to the film's subversive qualities in a repressive era. (7) The misunderstanding also derives from an inherent difference between filmic and literary representation, between verbal suggestiveness and iconic specificity. In the novel, Macunaíma is transformed into a *príncipe lindo* (a beautiful prince); there is no racial specification. The film, in contrast, is constrained to choose actors for roles, and actors come equipped with racial characteristics. Thus, the fablelike evocativeness of "comely prince" gives way to the physical presence of the white actor Paulo José, chosen for his Thespian talents and not for his whiteness, but leading to racial misreadings. At the most, the director might be accused not of racism, but rather of insensitivity; first, for appearing to posit a link between blackness and ugliness (a link with very painful historical and intertextual resonances for people of color), and second, for failing to imagine the ways that his film might be read in non-Brazilian contexts. At the same time, the metaphor of the Brazilian "family," common to both novel and film, should not be seen as entirely innocent, because the national ideology of the mixed family glosses over the fact that the metaphor has historically relegated black Brazilians to the status of "poor cousins" or "adopted children." But such a critique should begin only *after* the film has been understood within Brazilian cultural norms, and not as the application of an a priori schema rooted in the discourses of another national culture.

That films on some level reflect ambient social life and ideologies should not lead us to a naive mimeticism. For example, Brazilian films, taken as a whole, do not reflect the majority status of its black, mulatto, and mestiço citizens. Although the majority population of Rio de Janeiro, the chief center of film production in the silent era, was black and mestiço, this demographic fact is not reflected in the films of the period; Afro Brazilians thus constituted a "structuring absence." On another level, this very absence really "reflected," if not the demographic reality, at least the real power situation in Brazil. As Abdias do Nascimento puts it in relation to Brazilian theater: "the white monopoly on the Brazilian stage reflects the white monopoly on land, on the means of production, on political and economic power, on cultural institutions."[8] In demographic terms, *Dona Flor e Seus Dois Maridos* (Dona Flor and

Her Two Husbands, 1976) portrays a Bahia considerably less black than the real one; Disney's *The Three Caballeros* (1945) portrays a Bahia without any blacks at all. Antunes Filho's *Compassso de Espera,* to take a different example, reflects on racial repression in Brazil, yet the film's protagonist, a black poet and advertising agent closely allied with the São Paulo elite, is, sociologically, a highly atypical figure. But the idea is not to demand point-for-point demographic adequation, only to be aware of the social stratifications informing representation.

The cinema forms part of a larger spectrum of media representations. Blacks are vastly underrepresented in the Brazilian mass media.[9] As the film *Mulheres Negras* (Black Women of Brazil, 1986) points out, TV commercials, news programs, and advertisements are more evocative of Europe than of a mestiço country. Whereas African Americans, a demographic minority, are highly visible in U.S. media, Afro Brazilians, a demographic majority, are virtually invisible in Brazil. There is no equivalent in Brazil to the Black Entertainment Network, no Cosby or Oprah. A 1988 analysis of images of blacks in advertising found that out of 203 ads from TV and weekly newsmagazines, blacks appeared in only 9.[10] The blond TV star Xuxa, with her fair skin, blond hair, and blue eyes, seems to incarnate a certain ego ideal for the country.[11] Even in Salvador, the most Africanized city in Brazil, the news anchors tend to be light skinned. Most prime-time TV soap operas and miniseries, similarly, have focalized white protagonists while relegating black characters to the margins, although recently some miniseries—*Zumbi, Sinhá Moça, Xica da Silva*—have foregrounded African Brazilian themes, often in costume dramas set in the times of slavery.

The most striking absence within Brazilian cinema is that of the black woman. The *chanchadas* feature Afro Brazilian male performers, but very few black women. The romantic involvements of black men in Brazilian films (e.g., Jorge in *Compasso de Espera*) tend to be with white women, a portrayal consistent with a tendency in real life for upwardly mobile blacks to link up with lighter-skinned partners. Cinema Novo features a number of black women's roles (Cota in *Barravento,* the mistress in *A Grande Feira* [Big Market, 1962]), but they are rarely the political or social equal of the male characters. Adaptations of novels often cast white actresses for what in the source novels were mulatta roles: Bete Faria as Rita Bahiana in *O Cortiço* (The Tenement, 1974) Sônia Braga as Gabriela in *Gabriela.* Only a few rare films feature prestigious white men in love with black women, notably Carlos Diegues's *Xica da Silva* (1976) and Orlando Senna's *Diamante Bruto* (Rough Diamond, 1977), a film about a TV star who returns to his native Minas to find his long-lost love. Even the films by (male) Afro Brazilian directors tend to neglect the black woman. The black poet Saul, in Waldyr Onofre's *As Aventuras Amorosas de um Padeiro* (Amorous Adventures of a Baker, 1975) falls in love with white Rita, not with a black woman (see photo 124). The posited alliance between black men and white women ends up leaving black women without male allies, while ignoring solidarity among black women themselves. Documentaries such as *Mulheres Negras*, not surprisingly, try to take up the "slack" in representation. The other major striking absence is of black gays and lesbians, one of the few exceptions being the transvestite mafioso protagonist of *Rainha Diaba*. Black gays appear briefly in a number of films (e.g., *Toda Nudez Sera Punida* [All Nudity Will Be Punished, 1978]) but usually in caricatural or ephemeral roles. Moreover, gay characters "die off" with suspect rapidity and regularity. Here, too, the documentary and fiction shorts by such directors as Eunice Guttman and Karim Ainouz take up the representational slack.

124. Rita and Saul in *As Aventuras Amorosas de um Padeiro* (1975)

A privileging of social portrayal, plot, and character often leads to a slighting of the specifically cinematic mediations of the films: narrative structure, genre conventions, cinematic style. Eurocentric discourse in film may be relayed not by characters or plot but by lighting, framing, mise-en-scène, music. Some basic issues of mediation have to do with the *rapports de force,* the balance of power as it were, between foreground and background. In the visual arts, space has traditionally been deployed to express the dynamics of authority and prestige. The cinema translates such correlations of social power into registers of foreground and background, on-screen and off-screen, silence and speech. To speak of the "image" of a social group, we have to ask precise questions about images and sounds: How much space do the diverse characters occupy in the shot? Which of the characters are active and dynamic, which are merely decorative props? Do the eyeline matches identify us with one gaze rather than another? Whose looks are reciprocated, whose ignored? How do body language, posture, and facial expression communicate attitudes rooted in social hierarchies, attitudes of arrogance, servility, resentment, pride? Whose music dictates the emotional response? What homologies inform artistic and ethnic-political representation?

Many Brazilian films, in this sense, can be seen as staging the ambiguous protocols of "racial democracy." In the *chanchadas* white performers are foregrounded, along with an occasional black major or minor actor (Grande Otelo, Colé, Blecaute), with other people of color relegated to the barely observable background. Although African-inflected music and performance are a key presence in the *chanchadas,* that presence goes largely unacknowledged. They convey an epidermic simulacrum of "racial democracy" but ultimately "fix" blacks in a subaltern place. Moacyr Fenelon's musical *Tudo Azul* (Everything is Fine, 1951) illustrates this process quite clearly. The film is focalized around the dreams and frustrations of "white" characters, especially a songwriter romantically torn between his wife and a popular radio singer (Marlene). In a nightclub sequence, the two women encounter the singer Blecaute, already familiar to us from *Carnaval Atlântida* (1952), who is placed, barman-like, behind a counter. At the songwriter's request, he sings a popular carnival song, "Maria Candelária" (also the title of a famous Mexican film), while the white clubgoers dance enthusiastically. The white singer Marlene, meanwhile, sings another 1950s hit ("Lata d'água na Cabeça" [Carrying a Bucket of Water on Her Head]), which speaks of poor *faveladas* who lack running water. As José Gatti points out, the staging of the sequence "realizes" the racial conventions of the period. Blecaute socializes with the whites but also serves them. Marlene is shown in close-up in her middle-class apartment, while illustrative shots of black women in the favelas accompany her singing. The white woman singer "speaks for" the black women, much as the white male filmmaker speaks for and places blacks in general. The representation is of blacks and whites living in apparent harmony, but with the subaltern status (barman, entertainer, *favelado*) of the blacks taken for granted."

In the classical musicals, then, Afro Brazilians constituted not only a suppressed historical voice but also a literally suppressed ethnic voice, authorizing a Euro Brazilian signature on what were basically African American cultural products. In a power-inflected form of ambivalence, the same dominant society that "loves" ornamental snippets of black culture excludes the black performers who might best incarnate it. Like Hollywood musicals, many Brazilian musicals thematize the struggle between "high" culture (opera, legitimate theater, ballet) and "low" culture (vaudeville, popular music), a struggle that is *also* racial. A sequence from *De Pernas Prò Ar* (Upside Down, 1957) makes this racialized hierarchy explicit. The sequence begins with blacks in African costume dancing Afro-style to a polyrhythmic *batucada* and then segues to big band music and "sophisticated" dance, in which tuxedoed whites literally expel the black performers. In this choreographed version of social Darwinism, black artists seem to shrink in fright at the vision of a seemingly more powerful form of music.

In terms of the cinema, blacks and indigenous people have had only a minimal role in scripting, directing, and producing Brazilian films. There is no equivalent in Brazil to 1930s black independent directors like Oscar Micheaux and Spencer Williams, or to Native American directors like Bob Hicks. Although the 1970s witnessed the emergence of a handful of black directors (Haroldo Costa, Antônio Pitanga, Waldyr Onofre, Odilon Lopes, Zózimo Bulbul), few of them have managed to make second features. Their films, furthermore, have not enjoyed the degree of success generated by the films of African American directors such as Spike Lee, Charles Burnett, Mario van Peebles, Julie Dash, Robert Townsend, Bill Duke, and the Hughes Brothers in the United States, although this lack of success doubtless has more to do with the general crisis of the Brazilian film industry than with any special hostility toward black directors.[13] Nor do the films by black directors necessarily spotlight racial issues. Questions therefore arise: In what way do these black directors foreground, or elide, black experience and concerns? How does their self-representation differ from the representations proffered by their white colleagues? The answer is that their representations, while slightly more sympathetic to blacks, do not differ greatly from the films of sympathetic white directors such as Nelson Pereira dos Santos. And then the question becomes: are black Brazilian directors less angry or race-conscious than Afro American directors? Or is their anger simply repressed from within or rendered taboo from without?

In both the United States and Brazil, the situation within the film industry mirrors that of the country as a whole. Blacks are visible, especially as performers, but they are seldom in control of their own image. The major area in which blacks have worked is not as directors but as actors. We have discussed the work of Sebastião Prata ("Grande Otelo"), Antônio Pitanga, Milton Gonçalves, Zózimo Bulbul, Eliezer Gomes, and Zezé Motta. We have not mentioned Jorge Coutinho, Marcílio Faria, Aurea Campos, Francisca Lopes, Samuel dos Santos, and many others. While Grande Otelo became "king of the chanchadas" in the 1940s and 1950s, Ruth de Souza played the maid in the films of Vera Cruz. Black performers like Antônio Pitanga (*Barravento, Ganga Zumba,* and *A Grande Cidade* [The Big City, 1965]), Marcos Vinícius (*Xica da Silva, J.S. Brown: O Último Heroi* [J.S. Brown: The Last Hero, 1979]), Milton Gonçalves (*Macunaíma, Eles Não Usam Black Tie* [They Don't Wear Black Tie, 1981]), Zózimo Bulbul (*Terra em Transe* [Land in Anguish, 1967], *Compasso de Espera*), and Zezé Motta (*Xica da Silva, A Força do Xangô* [The Power of Xangô, 1979]) meanwhile developed distinguished careers within Cinema Novo. Performance, too, it is important to remember, has subversive potential. At times a black actor can undermine the intentions of a white-dominated film. In a Hollywood context, Donald Bogle focuses on the ways African American performers have "signified" and subverted the roles forced on them, battling against confining types and categories, a battle homologous to the quotidian struggle of three-dimensional blacks against the imprisoning conventions of an apartheid-style system. At their best, black performances undercut stereotypes by individualizing the type or slyly standing above it, playing against script and studio intentions, turning demeaning roles into resistant performance.[14] Grande Otelo, in this same spirit, claimed in interviews

125. Costinha (Crusoé) and Otelo (Friday) in *As Aventuras de Robinson Crusoé*

that he always tried to put "a little resistance" even into demeaning roles. In *As Aventuras de Robinson Crusoé*, the 1978 Brazilian version of *The Adventures of Robinson Crusoe*, where Grande Otelo plays "Friday," for example, Otelo subverts Daniel Defoe's colonialist classic by playing a Friday who refuses to accept the colonizer's power to name: "*Me* Crusoé," Otelo repeatedly tells the Englishman, "*you* Friday!" (photo 125).

The choice of actors is central to the issue of racial self-representation. Third World and minoritarian peoples in Hollywood have with great regularity been represented not by themselves but rather by white actors in blackface (Jeanne Crain in *Pinky* [1949]), in redface (Jeff Chandler in *Broken Arrow* [1950]), in yellowface (Paul Muni in *The Good Earth* [1937]), and brownface (Charlton Heston in *Touch of Evil* [1948]). The choice of white actors to play people of color thus inevitably raises the question of racial discrimination. In the United States, furthermore, black actors and actresses have tended to be invited to perform only those roles previously designated as "black," under the tacit assumption that roles such as astronaut, doctor, lawyer are not to be played by blacks unless so designated; the implicit norm is whiteness. The Brazilian situation is both similar and distinct in this respect. As we saw in the case of *Gimba*, there have been occasional complaints about the bypassing of black actors for certain roles. When Brazilian playwright Nelson Rodrigues, in the 1940s, presented *O Anjo Negro,* a play with a black protagonist, he was shocked to be told by the Municipal Theater that he would have to cast a white in blackface. Zezé Motta, similarly, recalls the intense pressure put on Carlos Diegues to cast a light-skinned mulatta for *Xica da Silva.*[15] But usually, for good or for ill, Brazilian casting seems less race-conscious than in North America. Black actors are not usually thought of as somehow incarnating the black race; nor are they read by the audience in such a light. The black actor Marcos Vinícius in *J.S. Brown: O Último Heroi* plays a Brazilian who adores American detective films and therefore changes his name João da Silva to J. S. Brown (photo 126). Victim of an imported aesthetic, he wears detective-style trench coats even in the tropics. But the actor's blackness is irrelevant to the film's allegory of alienation; the protagonist could have been portrayed by a white actor without significantly altering the film. In this sense, certain "negative" roles played by Afro Brazilians in Brazilian cinema can paradoxically be a positive sign; the very lack of self-consciousness about whether an image is positive or negative signifies the assumption that the choice of actors is not always "allegorical," that actors do not always encapsulate their race.

A purely epidermic, chromatic "physiognomist" approach simply does not work in the case of Brazilian cinema, and not only because of the practical problem of defining who is "black." In Brazil, the corporeal and the cultural are often delinked, a process that began already with the deculturation and Europeanization of the Indians. But the reverse process, that is, the Africanization of the Europeans, has also taken place. Thus some Brazilians with European features can be deeply involved in African or indigenous culture, and, conversely, people with African or indigenous features can feel little affinity for indigenous or Afro Brazilian culture. An ethnocentric vision based on American cultural patterns often leads to the "racializing" of filmic situations Brazilians would not see as racially connoted. The differing racial spectrum at times leads to cultural misunderstandings. For Brazilian audiences, certain American films that treat racial discrimination, for example, *A Soldier's Story* (1984), are confusing because in those films some of the characters portrayed as victimized by racial discrimination are played by actors that for Brazilians are not "black." The converse also applies; American and European viewers can misperceive the racial implications of Brazilian films because of a confu-

126. Marcus Vinícius in *J.S. Brown: O Último Heroi (1979)*

sion over who is black, a proof if ever one was needed that race is a historically constructed category.

Glauber Rocha's *Deus e Diabo na Terra do Sol* (literally God and the Devil in the Land of the Sun; released as Black God, White Devil; 1964), provides a particularly telling example of these processes. The millennial cult leader Sebastião in the film is played by the black actor Lídio Silva (see photo 127), even though the historical prototypes for the role (a series of millenarian leaders) were not black. Although the film never calls attention to racial issues, the English translation of the film's title—*Black God, White Devil*—"racializes" and Manicheanizes the Portuguese original, thus encouraging a reading of the black character Sebastião as an emblem of the black race as a whole. At the same time, perception of the racial dimension of a film like *Deus e Diabo na Terra do Sol* can change. Although in Brazil the issue of race had been regarded as irrelevant during more than 15 years following the film's release, the black character suddenly became the object of a polemic during a 1981 seminar on "Cinema and Decolonization" sponsored by SECNEB (Bahian Society for the Study of Black Culture). SECNEB member Marco Aurélio Luz objected that the black character's ritual murder of a child shaped a negative image of blacks, characterizing him as primitive and dangerous. José Carlos Avelar, meanwhile, found this racializing "absurd," arguing that the image of Se-

127. Sebastião (Lídio Silva) in *Deus e o Diabo na Terra do Sol* (1964)

bastião is not of a black man per se, but part of an allegorical portrayal of the country as a whole. For Ismail Xavier, similarly, Sebastião "does not represent black culture . . . his acts must be analysed as constructed by the film, and not in terms of the cultural and ethnic origins of the actor."[16] A multidimensional analysis of Sebastião's role, then, would have to take into account not only the ethnic traits of actor and role but also the narrative structure of the film, the historical prototypes for the character, and the possibilities of reading or misreading on the part of the spectator. Although the actor is undeniably black, and while the role is undeniably negative in certain respects, it is also worth noting that the religious practices are in no sense African; rather, they reference a millennialist tradition with Catholic/Iberian antecedents, the product of social oppression in the *sertão*. Neither the film nor the characters in the film, furthermore, call attention to Sebastião's blackness. The fact that most of his followers are dark-skinned mestiços also serves to play down Sebastião's racial difference.

The Lessons of Anthropophagy

I have tried here to take a comparative, diasporic, polycentric approach to Brazilian cinema, placing filmic representations in the broader context of the multiracial societies of the Americas. Within this approach, I have endeavored to see issues of racial representation within a complex and multivalent relationality, registering the structural analogies underlying dominant representations of marginalized groups, along with the interplay of social and sexual displacements, projections, allegories, and dialogisms among the diverse communities. The comparative approach, I would argue, works both broadly and in relation to specific films. A film such as *Macunaíma,* for example, can be seen as part of a broader Pan-American genre—the racial transformation film—which is ultimately a product of a hemispheric "magic realism" that thrives on real-life cultural disjunctions coexisting in the same time and space. In this sense it is comparable to Woody Allen's *Zelig* (1983), another film in which a character duplicates himself in miraculous feats of ethnic doubling. Born white and Jewish, Woody Allen's chameleon-man protagonist subsequently becomes Native American, African American, Irish, Italian, Mexican, and Chinese, just as Macunaíma is born black and Indian, yet becomes white and Portuguese. Like Macunaíma, Zelig too might be called a "hero without any character," both in a characterological and in an ethnic sense. Both Macunaíma and Zelig personify the cultural "heteroglossia" or "many-languagedness" of the cultures from which they emerge. They resemble their cities (New York and São Paulo), which are, like the characters themselves, the sites of constant metamorphosis, disintegration, assimilation, and renewal. Both cities received parallel waves of immigrants, often from the same countries (Germans, Italians, Jews from Eastern Europe, Arabs from the Middle East, Chinese, Japanese, and so forth), just as both received as well "internal immigrants," such as blacks from the South, in the case of New York, and blacks from Bahia and Minas, in the case of São Paulo. Both cities have their Italian neighborhoods (Little Italy in New York, Bras and Bexiga in São Paulo), their turn-of-the-century Jewish communities (the Lower East Side; Bom Retiro), and their Asiatic communities (Chinatown; Liberdade). As chameleon men who literally *become* their ethnic neighbors, Zelig and Macunaíma each illustrate the opportunistic appropriations typical of a mobile, heteroglot culture. Both characters exemplify the process by which diverse ethnicities meet, clash, and interact; their metamorphoses simply render palpable the constant process of synchresis that occurs when ethnicities brush against and rub off on one another in a context of cultural "many-languagedness."[17]

But the "racial transformation" theme goes beyond *Zelig* and *Macunaíma*. American films such as *Black Like Me* (1964), *Watermelon Man* (1970), *Soul Man* (1986), *True Identity* (1987), and *Made in America* (1993) all play on the same trope of ethnic metamorphosis. Sandra Bernhard, in the opening sequence of *Without You I'm Nothing* (1989), sings "My skin is black" and is lit and dressed so as to appear black. As Masha in Scorsese's *The King of Comedy* (1983), the same actress speaks of wishing she were black, much as Woody Allen, in *Annie Hall* (1977), suggests that smoking grass makes white college students think they've become Billie Holliday. In Brazil, innumerable films have white Brazilians (e.g., Ney Santana in *O Amuleto de Ogum* [Amulet of Ogum, 1974], the *capoeira* player in *Cordão de Ouro* [Gold Belt, 1977]) become "possessed" by African culture. But the trope is hardly limited to film. In Brazil, (white) singer Joyce sings, "sou mulata" (I'm a mulatta), while Caetano Veloso, in *Araçá Azul,* says punningly: "sou mulato nato / no sentido lato / mulato democrático do litoral" (I am mulatto born / mulatto in the broad sense / the democratic mulatto from the coast). In the United States, Lou Reed sings "I Wanna Be Black" on the album *Street Hassle* (1979), just as the all-white rap group Young Black Teenagers speaks of being "Proud to be Black," arguing that "Blackness is a state of mind." Indeed, "cultural mulattoes," such as Prince, Madonna, Michael Boulton, Michael Jackson, and Maria Carey, are at the cutting edge of American pop culture.

Brazilian popular culture draws on the contradictory processes of the diverse and coimplicated communities that make up Brazil. At times the cultural juxtapositions and counterpoints within Brazilian cinema are surprising, even disconcerting. Arthur Omar's *Triste Trópico* (1977) superimposes recordings of Hitler's speeches on slowed-down images of blacks celebrating carnival, in a counterpoint that disturbs precisely because the relation between sound and image is not clearly interpretable as one either of total opposition or of total alliance (photo 128). A similar counterpointing of blackness and Nazi discourse occurs in Sílvio Back's *Aleluia Gretchen* (1976), a film about the Nazi-sympathizing German community in the South of Brazil during the 1930s. In one sequence, the black servant character Repo dresses up as Santa

128. Arthur Omar's *Triste Trópico* (1977)

Claus while regarding himself in the mirror. He tries on a white wig, reminiscent of the aristocratic wigs from the samba pageants and performs samba steps around the room. He passes talcum powder over his face until he becomes completely white, thus literalizing the "ideology of whitening." He repeats German words ("Ja, Jawohl, Fertig, Bitte, Danke"), all of which have to do with etiquette and submission. His performance of colonial mimicry pays homage to the "Aryanization" favored by right-wing Germans in Brazil. He becomes, as Flora Sussekind puts it, "the obedient caricature of an alien identity and culture."[18] But as he observes the Kranz family at the dinner table, tears run down his cheeks, disfiguring his makeup and bearing witness to the psychic trauma evoked by Fanon's title *Black Skin, White Masks*. The cultural counterpoint of the final picnic sequence, in contrast, introduces a note of hope, when German music is interrupted by a carnival *batucada* led by Repo; after initial reluctance, the picnickers begin to dance. Afro Brazilian culture, it is implied, will eventually triumph over racist ideology.

Another way that Brazilian culture is figured as a mixed site is through the metaphor of garbage. For the late 1960s Udigrudi (Underground) filmmakers, the garbage metaphor captured the sense "of marginality, of being condemned to survive within scarcity, of being the dumping ground for transnational capitalism, of being obliged to recycle the materials of the dominant culture."[19] In an Afro-diasporic context, the "garbage aesthetic" evokes the ways that blacks in the New World, largely deprived of social and economic power, have managed to transmogrify waste products into art, teasing beauty out of the very guts of deprivation, whether through the musical use of throwaway metal (the steel drums of Trinidad), the culinary use of throwaway parts of animals (soul food, *feijoada*), or the use in weaving of throwaway fabrics (quilting). All these bricolage aesthetics have in common a notion of discontinuity—a quilt is made of scraps exemplifying diverse styles and materials—whence their link with artistic Modernism as an art of discontinuity and with postmodernism as an art of recycled trash and pastiche. At the same time, garbage can be seen as a polysemic signifier that can be read literally (garbage as a source of food for poor people; garbage as the site of ecological disaster; garbage as the diasporized, heterotopic space of the promiscuous mingling of the rich and the poor, the industrial and the artisanal, the national and the international, the local and the global). Or garbage can be read metaphorically as a figure for social indictment—poor people treated like garbage, garbage as the "dumping" of pharmaceutical products or of "canned" TV programs. Alternately, garbage can be an allegorical text to be deciphered, a form of social colonics where the truth of a society can be "read" in its waste products.

Two recent documentaries literalize the theme of garbage. Eduardo Coutinho's documentary *Boca de Lixo* (literally "mouth of garbage, but translated as "The Scavengers," 1992) directly links it to the "aesthetics of garbage," since the phrase "mouth of garbage" refers to the Sao Paulo red-light district where the Udigrudi films were produced. The film centers on impoverished Brazilians who survive thanks to a garbage dump outside of Rio (photo 129), against the backdrop of the outstretched arms of the Christ of Corcovado. Here the camera is witness to social misery. Ferreting through the garbage, the participants perform a triage of whatever is thrown up by the daily lottery of ordure, sorting out plastic from metal from food for animals. Since many of the faces are female and dark-skinned, the film reveals the feminization of poverty and the racialization of misery. Here we see the end point of an all-permeating logic of commodification, logical telos of the consumer society and its ethos of planned obsolescence. In this squalid phantasmagoria, the same commodities that had been fetishized by advertising are now shorn of

129. Eduardo Coutinho's *Boca de Lixo* (1992)

their aura of charismatic power. We are confronted with the seamy underside of globalization as the film gives the lie to facile versions of one world under a consumerist groove. The world of transnational capitalism and the "posts," we see, is more than ever a world of constant, daily immiseration. Here we see the hidden face of the global system, that which is masked by the innocuous pronouncements of the IMF and the euphoric nostrums of "globalization."

Rather than take a miserabilist approach, Coutinho shows us people who are inventive, ironic, and critical, who tell the director what to look at and how to interpret what he sees. The garbage dwellers repeatedly insist that "Here nobody steals," as if responding to the accusations of imaginary middle-class interlocutors. Instead of the suspect pleasures of a condescending "sympathy," the middle-class spectator is obliged to confront vibrant people who dare to dream and to talk back and even criticize the filmmakers. Not outcasts or pathetic people, the film's subjects exist on a continuum with Brazilian workers in general. They encapsulate the country as a whole: they have held other jobs; they have worked in other cities; they have labored in the homes of the elite. They have "lines out" to the center; they disprove what Janice Perlman calls the "myth of marginality." A homespun philosopher in the film tells the filmmakers that garbage is a beginning and an end in a cyclical principle of birth and rebirth—what goes around comes around. Garbage is shown as stored energy, containing in itself the seeds of its own transformation. Garbage becomes a form of social karma, the deferred rendezvous between those who can afford to waste and those who cannot afford not to save what has been wasted. Those who live off garbage also decorate their homes with it. While the elite wastes food almost as a matter of principle, the poor are obliged to lick their own plates, and those of others, clean. Here we have garbage as social precipitate, a residue of social inequities.

Jorge Furtado's *Ilha das Flores* (Isle of Flowers, 1989), meanwhile, brings the "garbage aesthetic" into the postmodern era, while also demonstrating the cinema's capacity as a vehicle for political and aesthetic reflection. Described by its author as a "letter to a Martian who knows nothing of the earth and its social systems," Furtado's short uses Monty Python–style animation, archival footage, and parodic-reflexive documentary techniques to indict the distribution of wealth and food around the world. The "isle of flowers" of the title is a Brazilian garbage dump where famished women and children, in groups of 10, are given five minutes to scrounge for food. But before we get to the garbage dump, we are given the itinerary of a tomato from farm to supermarket to bourgeois kitchen to garbage can to the "Isle of Flowers." Furtado's edited collage is structured as a social lexicon or glossary, or better surrealist enumeration of key words such as "pigs," "money," and "human beings." Human beings, for example, are defined as "biped animals with highly developed telencephalon and opposable thumbs." And the definitions are interconnected and multichronotopic; they lead out into multiple historical frames and historical situations. In order to follow the trajectory of the tomato, we need to know the origin of money: "Money was created in the seventh century before Christ. Christ was a Jew, and Jews are human beings." We then move swiftly to the photographic residue of the Holocaust, where Jews, garbagelike, are thrown into death camp piles. (The Nazis, we are reminded, were also fond of recycling.) Throughout, the film moves back and forth between minimalist definitions of the human—those bipeds with telencephalon and opposable thumbs—to the lofty ideal of freedom evoked by the film's final citation from Cecília Meireles's *Romanceiro da Inconfidência:* "Freedom is a word the human dream feeds on, that no one can explain or fail to understand."

But this summary gives little sense of the experience of the film, of its play with documentary form and expectations. First, the films visuals—old TV commercials, newspaper advertisements, health care manuals—themselves constitute a kind of throwaway, visual garbage. (In the silent period of cinema, we are reminded, films were seen as transient entertainments rather than artistic durables and therefore as not worth saving; they were even recycled for their lead content during World War I.) Second, the film, whose preamble states that "this is not a fiction film," mocks the positivist mania for factual detail by offering useless, gratuitous precision: "We are in Belem Novo, city of Porto Alegre, state of Rio Grande do Sul. More precisely, at thirty degrees, twelve minutes and thirty seconds latitude south, and fifty one degrees eleven minutes and twenty three seconds longitude west." The film also parodies the conventions of the educational film, with its authoritative voice-over and quizlike questions ("What is a history quiz?"). The overture music is a synthesized version of the theme song of "Voice of Brazil," the widely detested official radio program that has been annoying Brazilians since the days of Vargas. Humor becomes a kind of trap; the spectator who begins by laughing ends up, if not crying, at least reflecting very seriously. Opposable thumbs and highly developed telencephalon, we are told, have given "human beings the possibility of making many improvements in their planet"; a shot of a nuclear explosion serves as illustration. Furtado invokes the old carnival motif of pigs and sausage, but with a political twist; here the pigs, given inequitable distribution down the food chain, eat better than people. In this culinary recycling, we are given a social examination of garbage; the truth of a society is in its detritus. The socially peripheral points to the symbolically central. Rather than having the margins invade the center as in carnival, here the center creates the margins, or better, there are no margins; the tomato links the urban bourgeois family to the rural poor via the sausage and the tomato within a web of global relationality.

The trope of garbage is also symptomatic of the postmodern and postcolonial moment. If Third Worldist discourse drew sharp lines between Europe and non-Europe, First World and Third World, oppressor and oppressed, contemporary discourse is less binary. With post–Third Worldism, such binaristic dualisms give way to a more nuanced spectrum of subtle differentiations, in a new set of global regimes where First World and Third World are mutually imbricated. Notions of ontologically referential identity metamorphose into notions of a conjunctural play of identifications. Once rigid boundaries are now presented as more porous; imagery of barbed-wire frontiers have mutated into metaphors of fluidity and crossing. Colonial metaphors of irreconcilable dualism give way to postcolonial tropes drawing on the diverse modalities of mixedness: religious (syncretism); biological (hybridity); human-genetic *(mestiçagem);* and linguistic (creolization). The tropicalist movement of the late 1960s, picking up from the modernists' mix of futurism and primitivism, anticipated the "posts" with its diverse tropes of mixing, its musical minglings of electric guitar and *berimbau,* its creative syntheses of bossa nova, traditional samba, and northeastern music. The composer-singer Gilberto Gil's 1989 song "From Bob Dylan to Bob Marley: A Provocation Samba" evokes these issues of hybrid identity by setting into play a number of broad cultural parallels and contrasts, between Jewish symbiology and Jamaican Rastafarianism, between the Inquisition's anti-Semitism and the European suppression of African religions ("When the Africans arrived on these shores / there was no freedom of religion"), ultimately contrasting the progressive syncretism of a Bob Marley (who died "because besides being Black was Jewish") from the alienation of a Michael Jackson, who "besides turning white . . . is becoming sad." Gil celebrates syncretism and hybridity, but articulates them in relation to the asymmetrical power relations engendered by colonialism. For oppressed people, artistic syncretism is not a game but a sublimated form of historical pain, an exercise, as Gil puts it, both of "resistance" and "surrender."

As descriptive catchall terms, "hybridity" and "syncretism" fail to discriminate between the diverse modalities and "compromise formations" of hybridity: colonial imposition, obligatory assimilation, political co-optation, cultural mimicry, and so forth. Elites have always made co-optive top-down raids on subaltern cultures, while the dominated have always parodied and "signified" as well as emulated elite practice. Hybridity, in other words, is power-laden and asymmetrical. It is also co-optable. In Brazil, as in many countries in Latin America, national identity has often been *officially* articulated as hybrid and syncretic, through hypocritically integrationist ideologies that have glossed over subtle racial hegemonies.

Latin America has been fecund in tropes of aesthetic innovation: Gabriel García Márquez's "magic realism," Alejo Carpentier's "lo real maravilloso americano," Rocha's "aesthetic of hunger," the Underground's "aesthetics of garbage," Paul Leduc's "salamander" (as opposed to dinosaur) aesthetic, Guilhermo del Toro's "termite terrorism," Julio García Espinosa's *cine imperfecto,* Arturo Lindsay's "santería aesthetics," and Caetano and Gil's "tropicália." Many of these alternative aesthetics have in common the twin anthropophagic notions of revalorizing what had been seen as negative—even "magic realism" inverts the traditional condemnation of magic as irrational superstition—and of turning strategic weakness into tactical strength, teasing an aggressive beauty out of the very guts of misery. The Brazilian "anthropophagic" movement, as we saw earlier, called for an art that would devour European techniques in order to better struggle against European domination. And if we substitute "dominant" and "alternative," or "mass" and "popular," for "Europe" and "Brazilian," we begin to glimpse the contemporary relevance of their critique. By appropriating an existing discourse for its own ends, anthropophagy *assumes* the force of the dominant discourse only to deploy that force, through a kind of artistic jujitsu, *against* domination, stealing elements of the dominant culture and redeploying them in the interests of oppositional praxis.

In Brazilian art, syncretism has been an absolutely crucial thematic and aesthetic resource. Historically, Brazilian architects and artisans, many of them black, "tropicalized" the Iberian Baroque church style, for example, by turning grapes into pineapples. The Afro-Muslim architect Manoel Friandes, as Henry Drewal points out, infused the austere Christian exterior of the "Church of Lapinha" in Salvador with an "exuberant Islamic presence" through Moorish arches, decorative tiles, and Arabic script.[20] Brazilian cinema, in the wake of this perennial tradition, also proliferates in the signs and tokens of syncretism, deploying "multi-temporal heterogeneity" (Néstor García Canclini) as a means for achieving a renovated aesthetic. The opening sequence of *Macunaíma,* for example, shows a family whose names are indigenous, whose epidermic traits are African and European and mestiço, whose clothes are Portuguese and African, whose hut is *mameluco,* and whose manner of giving birth is indigenous. The tensions between Catholicism and *candomblé,* in *Pagador de Promessas,* similarly, are evoked through the manipulation of cultural symbols, setting in motion a cultural battle, for example, between *berimbau* and church bell, thus synecdochically encapsulating a larger religious and political struggle. *Tenda dos Milagres* counterposes opera and samba to metaphorize the larger conflict between Bahia's white elite and its subjugated mestiços, between ruling-class science and Afro-inflected popular culture. Thus Brazilian cinema at its best orchestrates not an innocuous pluralism, but rather a strong cultural counterpoint between in some ways incommensurable yet nevertheless thoroughly coimplicated cultures. The final shot of *Terra em Transe* exemplifies this process brilliantly. As the film's protagonist Paulo wields a rifle in a Che Guevara–like gesture of quixotic rebellion, we hear a soundtrack composed of Villa-Lobos, *candomblé* chants, samba, and machine-gun fire. The mix, in this feverish bricolage, is fundamentally unstable; the Villa-Lobos music never really synchronizes with the *candomblé* or the gunfire. We are reminded of Alejo Carpentier's gentle mockery of the innocuous juxtapositions of the European avant-gardists—for example, Lautreamont's "umbrella and a sewing machine on a dissecting table"—which Carpentier contrasts with the explosive counterpoints of indigenous, African, and European cultures thrown up daily by Latin American life and art.

Rather than merely reflect preexisting syncretisms, Brazilian cinema at its best actively syncretizes cultural forces in ways that reflect the subterranean workings of Afro-diasporic energy. Also interesting in aesthetic terms is the link between African religions and "magic realism," a link prefigured in Carpentier's earlier vodun-inspired notion of "lo real maravilloso." In their attempts to forge a liberatory film language, both African and Brazilian artists have drawn on popular religion and ritual magic, elements less "pre-modern" (a term that embeds modernity as telos) than "para-modern." The question of cinematic "magic" illustrates the pitfalls of imposing a linear narrative of cultural "progress" in the manner of "development" theory, which sees people in traditional societies as mired in an inert preliterate past, incapable of change and agency. Within a palimpsestic aesthetic, the artistic reinvoicing of tradition can serve purposes of *collective* agency in the present. In *A Deusa Negra* (The Black Goddess, 1978) and *Macunaíma,* as in many African films such as *Yeelen* (1987), *Jitt* (1992), and *Kasarmu Ce* (This Land is Ours, 1991), magical practices become an aesthetic resource, a means for breaking away from the linear, cause-and-effect conventions of Aristotelian narrative poetics, a way of defying the "gravity," in both senses of that word, of chronological time and literal space. The values of African religious culture inform films like *A Força de Xangô* and *Amuleto de Ogum.* A film such as *A Deusa Negra* synthesizes the modern and the traditional through an Afro-magical *egungun* aesthetic, that is, an aesthetic that invokes the spirits of the ancestors as embodiments of personal and collective history, in a transgenerational approach that mingles past (slavery, the *quilombos*) and the present.[21]

All of the world's cultures have washed up on the shores of Brazil. What triggers optimism even in this crisis-ridden period is Brazil's constitutive multiculturalism, its chameleonic *disponibilité*, its permeability to Africa, Europe, and indigenous America. As a country both "occupying" and "occupied" (Paulo Emílio Salles Gomes's formulation), no culture, ultimately, is completely alien to Brazil, whence its ability to play on a wide spectrum of cultural repertoires. Brazilian art reflects an ability to move between linguistic-cultural worlds, to negotiate multiple identities in a manner reminiscent of the playful dance of identities characteristic of carnival and *candomblé*. Although the country's class structures are ossified and sclerotic, its cultural structures are open and porous. Not all of the arts have "translated" this cultural "availability" in the same way, of course. Brazilian music, perhaps more than the cinema, has managed to produce an aesthetic synthesis at once Brazilian and international, popular and experimental, accessible and complex. Brazilian music has also been more successful, both nationally and internationally, than Brazilian cinema. Unlike Brazilian cinema, Brazilian popular music consistently outsells non-Brazilian music. Not coincidentally, Brazilian music has also been both more Africanized and more confidently cosmopolitan than Brazilian cinema, more capable of positing strong cultural counterpoints. (In the lyrics of Gilberto Gil, Caetano Veloso, Milton Nascimento, Djavan, Gal Costa, Marisa Monte, it is also less masculinist and homophobic.) Brazilian music forms part of an endlessly creative multidirectional flow of musical ideas that moves back and forth around the "Black Atlantic," generating such hybrids as jazz-samba, samba-rap and samba-reggae, and reforenge (a blend of rock, merengue, and forró). Afro-diasporic music displays an anthropophagic capacity to absorb influences, including Western influences, while still being driven by a culturally African bass-note. Pop musician intellectuals like Chico Buarque de Holanda, with his samba allegories; Gilberto Gil, with his musical essays on the politics of syncretism; and Caetano Veloso, in songs like "Something is Out of Order in the New World Order," provide a model of pleasurable, danceable political-artistic praxis.[22] "Popular" in both the box-office sense and the Bakhtinian carnivalesque sense, they constitute a contemporary version of Antonio Gramsci's "organic intellectuals." Brazilian musical groups like Olodum and Ilê Aiyê, meanwhile, not only make their own music videos but also create community schools for practical and anti-Eurocentric education, while constructing "carnival factories" to provide jobs.[23] The work of these groups is registered in Paulo Cesar Soares's *Bahia de Todosos Ritmos* (Bahia of All Rhythms, 1996). Their audio-visual-musical texts demonstrate art's capacity to give pleasurable form to social desire, to open new grooves, to mobilize a sense of possibility, to shake the body-politic, to appeal to deeply rooted but socially frustrated aspirations for new forms of work and festivity and community, crystallizing desire in a popular and mass-mediated form.

Brazilian music, then, has been the least colonized and the most African-ized branch of Brazilian popular culture, as well as the most successful in dis-seminating itself not only within Brazil but also around the world. Brazil's "export quality" music—and here the export is of "cooked" not "raw" prod-ucts—reverses the artistic current; it influences world music, it is constantly plagiarized and borrowed.[24] Can one imagine "fusion" or disco, for example, without the Brazilian stimulus? In music, Brazilian and American artists meet as equals. When Jobim collaborates with Sinatra, or João Gilberto with Stan Getz, or Milton Nascimento with Pat Metheny, or Gilberto Gil with Stevie Wonder, or Hermeto Paschoal with Miles Davis, there is no question of sub-ordination or dependency. Obviously the artistic and commercial success of Brazilian popular music also has to do with other factors: that music does not depend on a vast infrastructure, that musical production is less expensive than cinematic production, and that music has inserted itself in a distinct manner into the global economy. Whereas Hollywood dominates Brazilian film exhi-bition, multinational corporations find it convenient to promote Brazilian music. Nevertheless, some dimensions of this differential success transcend political economy. Brazilian music is not overshadowed by the charismatic charm of the dominant Hollywood aesthetic; in popular music, the dominant aesthetic *is* Afro-diasporic. Brazilian music is thus less intimidated by the hegemonic model. Consequently, while Brazilian cinema has either slavishly imitated Hollywood (the case of Vera Cruz) or violently rejected it (early Cin-ema Novo), it has not in general anthropophagically absorbed its power as a form of "media jujitsu."[25]

Waxing speculative for a moment, we might ask what would be the filmic equivalent to the kinds of "lateral syncretisms" to be found in the mutually enriching collaborations between the diverse modalities of Afro-diasporic music? What would be the counterpart in the cinema of the rich synthesis of touching melody, complex harmony, poetic lyrics, and varied rhythms offered by Brazilian popular music? Where are the cinematic equivalents to musicians like Gilberto Gil and Caetano Veloso (photos 130a and 130b), who not only practice syncretic forms of music but also thematize syncretism within their lyrics?[26] What if Brazilian cinema were to use sound and music more innovatively? (The film was terrible, goes the perennial lament, but the soundtrack was wonderful.) What if Brazilian films went beyond merely "including" music to "becoming" music on the Afro Brazilian model, creating kinetic, percussive, polyrhythmic arrangements of images and sounds? When will Brazilian cinema be as confidently intertextual, as playfully cannibalistic and as pleasurable as Brazilian music? What if the cinema were to develop an improvisational "aesthetic of mistakes," one that absorbed the African tradition of tolerance toward "acoustically illogical and unclear sounds, sounds not sus-

130a/130b. Tropical Anthropophagy: Caetano Veloso

ceptible to total control,"[27] an aesthetic of cybernetic sampling and diasporic bricolage, an anthropophagic aesthetic that devours the best of world cinema but reelaborates it "with autonomy," as Oswald de Andrade had already suggested?

Despite substantial obstacles, Brazilian cinema has accomplished an enormous amount. Innumerable documentaries and many features have given voice to people of color and provided glimpses of Brazilian history from a multicultural perspective. Nonetheless, Brazilian cinema has rarely achieved the proud and open-ended synthesis typical of Brazilian popular music. Indeed, it has yet to become truly and consistently, as opposed to superficially and sporadically, "polyphonic," not only in cinematic terms (the contrapuntal call-and-response play of track against track and genre against genre), but also in cultural terms of the interplay of socially generated voices. The overall trajectory from the "white" cinema of the silent period to the undoubtedly multicolored cinema of today does point, thankfully, to the progressive deployment of more social and cultural voices, even if that process has been less thoroughgoing than one might have hoped. The challenge now is to go beyond the mere inclusion of individual representatives of the diverse groups, to go beyond even a concern with positive and negative images, in order to present diverse community perspectives, to stage, as it were, the polyphonic clashes and harmonies of Brazilian cultural diversity. True cinematic polyphony will emerge, most probably, only with the advent of political equality and cultural reciprocity among the diverse communities. But until the advent of such a utopian moment, cultural and political polyphony can be evoked, at least, through the proleptic procedures of "anticipatory" texts, texts at once militantly imaginative and resonantly multivoiced, with their eyes and ears always open to the long-term possibilities of change.

NOTES

∞

Historical Preamble

1 In the racist view, Brazil is seen as racially mixed and therefore degraded. On a 1868 trip through Brazil, Harvard professor Louis Agassiz spoke of a "degraded people, a mongrel crowd as repulsive as mongrel dogs." Quoted in Fredrick B. Pike, *The United States and Latin America: Myths and Stereotypes of Civilization and Nature* (Austin: University of Texas Press, 1992), p. 144.

2 For the diverse estimates of the native population of Brazil at the time of European conquest, see Manuela Carneiro da Cunha, ed. *História dos Índios no Brasil* (São Paulo: Companhia das Letras, 1992).

3 See Claude Lévi-Strauss, "Saudades do Brasil," *The New York Review of Books,* 42 (December 21, 1995).

4 I borrow the definitions of "multination" and "polyethnic" from Will Kymlicka, *Multicultural Citizenship* (Oxford: Clarendon Press, 1995), p. 6.

5 See Pike, *The United States and Latin America*, p. 162.

6 There exist various theories about the provenance of the word *mamelucos*. Some trace it to *maloca,* the Tupi word for house or dwelling. Others trace it to a word used by the Portuguese in the Middle Ages to refer to mestiços and Moors. Others trace it to Arabic *mamluk,* meaning slave, servant.

7 See Ronaldo Vainfas, *A Heresia dos Índios* (São Paulo: Companhia das Letras, 1995), p. 158.

8 Quoted in Pike, *The United States and Latin America,* p. 114.

9 See ibid., p. 120.

10 On Indian names, see Jack Weatherford, *How Indians Enriched America* (New York: Ballantine, 1991). On Native American names in New York City, see Robert Steven Grumet, *Native American Place Names in New York City* (New York: Museum of the City of New York, 1981).

11 See Donald A. Grinde Jr., and Bruce E. Johansen, *Exemplar of Liberty: Native America and the Evolution of Democracy* (Los Angeles: American Indian Studies Center, UCLA, 1991) and Bruce E. Johansen, *Forgotten Founders: How the American Indian Helped Shape Democracy* (Boston: Harvard Common Press, 1982). Both of these books carefully and quite cautiously document

the Native American influence on American institutions, usually citing the founding fathers themselves.

12   See Kenneth C. Davis, "Ethnic Cleansing Didn't Start in Bosnia," *New York Times* (September 3, 1995), p. 6.

13   Fluent in Tupi, Humberto Mauro later supplied the Tupi dialogue for dos Santos's *Como Era Gostoso Meu Francês* (How Tasty Was My Little Frenchman, 1971).

14   See Ivan van Sertima, *They Came before Columbus* (New York: Random House, 1975).

15   A 1992 samba pageant presentation, Kizombo, also called attention to the putative pre-Columbian arrival of Africans in the New World, both in the lyrics and through gigantic representations of the Mexican Olmec statues with their clearly Negroid features.

16   Mary Louise Pratt, *Imperial Eyes: Travel Writing and Transculturation* (London: Routledge, 1992), p. 7.

17   I place "red," "white," and "black" in quotation marks because the identification of specific races with colors is ultimately a chromatic trope. Since racial categories are socially and historically constituted, I will be using Portuguese terms for the Brazilian context and English terms for the U.S. context.

18   Patrick Henry, William Byrd, and Thomas Jefferson all recommended intermarriage with Indians as a means of integration. During the governmental incursions on Cherokee land in the wake of the discovery of gold in 1828, religious groups (Methodists, Baptists, Presbyterians, and Moravians) attacked the incursions and suggested "intermarriage as a force for improvement," but their proposals were rejected by the federal government. See Theodore W. Allen, *The Invention of the White Race* (London: Verso, 1994), p. 33, and Gary Nash and Richard Weiss, *The Great Fear: Race in the Mind of America* (New York: Holt, Rinehart and Winston, 1976).

19   See Doris Sommer, *Foundational Fictions: The National Romances of Latin America* (Berkeley and Los Angeles: University of California Press, 1991).

20   For a discussion of transracial male bonding in American literature, see Leslie Fiedler, *Love and Death in the American Novel* (New York: Criterion, 1960).

21   The Olavo Bilac phrase is found in his *Poesias* (Rio de Janeiro: Alvez, 1964). The fundamental reference for Gilberto Freyre is *Casa Grande e Senzala,* published in English as *The Masters and the Slaves,* trans. Samuel Putnam (New York: Knopf, 1956).

22   See Dain Borges, "Intellectuals and the Forgetting of Slavery in Brazil," *Annals of Scholarship* (September 1994).

23   I am grateful to Lula Buarque de Hollanda, who worked as a research coordinator on the project, for giving me a copy of the script of the proposed film.

24   Interview with Joaquim Pedro de Andrade, *Imagems,* no. 3 (December 1994).

25   Quoted in Paulo Sotero, "Jirinovski do Patomac abala Nave Republicana," *O Estado de São Paulo* (February 25, 1996), A18. Two recent American books, Peter Brimelow's *Alien Nation,* and Michael Lind's *The Next American Nation,* also speak in panicked terms of the "danger" of the "Brazilianization" of the United States. For Brimelow, the danger is of ethnic decomposition and the loss of Anglo European hegemony. For Lind, the danger is of the explosive social tensions generated by an informal caste system in which whites dominate the top of the hierarchy and blacks and mulattoes inhabit the bottom. These analyses ignore the positive potentialities of "Brazilianization," while scapegoating Brazil for what are really the consequences

of capitalism. In a response to the Lind book, Zuenir Ventura points out the irony that "Ameri cans love capitalism and tell everybody to practice it, yet when the system generates major social flaws they blame it on 'Brazilianization,' as if we Brazilians invented the system." See "O Pior do Brasil para os EUA," in *Jornal do Brasil* (July 15, 1995), p. 5.

26 Darcy Ribeiro, *O Povo Brasileiro: A Formação e o Sentido do Brasil* (São Paulo: Companhia das Letras, 1995), p. 448.

27 See Ali Mazrui, "Global Africa in Flux: The Dialectic of Diversity in the Black World," in Carlos Moore, ed. *African Presence in the Americas* (Trenton, N.J.: Africa World Press, 1995). "In no other country in the world," Mazrui writes, "is the totality of both the African and the Black experience studied on a wider scale and by more scholars than in the United States" (p. 236).

28 Ribeiro, *O Povo Brasileiro*, p. 239.

29 Ella Shohat and I explore this larger topic in our *Unthinking Eurocentrism: Multiculturalism and the Media* (London: Routledge, 1994).

30 Quoted in Abdias do Nascimento and Elisa Larkin Nascimento, *Africans in Brazil: A Pan-African Perspective* (Trenton, N.J.: Africa World Press, 1992), p. 9.

31 For more on "submerged ethnicity," see Stam and Shohat, *Unthinking Eurocentrism* (London: Routledge, 1994).

32 Among the critics who have problematized the notion of "whiteness" are Coco Fusco, Richard Dryer, Toni Morrison, Caren Kaplan, Hazel Carby, and Ruth Frankenberg.

33 See João Carlos Rodrigues's useful essay "O Índio Brasileiro e o Cinema," in *Cinema Brasileiro e Estudos* (Rio: Embrafilme/Funarte, 1980).

34 Among the various U.S. distributors and institutions that handle the films and videos mentioned here are New Yorker Films, Cinema Guild, CineWorld, First Run Features, International Film Circuit, the International Media Resource Exchange, Kino International, Miramax, New Line Cinema, Wendy Leidel, Samuel Goldwyn, Video Data Bank, Videoteca del Sur, and Women Make Movies. The Latin American Curriculum Resource Center at Tulane University and the Latin American Video Archive in New York (Karen Ranucci) also distribute Brazilian videotapes for classroom use. At the same time, scholars such as Randal Johnson at UCLA, Julianne Burton at U.C. Santa Cruz, Bob Tolman at the University of Mexico, and Nelson Vieira at Brown University, have been developing media archives devoted to Latin American Cinema in general and Brazilian Cinema in particular.

1 Comparative Diasporas

1 The issue of Brazil's image came up recently when a Rio judge issued an injunction that would have prohibited Spike Lee from filming a Michael Jackson music video in a favela because filming it in that location would have harmed Rio's "image." Spike Lee protested that Brazil was conducting itself "like a Banana Republic," and permission to film was ultimately granted. See "Rio Frets as Michael Jackson Plans to Film Slum," *New York Times,* International Section (February 11, 1996), p. 3.

2 Interestingly, the leaders of the independence movements in both countries were slaveholders

who made ambiguous gestures toward the idea of abolishing slavery. While preparing the "Declaration of Independence," Thomas Jefferson, who was reputed to have a black mistress (Sally Hemmings), wrote a clause condemning the slave trade, but the clause was eliminated from the final document, just as he withheld publication of his "Notes on Virginia," where he described slavery as a cruel institution. In Brazil, the conspirators of the Inconfidência Mineira, the abortive eighteenth-century revolt against Portuguese colonialism (registered in Joaquim Pedro de Andrade's *Os Inconfidentes* [The Conspirators, 1971]), also discussed the possibility of abolition, but the conspirators never reached power. The postindependence Constitution of 1823, although partially inspired by the ideas of Jean-Jacques Rousseau, still embraced a slavery repudiated by the Swiss philosophe.

3   Warren Dean, "O Village Já Foi Brasileiro," *Folha de São Paulo* (May 13, 1987), A31.

4   See Eugene Genovese, *In Red and Black* (Knoxville: University of Tennessee Press, 1984), p. 23.

5   Marvin Harris, *Patterns of Race in the Americas* (New York: Greenwood, 1964), p. 86.

6   See Carl N. Degler, *Neither Black nor White: Slavery and Race Relations in Brazil and the United States* (Madison: University of Wisconsin Press, 1986), p. 72.

7   Some of the key texts in the first wave of the comparative slavery debate are Frank Tannenbaum, *Slave and Citizen* (New York: Knopf, 1947); Stanley Elkins, *Slavery: A Problem in American Institutional and Intellectual Life* (Chicago: University of Chicago Press, 1959); Eugene D. Genovese, *The World the Slaveholders Made* (New York: Vintage, 1971); *Roll Jordan Roll: The World the Slaves Made* (New York: Pantheon, 1974); and Herbert Gutman, *The Black Family in Slavery and Freedom* (New York: Pantheon, 1976).

8   On the Quakers, see Stewart J. Brewer, *Holy Warriors: The Abolitionists and American Slavery* (New York: Hill and Wang, 1981), p. 23.

9   See Thomas E. Skidmore, *Preto no Branco: Raça e Nacionalidade no Pensamento Brasileiro* (Rio de Janeiro: Paz e Terra, 1989), p. 217.

10   Thomas E. Skidmore makes this point in "O Negro no Brasil e nos Estados Unidos," *Argumento* no. 1 (1973).

11   Ibid.

12   While making *Gaijin* (1980), her film about Japanese immigrants to Brazil, Tizuka Yamasaki discovered that she had to use Japanese performers to play the leading roles, since Japanese Brazilians had developed overly expansive and loose "Brazilian" body language that made them unconvincing as Japanese.

13   Basil Davidson, *African Kingdoms* (New York: Time-Life Books, 1966), p. 174.

14   Lélia Gonzalez made the comment in a guest lecture at NYU in the mid-1980s.

15   Darcy Ribeiro, in *O Povo Brasileiro*, is one of many writers who point this out.

16   Roger Bastide, *The African Religions of Brazil: Towards a Sociology of the Interpretation of Civilizations* (Baltimore and London: Johns Hopkins University Press, 1978), pp. 247–348.

17   My account is obviously indebted to the opening paragraph of Robert Farris Thompson's *Flash of the Spirit: African and Afro-American Art and Philosophy* (New York: Random House, 1983), p. xiii.

18   Innumerable documentaries and video clips pay homage to Afro Brazilian music. Apart from David Byrne's *Ilê Aiyê/Angola,* the films include Roberto Moura's *Chega de Demanda, ou Cartola* (1973); Carlos Tourinho's *Escola de Samba* (1978); Antônio Carlos Fontoura's *Heitor dos Prazeres*

(1965); Geraldo Miranda's *A Hora e a Vez do Samba* (1973); Luis Ferro's *Karnaval Ijexá* (1988); Leon Hirszman's *Nelson do Cavaquinho* (1971); Manuel Gimenez's *Nossa Escola de Samba* (1965); Rubens Confete and Ney Lopes's *Partido Alto* (1973); and João Carlos Horta's *Pixinguinha* (1969).

19 Quoted in Eduardo Silva, *Prince of the People: The Life and Times of a Brazilian Free Man of Colour* (London: Verso, 1993), p. 20.

20 See Decio Freitas, *Palmares: A guerra dos Escravos* (Rio de Janeiro: Graal, 1978), p. 73.

21 For more on recent archaeological research into Palmares, see Ricardo Bonalume Neto, "O Pequeno Brasil de Palmares: Escavaçoes Arquelogiças Sugerem Que o Quilombo de Zumbi Era Multiétnico Como um Pequeno Brasil," *Folha de São Paulo* (June 4, 1995), pp. 5–16

22 See James Brook, "Brazil Seeks to Return Ancestral Lands to Descendants of Runaway Slaves," *New York Times* (August 15, 1993), p. 3.

23 Howard Winant, *Racial Conditions: Politics, Theory, Comparisons* (Minneapolis: University of Minnesota Press, 1994), p. 118.

24 On this subject, see Theodore W. Allen, *The Invention of the White Race,* vol. 1 (London: Verso, 1994).

25 See Peter Fry's review of Michael Hanchard's *Orpheus and Power,* in *The Times Literary Supplement* (December 8, 1995).

26 I would like to thank Arlindo Castro for pointing out the link to the iconography of the high school text books.

27 Oracy Nogueira, *Tanto Preto Quanto Branco: Estudos de Relações Raciais* (São Paulo: T. A. Queiroz, 1985), p. 21.

28 Statistics cited in José Oscar Beozzo, *Situação do Negro na Sociedade Brasileira* (Petrópolis, Brasil: Vozes, 1984), pp. 563–564.

29 The demographer Elza Berquo, from Brazilian Center of Analysis and Planning (CEBRAP), groups *pretos* and *pardos* together for political reasons, in order to "strengthen the protesting power of this segment of the population." *Folha de São Paulo* (June 25, 1995), p. 37.

30 See Michael George Hanchard, *Orpheus and Power: The Movimento Negro of Rio de Janeiro and São Paulo, Brazil, 1945–1988* (Princeton, N.J.: Princeton University Press, 1994), p. 62.

31 In Brazil, the top 10 percent of income earners enjoy 51.3 percent of all income. See Anthony W. Pereira, "Latin America in the Era of Hot Money," *Dissent* (Winter 1996), p. 48.

32 See *Folha de São Paulo* (June 25, 1995), p. 12.

33 Frantz Fanon, "Racism and Culture," in *Présence Africaine,* nos. 8–10 (1956).

34 To borrow and slightly modify Helen Page's definition of white supremacy, racism in Brazil is an "ideological, structural and historical stratification process," whereby Euro Brazilians sustain, to their own best advantage, "the dynamic mechanics of upward and downward mobility or fluid class status over the non-European populations." Quoted in Loretta Ross, "White Supremacy in the 1990s," in *Eyes Right: Challenging the Right Wing Backlash* (Boston: South End, 1995), pp. 172–173.

35 Alejandro Lipschutz, *El Indiamericanismo y el Problema Racial en las Americas* (Santiago, Chile, 1994), p. 75; quoted in Fredrick B. Pike, *The United States and Latin America: Myths and Stereotypes of Civilization and Nature* (Austin: University of Texas Press, 1992), p. 13.

36 Michael Hanchard, *Orpheus and Power,* p. 6.

37 Roger Bastide, *As Americas Negras* (São Paulo: Difel, 1974), p. 285.

38   See *Folha de São Paulo* (June 25, 1995).

39   See Fernando Conceição, "O Negro debaixo do Tapete," *Folha de São Paulo* (March 26, 1995), p. 3 (illustrated).

40   The African American musician, painter, and teacher Lloyd MacNeill pointed out to me that whenever Brazilians would boast about their "foot in the kitchen," he would say: "Yes, that's obvious from your features." At that point, he reports, many Brazilians suddenly shift ground and deny their black inheritance, or at least the idea that it might be "visible."

41   Pierre Van den Berghe suggestively distinguishes between two "ideal types" of race relations: paternalist à la Brasil and competitive à la the United States. In the former, miscegenation is tolerated; in the latter it is condemned. In the former, prejudice is not sexually obsessed, whereas in the latter it comes charged with frustrations, aggression, sadism, fear of castration. In the former, racism is "soft"; in the latter it is virulent. Van den Berghe's ideas are summarized in Roger Bastide, *Le Prochain et le Lointain* (Paris: Cujas, 1970), p. 101.

42   See *New York Times* (December 10, 1995), Metro Report, p. 49.

43   Peter Fry adopts an anthropological stance toward the "myth" of racial democracy, seeing myth not as false consciousness but rather as "ordered systems of thought which enshrine and express fundamental understandings about society." See his review of Hanchard's *Orpheus and Power.*

44   See Stuart Hall, "The Whites of Their Eyes: Racist Ideologies and the Media," in George Bridges and Rosalind Brundt, eds., *Silver Linings: Some Strategies for the Eighties* (London: Lawrence & Wishart, 1981), p. 36.

45   Nelson do Valle Silva and Carlos Hasenbalg, *Relações Raciais no Brasil Contemporâneo* (Rio de Janeiro: Rio Fundo, 1992), p. 151.

46   See Anani Dzidzienyo, *The Position of Blacks in Brazilian Society.* UN Minority Rights Report no. 7 (London: Minority Rights Group, 1971), p. 14.

47   See Joel Kovel, *White Racism: A Psychohistory* (New York: Columbia University Press, 1984).

48   See "Brasil, uma Nação Inconclusa," *Folha de São Paulo* (June 25, 1995).

49   See "Cem Anos, sem Qause Nada," *Veja* (April 20, 1988).

50   Dzidzienyo, *The Position of Blacks in Brazilian Society,* p. 5.

51   The etiquette of race at one historical point even applied in the world of soccer. According to Mário Filho, black soccer players had to play a cleaner game than whites: "When they had to take the ball away from a white player, they did it with visible *delicatesse,* or let the white pass." Mário Filho, *O Negro no Foot-ball Brasileiro* (Rio de Janeiro: Imaos Pongetti, 1947), p. 97.

52   See Hanchard, *Orpheus and Power.*

53   On convergence, see the work of Howard Winant *(Racial Conditions)* and of Michael Hanchard. Hanchard distinguishes between the "Africanist" orientation of cultural groups such as the Olodum Theater Group and the "Americanist" orientation of the explicitly political groups. See *Orpheus and Power* (Princeton, N.J.: Princeton University Press, 1994).

54   See Winant, *Racial Conditions,* p. 158.

55   From Sílvio Romero, "A Emancipação dos Escravos," in *O Mínitor* (August 1881); quoted in Brookshaw, *Raça e Cor na Literatura Brasileira* (Porto Alegre: Mercado Aberto, 1983), p. 43.

56   Hanchard, *Black Orpheus,* p. 142.

57   See José Carlos Avellar, "O Brasil por Conta de Nós Próprio," in Jaime Rodrigues et al., *O Brasileiro de Novo nas Telas* (Rio de Janeiro: Cultural Department of the State University of Rio de Janeiro, 1993), pp. 17–25.

2. The Structuring Absences of Silent Cinema

1   "There was a lot of resistance," Pixinguinha recalled, "I was never refused entrance because of my color, but that's because I never abused the situation." When socialites like Guinle would invite him to dinner, Pixinguinha continues, "I understood that he was just being nice and I knew that he didn't expect me to accept his invitation. So I too would be nice and not accept." See Roberto Moura, *Tia Ciata e a Pequena África no Rio de Janeiro* (Rio de Janeiro: Biblioteca Carioca, 1995), p. 84. Pixinguinha's account of negotiating the complex racial codes of 1920s and 1930s Rio give a glimpse into the operative "racial etiquette" of the time.

2   See Joseph Page, *The Brazilians* (Reading, Mass.: Addison-Wesley, 1995), p. 72.

3   The published notices about Benjamin de Oliveira and the Spinelli Circus are gathered in Vicente de Paula Araújo, *Salões, Circos e Cinemas de São Paulo* (São Paulo: Perspectiva, 1981). See pages 74, 88, 93, 268, 270.

4   See Araújo, *Salões, Circos e Cinemas de São Paulo*, p. 116.

5   Jorge J. V. Capellaro and Victoria G. J. Capellaro, *Vittório Capellaro: Italiano Pioneiro de Cinema Brasileiro* (Rio: Cadernos de Pesquisa, CPCB, 1986), p. 23.

6   Quoted by Roberto Moura, "A Bela Época," in Fernão Ramos, ed., *História do Cinema Brasileiro* (São Paulo: Art Editora, 1987), p. 48.

7   Paul Gilroy, *The Black Atlantic: Modernity and Double Consciousness* (Cambridge: Harvard University Press, 1993).

8   Quoted in Skidmore, *Preto no Branco*, p. 155.

9   Quoted in Thomas E. Skidmore, *Black into White* (New York: Oxford University Press, 1974), p. 17.

10 See Skidmore, *Preto no Branco*, p. 136.

11 Ibid., p. 205.

12 Cited in Darcy Ribeiro, *Aos Trancos e Barrancos: Como o Brasil Deu no Que Deu* (Rio de Janeiro. Editora Guanabara, 1985), item. 363.

13 Based on information from the censors, cited in Ramos, *História do Cinema Brasileiro*, p. 107.

14 *Cinearte*, Rio de Janeiro (June 18, 1930).

15 This aesthetic stance existed on a continuum with elite attitudes in everyday social life. For example, in 1908, writer Monteiro Lobato expressed repulsion at seeing Cariocas on their way home from work: "How can we fix these people? What terrible problems the poor African negro, in his unconscious vengeance, has created for us here. Perhaps salvation will come from São Paulo and other zones with higher injections of European blood. The Americans saved themselves from miscegenation by creating the barrier of racial prejudice. That barrier exists here as well, but only among certain classes and in certain areas. In Rio it doesn't exist." Passages from Monteiro Lobato's *A Barca da Gleyre* quoted in Skidmore, *Preto no Branco*, p. 199.

16 *Cinearte* (December 11, 1929), p. 28.

17 In 1926, while making the second version of *O Guarani*, Vittório Capellaro did use some Indian performers. The director and actor Tácito de Souza were detained by the Santos police for "showing the Bananal Indians, when there is so much progress to show." The two were released only after direct intervention by Coronel Rondon. See João Carlos Rodrigues, "O Índio Brasileiro e o Cinema," in *Cinema Brasileiro e Estudos* (Rio: Embrafilme/Funarte, 1980), p. 183.

18 Many Brazilian writers have either seriously proposed (e.g., Plínio Salgado in the 1930s), or parodied (Lima Barreto in *O Triste Fim de Policarpo Quaresma*), the idea of the indigenous language Tupi as the official national language.

19 See Benedita Gouveia Damasceno, *Poesia Negra no Modernismo Brasileiro* (Campinas, Brasil: Pontes, 1988), p. 40.

20 See Antônio Cândido, "Literature and the Rise of Brazilian National Self-Identity," *Luso-Brazilian Review* 5 (June 1968), p. 36.

21 Quoted in Ramos, *História do Cinema Brasileiro*, p. 74. Excerpts from some of these documentaries form part of Sílvio Back's 1995 documentary *Yndio do Brasil*.

22 Randal Johnson has pointed out to me that the modernist painter Menotti del Picchia and his mother had their own production company.

23 Oswald de Andrade, "Conversando com Oswald de Andrade," *Gazeta do Povo* (1950), cited in Maria Eugenia Boaventura, *A Vanguarda Antropofágica* (São Paulo: Ática, 1985), p. 31.

24 For more on modernist "anthropophagy," see Robert Stam, "Of Cannibals and Carnivals," in *Subversive Pleasures: Bakhtin, Cultural Criticism and Film* (Baltimore: Johns Hopkins University Press, 1989).

25 For an English version of the "Cannibalist Manifesto," see Leslie Bary's excellent introduction to and translation of the poem in *Latin American Literary Review* 19 (July–December 1991).

26 Alfred Jarry in his "Anthropophagie" (1902) spoke of that "branche trop négligée de l'anthropophagie" and in "L'Almanach du Père Ubu" addressed himself to "amateur cannibals." The Dadaists entitled one of their organs *Cannibale,* and in 1920 Francis Picabia issued the "Manifeste Cannibale Dada."

27 Augusto de Campos, *Poesia, Antipoesia, Antropofagia* (São Paulo: Cortez e Moraes, 1978), p. 121.

28 Oswald de Andrade's various manifestoes are collected in *Do Pau-Brasil à Antropofagia às Utopias* (Rio de Janeiro: Civilização Brasileira, 1972).

29 The modernist rehabilitation of non-European culture, as David Brookshaw points out, was essentially artistic. The modernists did not intervene politically on behalf of the black masses or in favor of tribes threatened with extinction. See David Brookshaw, *Raça e Cor na Literatura Brasileira* (Porto Alegre: Mercado Aberto, 1983), p. 96.

30 Oswald de Andrade, "L'Effort Intellectuel du Brésil Contemporain," *Revue de l'Amérique Latine,* no. 5 (May–August 1923).

31 Raul Bopp, *Poemas Negros* (Rio de Janeiro: Ariel, 1932), p. 8.

32 Mário de Andrade, *Poesias Completas* (São Paulo: Martins, 1972), pp. 32–33.

33 See Theodor Koch-Grunberg, *Vom Roroima Zum Orinoco: Ergebnisse einer Reise in Nord Brasilien und Venezuela in den Jahren 1911–1913,* vol. 2, *Mythen und Legenden der Taulipang und Arekuna Indianer* (Stuttgart: Strocker & Schroder, 1924).

34 The English translation of *Macunaíma,* unfortunately, conveys little of this. The key phrase "Ai que preguiça," in the Portuguese of the novel an expression of delicious languor, becomes in the English version "What a fucking life!" We still await an English translation that would transpose the culturally polyphonic prose-poetry of Mário de Andrade's novel into an equally polyphonic English, drawing on indigenous words, African American slang, and immigrant speech.

35 Quoted in M. Cavalcanti Proenca, *Roteiro de Macunaíma* (Rio de Janeiro: Civilização Brasileira, 1969), p. 17.

36 On the indigenous African amalgam see Mário de Andrade, *Música de Feitiçaria no Brasil* (Belo Horizonte, Brasil: Itataia, 1983), p. 26. On the Euro-Catholic and African synthesis, see Mário de Andrade, *O Turista Aprendiz* (São Paulo: Duas Cidades, 1976), pp. 248 249.

37 From de Andrade, *Poesias Completas,* but paraphrased in David T. Haberly, *Three Sad Races: Racial Identity and National Consciousness in Brazilian Literature* (Cambridge: Cambridge University Press, 1983), p. 138.

38 For more on the Bakhtinian conception of polyphony, see Mikhail Bakhtin, *Problems of Dostoevsky's Poetics* (Minneapolis: University of Minnesota Press, 1984).

39 See Mário de Andrade, *A Escrava Que Não É Isaura,* in *Obra Imatura* (São Paulo: Martins, 1972), p. 268.

40 I further explore the analogies between São Paulo and New York, and between *Macunaíma* and *Zelig,* in "A Tale of Two Cities: Cultural Polyphony and Ethnic Transformation," *East-West Film Journal* 3, no. 1 (December 1988).

41 See de Andrade, *Poesias Completas,* pp. 203–204.

42 See de Andrade, *Obra Imatura,* p. 266. For discussion of de Andrade's "harlequinate" iden-tity, see David T. Haberly, *Three Sad Races.* For a discussion of the racial question within Modernism, see Zita St. Aubyn Nunes, *"Os Males do Brasil": Antropofagia e a Questão da Raça* (Rio: SIEC, 1989).

43 Abdias do Nascimento, who met with Mário de Andrade in the 1930s, describes him, some-what harshly, as a "typical product of Brazilian racial ideology; one of those mulattoes who spend their lives passing and would never admit to any African identity." See Abdias do Nasci-mento and Elisa Larkin Nascimento, *Africans in Brazil,* p. 25.

44 This and the following quote are from de Andrade, *Poesias Completas* (São Paulo: Martins, 1972), 000 and 000.

45 De Andrade, *O Turista Aprendiz,* p. 305.

46 See "O Desafio Brasileiro," in *O Empalhador de Passarinho* (São Paulo: Martins, 1972).

47 Positivist intellectuals at the time were revolted by an article by the German Von Ihering, director of the Museu Paulista, in which he preached the extermination of the Indians in the name of progress and civilization. His racist cry was provoked by what he saw as the "failure" of the army to help his colonizing German compatriots in their confrontation with the indig-enous peoples.

48 See Skidmore, *Preto no Branco,* p. 85.

49 See Fredrick B. Pike, *The United States and Latin America: Myths and Stereotypes of Civilization and Nature* (Austin: University of Texas Press, 1992), pp. 202–203.

50 Guimarães, Bernardo. *A Escrava Isaura* (Rio de Janeiro: Editora Ouro, 1961), p. 24.

3. *Carmen Miranda, Grande Otelo, and the* Chanchada

1 For Abdias do Nascimento, these fora were dominated by the "pomp and circumstance of white scholars and scientists." See Abdias do Nascimento and Elisa Larkin Nascimento, *Afri-cans in Brazil,* p. 37.

2 Emília Viotti da Costa, *Brazilian Empire: Myths and Histories* (Chicago: University of Chi-cago Press, 1985), p. 239.

3   Clóvis Moura is quoted in Martiniano J. Silva, *Racismo à Brasileira* (Brasília: Thesaurus, 1987), p. 180.

4   Hanchard, *Orpheus and Power,* pp. 43, 47.

5   Quoted in Skidmore, *Preto no Branco,* p. 225.

6   Nanal, quoted in Ana Maria Rodrigues, *Samba Negro, Espoliação Branca* (São Paulo: HUCITEC, 1984), p. 29.

7   Quoted in Sérgio Cabral, *As Escolas de Samba do Rio de Janeiro* (Rio de Janeiro: Limiar, 1996), p. 97.

8   Quoted in Cabral, pp. 71–72.

9   Alex Viany, *Introdução ao Cinema Brasileiro* (Rio de Janeiro: MEC/INL, 1959), pp. 107–108.

10 From Jorge Amado's review in *Boletim de Ariel,* but cited in Viany, *Introdução ao Cinema Brasileiro,* p. 145.

11 Quoted in Sérgio Augusto, *Este Mundo É um Pandeiro: A Chanchada de Getúlio a JK* (São Paulo: Cinemateca Brasileira/Companhia das Letras, 1989), pp. 18–19.

12 Quoted in Augusto, *Este Mundo É um Pandeiro,* p. 18.

13 It is interesting to compare other 1930s musical films from the other countries of the Americas in terms of their racial representations. The Argentinean film *Tango* (1933) features one black woman dancing in a crowd of tango dancers. The Cuban film *El Romance del Palmar* (1938), the product of a multiracial society very much like Brazil's, features whites in leading roles but also includes black musicians.

14 Henry Louis Gates Jr. notes the iconographic links between blackness, the harlequin, and the minstrel figure, whereby the "inherent nobility of Harlequin the Black Clown [became] transformed by degrees into the ignoble black minstrel figure." See Gates, *Figures in Black* (New York: Oxford University Press, 1987), pp. 51–53.

15 My discussion here is indebted to Ella Shohat's analysis, first published in her essay "Gender and the Culture of Empire" and subsequently included in our coauthored *Unthinking Eurocentrism.*

16 See Antônio Risério, *Caymmi: Uma Utopia de Lugar* (São Paulo: Perspectiva, 1993), p. 31.

17 See Zeca Ligiero, *Carmen Miranda: An Afro-Brazilian Paradox,* unpublished and as yet undefended dissertation for Performance Studies, NYU. The most informed analysis available of Carmen Miranda's African roots, Ligiero's study will soon be published by Temple University Press.

18 The characterization by Jorge Amado is part of a series of homages to Grande Otelo after his death and included in *Écrans d'Afrique* (3d–4th trimester, 1993), p. 34.

19 Ibid., p. 36.

20 See *Jornal do Brasil* (November 27, 1993), p. 7. The notion of an elite *gafieira* is somewhat oxymoronic in the sense that the very word *gafieira* is self-mocking, coming from "gaffe," that is, the *gafieira* was a place where people committed gaffes.

21 Jean-Claude Baker and Chris Chase, *Josephine: The Hungry Heart* (New York: Random House, 1993), p. 163.

22 The only biography of Grande Otelo is Roberto Moura's thoroughly researched and insightful *Grande Otelo* (Rio de Janeiro: Relume/Dumara, 1996). Otelo worked with Moura on a script about the *gafieiras* (club elite) and also performed in Moura's *Katharsys: História dos Anos 80* (Katharsys: Tales from the 1980s, 1994).

23 Quoted in Rosángela de Oliveira Dias, *O Mundo como Chanchada: Cinema e Imaginário das Classes Populares na Década de 50* (Rio de Janeiro: Dumará, 1993), p. 9.

24 See Augusto, *Este Mundo É um Pandeiro*, p. 107.

25 The impression of Welles as American agent derives, perhaps, from the early period of Welles's stay in Brazil, when he appeared to have close connections with the populist, autocratic Vargas government, connections that did not help Welles when he started to offend the regime by filming the favelas.

26 See Augusto, *Este Mundo É um Pandeiro*, p. 192.

27 See ibid., p. 130.

28 Interview with Grande Otelo, *Positif*, no. 314 (April 1987), p. 48.

29 Quoted in Augusto, *Este Mundo É um Pandeiro*, p. 131.

30 Quoted in ibid., p. 132.

31 Ibid., p. 175.

32 Vinícius de Moraes, *O Cinema de Meus Olhos* (São Paulo: Companhia das Letras, 1991), p. 264.

33 Quoted in João Luiz Vieira, "A Chanchada e o Cinema Carioca," in Ramos, ed. *História do Cinema Brasileiro*, p. 163.

34 For an incisive discussion of the Brazilian parodies, see João Luiz Vieira, *Hegemony and Resistance: Carnival and Parody in Brazilian Cinema*, Ph.D. diss., NYU, 1982.

35 "Cinema Brasileiro Entre Aspas," *Revista Anhembi* (São Paulo), 20, no. 58 (September 1955).

36 Silvyano Cavalcanti Paiva, "Nudismo, Macumba, e Malandragem," *A Cena Muda* (January 31, 1952), p. 11.

37 Vieira, *Hegemony and Resistance*.

38 Eartha Kitt reported Orson Welles's words on an afternoon talk show in 1993.

39 In *Mandarim* (Mandarin) the contemporary musical elite represents the 1930s musical elite: Chico Buarque plays Noel Rosa, Gal Costa plays Carmen Miranda, and Maria Betânhia creates a fusion of Aracy de Almeida and Marília Batista.

40 See James Snead, *White Screen/Black Images* (London: Routledge, 1993).

41 *Meus Amores no Rio* even has a blackface number, in which Susana Freyre and Jardel Filho do a *boneca de pixe* (tar baby) number.

42 Otelo makes remarks to this effect in the BBC documentary about *It's All True*.

43 In interviews, Otelo called for a kind of black capitalism and mutual support. "I think that we should shake up those blacks who rise on the social ladder and come to occupy key positions and who, whether out of fear or because they already suffered too much, decide to hide or wash their hands. In the final analysis, every ethnic group in Brazil has organized." Otelo seems ambivalent about Brazilian racism, arguing on the one hand that there is less racism in Brazil because all Brazilians have partial black ancestry—"I only believe that a Brazilian is really white when I've seen photos of all his grandparents"—and lamenting on the other the fact that he has always had to struggle harder than a white actor would have. He was rarely paid the money due him, he says, and expresses the common complaint of black performers throughout the diaspora that blacks have to work twice as hard to get what whites get as a matter of course. He has also insisted in interviews on the importance of black celebrities' marrying black women, rather than the white women who seek out black celebrities. Quotations here are taken from an interview with Grande Otelo in *O Estado de São Paulo* (June 10, 1978).

44 When asked why it was only in the 1960s that he became concerned about black issues, Otelo
answered that he had always been concerned but that it was only recently that the black community began to pressure him to make a more vocal commitment. Otelo contrasted his own
attitude with that of another black celebrity—Pelé. "I want to unite the blacks of Brazil, including those who are abroad like Pelé. I would like Pelé to feel black and join with his people
in this struggle." Nestor de Holanda, "Da Favela para Hollywood," *A Cena Muda* (February
11, 1942).

4. Pan-American Interlude

1 Documents cited, when no other source is mentioned, are generally from the Welles collection at the Lilly Library of Indiana Library.

2 See Jonathon Rosenbaum and Bill Krohn, "Orson Welles in the U.S.: An Exchange," *Persistence of Vision*, no. 11 (1995), p. 95.

3 Catherine Benamou's dissertation on *It's All True* (Cinema Studies, NYU, 1997) comprises a
thoroughly researched study of the textual, intertextual, and contextual aspects of the film.

4 See Charles Higham, *The Films of Orson Welles* (Berkeley and Los Angeles: University of Cali-
fornia Press, 1971); Higham's *Orson Welles: The Rise and Fall of an American Genius* (New
York: St. Martin's Press, 1985); and John Russell Taylor, *Orson Welles: A Celebration* (Boston:
Little, Brown & Co., 1986).

5 Higham, p. 332.

6 In her dissertation on *It's All True,* Benamou delineates the major causes alleged for the film's
noncompletion—(1) the film's cost, which would have put RKO back "into the red"; (2)
Welles's alleged ties to the Communist Party; (3) Welles's alleged lack of discipline and his
financial irresponsibility; and (4) the *jangada* incident in which the hero Jacaré disappeared—
and systematically refutes each in great detail and with great cogency. Benamou based her
account on extensive archival research in the United States, Brazil, and Mexico and on interviews with such key figures as Grande Otelo, Herivelto Martins, Edmar Morel, George Fanto,
and many others. One looks forward to the publication of this indispensable work.

7 See Taylor, *Orson Welles: A Celebration,* p. 64.

8 Taylor, *Orson Welles: A Celebration,* p. 65.

9 See Higham, *The Films of Orson Welles,* p. 87.

10 Higham, *Orson Welles: The Rise and Fall of an American Genius,* p. 199.

11 Even those critics not especially hostile to Welles make egregious errors concerning Brazil and
Brazilians. Frank Brady, for example, calls Grande Otelo a "dwarf" and, perhaps confusing
Rio de Janeiro with Santiago de Chile, speaks of "snowcapped mountains visible from down-
town [Rio]," which would certainly surprise most Cariocas. See Frank Brady, *Citizen Kane*
(New York: Charles Scribners, 1989), p. 335.

12 See *Cine-Rádio Jornal* (March 6, 1942).

13 See *Cine-Rádio Jornal* (June 3, 1942).

14 See *Cine-Rádio Jornal* (April 22, 1942).

15 We find a similar insistence on linguistic reciprocity in Welles's radio broadcasts from Latin

America. In "The Bad Will Ambassador," for example, a kind of *Ugly American avant la lettre,* Welles offers a satirical portrait of an arrogant American businessman who has trouble with "those strange Latin names." At one point, he asks of someone if they speak English, to which his Latin American interlocutor replies "No, Sir, only Spanish and Portuguese," provoking the American's comment: "That's all right, he'll have time to get an education."

16 See *Cine-Rádio Jornal* (February 11, 1942).

17 See *Cine-Rádio Jornal* (April 22, 1942).

18 Vinícius de Moraes, "Orson Welles em Filmagem," in *O Cinema de Meus Olhos,* p. 63.

19 From "Some Notes from a Research on Welles in Brazil," by Heloísa Buarque de Holanda with research assistance by Ana Rita Mendonça, notes sent as a contribution to the Welles Conference held at NYU in May 1988.

20 See Andrew Sarris, *Village Voice* (May 5, 1988).

21 See *A Noite* (April 10, 1942).

22 See *Cine-Rádio Jornal* (February 11, 1942).

23 See, for example, *Cine-Rádio Jornal* (June 3, 1942).

24 See Filmar Morel, *Vendaval da Liberdade: A Luta do Povo pela Abolição* (São Paulo: Global, 1988), where Morel, one of Welles's collaborators, speaks of the role of *jangadeiros* in the abolitionist struggle.

25 The information about Jacaré's imprisonment came from his son, José "Guaiuba" Olímpio Meira, in an interview with Bill Krohn in Fortaleza, January 1993.

26 Sérgio Cabral mentions one antecedent journalistic article, Egídio de Castro e Silva's "O Samba Carioca," published in *Revista Brasileira de Música* (vol. 6 [1939], pp. 45–48). See Sérgio Cabral, *As Escolas de Samba do Rio de Janeiro* (Rio de Jeneiro: Limiar, 1996), p. 120.

27 "Carnaval," *Careta* (February 21, 1942), p. 22.

28 Taped interview with Alex Viany conducted by Heloísa Buarque de Holanda.

29 Vinícius de Moraes, "Grandeza de Otelo," in *O Cinema de Meus Olhos,* p. 263.

30 In conversations with Catherine Benamou, Grande Otelo expressed appreciation for the fact that Welles allowed him to explore different facets of his creative personality. See Benamou, Ph.D. diss.

31 Otelo speaks of Welles's interview in *Le Figaro* in which Welles criticized the Marcel Camus film *Otália da Bahia* (1976), claiming that the film's only redeeming feature was a performance by Grande Otelo. See *Filme Cultura,* no. 40 (August–October 1982), p. 9.

32 The note was apparently sent to Otelo via Gregg Toland, who was present at the inauguration of the Atlântida Studio in 1941. See Roberto Moura, *Grande Othelo,* pp. 46–47.

33 Interview with Grande Otelo and Herivelto Martins conducted by Alex Viany, available in the Rio de Janeiro Cinematheque, Museu de Arte Moderna.

34 Grande Otelo describes this interweaving, where he and Linda Batista sing the same song but from two different social sites, in an interview included in Rogério Sganzerla's 1985 film *Nem Tudo É Verdade* (It's Not All True).

35 For a critique of Disney's Latin American films, see Julianne Burton-Carvajal, "Surprise Package: Looking Southward with Disney," in Eric Smoodin, ed., *Disney Discourse: Producing the Magic Kingdom* (New York: Routledge, 1994).

36 From Welles's notes on "Problems of Photographing Carnaval," from the Lilly Archive.

37 "Orson Welles' Almanac," *New York Post* (February 13, 1945).

38   In the same period, the story of Haiti's postrevolutionary King Christophe inspired intertextual
     variations not only by Welles but also by Eugene O'Neill and W. E. B. Dubois, while Katherine
     Dunham used Vodou ritual as a renovating source for modernist dance. See Kate Ramsey,
     "Vodou and Nationalism: The Staging of Folklore in Mid-Twentieth Century Haiti," *Women
     and Performance* 7, no. 2, Issue 14–15 (1995).

39   See *Cine-Rádio Jornal* (February 11, 1942).

40   See *Jornal do Brasil,* Caderno B (1985).

41   Viany interview of Martins and Otelo.

42   Bill Krohn recalls that the Brazilian filmmaker Rogério Sganzerla took him to the specific bar
     where this incident occurred. See Rosenbaum and Krohn, "Orson Welles in the U.S.," p. 95.

43   See Barbara Leaming, *Orson Welles* (New York: Viking Penguin, 1985), pp. 402–404. In the
     Lilly Library Welles collection, one can read various letters of response, ranging from racist
     diatribes to grateful letters from black Americans. A letter from one Edna Fraser (July 13,
     1946) asks rhetorically: "How would you feel if Negro men whistle at [your daughters]? . . .
     Would you consent to your lovely daughters being touched by negroes?" If "you are advocat-
     ing [miscegenation]," she warns, "then as I have loved and admired, so should I despise and
     loathe the very sound of your voice and name." Letters from blacks, in contrast, stress appre-
     ciation and solidarity. Norma Keene (August 7, 1946) writes: "you can't imagine just how
     much I, as well as thousands of Colored people whom I'm sure listen to your program every
     Sunday, appreciate what it is you are planning to do . . . appreciate because whoever that
     policeman was he should be brought to justice the same as the War Criminals were."

44   See Edmar Morel, "O Orson Welles Que Conheci," *Tribuna de Imprensa* (Rio de Janeiro,
     March 12, 1987).

45   Quoted by Servulo Siqueira, in "Tudo É Verdade," *Folha de São Paulo* (December 2, 1984).

46   Catherine Benamou, in her dissertation, points out that in 1929 Shores directed a feature for
     RKO entitled *Jazz Age* about the corrupting influence of jazz on children.

47   One hears echoes of this early hostility in the present-day words of Reginald Armour, then
     executive secretary to George Schaeffer, as registered in the BBC documentary *The RKO Story.*

48   Catherine Benamou points out that RKO was relatively weak-kneed about the opposition of
     racist white southerners. Other studios, such as MGM, were not so easily intimidated.

49   Wilson is interviewed in the BBC documentary *The RKO Story.*

50   Quoted in Cabral, *As Escolas de Samba do Rio de Janeiro,* pp. 134–135.

51   See *Meio Dia* (April 2, 1942).

52   See Gatinha Angora, "Of Good Intentions," *Cine-Rádio Jornal* (May 20, 1942).

5. Vera Cruz

1   Quoted in Ricardo Gaspar Muller, "O Teatro Experimental do Negro" (unpublished paper).

2   Abdias do Nascimento, Preface to *Sortilégio II (Mistério Negro de Zumbi Redivivo)* (Rio de
     Janeiro: Paz e Terra, 1979), p. 28.

3   Abdias do Nascimento and Elisa Larkin Nascimento, *Africans in Brazil,* p. 26.

4   See Abdias do Nascimento, *Sortilégio II,* p. 49. Although critical of racism in the United States,

do Nascimento does credit the United States with recognizing the "merit of my work." He and the Black Experimental Theater are the subject of a documentary, Daniel Caetano's *Teatro Negro*.

5   Quoted in Maria Rita Galvão and Jean-Claude Bernardet, *Cinema. Repercussões em Caixa de Eco Ideológica* (São Paulo: Brasiliense, 1983), p. 150.

6   Quoted in Maria Helena Machado, *O Plano e o Pânico: Os Movimentos Sociais na Década da Abolição* (São Paulo: UFRJ/EDUSP, 1994), p. 13.

7   Ibid. p. 150.

8   Quoted in Machado, *O Plano e o Pânico*, p. 101.

9   Ibid., p. 163.

10 See Skidmore, *Preto no Branco*, p. 33.

11 See Carl N. Degler, *Neither Black nor White*, p. 84.

12 *Uncle Tom's Cabin*, published in English in 1851, was translated into Portuguese in 1853 and later presented in Rio (1876) to great acclaim. There were also abolitionist novelists in Brazil, many of whom wrote under pseudonyms to avoid arrest. José de Alencar's *Mãe*, for example, was written under a pseudonym. Needless to say, abolitionist and liberationist movements in one part of the black Atlantic world always had repercussions elsewhere, as for example in the panic that spread through the slave-holding world after Toussaint l'Ouverture's revolution in Haiti in 1815. At one point in *Sinhá Moça*, a character warns that if Brazil continues slavery it will be rent by civil war as the United States had been.

13 Princesa Isabel, author of the Lei Áurea ending slavery, herself hailed abolitionism as a majority movement, "applauded by all classes, with admirable examples of abnegation on the part of slaveholders." Quoted in Moura, *Tia Ciata e a Pequena África no Rio de Janeiro*, p. 19.

14 Machado, *O Pleno e o Pânico*, p. 144.

15 The sequence's juxtaposition of religious mass with political torture is one of many cases of ironic juxtaposition: the opening sequence contrasts elegant conversation in the first-class train compartments with the desperate flight of the fugitive slave outside; the party sequence shuttles between images of waltzing well-dressed whites in the Big House with images of slaves plotting revolt in the *senzala*.

16 A photo from the João de Orleans e Bragança Collection shows just such a celebration, revealing a huge mass of people in São Cristovão celebrating the abolition of slavery.

17 See *Revista Anhembi*, "Cinema de 30 Dias" (July 1953), p. 132.

18 See Júlio José Chiavenato's summary of Nabuco's arguments in *O Negro no Brasil: Da Senzala a Guerra do Paraguai* (São Paulo: Brasiliense, 1980), p. 213.

19 On the use of lighting to foil black and white performers in a manner flattering to whites, see James Snead, *White Screen/Black Images* (London: Routledge, 1993).

20 The Milton Nascimento song "Morror Velho" tells a similar tale of black and white buddies playing together on the *fazenda*. The white son of the *fazendeiro* goes off to the big city, promising eternal friendship, but when he returns he is different and has a University degree: "And now on the *fazenda* he's the boss / and his old comrade / now no longer plays; he works." I would like to thank Arlindo Castro for calling this song to my attention.

6. The Favela

1 Quoted in Maria Rita Galvão and Jean-Claude Bernardet, *Cinema: Repercussões em Caixa de Eco Ideológica* (São Paulo: Brasiliense, 1983), p. 248.

2 In the journal *Retrospectiva* (1954), quoted in Galvão and Bernardet, *Cinema: Repercussões em Caixa de Eco Ideológica*, p. 136.

3 Interview with Gerald O'Grady in *Nelson Pereira dos Santos: Cinema Novo's Spirit of Light*, brochure for the 1995 retrospective of dos Santos's work at the Walter Reade Theater, New York City, prepared by the Film Society of Lincoln Center and the Harvard Film Archive, under the direction of Gerald O'Grady.

4 *A Marcha* (October 7, 1955), p. 13.

5 Angela Maria was then and is still now a very popular singer. In 1957 she sang on a São Paulo TV show together with Louis Armstrong.

6 One is reminded of rock 'n' roll's commercialization of black rhythm-and-blues and even of Rod Stewart's "borrowing" of the musical theme of Jorge Bem's *Taj Mahal,* a homage to the black North American singer, for his individualist and lucrative "Do You Think I'm Sexy?"

7 There are various explanations for why samba groups came to be called "schools," for example, that the expression began as a joke, that is, sambistas would refer to getting their diploma from the samba school (roughly like the American expression "school of hard knocks"), or that there was, literally, a school near one of the first samba schools. The samba schools historically came from the *favelas,* most of them situated in the Zona Norte of Rio, not near the beaches of Zona Sul. (*Black Orpheus* romanticizes by choosing the favelas with the most picturesque vistas.) There are scores of officially recognized samba schools in Rio. Their performances, at the time of *Black Orpheus* in the streets and nowadays in the *sambodromo,* run without interruption over many days. The schools feature thousands of performing members who collectively construct the pageant; they choose a theme (allegorical, historical, topical), compose songs, choreograph dances, write lyrics, and develop rhythms. Each samba school has its flag and its colors—Salgueiro, for example, is red and white, Portela is blue and white, Mangueira is pink and green—and Cariocas root for them as they might for a soccer team. Although North American critics saw the spectacle as frenzied, it is in fact highly organized, as it would have to be given the complex logistical problems involved in moving thousands of performers and floats down a stretch of asphalt.

8 See José Eduardo Homen de Nello, *Música Popular Brasileira* (São Paulo: UDESP, 1976), p. 59.

9 Vinícius de Moraes, preface to the second edition of *Orfeu da Conceição* (Rio de Janeiro: Dois Amigos, 1967), p. 2.

10 See Perrone, *Masters of Contemporary Brazilian Song: MPB 1965–1985.* Austin: University of Texas Press, 1989.

11 Abdias do Nascimento and Elisa Larkin Nascimento, *Africans in Brazil*, p. 46.

12 On *negrismo,* see Benedita Gouveia Damasceno, *Poesia Negra no Modernismo Brasileiro* (Campinas: Pontes, 1988).

13 For more on the Orpheus tradition in relation to the film see Charles Perrone, "Don't Look Back: Myths, Conceptions, and Receptions of *Black Orpheus,*" a paper presented at the Latin American Cinema Studies Conference held at Tulane in October 1996. In independent re-

search, Perrone and I came to very similar conclusions about the film, although our emphases are distinct.

14 According to Ruy Castro, Abdias do Nascimento accused de Moraes of "exploiting black people." De Moraes then fired do Nascimento and substituted white actor Chico Feitosa in blackface. See Ruy Castro, *Chega de Saudade: A História e as Histórias da Bossa Nova.* (São Paulo: Companhia das Letras, 1990), p. 124.

15 The participation of the Black Experimental Theater in *Black Orpheus* was somewhat ironical and ambivalent. In one sense, the film advanced the group's goal of valorizing the work of black actors. In another sense, however, it went against the group's critique of Eurocentric ideas. For Abdias do Nascimento, theater itself was primordially African in that Egyptian theater preceded Greek. His own creative work, such as the play *O Sortilégio*, tended to privilege the Yoruba pantheon of the *orixás* rather than the Greek pantheon.

16 I am indebted to Dan Dawson for this information concerning the possible African origins of the religious use of feathers.

17 Octávio Bonfim in *O Globo* (August 25, 1959).

18 Quoted in José Castello, *Vinícius de Moraes: O Poeta da Paixão, Uma Biografia* (São Paulo: Companhia das Letras, 1994), p. 262.

19 Walter de Silveira, "*Orfeu do Carnaval:* Um Filme Estrangeiro," in *Fronteiras do Cinema* (Rio de Janeiro: Coleção Tempo Novo, 1974), p. 106.

20 Ibid., p. 108.

21 See Sábato Magaldi, "*Orfeu*—Peça e Fita," in the Suplemento Literário of *Estado de São Paulo* (August 15, 1959).

22 Novais Teixeira, "O Brasil no *Orfeu Negro*," *O Estado de São Paulo* (June 13, 1959).

23 See B. J. Duarte, "Uma Questão de Cultura," in *Folha da Manhã* (May 24, 1959).

24 Paul V. Beckley, *New York Herald Tribune* (December 22, 1959).

25 Bosley Crowther, *New York Times* (December 22, 1959).

26 Bosley Crowther, *New Yorker* (July 11, 1959), p. 41.

27 See Moniz Viana, "Orfeu do Carnaval," *Tribuna da Imprensa* (September 16, 1959).

28 A number of indices point to the identity of Clauder/Glauber. First, Glauber was a practicing critic at the time. Second, everything in the essay about *Black Orpheus* is consistent with Glauber's radical view about the politics and aesthetics of film at that time. Third, the essay's language anticipates Glauber's "Aesthetic of Hunger" (1965). Finally, the opposition of "metaphysics" and "hunger" anticipates key lines of dialogue in Glauber Rocha's *Terra em Transe*. When the protagonist-narrator, quoting Chateaubriand, speaks of the "Hunger of the Absolute," the leftist activist character Sara responds simply, "Hunger." It is not clear why Glauber would have chosen to use a pseudonym, but one can note that the same practice was not unknown among the French New Wave filmmakers; Jean-Luc Godard, for example, signed many articles Hans Lucas.

29 See Clauder Rocha, "*Orfeu:* Metafísica da Favela," *Jornal do Brasil* (October 24, 1959).

30 Among the many North American musicians who passed through Brazil in this period and who collaborated with Brazilians were Nat King Cole, Sarah Vaughan, Lena Horne, Frank Sinatra, Charlie Byrd, Stan Getz, Herbie Mann, Billy Eckstine, Sammy Davis Jr., and Tony Bennett. See Castro, *Chega de Saudade.*

31 *Black Orpheus* has had some interesting progeny. A recent German film, Doris Dorrie's *Nobody*

Loves Me (1991), features a bicultural character (from Nigeria but fluent in German) named Orpheus and is set against the backdrop of German carnival. Carlos Diegues has also contemplated the possibility of a remake of *Black Orpheus.*

32 Camus said, for example, that "in Bahia, 60% of the population wakes up without knowing if they're going to eat that day, and yet these same people know how to laugh, sing, and amuse themselves." The comments are taken from the promotion notes distributed to Brazilian exhibitors.

7. Intimations of Blackness

1 The review was published in the Salvador newspaper *Diário de Notícias,* and is held in the cinematheque files in Rio (File 188).

2 In this same period, in 1961, interestingly enough, Carolina de Jesus, a São Paulo *favelada,* published her *Quarto de Despejo* (translated into English as *Child of the Dark*), perhaps the first direct literary testimonial about the social misery in which millions of Brazilians lived. In São Paulo, Amir Haddad adopted the book for the theater, using black actors from the favelas, along with Ruth de Souza, who physically resembled the author-protagonist of *Quarto do Despejo.* (Carolina de Jesus's daughter reports that her mother went to opening night and shouted, "It's wrong! It's wrong!") The book generated several film projects in the United States, East Germany, and Italy. See José Carlos Sebe Bom Meihy and Robert M. Levine, *Cinderela Negra: A Saga de Carolina Maria de Jesus* (Rio de Janeiro: UFRJ, 1994).

3 Estevam's essay is included in Randal Johnson and Robert Stam, eds., *Brazilian Cinema* (New York: Columbia University Press, 1995).

4 Jean-Claude Bernardet, *Brasil em Tempo de Cinema* (Rio de Janeiro: Ed. Civilização Brasileira, 1967).

5 I am indebted to Vivian Sobchack's analysis on film noir in her as-yet-unpublished essay "Lounge Time: Postwar Crises and the Chronotope of Film Noir" (given to me by the author).

6 Gomes was orphaned at age 16 and had to work in a hardware store during the day and as a stevedore at night in order to support his seven younger brothers. After the success of *Assalto ao Trem Pagador,* he was sent by Itamaraty (Foreign Ministry) to the Cannes Film Festival and was subsequently invited to perform in a number of European films, as well as to participate in the 1966 Black Arts Festival in Dakar.

7 Bernardet, *Brasil em Tempo de Cinema* (Rio de Janeiro: Civilização Brasiliera, 1967).

8 The protestors listed Breno Melo, Luiza Maranhão, Léa Garcia, Lourdes de Oliveira, Ruth de Souza, Rubem Campos, Jorge Coutinho, Marcílio Faria, Djalmo Ferrcira, Sebastião de Oliveira, Grande Otelo, Zeni Pereira, Jaciara Sampaio, Aurea Campos, Abdias do Nascimento, Nilsa Bentes, Aparecida Roisa, Francisco Lopes, Gessi Jesse (the future wife of Vinícius de Moraes), Milton Gonçalves, Samuel dos Santos, Eliezer Gomes, and many others.

9 The theme of tensions over race and sexuality animates another film, not part of the Cinema Novo movement, Glauro Couto's *Os Vencidos* (The Vanquished, 1964). In the film a millionaire real-estate speculator becomes angry when his lover falls in love with a handsome black fisherman played by Breno Mello (the Orpheus of *Black Orpheus*).

8. Afro Brazilian Religion and the Bahian Renaissance

1 Cited in Joseph M. Murphy, *Working the Spirit* (Boston: Beacon Press, 1994), p. 214, n. 21.

2 See Risério, *Caymmi: Uma Utopia de Lugar*, p. 111.

3 For a critique of Eurocentric language concerning African religions, see John S. Mbiti, *Africans Religions and Philosophy* (Oxford: Heinemann, 1969).

4 Muniz Sodré, *Cultura Negra e Ecologia* (Rio de Janeiro: Papéis Avulsos/Centro Interdisciplinar de Estudos Contemporaneos 1985).

5 See Karin Barber, "Yoruba Oriki and Deconstructive Criticism," *Research in African Literature* 15 (Winter 1984).

6 See also Alfredo Bosi's brilliant analysis of the confrontation between Catholicism and Tupi Guarani religion in his *Dialética da Colonização* (São Paulo: Companhia das Letras, 1992). I do not mean to posit a unitary or homogenous Christianity, for in fact the mystical-rationalist divide exists within all religions.

7 I first heard this phrase in conversation with my friend Tomas Lopez-Pumarejo.

8 For positive portrayals of African religions, we must look to African (*A Deusa Negra* [The Black Goddess, 1978]) Brazilian (*A Força de Xangô* [The Power of Xangô, 1979]), and Cuban (*Patakin*) features and to documentaries such as Angela Fontanez's *The Orixá Tradition*, Lil Fenn's *Honoring the Ancestors,* Maya Deren's *The Divine Horsemen,* and Gloria Rolando's *Oggun*.

9 Georges Lapassade and Marco Aurélio Luz argue this position in *O Segredo da Macumba* (Rio de Janeiro: Paz e Terra, 1972). See also Marco Aurélio Luz, *Cultura Negra e Ideologia do Recalque* (Rio de Janeiro: Achiame, 1983).

10 For a psychoanalytic approach, see Ernesto M. La Porta, *Estudo Psicanalítico dos Rituais Afro-Brasileiros* (Rio de Janeiro: Atheneu, 1979).

11 See Sheila Walker, *Black Scholar* 8 (September 1975), p. 29.

12 Harold Bloom, *The American Religion* (New York: Simon & Schuster, 1992), p. 245.

13 According to a Bahian popular a normal mother "has" children but a mother of the saints "makes" children, that is, the children of the saints. See Antônio Risério, *Caymmi: Uma Utopia de Lugar*, p. 97.

14 Ruth Landes, *The City of Women* (New York: Macmillan, 1947).

15 For a discussion of homosexuality within *candomblé*, see J. Lorand Matory, "Homens Montados: Homosexualidade e Simbolismo da Posessão nas Religiões Afro-Brasileiras," in João José Reis, ed., *Escravidão e Invenção da Liberdade* (São Paulo: Brasiliense, 1988).

16 On occasion, white tourists visiting *candomblé* can be suddenly taken over by "wild trance." See Serge Bramly, *Macumba: Forces Noires du Brésil* (Paris: Seghers, 1975).

17 Roger Bastide, *Estudos Afro-Brasileiros* (São Paulo: Perspectiva, 1973), p. 281.

18 Thompson, *Flash of the Spirit*, pp. 5–7.

19 See Henry Louis Gates Jr., *The Signifying Monkey* (New York: Oxford University Press, 1988).

20 Arturo Lindsay, ed., *Santería Aesthetics in Contemporary Latin American Art* (Washington and London: Smithsonian, 1996), preface, p. xx.

21 See Anselmo Duarte, *Adeus Cinema* (São Paulo: Editora Massão Ohno, 1993), p. 84.

22 See ibid. Duarte also reports that Buñuel suggested that Duarte receive his prize in a bathing suit, to protest against the de riguer tuxedo. When he refused, according to Duarte, Buñuel himself, then 62, went to the festivities in a bathing suit but was barred at the door.

23 Anselmo Duarte, *Adeus Cinema,* pp. 95–96.

24 Ibid., p. 94.

25 Ismail Xavier, *Sertão Mar: Glauber Rocha e Estética da Fome* (São Paulo: Brasiliense, 1983).

26 The *New York Times* film critic Bosley Crowther, in his review (September 29, 1963) of *Pagador de Promessas,* gave remarkably inaccurate and ethnocentric accounts of crucial scenes from the film. According to Crowther, a "swarm of pagan dancers stage a stomping, swirling riot" and "Negroes and Indians come on and crowd the stage with wiggle dancing and the music of drums and guitars." Apart from the fact that there are no guitars in sight, the "wiggle dancing" is usually referred to as samba, and the bestial "swarm" of Negroes and Indians, who are not so easily distinguishable as Crowther's account suggests, is simply an ethnically mixed group of Brazilians enjoying themselves in the carnivalesque fashion common in Salvador.

27 José Gatti offers a thorough account of the production process of *Barravento* in his *Barravento: A Estréia de Glauber* (Florianópolis: Editora da UFSC, 1987). The same issues are taken up again in José Gatti's as-yet-unpublished doctoral dissertation, completed at NYU in 1995, entitled "Dialogism and Syncretism in the Films of Glauber Rocha."

28 Glauber Rocha, *Revolução do Cinema Novo* (Rio de Janeiro: Alhambra/Embrafilme, 1981), p. 307.

29 Ibid., p. 13.

30 Interview with Pitanga quoted in Celso Prudente, *Barravento — O Negro como Possível Referencial Estético no Cinema Novo de Glauber Rocha* (São Paulo: Nacional, 1995), p. 38.

31 Actor Antônio Pitanga, the Firmino of the film, recalls that the fishermen were so worried about the real-life boss and net owner that they were careful not to pronounce any rebellious words from the script when he was nearby. See José Gatti, *Barravento: Estréia de Glauber,* p. 29.

32 The promotional literature for the film had a slightly different emphasis, placing less stress on the alienating role of religion and more on the slavelike conditions in which the fishermen live. The notes begin: "After the abolition of slavery, black Brazilians still remain in a certain sense slaves."

33 See José Gatti, "Dialogism and Syncretism in the Films of Glauber Rocha," p. 113. See also Juana Elbein dos Santos, *Os Nagô e a Morte: Pade, Asese e o Culto Egun na Bahia* (Petrópolis, Brasil: Vozes, 1976).

34 Abdias do Nascimento offers this definition in an interview in Raquel Gerber Beatriz Nascimento's documentary *Ori* (1989).

35 See Xavier, *Sertão Mar,* p. 41.

36 For Xavier's excellent analysis of *Barravento,* see ibid.

37 Ibid., p. 31. It is also worth pointing out that if Rocha at the time of the film's making took a distant, critical attitude toward *candomblé,* in subsequent years he moved toward a more approving and identificatory attitude. In a statement made in 1971 in New York, Rocha's language of magic links African spirituality to artistic revolution, while completely inverting the Eurocentric view of African religion as "witchcraft": "Revolutionary art," he wrote, "should constitute a kind of magic which can enchant people to the point that they can no longer live in this absurd reality. Borges, going beyond this reality, wrote the most liberatory irrealities of our time. His esthetic is that of dream. For me, his work provides a spiritual illumination which helps dilate my Afro-Indian sensibility in the direction of the original myths of my race."

This race, poor and apparently without a future, elaborates in mysticism its moment of freedom. The Afro-Indian combats the colonizing mysticism of Catholicism, which is nothing more than the witchcraft of repression and the moral redemption of the rich." See Rocha, *Revolução do Cinema Novo*, p. 111.

38 Gatti, "Dialogism and Syncretism in the Films of Glauber Rocha," p. 187.

39 Rocha's manifesto is included in Johnson and Stam, *Brazilian Cinema*, pp. 69-71.

40 Anthropologist Luiz Mott published an article in *Bahia Hoje* arguing that Zumbi was gay. As evidence, he offered five "clues": the fact that Zumbi had no wife; that he did not take advantage of polygamy as something offered to warrior chiefs; that he was called *sueca* (gay); that he was a descendant of the Jagas group from Angola, a tribe known to include homosexuals; and that he was brought up by a priest, with whom he is supposed to have been sexually involved. The form of Zumbi's death--being castrated and having his penis placed in his mouth—was a typical manner of punishing homosexuals. Black activists, meanwhile, tried to rebut Mott's argument, saying that Mott confused *sueca* with *sueco*, that is, the word for "invisible" in Bantu, and offering other arguments.

41 Rocha, *Revolução do Cinema Novo*, p. 234.

9. From Auto-Critique to Anthropophagy

1 It was Jean-Claude Bernardet, in *Brasil em Tempo de Cinema*, who first pointed out the frequency of the magister ludi figure in early Cinema Novo.

2 Sábato Magaldi addresses this theatrical tradition in his *Panorama do Teatro Brasileiro* (Rio de Janeiro: MEC/SNT, 1977).

3 The first version of *Terra em Transe*, Jose Gatti points out, featured a number of Jewish characters. One, named Salomão Jordan, had a character that evoked parallels with the prominent Jewish journalist Samuel Wainer, who had opposed the 1964 coup. The militant Sara was also to have been of partial Jewish background, and her boyfriend was to have died in Germany trying to rescue his parents from the Nazis. The final version bears almost no traces of this Jewish emphasis. José Gatti also notes that Rocha shared a jail cell with Jewish novelist Carlos Heitor Cony, whose novel *Pesach* deals with politicized Jewish intellectuals from Rio.

4 Black actor Zózimo Bulbul appears in *Terra em Transe* as a direct sound technician recording the dialogues around him, in a role that prefigures his own future vocation as the cineaste-author of films like *Alma no Olho* (Soul in the Eye, 1976) and *Abolição* (Abolition, 1988)

5 The quotation from "Anthropophagie" appears in Augusto de Campos, *Revista de Antropofagia* (Sao Paulo: Divisão de Arquivo do Estado de São Paulo, 1984), p. 1. For "Almanachs du Père Ubu," see Alfred Jarry, *Tout Ubu* (Paris: Librairie Générale Française, 1962).

6 Oswald de Andrade's vision is confirmed by Pierre Clastres's anthropological research into the same Brazilian indigenous groups of which Andrade spoke. Clastres describes these groups as tropical "affluent societies" (not in the contemporary sense but in the sense of having surplus food) and as societies without social hierarchy or political coercion. See Pierre Clastres, *Society against the State* (New York: Zone Books, 1987).

7 See ibid. for a critique of the ethnocentrism of a classical anthropology accustomed to conceiving political power in terms of hierarchized and authoritarian relations of command and

obedience and therefore incapable of theorizing Tupinambá culture and society.

8   Quoted in de Campos, *Poesia, Antipoesia, Antropofagia* (São Paulo: Cortez e Moraes, 1978).

9   Joaquim Pedro de Andrade made many films related to the modernist movement: *O Poeta do Castelo* (The Poet from the Castle, 1959), a short about the modernist poet Manuel Bandeira (with whom Mário de Andrade exchanged letters); the feature *O Padre e a Moça* (The Priest and the Girl, 1965), which adopts a poem by another modernist, Carlos Drummond de Andrade; and *O Homem do Pau-Brasil* (The Brazil-Wood Man, 1982), inspired by the other *monstre sacré* of Modernismo, Oswald de Andrade.

10 For this and preceding quote, see Johnson and Stam, *Brazilian Cinema*, 82–83.

11 See Mikhail Bakhtin, *Rabelais and His World,* trans. H. Iswolsky (Cambridge: MIT, 1968), p. 308.

12 See Ismail Xavier, *Alegorias do Subdesenvolvimento: Cinema Novo, Tropicalismo, Cinema Marginal* (São Paulo: Brasiliense, 1993).

13 Quoted in Heloísa Buarque de Holanda, *Macunaíma: Da Literatura ao Cinema* (Rio de Janeiro: José Olympio/Embrafilme, 1978), p. 122.

14 For a thoroughly researched and closely observed textual analysis of *Macunaíma,* see Randal Johnson, "Cinema Novo and Cannibalism: *Macunaíma,*" in Johnson and Stam, *Brazilian Cinema,* pp. 178–190.

15 See Xavier, *Alegorias do Subdesenvolvimento: Cinema Novo, Tropicalismo, Cinema Marginal,* pp. 139–160.

16 For a Bakhtinian analysis of the carnivalesque aspects of *Macunaíma,* see Robert Stam, *Subversive Pleasures: Bakhtin, Cultural Criticism and Film* (Baltimore: Johns Hopkins, 1989).

17 I am indebted to Arlindo Castro for making this point.

18 See William Arens, *The Man-Eating Myth: Anthropology and Anthropophagy* (London: Oxford, 1979).

10. Afro/Indigenous Celebration

1   On black militancy in this period, see Hanchard, *Orpheus and Power,* and Pierre-Michel Fontaine, ed. *Race, Class, and Power in Brazil* (Los Angeles: Center for Afro-American Studies UCLA, 1985), especially articles by Fontaine, J. Michael Turner, and Lélia Gonzales. On the *afoxé* groups in Bahia, see Christopher Dunn, "Afro-Bahian Carnival: A Stage for Protest," *Afro-Hispanic Review* 11, nos. 1–3 (1992).

2   Quoted in Hanchard, *Orpheus and Power,* p. 115.

3   In conversation with the author.

4   My informant concerning Dom Salvador was the musician and Rutgers arts professor Lloyd MacNiel.

5   In the 1970s, I had the disconcerting experience of realizing the Brazilian censors had plagiarized my own work. A series of essays on Jean-Luc Godard that I had published in the Literary Supplement of the *Estado do São Paulo* in 1971, in which I examined with approval the cinematic strategies of his revolutionary cinema (contradiction between sound and image, etc.), was used, without citation, as a guide for censors as to what techniques to look out for and censor as "subversive."

6   Interestingly, a novel from the same period, *Esperando a Falecida,* by the black author Osvaldo de Camargo makes reference to Sidney Poitier: "the gigantic negro, much beloved by whites, the perfect policeman, the summa. How I love Sidney! How I hate Sidney!" Quoted in Brookshaw, *Raça e Cor na Literatura Brasileira* (Porto Alegre: Mercado Alberto, 1983), p. 216.

7   See Bastide, *Le Prochain et le Lointain,* p. 25.

8   See "O Boom Umbandista," *Veja* (January 7, 1981), p 4041. Diana Brown's estimates are somewhat lower. See her *Umbanda: Religion and Politics in Urban Brazil* (New York: Columbia University Press, 1994), p. xvi.

9   See Bastide, *The African Religions of Brazil.*

10 See Isabel Castellanos, "Religious Acculturation in Cuba," in Lindsay, *Santería Aesthetics in Contemporary Latin American Art,* p. 46.

11 Tenório helped nurture along his own mythology through a bit of trickery. He would hand people his gun, ask them to fire at him twice, which they would do, and yet he would escape unscathed. He would then fire a third bullet to show it was loaded; the first two bullets, obviously, were blanks.

12 See Nelson Pereira dos Santos, "O Cinema e a Cultura Popular," in *Jornal do Brasil* (February 23, 1975).

13 When I was teaching on a Fulbright at Federal University in Niterói in 1995, one of my students, André Luiz Sampaio, presented a paper (and a videotape) that consisted of an *umbanda pai de santo* (Ogum Jessi Jessi Patecuri) interpreting specific sequences from *O Amuleto de Ogum.* Such an exercise reveals that *umbanda* is a hermeneutic system like any other.

14 One often hears in Brazil of people with problems who tried psychoanalysis or conventional therapy to no avail, but who resolved their problems through *umbanda.*

15 Nívio Ramos Sales, *A Prova de Fogo* (Rio de Janeiro: Esquina, 1981), p. 13.

16 Actor Zózimo Bulbul reports that Antônio Carlos Fontoura considered him for the title role, but that he was "too handsome to represent a marginal." See interview with Zózimo Bulbul in *Filme Cultura,* no. 40 (August–October 1982), p. 16.

17 Brazilian filmmaker Karim Ainouz is currently scripting a feature film devoted to Madame Satan.

18 From the press brochure released on the film.

19 Interview with Waldyr Onofre, *Ultima Hora* (June 12, 1976).

20 Interview with Waldyr Onofre, *Movimento* (June 21, 1976).

21 For the favorable comments on the film, see interview with Zózimo Bulbul in *Filme Cultura,* p. 17.

22 See Manuela Carneiro da Cunha, *Negros Estrangeiros: Os Escravos Libertos e Sua Volta à África* (São Paulo: Brasiliense, 1985).

23 In life, too, Pitanga has always been politically and culturally active. Indeed, he is now an elected politician married to another black politician, Congresswoman Benedita da Silva. Even when desperate for work, Pitanga never accepted "service roles." Pitanga is widely traveled, including to Africa where he conversed with Leopold Senghor and Kwame Nkrumah, and where he discovered a "new, free Africa." See "Meu Filme É uma Alegoria," interview with Pitanga in the *Correio do Povo* (August 3, 1978).

24 See Rocha, *Revolução do Cinema Novo.*

25 Interview with Pitanga, *Lux Jornal* (June 19, 1979).

26 Eduardo de Oliveira points out that many of those who fought for black liberation in São

Paulo were mulattoes. See "O Mulato: Um Obstáculo Epistemológico," *Argumento* 1, no. 3 (1973), pp. 65–73.

11. Toward the Present

1   Glauber Rocha, "Cinema Novo: O Delírio de um Gol por Cima da Carne Seca," *Status,* no. 26 (September 1976), p. 128.

2   Chiavenato, *O Negro no Brasil* (São Paulo: Brasiliense, 1980), p. 21.

3   Some freed blacks came to acquire slaves themselves.

4   Interview with Diegues, *Filme Cultura,* no. 40 (August–October 1982), p. 13.

5   See Rocha, *Revolução do Cinema Novo,* pp. 326–330.

6   See Randal Johnson, *Cinema Novo x 5: Masters of Contemporary Brazilian Film.* (Austin: University of Texas Press, 1984), pp. 75–81.

7   *Xica da Silva* was publicly protested during its commercial run in San Francisco.

8   Beatriz Nascimento, "A Senzala Vista da Casa Grande," *Opinião* (October 15, 1976), p. 20.

9   Ibid.

10 I am indebted to Mia Mask's comments on this aspect of the film.

11 Sílvia Oroz, *Carlos Diegues: Os Filmes Que Não Filmei* (Rio de Janeiro: Rocco, 1984), p. 115.

12 See Randal Johnson, "Carnivalesque Celebration in *Xica da Silva,*" in Randal Johnson and Robert Stam, eds., *Brazilian Cinema* (East Brunswick, N.J.: Associated University Presses, 1982), p. 216.

13 Oroz, *Carlos Diegues,* p. 129.

14 The very genesis of *Ladrões de Cinema* had to do with this disproportion of power between First and Third World filmmakers. One of Cony's friends was hired by an American production company to film the final round of a golf competition. The film crew was sophisticated and well equipped, with five 35-mm cameras, the director orchestrating the shoot through a walkie-talkie. The friend's job was to film the final hole, letting the film roll until the golf ball entered the hole. Nervous about wasting so much film, the friend stopped the camera during moments of inaction; yet the director ordered him to keep the cameras rolling. The story reveals the disadvantaged situation of Brazilian filmmakers, who lack the resources to realize projects infinitely more interesting than a golf match.

15 In contrast, Marcel Camus paid $100,000 for his Jorge Amado adaptation (*Pastores da Noite* [Shepherds of the Night, 1977]) and Bruno Barreto paid $20,000 for *Dona Flor e Seus Dois Maridos* (Dona Flor and Her Two Husbands, 1976).

16 See Manuel Raimundo Querino, *The African Contribution to Brazilian Civilization,* Center for Latin American Studies, Arizona State University, Special Studies no. 8 (1978).

17 Cited in Chiavenato, *O Negro no Brasil,* p. 170.

18 For an excellent biography plus auteur study of Nelson Pereira dos Santos, see Helena Salem, *Nelson Pereira dos Santos: O Sonho Possível do Cinema Brasileiro* (Rio de Janeiro: Nova Fronteira, 1987).

19 Not everyone is so favorably inclined toward Amado, however. Abdias do Nascimento denounces him as an exploiter of black culture.

20 The term itself, in my view, reflects a neocolonized inferiority complex. It encodes the idea that there is something anomalous about non-Brazilians finding Brazil a worthy object of study. The French, the English, the Americans, find it normal that international scholars are interested in their national cultures and therefore have no terms like "Frenchist," "Englishist," and so on.

21 See Amado's preface to Haroldo Costa, *Fala Crioulo* (Rio de Janeiro: Record, 1982), p. 15.

22 Teófilo de Queiroz Jr., quoted in Abdias do Nascimento, *O Quilombismo* (Petrópolis: Vozes, 1980), p. 237.

23 For an excellent critique of the film, see Joan Dassin's *"Tent of Miracles,"* included in *Nelson Pereira dos Santos: Cinema Novo's Spirit of Light,* brochure for the 1995 retrospective of dos Santos's work at the Walter Reade Theater, New York City, prepared by the Film Society of Lincoln Center and the Harvard Film Archive, under the direction of Gerald O'Grady.

24 This homage to Indians also exists in the *caboclo* figure in *umbanda,* as well as in the names of samba groups like Cacique de Ramos and carnival *blocos* like the Apaches. An obvious comparison case would be the Mardi Gras Indians in New Orleans, a city that long banned blacks from wearing masks on Mardi Gras Day and where Indian "war paint," according to George Lipsitz, allowed African Americans to "problematize the binary system of racial categorization in the U.S." See George Lipsitz, *Dangerous Crossroads* (London: Verso, 1994), p. 72.

25 Quoted in José Gatti, "Dialogism and Syncretism in the Films of Glauber Rocha," p. 187.

26 See Preston E. Jones, *Latin America* (New York: Lothrop, Leed-Shepard, 1942), pp. 399–400, quoted in G. Harvey Summ, ed. *Brazilian Mosaic* (Wilmington: Scholarly Resources, 1995), p. 21.

27 See Júlio José Chiavenato, *O Negro no Brasil,* pp. 146–147.

28 In some regions of Brazil, roughly half of the free blacks had purchased their own freedom. See João José Reis, *Negociação e Conflito: A Resistência Negra no Brasil Escravista* (São Paulo: Companhia das Letras, 1989), p. 17.

29 Carlos Diegues described *Quilombo* as a "kind of science fiction film, in the sense that I was not just interested in recounting what had happened in my country, but in projecting the future." See Carlos Diegues, "Choosing between Legend and History: An Interview," *Cineaste* 15 , no. 1 (1986), p. 12.

30 On the situation of homeless children in Brazil, see Gilberto Dinnerstein, *Brésil: La Guerre des Enfants* (Paris: Fayard, 1991), pp. 25–26.

31 In February 1996, Spike Lee was told by a judge that he could not film a music video alluding to violence against street children in Rio because it would be "denigrating to the image of Brazil." "Rio Frets as Michael Jackson Plans to Film Slum," *New York Times,* International Section (February 11, 1996), p. 3.

32 Cinema Novo's elision of the working class was first pointed out by Jean-Claude Bernardet in his *Brasil em Tempo de Cinema.*

33 These passages are quoted in Sílvio Back, *República Guarani* (Rio de Janeiro: Paz e Terra, 1982), p. 37.

34 See, for example, David MacDougall, "Beyond Observational Cinema," in Paul Hockings, ed., *Principles of Visual Anthropology* (The Hague: Moutour 1975).

35 See Faye Ginsburg, "Aboriginal Media and the Australian Imaginary," *Public Culture* 5 (Spring 1993).

The Potentials of Polyphony

1 For more on Bakhtinian theories and their relevance for the media, see Robert Stam, *Subversive Pleasures: Bakhtin, Cultural Criticism and Film* (Baltimore: Johns Hopkins, 1989).

2 See Degler, *Neither Black nor White*, p. 122.

3 In 1975, the Congress of Brazilian Women made the following statement about the mulatta figure: "Brazilian black women inherited a cruel legacy: that of being the object of pleasure of the colonizers. It is the fruit of this cowardly crossing of blood that is now proclaimed the 'only national product worthy of export: the Brazilian mulatta.' But if the quality of the 'product' is said to be high, the treatment she receives is extremely degrading and disrespectful." Quoted in Abdias do Nascimento, *O Genocídio do Negro Brasileiro: Processo de um Racismo Mascarado* (Rio de Janeiro: Paz e Terra, 1978), pp. 61–62.

4 See Teófilo de Queiroz Jr., *Preconceito de Cor e a Mulata na Literatura Brasileira* (São Paulo: Atica, 1975), p. 122.

5 Quoted in Abdias do Nascimento, *Quilombismo*, p. 239.

6 Muniz Sodré, "Mulata da Melhor Mulataria?" *Isto É* (November 23, 1977), p. 46.

7 See Ella Shohat and Robert Stam, *Unthinking Eurocentrism*.

8 Quoted in Flora Sussekind, *O Negro como Arlequim: Teatro e Discriminação* (Rio de Janeiro: Achiame, 1982).

9 See Zelbert Moore, "Reflections on Blacks in Contemporary Brazilian Popular Culture in the 1980s," in *Studies in Latin American Popular Culture*, vol. 7 (1988), pp. 213–226.

10 Carlos Hasenbalg and Nelson do Valle Silva, "As Imagens do negro na publicidade," in *Estrutura Social, Mobilidade e Raça* (São Paulo: Vértice, 1988), pp. 185–188.

11 See Amelia Simpson, *Xuxa: The Mega-Marketing of Gender, Race, and Modernity* (Philadelphia: Temple University Press, 1993).

12 See José Gatti, "Dialogism and Syncretism in the Films of Glauber Rocha."

13 Seminars and colloquia on Latin American cinema often lapse into ritualistic denunciations of Hollywood. What is lost is the sense that Hollywood is not a monolith and that the natural allies of Brazilian and Third World filmmakers, and in some cases their spiritual children, are the independent critical filmmakers in the United States and other First World countries, for example, Spike Lee, Julie Dash, John Sayles, Marlon Riggs, Isaac Julien, and so forth.

14 Donald Bogle, *Toms, Coons, Mulattoes, Mammies and Bucks: An Interpretive History of Blacks in American Films.* (New York: Continuum, 1989), p. 36.

15 *Afinal* (July 23, 1985), p. 8.

16 See *Filme Cultura*, no. 40 (August–October 1982), p. 23.

17 For more on *Zelig*, see Robert Stam and Ella Shohat, "*Zelig* and Contemporary Theory: Meditation on the Chameleon Text," *Enclitic* 9, nos. 1–2 (1987).

18 See Sussekind, *O Negro como Arlequim*, p. 17.

19 Ismail Xavier, *Allegories of Underdevelopment: From the "Aesthetics of Hunger" to the "Aesthetics of Garbage*," Ph.D. diss., NYU, 1982.

20 Henry Drewal, "Sign, Substance, and Subversion in Afro-Brazilian Art," in Arturo Lindsay, ed., *Santería Aesthetics in Contemporary Latin American Art*, p. 266.

21 *Egungun,* as practiced in Brazil, calls up representations of male ancestors. It was founded, interestingly, as a response to the preponderant role of women in *candomblé*. For a documentary presentation of *egungun*, see the Carlos Brasbladt film entitled, simply, *Egungun* (1982).

22 For more on Brazilian popular music, see Charles A. Perrone, *Masters of Contemporary Brazilian Song: MPB 1965–1985* (Austin: University of Texas Press, 1989), and Robert Stam, *Subversive Pleasures*.

23 Jeff Decker develops the notion of rap artists as "organic intellectuals" in his "The State of Rap," *Social Text* 34 (1993). The expression strikes me as equally if not more appropriate to the Brazilian artists mentioned here. The Brazilian artists have also avoided the homophobia and misogyny that have often marred rap music.

24 On this subject, see Christopher Dunn's fascinating interview ("The Tropicalist Rebellion") with Caetano Veloso in *Transition* Issue 70, vol. 6, no. 2 (1996).

25 Brazilian colloquia on the current situation of the cinema routinely feature ritualistic denunciations of Hollywood; one rarely hears of the possibilities of parodistic cannibalization and ironic recyclage. Nor does one hear about the possible affinities with Afro-diasporic or indigenous cinemas or about analogies to the projects of such filmmakers as Spike Lee, Julie Dash, Isaac Julien, and Marlon Riggs, who are in some ways the spiritual children of Third World cinemas like Brazil's.

26 Paul Simon is a relative latecomer to this mode of music; his *Rhythm of the Saints* offers not "strong syncretism," but rather a kind of mismatch where individualist "sensitive poet" lyrics do not so much play off as contradict the collective energies of the *baturadas* of Olodum. At the same time, those who accuse Paul Simon of "stealing" would presumably not argue the converse, that John Coltrane "stole" the music of "My Favorite Things," for example. The issue is not of ethnic copyright but of the concrete successes or failures of specific collaborations.

27 See Christopher Small, *Music of the Common Tongue* (London: Calder Press, 1987).

SELECTIVE BIBLIOGRAPHY

∞

Alvim, Clara. *Os Discursos sobre o Negro no Século XIX: Desvios da Enunciação Machadiana*. Rio de Janeiro: Papéis Avulsos, 1989.

Andrade, Mário de. *Macunaíma: O Herói Sem Nenhum Caráter*. Rio de Janeiro: Edição Crítica, 1978.

_____. *Música de Feitiçaria no Brasil*. Belo Horizonte, Brasil: Itataia, 1983.

_____. *Macunaíma*. Trans. E. A. Goodland. New York: Random House, 1984.

Araújo, Vicente de Paula. *A Bela Época do Cinema Brasileiro*. São Paulo: Perspectiva, 1976.

_____. *Salões, Circos e Cinemas de São Paulo*. São Paulo: Perspectiva, 1981.

Augusto, Sérgio. *Este Mundo É um Pandeiro: A Chanchada de Getúlio a JK*. São Paulo: Cinemateca Brasileira/Companhia das Letras, 1989.

Avellar, José Carlos. *Imagem e Som, Imagem e Ação, Imaginação*. Rio de Janeiro: Paz e Terra, 1982.

_____. *O Cinema Dilacerado*. Rio de Janeiro: Alhambra, 1986.

Azevedo, Célia Maria Marinho de. *Onda Negra, Medo Branco: O Negro no Imaginário das Elites—Século XIX*. Rio de Janeiro: Paz e Terra, 1987.

Azevedo, Eliane. *Raça: Conceito e Preconceito*. São Paulo: Ática, 1987.

Azevedo, Thales de. *Democracia Racial: Ideologia e Realidade*. Petrópolis, Brasil: Vozes, 1975.

Bacelar, Jeferson. *Etnicidade: Ser Negro em Salvador*. Salvador, Brasil: Ianama/Programa de Estudos do Negro na Bahia (PENBA), 1989.

Back, Sílvio. *República Guarani*. Rio de Janeiro: Paz e Terra, 1982.

Barnes, Sandra T., ed. *Africa's Ogun: Old World and New*. Bloomington and Indianapolis: Indiana University Press, 1989.

Bastide, Roger. *Le Prochain et le Lointain*. Paris: Cujas, 1970.

_____. *Estudos Afro-Brasileiros*. São Paulo: Perspectiva, 1973.

_____. *The African Religions of Brazil: Towards a Sociology of the Interpretation of Civilizations*. Trans. Helen Sebba. Baltimore and London: Johns Hopkins University Press, 1978.

Bastos, Abguar. *Os Cultos Mágico-Religiosos no Brasil*. São Paulo: Hucitec, 1979.

Bernardet, Jean-Claude. *Brasil em Tempo de Cinema*. Rio de Janeiro: Ed. Civilização Brasileira, 1967.

_____. *Trajetória Crítica*. São Paulo: Polis, 1978.

_____. *Cineastas e Imagens do Povo*. São Paulo: Brasiliense, 1985.

Bernardet, Jean-Claude, José Carlos Avellar, and Ronald F. Monteiro. *Anos 70*. Rio de Janeiro: Europa Empresa, 1979–1980.

Bernardet, Jean-Claude, and Teixeira Coelho, eds. *Terra Em Transe, Os Herdeiros: Espaços e Poderes*. São Paulo: Com-Arte, 1982.

Bern, Zila. *Qual É: A Questão da Negritude*. São Paulo: Brasiliense, 1984.

_____. *Introdução: A Literatura Negra*. São Paulo: Brasiliense, 1988.

Birman, Patrícia. *O Que É Umbanda*. São Paulo: Brasiliense, 1983.

_____. *Beleza Negra*. Rio de Janeiro: Papéis Avulsos, 1989.

Blackburn, Robin. *The Making of New World Slavery*. London: Verso, 1997.

Boal, Augusto. *Theater of the Oppressed*. New York: Theater Communications Group, 1979.

Boaventura, Maria Eugenia. *A Vanguarda Antropofágica*. São Paulo: Ática, 1985.

Bogle, Donald. *Toms, Coons, Mulattoes, Mammies, and Bucks: An Interpretive History of Blacks in American Films*. New York: Continuum, 1989.

Bolderston, Danniel and Donna J. Guy. *Sex and Sexuality in Latin America*. New York: NYU Press, 1997.

Borges, Luiz Carlos R. *1960–1980: Cinema à Margem*. Campinas: Papirus, 1983.

Bramly, Serge. *Macumba: Forces Noires du Brésil*. Paris: Seghers, 1975.

Brasil, Assis. *Cinema e Literatura*. Rio de Janeiro: Tempo Brasileiro, 1967.

Brown, Diana. *Umbanda: Religion and Politics in Urban Brazil*. New York: Columbia University Press, 1994.

Browning, Barbara. *Samba: Resistance in Motion*. Bloomington and Indianapolis: Indiana University Press, 1995.

Cabral, Sérgio. *As Escolas de Samba do Rio de Janeiro*. Rio de Janeiro: Limiar, 1996.

Camargo, Suzana. *Macunaíma—Ruptura e Tradição*. São Paulo: Massão Ohmo/João Farkas, 1977.

Campos, Augusto de. *Poesia, Antipoesia, Antropofagia*. São Paulo: Cortez e Moraes, 1978.

Campos, Claudia de Arruda. *Zumbi, Tiradentes*. São Paulo: Perspectiva, 1988.

Campos, Haroldo de. *Morfologia do Macunaíma*. São Paulo: Perspectiva, 1973.

Cardosa, Ciro Flamarion S. *A Afro-America: A Escravidão no Novo Mundo*. São Paulo: Brasiliense, 1982.

Carneiro, Edison. *O Quilombo dos Palmares*. Rio de Janeiro: Civilização Brasileira, 1966.

_____. *Candomblés da Bahia*. Rio de Janeiro: Civilizaçao Brasileira, 1978.

Castello, José. *Vinícius de Moraes: O Poeta da Paixão, Uma Biografia*. São Paulo: Companhia das Letras, 1994.

Castro, Ruy. *Chega de Saudade: A História e as Histórias da Bossa Nova*. São Paulo: Companhia das Letras, 1991.

Catani, Afranio M., and José I. de Melo Souza. *A Chanchada no Cinema Brasileiro*. São Paulo: Brasiliense, 1983.

Cavalcânti, Alberto. *Filme e Realidade*. São Cristóvão, Rio de Janeiro: Artenova, 1977.

Cavalcanti, Mari Laura V. de Castro. *A Temática Racial No Carnaval Carioca: Algumas Reflexões*. Rio de Janeiro: Papéis Avulsos, 1989.

Chalhoub, Sidney. *Visões de Liberdade*. São Paulo: Companhia das Letras, 1990.

Cham, Mbye B. *Ex-Iles: Caribbean Cinema*. Trenton, N.J.: Africa World Press, 1991.

Cham, Mbye B, and Claire Andrade-Watkins, eds. *Blackframes: Critical Perspectives on Black Independent Cinema*. Cambridge: MIT Press, 1988.

Chiavenato, Júlio José. *O Negro no Brasil: Da Senzala a Guerra do Paraguai*. São Paulo: Brasiliense, 1980.

Churchill, Ward. *Fantasies of the Master Race*. Monroe, Maine: Common Courage Press, 1992.

Costa, Emília Viotti da. *Da Senzala a Colonia*. São Paulo: Brasiliense, 1989.

Costa, Haroldo. *Fala Crioulo*. Rio de Janeiro: Record, 1982.

Cripps, Thomas. *Slow Fade to Black*. New York: Oxford University Press, 1977.

——. *Black Film as Genre*. Bloomington and Indianapolis: Indiana University Press, 1979.

——. *Making Movies Black: The Hollywood Message Movie from World War II to the Civil Rights Era*. New York: Oxford, 1993.

Cunha, Manuela Carneiro da. *Negros, Estrangeiros: Os Escravos Libertos e Sua Volta à África*. São Paulo: Brasiliense, 1985.

——. *História dos Índios no Brasil*. São Paulo: Companhia das Letras, 1992.

Damasceno, Benedita Gouveia. *Poesia Negra no Modernismo Brasileiro*. Campinas, São Paulo: Pontes, 1988.

Damasceno, Caetana Maria. *Ritual e Conflito: Quando se Canta para Subir*. Papéis Avulsos, 1989.

Davis, Shelton H. *Victims of the Miracle: Development and the Indians of Brazil*. Cambridge: Cambridge University Press, 1977.

Degler, Carl N. *Neither Black nor White: Slavery and Race Relations in Brazil and the United States*. Madison: University of Wisconsin Press, 1986.

Deren, Maya. *Divine Horsemen: The Voodoo Gods of Haiti*. New York: Dell, 1970.

Diawara, Manthia. *African Cinema*. Bloomington and Indianapolis: Indiana University Press, 1992.

——. *Black American Cinema*. London: Routledge, 1993.

Diegues, Carlos. *Cinema Brasileiro: Idéias e Imagens*. Porto Alegre: Ed. da Universidade, 1988.

Downing, John D. H., ed. *Film and Politics in the Third World*. New York: Autonomedia, 1987.

Duarte, B. J. *Caçadores de Imagens: Nas Trilhas do Cinema Brasileiro*. São Paulo: Massão Onho/ Roswitha Kempf, 1982.

Dunn, Christopher John. *The Relics of Brazil: Modernity and Nationality in the Tropicalista Movement*. Ph.D. diss., Brown University, 1996.

Esteve, Michel, ed. *Glauber Rocha*. *Études Cinématographiques* nos. 97–99: Le Cinema Novo Brésilien. Paris, 1973.

Feijo, Martin Cesar. *Anabasis Glauber. Da Idade dos Homens a Idade dos Deuses*. São Paulo: Anabasis, 1991.

Feres, Nites Therezinha. *Leituras em Frances de Mário de Andrade*. São Paulo: Instituto de Estudos Brasileiros, 1969.

Fernandes, Florestan. *A Integração do Negro na Sociedade de Classes*. Vol. 2. São Paulo, Brasil, 1965.

——. *O Negro no Mundo dos Brancos*. São Paulo: Difusão Européia Do Livro, 1972.

Ferreira, Jairo. *Cinema de Invenção*. São Paulo: Max Limonad/ Embrafilme, 1986.

Filme Cultura. Ano XV –August–October 1982, no. 40. Special Issue on "Negro no Cinema Brasileiro."

Fontaine, Pierre-Michel, ed. *Race, Class, and Power in Brazil*. Los Angeles: Center for Afro-American Studies, UCLA, 1985.

Freitas, Byron Torres de, and Vladimir Cardoso de Freitas. *Os Orixás e o Candomblé*. Rio de Janeiro: Eco, 1967.

Freitas, Decio. *Palmares: A Guerra dos Escravos.* Rio de Janeiro: Graal, 1978.

Friar, Ralph and Natasha. *The Only Good Indian: The Hollywood Gospel.* New York: Drama Books, 1972.

Fusco, Coco. *Reviewing Histories: Selections from New Latin American Cinema.* Buffalo: Hallwalls, 1987.

Gabriel, Teshome H. *Third Cinema in the Third World: The Aesthetics of Liberation.* Ann Arbor, Mich.: University Microfilms International Research Press, 1982.

Gabriel, Teshome H., and Hamid Naficy, eds. *Otherness and the Media: The Ethnography of the Imagined and the Image.* Langhorne, Pa.: Harood, 1993.

Gagliardo, José Mauro. *O Indígena e a República.* São Paulo: HUCITEC, 1989.

Galembo, Phyllis. *Divine Inspiration: From Benin to Bahia.* Albuquerque: University of New Mexico Press, 1993.

Galvão, Maria Rita Eliezer. *Crónica do Cinema Paulistano.* São Paulo: Ática, 1975.

_____. *Burguesia e Cinema: O Caso Vera Cruz.* Rio de Janeiro: Civilização Brasileira, 1981.

Galvão, Maria Rita, and Jean-Claude Bernardet. *O Nacional e o Popular: na Cultura Brasileira.* São Paulo: Brasiliense, 1983.

Gates, Henry Louis, Jr. *The Signifying Monkey.* New York: Oxford University Press, 1988.

_____, ed. *"Race," Writing, and Difference.* Chicago: University of Chicago Press, 1986.

Gatti, José. *Barravento: A Estréia de Glauber.* Florianópolis: Editora da UFSC, 1987.

_____. "Dialogism and Syncretism in the Films of Glauber Rocha." Ph.D. diss. New York University, 1995.

Gerber, Raquel. *O Cinema Brasileiro e o Processo Político e Cultural: De 1950 a 1978.* Rio de Janeiro: Embrafilme, 1982.

_____. *O Mito da Civilização Atlântica: Glauber Rocha, Cinema, Política e a Estética do Inconsciente.* Petrópolis, Brasil: Vozes, 1982.

_____, ed. *Glauber Rocha.* Rio de Janeiro: Paz e Terra, 1977.

Gil, Gilberto. *Seleção de Textos, Notas, Estudos Biográfico, Histórico e Crítico e Exercícios por Fred de Goes.* São Paulo: Abril Educação, 1982.

Gilroy, Paul. *The Black Atlantic: Modernity and Double Consciousness.* Cambridge: Harvard University Press, 1993.

Goes, Fred de. *O País do Carnaval Elétrico.* São Paulo: Corrupio, 1982.

Gomes, Heloisa T. *As Marcas da Escravidão: O Negro e o Discurso Oitocentista no Brasil e nos Estados Unidos.* Rio de Janeiro: EFRJ, 1994.

Gomes, Paulo Emílio Salles. *Humberto Mauro, Cataguases Cinearte.* São Paulo: Perspectiva, 1974.

_____. *Cinema: Trajetória no Subdesenvolvimento.* Rio de Janeiro: Paz e Terra/Embrafilme, 1980.

_____. *Crítica de Cinema no Suplemento Literário.* Vol. 1. Rio de Janeiro: Paz e Terra/Embrafilme, 1981.

_____. *Crítica de Cinema no Suplemento Literário.* Vol. 2. Rio de Janeiro: Paz e Terra/Embrafilme, 1981.

_____. *Um Intellectual na Linha de Frente.* Rio de Janeiro: Brasiliense/Embrafilme, 1986.

Gonzaga, Alice. *50 Anos De Cinedia.* Rio de Janeiro: Record, 1987.

Guerra, Ruy, et al. *Le Cinema Novo Brésilien.* Paris: Lettres Modernes, 1972.

Guillermoprieto, Alma. *Samba.* London: Jonathan Cape, 1990.

Hanchard, Michael George. *Orpheus and Power: The Movimento Negro of Rio de Janeiro and São*

Paulo, Brazil, 1945–1988. Princeton, N.J.: Princeton University Press, 1994.

Hasenbalg, Carlos A. *Discriminação e Desigualdades Raciais no Brasil.* Rio de Janeiro: Graal, 1979.

Hess, David J., and Roberto da Matta, eds. *The Brazilian Puzzle: Culture on the Borderlands of the Western World.* New York: Columbia University Press, 1995.

Hobsbawm, Eric, and Terence Ranger, eds. *The Invention of Tradition.* Cambridge: Cambridge University Press, 1983.

Holanda, Heloisa Buarque de. *Macunaíma: Da Literatura ao Cinema.* Rio de Janeiro: José Olympio/Embrafilme, 1978.

_____. *Impressões de Viagem: CPC, Vanguarda e Desbunde, 1960/1970.* São Paulo: Brasiliense, 1980.

Holanda, Sérgio Buarque de. *Visão do Paraíso: Os Motivos Edenicos no Descobrimento e Colonização do Brasil.* São Paulo: Editora Nacional, 1985.

_____. *Raízes do Brasil.* Rio de Janeiro: José Olympio, 1988.

Jabor, Arnaldo. *Os Canibais Estão na Sala de Jantar.* São Paulo: Siciliano, 1993.

Johnson, J. *Macunaíma: From Modernism to Cinema Novo.* Ann Arbor, Mich.: University Microfilms International, 1977.

Johnson, Randal. *Literatura e Cinema: Macunaíma: Do Modernismo na Literatura ao Cinema Novo.* São Paulo: T. A. Queiroz, 1982.

_____. *Cinema Novo x 5: Masters of Contemporary Brazilian Film.* Austin: University of Texas Press, 1984.

_____. *The Film Industry in Brazil: Culture and the State.* Pittsburgh: University of Pittsburgh Press, 1987.

Johnson, Randal, and Robert Stam, eds. *Brazilian Cinema.* New York: Columbia University Press, 1995.

Júnior, Manuel Diegues. *A África na Vida e na Cultura do Brasil.* Second World Black and African Festival of Arts and Culture, Lagos and Kaduna, Nigeria, 1977.

LaPorta, E. M. *Estudos Psicanalítico dos Rituais Afro-Brasileiros.* Rio de Janeiro: Atheneu, 1979.

Leal, Wills. *O Nordeste no Cinema.* Funape: Universidade Federal da Paraíba, 1982.

Leite, Dante Moreira. *O Caráter Nacional Brasileiro: História de uma Ideologia.* São Paulo: Pioneira, 1976.

Leopoldi, José Sávio. *Escola de Samba: Ritual e Sociedade.* Petrópolis, Brasil: Vozes, 1978.

Lima, Fernando Barbosa, et al. *Televisão and Video.* Rio de Janeiro: Jorge Zahar, 1985.

Lima, Lana Lage da Gama. *Rebeldia Negra e Abolicionismo.* Rio de Janeiro: Achiame, 1981.

Lindsay, Arturo, ed. *Santería Aesthetics in Contemporary Latin American Art.* Washington and London: Smithsonian, 1996.

Lipsitz, George. *Dangerous Crossroads.* London: Routledge, 1994.

Lody, Raul. *Candomblé: Religião e Resistência Cultural.* São Paulo: Ática, 1987.

Lopez, Helena Theodoro, et al. *Negro e Cultura no Brasil.* Rio de Janeiro: UNIBRADE/ UNESCO, 1987.

Luz, Marco Aurélio. *Cultura Negra e Ideologia do Recalque.* Rio de Janeiro: Achiame, 1983.

Lyons, Oren, John Mohawk, Vine Deloria Jr., Laurence Hauptman, Howard Berman, Donald Grinde Jr., Curtis Berkey, Robert Venables, et al. *Exiled in the Land of the Free: Democracy, Indian Nations, and the U.S. Constitution.* Santa Fe: Clear Light, 1992.

Machado, Maria Helena P.T. *Crime e Escravidão.* São Paulo: Brasiliense, 1987.

_____. *O Plano e o Pânico: Os Movimentos Sociais na Década da Abolição.* São Paulo: UFRJ/EDUSP, 1994.

Marotti, Giorgio. *Black Characters in the Brazilian Novel.* Los Angeles: Center for Afro-American Studies, University of California, 1987.

Martin, Michael T. *Cinemas of the Black Diaspora.* Detroit: Wayne State Press, 1995.

Matta, Roberto da. *Carnavais, Malandros e Heróis: Para uma Sociologia do Dilema Brasileiro.* 2d ed. Rio de Janeiro: Zahar, 1980.

Mattoso, Katia de Queirós. *Ser Escravo no Brasil.* São Paulo: Brasiliense, 1982.

Mauro, Humberto. *Sua Vida/Sua Arte/Sua Trajetória no Cinema.* Brasil: Artenova, 1978.

Meihy, José Carlos Sebe Bom, and Robert M. Levine. *Cinderela Negra: A Saga de Carolina Maria de Jesus.* Rio de Janeiro: UFRJ, 1994.

Moraes, Malu, ed. *Perspectivas Estéticas do Cinema Brasileiro (Seminário).* Brasil: Universidade de Brasília/Embrafilme, 1986.

Moraes, Vinícius de. *O Cinema de Meus Olhos.* São Paulo: Companhia das Letras, 1991.

Morel, Edmar. *Vendaval da Liberdade: A Luta do Povo pela Abolição.* São Paulo: Global, 1988.

Moreno, Antônio. *Cinema Brasileiro: História e Relações Com o Estado.* Niterói, Brasil: EDUFF, 1994.

Morse, Richard M. *O Espelho de Prospero: Cultura e Idéias nas Américas.* São Paulo: Companhia das Letras, 1988.

Mott, Maria Lucia de Barros. *Escritoras Negras: Resgatando a Nossa História.* Rio de Janeiro: Papéis Avulsos/UFRJ, 1989.

Moura, Clóvis. *Os Quilombos e a Rebelião Negra.* São Paulo: Brasiliense, 1981.

_____. *Rebeliões da Senzala.* São Paulo: Editora Ciências Humanas, 1981.

_____. *Brasil: Raízes do Protesto Negro.* São Paulo: Global, 1983.

_____. *Quilombo: Resistência ao Escravismo.* São Paulo: Ática, 1987.

Moura, Roberto. *Tia Ciata e a Pequena África no Rio de Janeiro.* Rio de Janeiro: Biblioteca Carioca, 1995.

_____. *Grande Otelo.* Rio de Janeiro: Relume/Dumara, 1996.

Mukuna, Kazadi wa. *Contribuição Bantu na Música Popular Brasileira.* São Paulo: Global, 1983.

Munanga, Kabengele. *Negritude: Usos e Sentidos.* São Paulo: Ática, 1986.

_____, ed. *Estratégias e Políticas Combaté à Discriminação Racial.* São Paulo: Edusp, 1996.

Nadotti, Nelson, and Carlos Diegues. *Quilombo: Roteiro do Filme e Crônica das filmagens.* Rio de Janeiro: Achiame, 1984.

Nascimento, Abdias do. *O Genocídio do Negro Brasileiro: Processo de um Racismo Mascarado.* Rio de Janeiro: Paz e Terra, 1978.

_____. *Sortilégio II (Mistério Negro de Zumbi Redivivo).* Rio de Janeiro: Paz e Terra, 1979.

_____. *O Quilombismo.* Petrópolis: Vozes, 1980.

Nascimento, Abdias do, and Elisa Larkin Nascimento. *Africans in Brazil: A Pan-African Perspective.* Trenton, N.J.: Africa World Press, 1992.

Neves, David E. *Cinema Novo no Brasil.* Petrópolis, Brasil: Vozes, 1966.

Novais, Fernando A., and Laura de Mello e Souza, eds. *Historia Da Vida Privada no Brasil: Cotidiano e Vida Privada na América Portuguesa.* São Paulo: Companhia das Letras, 1997.

Nogueira, Oracy. *Tanto Preto Quanto Branco: Estudos de Relações Raciais.* São Paulo: T. A. Queiroz, 1985.

Noronha, Jurandyr. *No Tempo da Manivela.* Rio de Janeiro: Kinart, Cinema e Televisão/Embrafilme, 1987.

Ortiz, Renato. *A Morte Branca do Feiticeiro Negro.* Petrópolis, Brasil: Vozes, 1978.

———. *Cultura Brasileira Identidade Nacional.* São Paulo: Brasiliense, 1985.

———. *A Moderna Tradição Brasileira.* São Paulo: Brasiliense, 1988

Oroz, Sílvia. *Carlos Diegues: Os Filmes Que Não Filmei.* Rio de Janeiro: Rocco, 1984.

Orser, Charles E., Jr. *In Search of Zumbi: Preliminary Archaeological Research at the Serra da Barriga, State of Alagoas.* Normal: Illinois State University Press, 1992.

Paranagua, Paulo Antonio, ed. *Le Cinéma Bresilien.* Paris. Editions du Centre Pompidou, 1987.

Parker, Andrew, Mary Russo, Doris Sommer, and Patricia Yaeger. *Nationalisms and Sexualities.* New York: Routledge, 1992.

Parker, Richard. *Bodies, Pleasures, and Passions: Sexual Culture in Contemporary Brazil.* Boston: Beacon, 1991.

Passek, Jean-Loup, ed. *Le Cinéma Brésilien.* Paris: Editions du Centre Pompidou, 1987.

Picchia, Pedro del, and Virginia Murano. *Glauber: O Leão de Veneza.* São Paulo: Escrita, 1981.

Pierson, Donald. *Negroes in Bahia: A Study of Race Contact in Bahia.* Chicago: University of Chicago Press, 1942.

Pierre, Sylvie. *Glauber Rocha.* Paris: Cahiers du Cinéma, 1987.

Perrone, Charles A. *Masters of Contemporary Brazilian Song: MPB 1965–1985.* Austin: University of Texas Press, 1989.

———. *Seven Faces: Brazilian Poetry Since Modernism.* Durham, N.C.: Duke University Press, 1996.

Prandi, Reginaldo. *Os Candomblés de São Paulo: A Velha Magia na Metropole Nova.* São Paulo: HUCITEC/Editora USP, 1991.

Price, Richard, ed. *Maroon Societies: Rebel Slave Communities in the Americas.* Baltimore and London: Johns Hopkins University Press, 1979.

Proença, M. Cavalcanti. *Roteiro de Macunaíma.* Rio de Janeiro: Civilização Brasileira, 1969.

Prudente, Celso. *Barravento—O Negro como Possível Referencial Estético no Cinema Novo de Glauber Rocha.* São Paulo: Nacional, 1995.

Queiroz, Maria Isaura Pereira de. *Roger Bastide: Sociologia.* São Paulo: Atica, 1983.

———. *Carnaval Brasileiro: O Vivido e o Mito.* São Paulo: Brasiliense, 1992.

Queiroz, Suely R. Reis de. *A Abolição da Escravidão.* São Paulo: Brasiliense, 1981.

Ramos, Alcida Rita. *Sociedades Indígenas.* São Paulo: Ática, 1986.

Ramos, Fernão. *Cinema Marginal (1968–1973): A Representação em Seu Limite.* São Paulo: Brasiliense, 1987.

———, ed. *História do Cinema Brasileiro.* São Paulo: Art Editora, 1987.

Ramos, José Mário Ortiz. *Cinema, Estado e Lutas Culturais (Anos 50/60/70).* Rio de Janeiro: Paz e Terra, 1983.

Reis, João José. *Rebelião Escrava no Brasil: A História do Levante dos Males (1835).* São Paulo: Brasiliense, 1986.

———. *Negociação e Conflito: A Resistência Negra no Brasil Escravista.* São Paulo: Companhia das Letras, 1989.

Rezende, Sidney, ed. *Ideário de Glauber Rocha.* Rio de Janeiro: Philobiblion, 1986.

Ribeiro, Darcy. *O Brasil como Problema.* Rio de Janeiro: Francisco Alves, 1995.

———. *O Povo Brasileiro: A Formação e o Sentido do Brasil.* São Paulo: Companhia das Letras, 1995.

Ribeiro, Darcy, and Carlos de Araujo Moreira Neto. *A Fundação do Brasil: Testemunhos 1500–1700.* Petrópolis, Brasil: Vozes, 1992.

Risério, Antônio. *Gilberto Gil: Expresso 2222.* Salvador, Brasil: Corrupio Comércio, 1987.

_____. *Cores Vivas*. Salvador, Brasil: Coleção Casa de Palavras, 1989.

_____. *Caymmi: Uma Utopia de Lugar*. São Paulo: Perspectiva, 1993.

_____. *Avant-Garde na Bahia*. São Paulo: Instituto Lina Bo/P. M. Bardi, 1995.

Risério, Antônio, and Gilberto Gil. *O Poético e o Político: E Outros Escritos*. Rio de Janeiro: Paz e Terra, 1988.

Roach, Joseph. *Cities of the Dead: Circum-Atlantic Performance*. New York: Columbia, 1996.

Rocha, Glauber. *Deus e o Diabo na Terra do Sol*. Rio de Janeiro: Civilização Brasileira, 1965.

_____. *Revisión Crítica del Cine Brasileño*. Madrid: Editorial Fundamento, 1971.

_____. *Revolução do Cinema Novo*. Rio de Janeiro: Alhambra/Embrafilme, 1981.

_____. *O Século do Cinema*. Rio de Janeiro: Alhambra/Embrafilme, 1983.

Rodrigues, Ana Maria. *Samba Negro, Espoliação Branca*. São Paulo: HUCITEC, 1984.

Rodrigues, João Carlos. *O Negro Brasileiro e o Cinema*. Rio de Janeiro: Globo, 1988.

Rodrigues, Nina. *Os Africanos no Brasil*. São Paulo: Editora Nacional, 1977.

Rubin, Vera, and Arthur Tuden. *Comparative Perspectives on Slavery in New World Plantation Societies*. New York: New York Academy of Sciences, 1977.

Saia, Luiz Henrique. *Carmen Miranda*. São Paulo: Brasiliense, 1984.

Said, Edward W. *Orientalism*. London: Routledge/Kegan Paul, 1978.

_____. *Culture and Imperialism*. New York: Knopf, 1993.

Salem, Helena. *Nelson Pereira dos Santos: O Sonho Possível do Cinema Brasileiro*. Rio de Janeiro: Nova Fronteira, 1987.

Sales, Nívio Ramos. *A Prova de Fogo: Posando para Retrato*. Rio de Janeiro: Esquina, 1981.

Salles, Francisco Luiz de Almeida. *Cinema e Verdade: Marilyn, Buñuel, Etc*. São Paulo: Companhia das Letras, 1988.

Santos, Joel Rufino dos. *O Que É Racismo*. São Paulo: Brasiliense, 1980.

Santos, Juana Elbein dos. *Os Nagô a e Morte: Pade, Asese e o Culto Egun na Bahia*. Petrópolis, Brasil: Vozes, 1976.

Saraceni, Paulo César. *Por Dentro do Cinema Novo: Minha Viagem*. Rio de Janeiro: Nova Fronteira, 1993.

Sayers, Raymond S. *The Negro in Brazilian Literature*. New York: Hispanic Institute in the United States, 1956.

Schneider, Cynthia, and Brian Wallis, eds. *Global Television*. New York: Wedge, 1988.

Schwarcz, Lilia K. Moritz. *De Festa Tamben se Vive: Reflexões sobre o Centenário da Abolição em São Paulo*. Rio de Janeiro: Papéis Avulsos/Centro Interdisciplinar de Estudos Contemporâneos, 1989.

_____. *O Espetáculo das Raças: Cientistas, Instituições e Questão Racial no Brasil 1870–1930*. São Paulo: Companhia das Letras, 1993.

Schwarcz, Lilia K. Moritz, and Lética Vidor, eds. *Negras Imagens*. São Paulo: Edusp, 1996.

Schwarcz, Lilia K. Moritz, and Renato da Silva Queiroz, eds. *Raça e Diversidade*. São Paulo: Edusp, 1996.

Schwartz, Jorge. *Vanguardas Latino-Americanas: Polêmicas, Manifestos e Textos Críticos*. São Paulo: EDUSP, 1995.

Schwarz, Roberto. *Que Horas São? Ensaios*. São Paulo: Companhia das Letras, 1987.

Shohat, Ella, and Robert Stam. *Unthinking Eurocentrism: Multiculturalism and the Media*. London: Routledge, 1994.

Silva, Eduardo. *Prince of the People: The Life and Times of a Brazilian Free Man of Colour.* London: Verso, 1993.

Silva, Martiniano J. *Racismo à Brasileira: Raizes Históricas.* Brasília: Thesaurus, 1987.

Silva, Nelson do Valle, and Carlos A. Hasenbalg. *Relações Raciais no Brasil Contemporâneo.* Rio de Janeiro: Rio Fundo, 1992.

Simpson, Amelia. *Xuxu. The Mega-Marketing of Gender, Race, and Modernity.* Philadelphia: Temple University Press, 1993.

Singh, Oseas, Jr. *Adeus Cinema.* São Paulo: Masão Ohno Editor, 1993.

Skidmore, Thomas E. *Preto no Branco: Raça e Nacionalidade no Pensamento Brasileiro.* Rio de Janeiro: Paz e Terra, 1989. English version: *Black into White: Race and Nationality in Brazilian Thought.* Durham: Duke University Press, 1993.

Smedley, Audrey. *Race in North America.* Boulder: Westview Press, 1993.

Sodré, Muniz. *Samba, O Dono do Corpo: Ensaios.* Rio de Janeiro: Codecri, 1979.

_____. *A Verdade Seduzida: Por um Conceito de Cultura no Brasil.* Rio de Janeiro: Codecri, 1983.

_____. *Cultura Negra e Ecologia.* Rio de Janeiro: Papéis Avulsos/Centro Interdisciplinar Contemporaneos, 1985.

_____. *A Máquina de Narciso: Televisão, Indivíduo e Poder no Brasil.* Rio de Janeiro: Achiame, 1987.

Sodré, Muniz, et al. *O Negro e a Abolição.* Revista de Cultura: Vozes, vol 73, April 1979.

Sommer, Doris. *Foundational Fictions: The National Romances of Latin America.* Berkeley and Los Angeles: University of California Press, 1991.

Souza, Marcio. *Breve História da Amazônia.* São Paulo: Marco Zero, 1994.

Souza, Paulo Cesar. *A Sabinada: A Revolta Separatista da Bahia 1837.* São Paulo: Brasiliense, S.A., 1987.

Stedman, Raymond William. *Shadows of the Indian.* Norman: University of Oklahoma Press, 1982.

Studies in Latin American Popular Culture. Vol. 7. Tucson: Department of Spanish and Portuguese, University of Arizona, 1988.

Sussekind, Flora. *O Negro como Arlequim: Teatro e Discriminação.* Rio de Janeiro: Achiame, 1982.

Tassara, Eda, ed. *O Índio/Ontem, Hoje, Amanha: Dossie do I Ciclo.* São Paulo: Memorial da América Latina: EDUSP, 1991.

Terra dos Índios de Zelito Viana. Rio de Janeiro: Embrafilme, 1979.

Thompson, Robert Farris. *Flash of the Spirit: African and Afro-American Art and Philosophy.* New York: Random House, 1983.

Unruh, Vicky. *Latin American Vanguards: The Art of Contentious Encounters.* Berkeley and Los Angeles: University of California Press, 1994.

Vainfas, Ronaldo. *America em Tempo de Conquista.* Rio de Janeiro: Zahar, 1992.

_____. *A Heresia dos Índios: Catolicismo no Brasil Colonial.* São Paulo: Companhia das Letras, 1995.

Ventura, Roberto. *Estilo Tropical: História Cultural e Polêmicas Literárias no Brasil 1870–1914.* São Paulo: Companhia das Letras, 1991.

Vianna, Hermano. *O Mundo Funk Carioca.* Rio de Janeiro: Zahar, 1988.

Viany, Alex. *Introdução ao Cinema Brasileiro.* Rio de Janeiro: MEC/INL, 1959.

Winant, Howard. *Racial Conditions: Politics, Theory, Comparisons.* Minneapolis: University of Minnesota Press, 1994.

Xavier, Ismail. *O Discurso Cinematográfico: A Opacidade e a Transparência.* Rio de Janeiro: Paz e Terra, 1977.

_____. *Sétima Arte: Um Culto Moderno.* São Paulo: Perspectiva, 1978.

_____. *Sertão Mar: Glauber Rocha e Estética da Fome.* São Paulo: Brasiliense, S.A., 1983.

_____. *Alegorias do Subdesenvolvimento: Cinema Novo, Tropicalismo, Cinema Marginal.* São Paulo: Brasiliense, 1993. English translation: *Allegories of Underdevelopment.* University of Minnesota Press, 1997.

Xavier, Ismail, et al. *O Desafio do Cinema: A Política do Estado e a Política dos Autores.* Rio de Janeiro: Jarge Zahar Editor, 1985.

Zamora, Lois Parkinson, and Wendy B. Faris, eds. *Magical Realism: Theory, History, Community.* Durham, N.C.: Duke University Press, 1995.

INDEX

∞

Robert Stam is Professor in the Department of Cinema
Studies at New York University. He is the author of several
books, including *Unthinking Eurocentrism: Multiculturalism
and the Media* (with Ella Shohat), *Subversive Pleasures:
Bakhtin, Cultural Criticism, and Film,* and *Brazilian Cinema*
(with Randal Johnson).

Library of Congress Cataloging-in-Publication Data
Stam, Robert. Tropical multiculturalism: a comparative
historyof race in Brazilian cinema and culture / Robert Stam.
p.   cm. — (Latin America otherwise)
Includes bibliographical references and index.
ISBN 0-8223-2035-5 (cloth: alk. paper).
ISBN 0-8223-2048-7 (pbk.: alk. paper)
1. Motion pictures—Brazil. 2. Race relations in motion
pictures. 3. Racism in motion pictures. I. Title. II. Series.
PN1993.5.B6S7   1997
791.43'75'0981—dc21   97-20233 CIP